FINANCIAL PLANNING HANDBOOK

A Portfolio of Strategies and Applications

Harold W. Gourgues, Jr.

New York Institute of Finance
A Prentice-Hall Company

Library of Congress Cataloging in Publication Data

Gourgues, Harold W.
  Financial planning handbook.

  Includes index.
  1. Finance, Personal—Handbooks, manuals, etc.
I. New York Institute of Finance. II. Title.
HG179.G715 1983   332.024   82–25963

ISBN 0–13–316398–9

This publication is designed to provide accurate and authoritative information in regard to the subject matter covered. It is sold with the understanding that the publisher is not engaged in rendering legal, accounting, or other professional service. If legal advice or other expert assistance is required, the services of a competent professional person should be sought.

—From a Declaration of Principles jointly adopted by a Committee of the American Bar Association and a Committee of Publishers and Associations

Printed in the United States of America

10 9 8 7 6 5 4 3 2

New York Institute of Finance
(NYIF Corp.)
70 Pine Street
New York, New York 10270

The business of life and the life of business provide, for me, an exhilarating two-way street. I dedicate this book to those who make it so.

I leave each day of work to return to a house that is made a home by my wife Geneva, daughter Katherine, and son Walter.

As each new day dawns, I leave them to join with a team of financial planning professionals to help others reach their financial destiny.

Just to have both ways to go is a rare opportunity. To be so attracted to both directions is a true blessing.

Contents

6
Step-By-Step Guide to
Measuring Your Client's Income Tax
Temperature, 91

7
How to Reduce or
Avoid Gift and Estate Taxes, 108

8
How to Make Risk Management Work, 128

III
FINANCIAL THERAPY
VIA ALTERNATIVE SOLUTIONS

9
Step-By-Step Guide to
Selecting the Proper Solutions
to Financial Problems, 155

10
Financial Planning Procedures for Building and
Managing Wealth, 169

11
Tax-Advantaged Investment Strategies for Repositioning Capital and Redirecting Discretionary Cash Flow, 196

12
Key Concepts for
Assuring Continued Financial Planning Success,
268

IV
MODEL FINANCIAL PLANS

Portfolio I
A Total Financial Plan
Prepared for:
Susan M. Lane, 283

Foreword

The newest wave of change in our society is most commonly recognized by the advances in computerization and the use of robotics. We are witnessing a decentralization of the labor force and tremendous improvements in the ability to transfer information that is needed to cope with today's activities. From the corner grocery store to the largest banks, the immediate access to information, products, and services reflects the increased sophistication facing today's consumer. But nowhere are these changes more evident than in the financial services industry.

Creating a sense of caution in the financial temperament of consumers are money market funds, commodities, limited partnership investments in oil, gas, real estate, equipment, agriculture and other items, wrap-around annuities, universal life insurance, gold, silver, coins, inflation, fluctuations in stock market and housing values, taxes and interest, and many other phenomena. Today's consumers are therefore more demanding of the organizations and people who serve their financial needs.

The capital markets, similarly buffeted by adverse economic forces, new consumer demands, and more competition have also entered a period of fundamental restructuring and revolutionary change. The last two years have been highlighted by a series of mergers and acquisitions among securities, insurance, real estate, banking, savings and loan, and retailing firms. As a result the traditional boundaries of these industries are disappearing, and a new offering of financial products and services is emerging.

The traditional roles of the consumer and the salesperson are disappearing. Today's society is demanding more than the sale of products. Financial planning is the new wave of activity that offers the stability and financial security that the consumer is seeking. It will not be the sale of products but planning, implementation, and periodic reviews of the goal setting process that will allow the financial services industry to serve the consumer of the future. The need for greater knowledge and understanding of the financial planning process is therefore critical not only for those who will succeed in the financial services industry, but also for those who will rely on them for success.

Mr. Gourgues' book is an outstanding and timely contribution to the industry. It provides a guide to understanding the total process and establishes a roadmap for those who want to pursue financial planning as a profession. Moreover, it demonstrates that financial planning is the process through which the consumer's hopes, dreams, and financial needs may be achieved.

In writing the book, Mr. Gourgues has presented the financial planning process in a clear and readily understandable format. His ideas regarding the segmentation of assets, use of a rate of return matrix, and implementation procedures are original and essential to the achievement of financial objectives. Financial planners and consumers alike should benefit from his presentation. If practiced as outlined by Mr. Gourgues, financial planning will provide a valuable service to our free enterprise system which, in the final analysis, will stand or fall according to its ability to offer financial security to those who use it.

WILLIAM B. SHEARER, JR.

Atlanta, Georgia

Preface

It is not astonishing at all that so many executives, business owners, and professionals approach middle or later age somewhere in or near a state of financial dependence. Almost always, it is more a case of failing to plan than it is a plan having failed. We find very successful individuals spending eight to eighteen *hours* a day guiding if not controlling $50,000, $5,000,000, or more of business assets or income—and then spending eight to eighteen *minutes* a day managing $50,000 to $5,000,000 of personal assets or income. While corporations may have detailed balance sheets, budgets, and five-year plans, their corporate heads do not know what they are worth today or what they can spend tomorrow. We find an extraordinary number of professionals mesmerized by what can aptly be called the "expertise transfer syndrome," which lulls, for instance, many doctors into believing that the ability to save life automatically translates itself into an ability to manage wealth. This syndrome can only be programmed to fail-sure. Its only cure is radical surgery—a major redirecting of the thinking of all who are involved in either the acceptance or delivery of this nation's incredible wealth of financial products and services. That redirection is what this book most seriously proposes and applies. Yet it sets out to be far more specific and immediately practical.

Before going into the scope of this book, let us finalize our commentary on financial entropy by citing one of the chief findings of a recent major study into the financial habits and attitudes of affluent America. SRI, Inc. (formally the Stanford Research Institute) reported in 1979 that affluent American households ($30,000 plus income) spend about 94% of their financial relationships with vendors of products (stocks, bonds, insurance, real estate, etc.) and services (banking, accounting, trust services, etc.) and only 6% in evolving strategies for the proper disposition of assets and income. SRI, Inc. also reported that only about 1% of the affluent have paid a fee for a comprehensive financial plan. We can assume, with little or no fear of contradiction, that few of the 1% have yet updated or revised their original plans—if, in fact, they were ever implemented in the first place. No wonder we see individual after individual traversing the financial stage of life as a disjointed puppet whose strings are being pulled in every direction by an average of thirty to forty vendors of products and services, few of which bear any meaningful relationship to each other. No wonder, too, we find an almost exponential rise in financial chaos with the increase in one's assets and/or income.

The answer that this book espouses is a logical, practical, and, most importantly, understandable approach to personal financial planning. While all that is proposed has been tested for several years with increasing success, experience has also proven that teaching both old and new practitioners and clients a whole new way of thinking can be most frustrating.

The major obstacles to redirecting thinking about personal financial planning are threefold. First, the overwhelming percentage of people in the financial services industries still think of financial planning as a product or administrative service, as opposed to a professional methodology for matching needs with product and service solutions. That is the major reason why so many different types of financial institutions fail in their first attempts at financial planning. Second, few of those who provide the vast array of valuable products and services are adequately trained or have professional backup to help them measure the client's true needs. Third, on the client side, it is the rare person who will face up to the need for comprehensive financial planning in advance of a major financial change of life. Financial planning, too, must seek to prevent more than just a cure.

This book proposes a very different approach to planning. It first defines financial planning as the ongoing process of:

1. examining one's current financial condition and relating it to one's lifetime and estate goals,
2. identifying the principal hurdles that act as obstacles to achieving one's multiple objectives, and
3. the objective selecting and implementing of both procedural and investment strategies for success.

It then sets forth, chapter by chapter, a segmented approach to using the financial planning process to better achieve the accumulation, preservation, and distribution of wealth.

More specifically, Section 1 demonstrates why and how to relate one's current financial condition to meaningful short-, intermediate-, and long-term goals. Section 2 shows how to measure, with mathematical exactitude, the principal financial problems. Section 3 provides innovative dimensions into the objective selection of solutions from the often confusing array of alternatives.

It must be reemphasized that this *Financial Planning Handbook* is anything but me-too. It is in fact a very bold but proven methodology for the creation and constant revision of a highly objective financial roadmap for individuals. It can therefore not be segmented into the typical chapters that axiomatically divide lifetime and estate planning books. Neither can it deal separately with trusts, investments, contracts, wills, or other products and services as separate major topics anymore than a book on the practice of medicine can be broken down into chapters on penicillin, chemotherapy, insulin, and open heart surgery. Certainly those are all highly usuable procedural and medicinal solutions to certain major medical problems. Yet the format of this book insists that we put the horse back in front of the cart so that financial ills will be identified well in advance of considering cures.

Finally, this book is written for all who are looking for solid basic techniques, tools, procedures, systems, strategies, and even forms that can be used in their own personal planning or for their clients. Contrary to the development of the medical profession, the cottage industry we know today as financial planning is rising from the synergism of a multitude of very specialized professional disciplines. Today's new horizons in financial planning point toward increasing generalization—toward more emphasis upon the meaningfulness of the financial roadmap than the mere attractiveness of a needless destination. Lending a hand toward that end while providing easy-to-apply, understandable techniques for formulating a plan for any season is what this book is designed to do for you.

Acknowledgments

How can you begin to acknowledge all who helped in the creation of a book like this when so much of what you are is a result of them?

Confessing to this attempt at the impossible, I'll begin with the Personal Financial Planning Department of Robinson Humphrey/American Express. It was there, as with no other professional group I have known, that a milieu developed—a laboratory for financial planning—in which comprehensive client problem solving could flourish. It is always people—quality people—who make great ideas blossom. Working with financial planning consultants like Jeannie Wright, Jim Valentine, Dick Saunders, Mary Pitts, Mel Locklear, Gary Nunn, David Channer, Eliot Brandy, and David Homrich means working with great people. They and the key support people like Tori Slater, Jean Redding, and their assistants made financial planning come alive at Robinson Humphrey/American Express. Without them, this book could never have been conceived.

More specifically, I wish to emphasize my deepest appreciation to Jeannie Wright, First Vice President and a first-class Director of Plan Creation at R-H, a long and faithful partner in financial planning. Her untiring assistance in making technical corrections and in helping to organize my thoughts had an immeasurable impact upon the development of this book.

It was then Olivia Lane, Editorial Consultant, who literally transformed many of my concepts into some semblance of order, who took the words and helped me to paint pictures you would understand and then use. I admire and thank her for that.

I wish to also thank Mr. William B. Shearer, Jr. of Dillard & Shearer, P.C. and Mr. Robert P. Goldberg of Alternman, Kritzer & Levick, P.C. for their valuable assistance, especially with the estate planning concepts discussed in Chapter 7. My special thanks also go to Ron Davis and *The Money Letter* for their permission to use various of my writings which had previously been published by them.

Finally, I owe a debt of sincere gratitude to two friends and associates who happen to be super typists—Rexiene Miller and Cheryle Reynolds.

HAROLD W. GOURGUES, JR.

Prologue

The oldest Greek book of record, *Works and Days*, pleaded for a return to times past, when life was simpler, less suspicious, and confusing, when one's perceptions were not illusions. Somehow, that's the way the distant but recollected past seems to the present. Twenty-twenty hindsight provides days gone by with such an air of simplicity.

Yesterday provides fewer hurdles to the comprehension of actions and reactions than does today. The past just sits there, available for certain scrutiny, harnessed and unmovable, just asking to be prioritized and weighed. But the present refuses to be quiet for a portrait. Its change is exponential. Problems and solutions are both in perpetual motion, multiplying and filled with seemingly endless disorder.

Planning one's financial future escapes not a particle of these philosophical truths. In no area of human endeavor are today's facts more vibrating, more complicated, more in need of organization. That is why we have spent these past three years—which have not exactly been the epitome of constancy—in pursuit of a practical statement of standards in financial planning. We tried to glance beyond the hot buttons of today. Instead, we strove for a consistency of principle in practice that would not easily yield to the aberrations of a rapidly changing society.

In so doing, all did not always develop as simply as was intended.

But take heart. Today's apparent complications in financial planning will, too, one day be viewed as simplicities of the past. To the heirs of this decade-old profession of financial planning, today's sophistications will appear as images in innocence. It is not that people lose their ability to be purposefully simple, they simply take on new perspectives. That is why we return to poignant reflections of the past. It is also what made the writing of a comprehensive treatment of a subject like financial planning fraught with danger for us, and hopefully very engaging for you who read it.

I

HOW TO EXAMINE YOUR CLIENT'S CURRENT FINANCIAL CONDITION

1

Key Ideas for Building Your Client's Financial Future

Planning for your client's total financial future can be a richly rewarding undertaking. It becomes all the more exciting a professional endeavor when you view it correctly from the very beginning.

Financial planning is the ongoing creation, implementation and updating of a financial road map designed to get clients from where they are to where they want to be. It can never be confused with any combination of individual or packaged financial products, investments, or services. These may all become appropriate vehicles to be used in the implementation of a plan. But they in themselves are clearly not the plan. Financial planning, instead, must be an evolving, growing, changing process of relating the current financial scenario to what the client would like it to be. To reach your client's financial destiny, the process must continually identify, with the precise mathematical tools that we'll show you, the procedures and investment vehicles that can be used, and the financial speed at which they must travel.

Key Idea No. 1: The financial planning process must continually seek to solve clearly identified lifetime and estate planning problems with objectively selected procedures and investment solutions.

It is a foregone conclusion, however, that it will be very difficult if not impossible for your client to ever reach his intended financial destiny unless specific aim is taken for it. He must know where he is now and then identify where he wants to be at specific intervals in the future. He must be willing to change his course from time to time as financial planning updates uncover new obstacles or eliminate old ones.

Macon, Georgia is about seventy-five miles south of Atlanta via Interstate 75. When in Atlanta and the goal is to attend a meeting in Macon one and one-half hours from now, the trip will probably be made safely by traveling 55 miles per hour, barring unforeseen circumstances. Driving much slower than that would mean not getting there in time. Speeding could mean both a waste of energy and time—just to wait upon arrival. It could also mean a traffic ticket and/or loss of life or limb. In that case, it may have been better never to have set out for Macon in the first place.

Three types of financial goals to aim for

Financial goal setting is no different. Sights must be set on a goal, but the goal must be both realistic and flexible.

THE KEY TO ACCUMULATING WEALTH

It's fine to have Macon for an objective, but trying to arrive via automobile in only one hour without taking undue risk is unrealistic. Traveling all the way on I-75 is also admirable, but it would be wise to allow some extra time in case there is an unexpected obstacle along that busy highway. It may even be necessary to use an alternate route if a major accident blocks passage.

Key Idea No. 2: When accumulating additional wealth is the prime goal, take aim for a specific target and then key in on the appropriate overall financial speed or risk level necessary for success.

THE KEY TO PRESERVING WEALTH

Conversely, there are those who are already in Macon, and who would simply like to stay there, financially speaking. Financial goal setting for them consists of making the most of what they have and where they are. There is then no sense in traveling at excessive speeds if they're already where they want to be. They may, however, decide to ride around a bit to have fun or just to keep up with things like the highway robbery we know as inflation. Even so, the obvious risks and potential rewards must always be carefully weighed.

> Key Idea No. 3: For those who are primarily concerned with preserving wealth, taking more than the necessary measured risk is pure folly.

THE KEY TO DISTRIBUTING WEALTH

Finally, there are those who have accumulated more than they believe they'll ever need. Their aim is to share some of it, always making certain that they are not providing someone else with the financial independence they worked so hard to achieve for themselves.

If they are gifting to charity, they can, of course, give away accumulated assets either all at once or a little at a time. The lure of lifetime recognition, coupled with both estate and income tax savings, can be very great. But they should never let the socially acceptable tax tail wag an immature economic puppy. It may be better to consider keeping the use of the asset while "living" and then transferring it to charity upon "leaving."

When gifting to family members, it may be wise to think twice before giving too much financial driving power too early to loved ones who cannot handle it. In such a case, it would be best to park the gifts in a trust with legal provisions that specify that the keys won't be available until the child or grandchild is of financial "driving age." Unfortunately there are no financial planning licensing laws for determining that age. It varies greatly from person to person. On occasion, that age is never reached, in which case over-gifting causes financial accidents and/or acts as a disincentive to success in a free enterprise environment.

> Key Idea No. 4: When the distribution of wealth is the major objective, take care not to create more problems for the future than are being solved for today.

How to gather data for determining your client's current financial condition

Few if any of us are very successful with very much for very long—if we do not base all that we do upon a handful of basic rules. One such fundamental rule in financial planning is that you must begin with all of the required financial data in the proper form. The design of a financial road map cannot possibly be more complete than the information upon which it is based.

The gathering of all information required for your client's financial examination is not viewed as the most exciting aspect of financial planning. We are all more interested in uncovering the problems and evolving interesting alternative strategies and techniques for solving them. But skimming over the crucial first stage of examining the total financial picture and its relationship to your client's desired financial future could be your biggest mistake. The importance of picturing *exactly* what the current financial pyramid looks like today, *as well as* what it should realistically be like tomorrow, cannot be over-emphasized.

FOUR CONSIDERATIONS IN MAKING ANY FINANCIAL DECISION

Once plan implementation begins, all of the procedural and investment vehicles used to achieve the desired goals should be chosen only after weighing four paramount considerations:

1. existing economics,
2. tax ramifications,
3. liquidity factors, and
4. the client's temperament.

Temperament is most difficult to pinpoint. That is why it is so crucial that any methodology used to gather data must provide so much more than just financial statistics.

Financial questionnaires that are used to accomplish this examination vary greatly from less than one page to virtual books. Either extreme is practically useless: The first creates no clear image; the second burdens you with meaningless redundancy. The questionnaire in Figure 1–1, which is completed on a hypothetical Dr. Tom Wright, offers a reasonable compromise between the typical formats that are more often too complicated than too simple. It will hopefully provide you with a practical guide to determining your client's current financial condition, as well as helping to recognize realistic current and future goals. Ironically, it is as useful for those clients who have overriding accumulation objectives as it is for those who desire to emphasize the preserving and/or distributing of wealth.

Finally, it can be completed, on average, in a couple of hours unless, as is often the case, there is uncertainty as to what is owned and what is being received, how it's owned and directed, or how it is risk-managed. For those who fit this description, spending more than two hours completing this questionnaire could be the most profitable several hours or days ever spent. It just might serve as a catalyst that will transform virtual chaos into an incipient semblance of financial order.

Key Idea No. 5: The first major step in the financial planning process is to determine the client's current financial position as well as his or her multiple goals. An appropriately designed financial questionnaire is the basic tool for achieving that end.

How the questionnaire helps to set specific and realistic goals for the future

Let us now see how Dr. Wright used the questionnaire to tell us what he's all about financially and personally, as well as to learn how we can use it to elicit Dr. Wright's true goals. The questionnaire, with all of the blanks and many of the margins filled in, becomes the point of departure for both current and future financial planning.

In more mature cases, where increased *and* increasing current spendable income and/or preservation of the estate are major goals, the gathered data will lead toward placing greater emphasis upon rearranging, almost immediately, the current financial pyramid.

Contrarily, when accumulation is the primary goal, the chief concern is not so much the positioning of existing investment assets as it is the directing of discretionary cash flow. In either case, first identifying the more general goal areas and then translating them into very specific and realistic targets are the tasks at hand. For illustrative purposes, we will study Dr. Thomas Wright's specific case.

Were Dr. Wright at or near financial independence in terms of net investment or potential net assets, the task would probably be to (1) improve upon the level and safety of his spendable income and (2) coordinate lifetime objectives with the estate planning goals. Because this is usually an easier task than creating an estate, and because most financial planning clients are still building their pyramids, we have purposely chosen to illustrate the questionnaire in setting goals, as indicated, via Dr. Wright's more typical "accumulation-oriented" case.

Note that the questionnaire begins by collecting very factual data. It then progresses into the statistics of what Dr. Wright has and what he is receiving, as well as how the assets and income are protected. It asks all the right questions about specific needs and goals, and finally deals almost exclusively with temperament. We notice, as is most frequently the case, that Dr. Wright's goals for the future can be categorized as follows:

FIGURE 1–1   *Dr. Wright's Questionnaire*

Total Investment
Planning
Confidential
Questionnaire

FIGURE 1–1 *(cont.)*

The very first step in the financial planning process is the examination of your total financial wherewithal. In addition to this questionnaire, the following documents are considered:

DOCUMENTS

☒   Copies of your last four years income tax returns and any gift tax returns.

☒   Copy of your will

☒   Copy of your spouse's will

☒   Copies of trust agreements or contracts (if applicable)

☐   Copies of business buy-sell agreements (if applicable)

☒   Others _(such as Personal Holding Co. documents)_

☐   _____

Your life, health, and other insurance policies should also be included for analyzing your present coverage.

PERSONAL INFORMATION

Client's Name __Thomas J. Wright__ _____ Social Security No. __123-45-6789__

Home Address __1385 Medical Hall Rd. NE, Atlanta, Ga 30319__ Phone __404-123-4567__

Business Address __2 Peachtree Bark St. NW, Atlanta, Ga 30303__ Phone __404-765-4321__

Date of Birth __9-23-36__ Birth Place __Macon, Ga.__

Occupation __Medical Doctor, Radiologist__ How Long? __14 years__

Who is your attorney? __Ken Reeves__

Who is your accountant? __Buddy Greene__

Do you have any other professional advisors of whom we should be aware? __Investment Broker, Bootsie__

__Carmichael; Banker, Reed Jones; CPCU, Mel Nunn.__

Date Information Obtained __January 1983__

(1)

FIGURE 1–1 *(cont.)*

FAMILY INFORMATION

Spouse _____ Mary _____ Date of Birth _Oct. 22, 1941_ Social Security No. _101-11-2131_

Occupation _____ Housewife _____ How Long? _16 years_

CHILDREN	DATE OF BIRTH	DEPENDENT	SELF-SUPPORTING
Jean	6-07-68	☒	☐
David	6-25-72	☒	☐
		☐	☐
		☐	☐
		☐	☐

Are all family members in good health? Yes _____ No __x__

If not, explain: _Jean is a juvenile diabetic, good health now but complications could set in_ _later, which I will want to help take care of financially._

Are any relatives other than spouse and children depending on you for support now or will need support in the future?

Yes _____ No __x__ If so, explain: _____

_____

Do you have any alimony or child support obligations? Yes _____ No __x__

If so, how much? _____ For how long? _____

Is your estate obligated to continue these obligations? _____

EDUCATION

Do you want to send your children to college? Yes __x__ No _____

How much do you estimate it will cost per child, per year? (In today's dollars) $ _5,000_

Have you set aside any assets for your children?   Yes __x__ No _____

Are they to be used for their college education?   Yes __x__ No _____

DESCRIBE:

CHILD	TYPE OF ASSET	AMOUNT	HOW HELD*
Jean **	Gas/Oil Drilling Prog.	$6,000 (Present Value)	Trust, Mary, trustee
	Growth Mutual Fund	10,000	
David	Gas/Oil Drilling Prog.	4,000 (Present Value)	Trust, Mary, trustee
	Growth Mutual Fund	6,000	

*Custodianship, trust or other. Give custodian, trustee, and donor: _Trustee, Mary; donor, Tom._

(2)

**I would like to concentrate now on bringing this up to $20,000 or more ASAP, since Jean is only 4 years away from college. My cost estimates may also be too low.

FIGURE 1–1 *(cont.)*

CASH RESERVES — FIXED DOLLAR ASSETS

	HUSBAND	WIFE	JOINT	YIELD
	-	-	-	-
Cash				
Checking Accounts	$ 3,000	$ 1,000	-	
Savings Accounts	8,000	-		
Credit Union				
Certificates of Deposit				
Deferred Annuities				
Government Bonds				
Notes Receivable				
Mortgages Receivable				
Other:				

HOME AND PERSONAL PROPERTY

Market value of your home $ _____165,000_____ Cost basis $_____135,000_____

Remaining mortgage $ __99,500__ Number of years __25__ Interest rate __9__%

Who is the owner? __Wife__

Do you have mortgage insurance in case of disability or death? Yes _____ No __x__ If so, how much? _____

PERSONAL PROPERTY	HUSBAND	WIFE	JOINT
Home furnishings			15,000
Automobiles			9,000
Silver, jewelry, coins			20,000
Clothing, furs			3,000
Antiques			1,000
Boat, airplane, trailer			2,000
Other_____			

REAL ESTATE

List all real estate holdings other than your home and those included under tax incentive investments. Use separate sheet if necessary.

Description	Market Value	Remaining Mortgage	Cost Basis	Gross Annual Income	Expenses, Depreciation (annual)	Owner	What are your plans for this property?
Lake House	60,000	30,500	50,000	-	-	Wife	hold for pleasure, appreciation

(3)

FIGURE 1–1　*(cont.)*

STOCKS, BONDS, AND MUTUAL FUNDS

Owner	No. Shares or Face Amount	Security Description	Listed or NASDAQ Symbol	Present Market Value	Total Cost	Annual Dividend	Coupon	Maturity Date
Myself	2599 shs	Tax-Managed Trust		12.00 or $31,185	$ 25,000	–	–	
Myself	$ 75,000	Municipal Bonds	OTC	65,000	75,000	–	5.6%	1987

TAX-INCENTIVE INVESTMENTS

Do you have any tax-incentive investments?
(Oil and gas exploration, real estate, cattle, coal, railway cars, etc.) Yes _X_ No ____

Description	Year Purchased	Amount Invested	Expected Annual Deductions	Present Value (if known)	Current Annual Income	Owner
Real Estate LTD.						
Partnership	1978	5,000	–	?	0	Myself
Partnership	1979	5,000	–	? (Over 10,000)	0	Myself
Gas/Oil Drilling*	1981	10,000	0	?	0	Myself
	1982	10,000	$2,000 in 83?		0	Myself

*$10,000 invested in 1980 was gifted to the children.

(4)

12

FIGURE 1–1   *(cont.)*

BUSINESS INTEREST OR PROFESSIONAL PRACTICE

Sole Proprietorship ☐   Sub-chapter S ☐
Partnership ☐   Corporation ☒

Business

I. Name __Wright Radiology Professional Corp.__ I.D. Number _____

II. Valuation

a). What is your estimation of the present market value of *your* share of the business?

__$30,000__

b). What do you estimate your estate would collect for the business (liquidation value)?

__$30,000__

or

Professional Practice

List the present value of *your* share of the following:

Checking Account _____$10,000_____

Accounts Receivable _____20,000 (1/2 probably collectable)_____

Equipment or Furniture _____10,000_____

Building _____–_____

Other _____–_____

Any liabilities? _____–_____

Would your estate be able to collect the above values? Yes _X_ No ____
If no, which ones would decrease and by how much?

__Could collect all but about 1/2 of the accounts receivable.__

Business or Professional Practice

Ownership:

Name	% of Ownership	Relationship (if any)
Dr. Thomas J. Wright	100%	

For Corporations Only:

Do you have any of the following corporate fringe benefit programs?

Pension Plan	Yes _X_ No ____
Profit Sharing Plan	Yes _X_ No ____
105(b) Medical Expense Reimbursement Plan	Yes _X_ No ____
Corporate Disability Plan	Yes _X_ No ____
Group Life Insurance	Yes _X_ No ____
Deferred Compensation Plan	Yes ____ No ____
Thrift or Salary Savings Plan	Yes ____ No ____

If not a corporation, have you ever considered incorporation?

If so, explain: _____

(5)

*I also own a Personal Holding Co. with a net worth of $66,000. $31,500 is a note from me and $34,500 is in blue chip stocks. This was originally a corporation that owned the pharmacy I bought from my father after graduating from pharmacy school.

FIGURE 1–1 *(cont.)*

Business or Professional Practice (Continued)

Employee Information (Complete for Employee Benefit Plan Proposals)

Name	Sex	Date of Birth	Employment Date	Full Time Part Time	Current Annual Compensation
Clara Florence Slater	F	1-1-30	1-1-70	Full-Time Sec'y	$12,000
Cheryle Miller	F	2-2-50	2-2-75	Med. Tech	$18,000

Disposition of Interest

What would happen to your business in the event of a long disability or your death? Would you want it retained by your heirs or sold or dissolved? __Dissolved__

Do you have a Buy-Sell or Stock Redemption Agreement? Yes ____ No __x__

What is the purchase price? $_____

Is there an escalation clause (to provide for increasing values)? Yes ____ No ____

Is your agreement funded? Yes ____ No ____

With what? _____ How much? _____

RETIREMENT INFORMATION

Type of Plan	Present Vested Interest	Value at Death	Beneficiary	Value of Voluntary Contributions	How Funded?	Monthly Retirement Income at Age ____
Keogh	$12,750 100%	Same	Wife	–	Corp. Bond Mutual Funds	?
I.R.A.						
Pension	$60,000 100%	Same	Wife	–	1/2 Common Funds 1/2 CD's	?
Profit Sharing	$80,750 100%		Wife	–	Stocks & Stock Mutual Funds	?
Thrift						
Salary Savings						

Are you satisfied with your retirement plan? Yes ____ No ____

Explain __Pension plan is administered by bank; profit sharing plan is administered by my brokerage firm. An average of about $5,000 went into my plans during previous years. I'd like that to be about $10,000 from now on.__

(6)

FIGURE 1–1   *(cont.)*

LIFE INSURANCE

If you do not send us your life insurance policies for an analysis, please complete the following for yourself and your spouse:

Insured	Face Amount	Company	Type	Issue Date	Cash Value	Annual Premium	Beneficiary	Owner
Myself	$ 50,000	1st Life	Group Term	1970	–	Pd by P.C.	Wife	Wife
Myself	$100,000	Hi Life	Whole Life	1968	$13,885	$ 1,500	Wife	Wife

HEALTH INSURANCE

Insured	Company	Disability Income	Benefit Period	Daily Benefit (Hosp.)	Major Med.	Acc. Death Benefit
Myself	1st Mutual	$ 1,500	5 years – after six months			
Family	BC–BS			Basic	$ 250,000	

OTHER INSURANCE

When was your property and casualty insurance last reviewed?____1977_____

Do you have personal excess liability coverage? Yes _X_ No ____ How Much? _$1,000,000_____

LIABILITIES

What other indebtedness do you have aside from mortgages previously mentioned?

	Total Amount	Due Date	Monthly Outlay	Obligor (Husb., Wife, Jt.)
Notes (Demand) 1st Atlanta Bank	$ 31,500	6 mos	–	Myself
Installment Obligations				
Cash Value Loans				
Taxes Payable	for cars, boat, down payment on lake house.			
Margin Accounts				
Other				

(7)

FIGURE 1–1 *(cont.)*

ESTATE INFORMATION

Do you have a will? Yes __X__ No ____ Date Drawn _____1975_____ Date Reviewed ____–____

What are the provisions of your will? __See attached—Basic two-trust marital deduction will.__

Does your spouse have a will? Yes __X__ No ____ Date Drawn ____Same____ Date Reviewed _____

What are the provisions of the will? __Same__

Do you expect any inheritances? __Yes__ Amount? __Small, less than $50,000__

Does your spouse expect any inheritances? ____Yes____ Amount? $250,000 or so, but everyone in her family lives forever. We're not counting on any of this in time to enjoy it.

Have you made any gifts to relatives? Yes __X__ No ____

When? __Past 3 years__ How Much? See children's assets, no gift taxes paid. Gave less than $6,000 per child per year.

Have you made any substantial gifts to any charities? Yes ____ No __X__

Are you interested in making such gifts? Yes ____ No ____

Now or in your will? __Now, and more later in will (if financial plan is successful) to Juvenile__ Diabetes Foundation.

TRUSTS

Have you created any trusts? Yes __X__ No ____

If yes, please give (a) type, (b) date created, (c) how it is funded, and (d) who is the beneficiary.

__Three years ago, I created irrevocable trusts (attached) for each of the children to contain__ assets given to them for college and other expenses that I am not legally required to provide.

Are you the beneficiary of any trusts? Yes ____ No __X__

If yes, please give (a) type, (b) donor, (c) annual income

(8)

16

FIGURE 1–1 *(cont.)*

CURRENT INCOME AND EXPENSES

Estimate of Current Year's Income   **Expenses**

Salary	$110,000	DEDUCTIBLE	
Bonus	_____	Interest	$ 15,000
Self Employment Income (Net)	_____	Taxes (Property, State Income)	8,000
Director or Trustee Fees	_____	Contributions	2,000
Pension, Annuity	_____	Other Deductible Expenses	3,500
		(Bus. Entertainment)	
Interest (Taxable)	1,250	NON DEDUCTIBLE	
Dividends **(from P.C.)**	4,760	Principal Reduction	1,500
Real Estate (Net)	-	Living	16,024 **
		(Other than deductible)	
Income from Sale of Asset	10,000*	Education	3,900
In PHC for '83 only			
(Basis $___0___)		Insurance Premiums	2,000
		F.I.T.	27,811
Social Security	-	Savings	0
Spouses Income	-	Investments	10,000
Other__**PHC**__	6,000	Other_**Disc. Cash Flow**_	36,475
Tax Free Income	4,200		
TOTAL	126,210*	TOTAL	126,210

*LTCG proceeds excluded from total since it stayed
in PHC.
Please give details of any installment sale income, capital gains or losses you expect this year. _____

Do you expect any significant changes in your income or expenses in the next 5 years? Yes ____ No ____ Please
explain **We are pleased with our current income status and have no big desire to improve on
the lifestyle we now enjoy. We're more interested in assurring ourselves of tomorrow's
standard of living.**

INCOME OBJECTIVES

RETIREMENT
At what age do you plan to retire? _**Whenever I feel like it.**_

What annual aftertax (spendable) income would you want at retirement? (In today's dollars) $ **55,000 or more
by no later than age 65. I'd like to be able to reach that earlier if possible. In fact, I'd
DISABILITY like to reach that level of independence as soon as possible without taking undue risk.**
If you became disabled, how much annual income would you and your family need to maintain your present

standard of living? $__**50,000**__

SURVIVOR'S INCOME
If you died today, what principal amount would you want to provide for:

Home Mortgage? $_____-_____ Education Fund? $_**15,000**_

Debts? $_**31,500**_____ Other $_____-_____

How much annual income would your family need to maintain their standard of living? $__**50,000**__

(9)

**Includes $2,170 of Social Security taxes plus $13,854 of other living expenses.

FIGURE 1–1   *(cont.)*

OVERALL FINANCIAL AND INVESTMENT CONCERNS

How would you best position your investment assets to coincide with your current investment temperament?

__10__% Very Conservatively. Conserving present capital is more important than making it grow.

__30__% Conservatively. High quality investments that provide an opportunity for appreciation and relative safety are important.

__50__% Subject to moderate risk. Aggressive growth is important.

__10__% Subject to high risk. Speculative growth is acceptable.

Do you have any preferences or objections to any particular investment areas?

Please explain ___I hate paying this much in taxes.___

Which of the following best describes your attitude towards your income needs?

☒ My present income is adequate for my needs.

☐ I need more current income.

☒ I can forgo current income to be better able to provide for future retirement income.

Indicate areas of major concern to you by rating numerically in order of importance:

__5__ Current Income   __2__ Education of Children

__4__ Retirement Income   __1__ Reduction of Current Income Taxes

__3__ Further Building of Estate   __7__ Reduction of Estate Taxes

__6__ Conservation of Assets for Heirs   ____ Other ___I want to save all the income taxes I can but I don't want to loose my money just to save taxes.___

What would you consider to be your primary financial objective or concern? ___Accumulate more assets for future income needs.___

Is there any thing else we should know? ___I am not anxious to gift more to my kids than they will need for college. I want them to have to work successfully.___

___I like to keep track of my investments but I would like someone else to be responsible for picking and managing them.___

(10)

1. FAMILY EDUCATION PLANS

Most families feel a moral if not legal need to develop their children's or grandchildren's future earning power and/or socio-economic stations in life. Education costs become, in many instances, a need that partially overrides lifestyle preferences. Providing for this increasingly expensive obligation therefore becomes an integral function of long-term planning. Obviously, the earlier the funding begins, the lesser the burden. The procedural or investment planning mechanism can, where appropriate, easily be lubricated via tax avoidance strategies. Dr. Wright, as can be seen on page 2, is well into a plan of action that can both be improved upon and better risk-managed.

2. LIFESTYLE AND INCOME

Usually some improvement in lifestyle is desired, simultaneous with a progression toward future financial independence. Page 9 in Dr. Wright's questionnaire is both revealing and unordinary. The Wright family enjoys a comfortable current lifestyle *and* is satisfied with it as is. That presents the Wrights with a unique ability to devote a considerable amount of discretionary cash flow to building their financial future. And they can do that while still funding the children's future education needs, which may well be understated in this questionnaire.

3. RETIREMENT INCOME

Dr. Wright's overriding objective is to be able to reach financial independence, which he defines as having after-tax income of $55,000. He desires this level of spendable income at least by age 65. But the *level*, in today's dollars, seems even more important than the specific age. The determination of how soon the Wrights can reach this goal becomes a prime objective of retirement income planning.

4. DISABILITY INCOME AND SURVIVOR'S INCOME

Dr. Wright also sees an important need to have at least $50,000 of spendable income in the event of his disability or premature death. While asset and income planning will provide for the Wright family if he lives in good health, a well conceived risk-management program is what will satisfy Dr. Wright's disability and/or survivor's income needs. These two aspects of planning go hand in hand, as the cost of one either adds or subtracts from the funds available for providing the other.

5. ESTATE PRESERVATION

Beyond mere survivor's income planning (see the capital needs analysis section in Chapter 8), all of us have some level of desire to reduce estate taxes and thereby conserve assets for heirs. Comprehensive long-term financial plans will devote a great deal of thought to the pros and cons of both the financial and psychological aspects for implementing these types of objectives.

In this area, more than any other, obtaining the solution is much easier than defining the problem and setting the proper objective. While saving estate and gift taxes may automatically sound ideal, it cannot be the controlling factor in estate planning anymore than saving income taxes can control lifetime investment planning. Over-emphasizing these tax savings may rob the living estate to pay—or rob—the heirs of the incentives to be productive in our free enterprise environment. On the other hand, heirs may be able to dispose of an estate in a more intelligent fashion than the people who brought us the postal service.

In any case, Dr. Wright has focused his aim very thoughtfully. He is basically saying to us that, after he has achieved all of his family's other objectives, he would perhaps consider techniques or strategies that would help transfer what is left to his heirs. But, to him, it is not an overriding objective.

Now, we can see that Dr. Wright has set fairly precise sights on what he wants his developing financial scenario to achieve. He, like most of us, can order his financial affairs so as to balance spending for today's luxuries with saving for tomorrow's necessities.

Key Idea No. 6: The financial questionnaire must be equally capable of: (1) providing insight into the current financial condition, (2) highlighting all of the objectives for the present and the future, and (3) describing the risks that can be taken to reach them.

The professional planner must fix firmly in his mind that the initial and careful gathering of data and listing of objectives in life or at death is but the beginning. The usefulness of that first major step is markedly enhanced via the construction of an orderly and graphic diagram for illustrating the *segmentation* of the current financial condition. Creating such a structural identification is what the following chapter will unfold for you.

2

How to Construct Your Client's Financial Pyramid

In the world of medicine, solutions to important health problems cannot be prescribed prior to the thorough examination of the patient. Financial planning is no different. It too must always start with as precise as possible an examination of your client's current financial condition. It is difficult, if not impossible, to even begin an orderly journey toward your client's chosen financial destiny, unless you know exactly where he or she is now. Consequently, a methodology for examining the present is almost as important as having the basic data. In the final analysis, the "output" can be no better than the completeness, accuracy, and intimacy of the "input."

Nothing is more frustrating than the discovery that procedural or investment directions were inappropriately suggested due to incomplete or erroneous input. What could possibly be more disappointing than to learn that important decisions were made without considering all of the detailed information that was actually provided to the planner? It is therefore crucial that total planning commence with detailed "financial disrobing" illustrated in easy to understand fashion.

You are hopefully already asking yourself the inevitable and very proper number one question: *Where and how do I begin?*

Two ways to get there

The first step is to design a system for translating the financial scenario— obtained from a questionnaire, a cold balance sheet, a cash flow analysis, and estate and death analysis—into an exciting, living financial pyramid. This new, more representative structure, as you will come to know, gives life to the concept that, financially speaking, clients exist in segments of both assets and cash flow, each of which must have a specific purpose. This chapter will show you that really only two things can be done to reach your client's financial goals:

1. position assets in line with the stated objectives, and
2. direct discretionary cash flow toward the anemic segments.

EXAMPLE:

> Assume that Joe Shearer has not yet entered the early stages of planning for his financial future. He is 32 years of age, married with two children, has investment assets of $15,000 held in a two-year 10% Certificate of Deposit at his local bank, and earns $36,000 as a promising young executive. His living expenses total $25,400.

How Cash Flow is Identified

Joe's income, federal income taxes, and discretionary cash flow are as follows:	
Salary	$ 36,000
Interest Income	1,500
	$ 37,500
Exemptions and Excess Itemized Deductions	(6,000)
Net Taxable Income	$ 31,500
Federal Income Tax	(5,514)
Social Security and State Income Taxes	(3,080)
Income After Taxes, Exemptions, and Excess Itemized Deductions	$ 22,906
Add: Exemptions and Excess Itemized Deductions	6,000

	$ 28,906
Less: Total Living Expenses	(25,400)
Reinvested Pretax Interest	(1,500)
Discretionary Cash Flow	$ 2,006

Two Tools for Reaching Financial Goals. Joe Shearer's two primary tools for arriving at his overall financial goals are: (1) the $15,000 accumulated when his spouse still worked, plus (2) the $2,006 of annual discretionary cash flow available for saving or investing after extracting the taxes due on the interest income.

How the Marginal Tax Bracket Affects Return. His current income places him in a 30% marginal or top tax bracket in 1983. His Certificate of Deposit therefore represents a true after-tax rate of return of 7.0% (10% times the complement of a 30% top bracket), assuming that his state does not tax interest income earned within the state. Joe is adding his $2,006 of investable cash flow to an equivalent investment, again compounding at an after-tax rate of return of 7.0%. At his current "financial speed," Joe's projected investment net worth at age 42, 10 years later, is as follows:

$15,000 @ 10% for 10 years	= $38,906
$2,006 per annum @ 7.0% for 10 years	= 27,716
Investment Net Worth at age 42	= $66,622

Note that you must compound the $15,000 at the full pretax 10% since the taxes on that return have already been extracted from the cash flow available for further investments. The cash flow must then be compounded at the effective after-tax rate since it is not subsequently decreased by the taxes due on the earnings that it produces during each of the 10 years of compounding.

A better way to reach for financial goals

Through the most elementary financial planning procedures, Joe then examined his segments of financial wherewithal. Next, he identified the following facts:

1. His discretionary cash flow was both too little and misguided toward too low a risk level in order to achieve his future asset/income objectives.

2. Income taxation was robbing his income of its total investment and reinvestment potential.

3. The current inflationary rate indicated a need to earn at least 10% after taxes so as not to travel backwards financially.

Further analysis indicated that the Shearers' proper investment positioning for the $15,000 would begin with $10,000 in cash reserves earning a tax-sheltered yield of 10% in a deferred annuity. Secondly, $5,000 should move to an income real estate partnership conservatively estimated to earn 5% tax-sheltered cash flow and 12% in growth and equity build-up after considering costs, leverage, and future capital gains taxes at today's tax rates. Joe's financial plan also resulted in the decision to decrease living expenses by $50 per month through careful budgeting, as follows:

Salary	$ 36,000
Interest Income	–0–
Exemptions and Excess Itemized Deductions	(6,000)
Net Taxable Income	30,000
Federal Income Tax	(5,064)
Social Security and State Income Taxes	(3,036)
Income After Taxes, Exemptions and Excess Itemized Deductions	21,900
Add: Exemptions and Excess Itemized Deductions	6,000
	27,900
Less: Total Living Expenses	(24,800)
Discretionary Cash Flow	$ 3,100

The improved $3,100 of investable cash flow is directed to a professionally managed pool of common stocks with a historical 12.0% total after tax rate of return.

The Shearer family's projected, after-tax investment worth is as follows:

$10,000 @ 10% for 10 years	$ 25,937
$5,000 @ 17% for 10 years	24,034
$3,100 per annum @ 12% for 10 years	54,401
Investment Net Worth @ at 42	$104,372
Previous Unplanned Projection	(66,622)
"Planned for" Improvement In Net Worth	$ 37,750

These projections, of course, assume that, for sake of example, the Shearers can reinvest all earnings at an after-tax internal rate of return equivalent to that estimated at the entry point. While this assumption may not in fact be the case, the illustration does serve to demonstrate how, in even an uncomplicated example, the planning process can make a big difference.

The simple recognition of what is available to work with, as well as how it is positioned and directed in relationship to taxation and inflation, can prevent your client's earning years from turning into yearning years. In Joe Shearer's case, planning produced a 56.7% projected improvement over what would have been his family's investment net worth in only 10 years.

How to use segmentation to take stock of your client

Before you can develop a logical method for portraying your client's current financial condition, you must thoroughly understand segmentation of assets and cash flow. One's current financial profile, as illustrated in the previous Joe Shearer example, consists of much more than just what is owned and owed. From a financial planning perspective, it is important that you begin to think in terms of segments of:

1. *assets* and how they are positioned, taxed, and risk-managed
   and
2. *income* (cash flow) and how it is directed, taxed, and protected.

Why is it so important to view your client's financial wherewithal in terms of both assets *and* cash flow? A basic financial fact of life is that your client's financial future will depend not only upon how you position current assets but also on how you first create and then direct discretionary cash flow. For those who are in the early to middle stages of accumulating wealth, the future will often depend far more heavily upon properly allocating annual cash flow than upon the positioning of existing assets.

There has been to date an over-emphasis among financial planners on dealing with currently owned investment assets and too little attention paid to the creation and subsequent direction of "savable or investable" segments of cash flow. This is true especially where accumulation is the overall objective. Conversely, when the preservation and/or distribution of existing assets are the prime planning objectives, there must at least be as much emphasis upon the management and positioning of existing assets as upon the disposition of discretionary cash flow.

Also, you must view both assets as well as cash flow as themselves existing in segments. With assets, a certain segment might have absolute safety of principal as the prime objective. Other segments will seek stability of principal and income. Others will seek growth of income or capital. Finally, as an extreme, segments of your capital may appropriately seek maximum growth via deep tax incentive investments with little or no concern for current income.

A multitude of segments of capital with varying objectives are both possible and probable in each case. The key is that each of the segments of capital should exist for a specific purpose. That purpose determines the investment or procedural objective, which in turn indicates the risk level that needs to be attached to it. The relative sizes of the various segments determine whether one is postured, in an overall sense, to primarily: (1) accumulate further assets, (2) preserve the purchasing power of what has already been accumulated, or (3) distribute within the family or to charities some or much of what has already been accumulated and preserved.

Discretionary cash flow must also be segmented, but in a slightly different sense. As existing segments of capital are examined and related to future goals, it becomes obvious that certain ones must gradually be fortified if goals are to be achieved. *The directing of the discretionary cash flow toward the necessary but inadequate segments frequently spells the difference between financial success and failure.*

You should therefore go no further without marking indelibly on your mind the principle of *segmentation*. Everyone exists financially in segments of assets *and* cash flow. You must further understand *that each segment of both must be assigned a purpose and therefore a risk level* if short-term, intermediate, and long-term objectives are to ever be met. During the diagnosis section of this book, you will gain insight into methods for determining how to accomplish these assignments of purpose and risk level, that is, how fast the segments should travel financially.

How to use the pyramid to paint a picture of the present

You do not have to read even one of the myriad books on pyramids to be somewhat in awe of those unique and ancient structures. The contrast between their seemingly simple lines and their mathematically complex and almost magical configuration is mind-boggling. Yet the paradoxical pyramid has come to be a rather useful format for portraying your financial condition.

The very appearance of the pyramid inspires solidness and order, and isn't that the type of financial structure we all seek? The pyramid, with its broad base and narrowing height, becomes an ideal graphical way of emphasizing the importance of laying the proper foundation beneath the building of a financial future. It allows beautifully for the segmentation of assets so that purposes can eventually be defined and risk levels assigned or reassigned. As you progress upward within the pyramid—in terms of height, increasing risk, and expected return—decreasing space devoted to higher risk is suggested. But most importantly, the pyramid enables the financial planner to more succinctly portray the client financially than is possible via the more traditional, sometimes confusing, coldness of a balance sheet.

To demonstrate the placement of assets into a pyramid, we will first look at the balance sheet of our imaginary 45-year-old Dr. Tom Wright who is married and has two children, ages 14 and 10. We will then transpose the assets into a pyramid, leaving spaces available for the placement of cash flow and its risk management, as we further develop the Wrights' total current financial structure.

HOW THE PYRAMID IS USED TO PORTRAY ASSETS

First recognize that it was necessary to collect the data to assemble the following balance sheet via the appropriate financial questionnaire illustrated in Figure 1–1. Also recall that it was our purpose to place equal if not greater emphasis upon the subjective goal-oriented portion of the data at that time.

A quick review of the balance sheet in Table 2–1 by an experienced planner would indicate that Dr. Wright probably has a host of potential problems and opportunities related to lifetime and estate planning. But that observation is not pertinent at this stage of the financial planning process. Our business now is the translation of the mere numbers of the balance sheet into a living financial pyramid that can serve multiple purposes. First, the pyramid provides the essence of order. The pyramid will more meaningfully portray the current financial condition. The particular methodology that we shall illustrate will provide an easy to understand starting point for your journey into the financial future. Figure 2–1 shows the financial pyramid that we would suggest for our imaginary Dr. Wright.

Several matters involving the use of this pyramid are worthy of discussion. The base segment is exactly what it implies; the foundation. Fundamental in financial planning is the provision for cash reserves for

TABLE 2–1
How to Determine Assets, Liabilities and Net Worth

Personal Balance Sheet for Dr. Tom Wright			
	Owned by Dr. Wright	Owned Jointly	Owned by Mrs. Wright
Assets:			
Checking Account	$ 3,000		$ 1,000
Savings Account	8,200		
Municipal/Corporate Bonds	65,000		
Life Insurance Cash Values (Net)			13,885
Common Stocks	31,185		
Real Estate			60,000
Keogh Plan	12,750		
Pension Plan	60,000		
Profit Sharing Plan	80,750		
Personal Holding Company	66,000		
Wright Radiology Professional Corporation	30,000		
Tax Incentive Investments	30,000		
Home			165,000
Personal Property		50,000	
Total Assets:	$386,685	$50,000	$239,885
Liabilities:			
Mortgage on Lake House			30,500
Mortage on Home			99,500
Demand Note	31,500		
Total Liabilities	$ 31,500		$130,000
Net Worth	$355,185	$50,000	$109,885
Combined New Worth			$515,070

emergencies, pending tax liability, and/or investment opportunities and estate liquidity. Equally important are the insurance contracts that may be necessary to protect income, perhaps the riskiest asset of all, against death and disability. There are also those contracts that protect other assets against damage, loss, and legal liabilities. And, of course, wills and contracts are quite fundamental in the current or eventual disposition of the entire pyramid.

Unfortunately, many young clients begin building their financial pyramids from the apex down instead from the bottom up. They will prematurely devote attention to the upper segments by directing assets or discretionary cash flow to more speculative investment areas before creating cash reserves and/or designing a risk-management system for protecting their existing assets and income sources. And we all know

FIGURE 2–1
The Financial Pyramid: Translating Dr. Wright's Balance Sheet

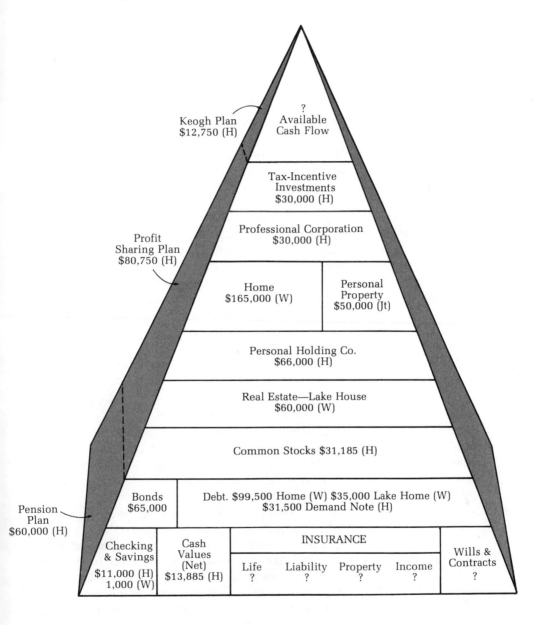

what chances a pyramid has of standing for very long on its apex. It is therefore imperative to begin building the financial pyramid exactly as you would build a house—from the bottom up.

As we move upward, above the foundation segments, risk and illiquidity usually increase, with the typical exception of home and personal property. From this point on, it is impossible to design a perfect order for everyone due to the uniqueness of each individual's financial holdings and temperament. While each planner will want to select the most applicable sequence, we recommend here that you construct the pyramid upward in the order in which assets might be liquidated in case of financial emergency.

As a result, cash reserves would be the very cornerstone, while bonds would usually appear before common stocks, and stocks would be positioned beneath most real estate. Investment or semi-investment real estate would appear before the home and personal property. The last assets, as we ascend the pyramid, would be the most illiquid, typically tax-incentive investments. Note that the qualified retirement plan assets are placed into a separate facet of the pyramid so as to emphasize their varying degrees of availability, liquidity, and risk levels.

Finally, the available cash flow must appear at the very apex of the pyramid in order to denote its very crucial and risky nature. It is also meant to key in on the importance of both protecting it and carefully directing it in ways that will facilitate reaching both short- *and* long-term objectives.

HOW THE PYRAMID IS USED TO DEPICT YOUR CASH FLOW

There are basically three directions for all of the segments of your cash flow or income. It can be spent, invested, and/or sent on a one-way trip to Fort Fumble in Washington, D.C. The well balanced financial plan will always assure that appropriate segments of cash flow are directed toward *all three*. Where further accumulation of wealth is the overall objective, it is the *rate of investing* that should have more to do with your getting there than the *rate of return on investments*.

For instance, most of the wealth that has been accumulated in Coca Cola stock is a result of individuals just deciding to invest than upon a decision to seek the lofty rate of return that the investment provided during its earlier periods of rapid growth. Many of the stories of individual success in owning gas and oil reserves, along with the attendant tax-benefited cash flow, are more a result of people simply salting away extra discretionary cash flow into acres of land than upon a decision to seek the extraordinary rate of return normally associated with gas/oil ventures and investments.

Example after example can be cited of financial success that resulted from simply keeping a greater part of all that is earned. On the other hand, I have seen few people who retired in dignity as a result of the specific selection of a given asset with cash that had been previously accumulated. *The great majority of clients will meet with far better-than-average financial success by developing an appropriate plan for first creating and then prudently directing a specific amount of annual discretionary cash flow.* This is not to imply that we can never ignore the management of our existing assets. It is, however, meant to emphasize proper personal cash flow management in a world of finance that places more importance upon *what to do with what one has than upon what to do with what one is getting.*

How to Determine Discretionary Cash Flow. While Chapter 4, "How To Create Discretionary Cash Flow," delves into the creation and measurement of discretionary cash flow, let us first look at Dr. Wright's cash flow scenario in general and then place the discretionary segment of it rightfully at the very top of the pyramid. See Table 2–2. After also discov-

TABLE 2–2
How to Determine Discretionary Cash Flow:
Cash Flow Analysis for Dr. Tom Wright

Income	
Salary	$110,000
Interest	1,250
Dividends from Professional Corporation*	4,560
40% of Net Long-Term Gains	4,000
Personal Holding Company (Subchapter S Corporation)	6,000
Business Deductions	(3,500)
Tax Incentive Investment Deductions	(10,000)
Adjusted Gross Income	$112,310
Less: Excess Itemized Deductionsons	(21,600)
($25,000 – $3,400)	
(Personal Exemptions)	(4,000)
Taxable Income	$ 86,710
Federal Income Tax Liability	(27,811)
Add: Tax Incentive Investment Deducations	10,000
Dividend Exclusion	200
Personal Exemptions	4,000
Tax Free Income	4,200
Excess Itemized Deducations	21,600
	$ 98,899
Less: Taxable Gain	(4,000)
Living Expenses	(48,424)
Discretionary Cash Flow	46,475
Less: Tax Incentive Investment Commitments	(10,000)
Remaining Discretionary Cash Flow	$ 36,475

*After the $200 dividend exclusion.

FIGURE 2–2
The Financial Pyramid: Determining Discretionary Cash Flow

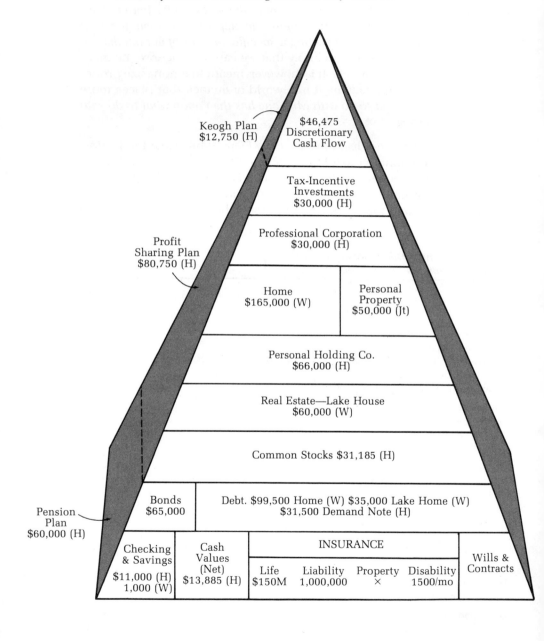

Keogh Plan
$12,750 (H)

$46,475
Discretionary
Cash Flow

Tax-Incentive
Investments
$30,000 (H)

Professional Corporation
$30,000 (H)

Profit
Sharing Plan
$80,750 (H)

Home
$165,000 (W)

Personal
Property
$50,000 (Jt)

Personal Holding Co.
$66,000 (H)

Real Estate—Lake House
$60,000 (W)

Common Stocks $31,185 (H)

Bonds
$65,000

Debt. $99,500 Home (W) $35,000 Lake Home (W)
$31,500 Demand Note (H)

Pension
Plan
$60,000 (H)

Checking
& Savings

$11,000 (H)
1,000 (W)

Cash
Values
(Net)
$13,885 (H)

INSURANCE

Life
$150M

Liability
1,000,000

Property
×

Disability
1500/mo

Wills &
Contracts

ering from the questionnaire that Dr. Wright has the specified levels of the various types of insurance protection, his financial pyramid can now be completed. (See Figure 2–2.)

How to Direct Segments of Cash Flow. Because we have not yet thoroughly diagnosed Dr. Wright's financial problems and objectives, it would be impossible to make appropriate comments about the positioning of the current assets or the directing of the $46,475 of cash flow after living expenses and taxes. Let us, however, simply demonstrate how the pyramid might be used to illustrate recommendations for the direction of the discretionary cash flow. *Assume* that the financial planner recommends that Dr. Wright continue to allocate his $46,475 just as he did during the previous year:

Tax Incentive investment committments	$10,000
Cash gifts to the children	6,000
Personal property purchases	16,975
Additional common stock purchases	8,000
Additions to cash reserves	2,500
Reduction of demand note	3,000
	$46,475

The plan for directing the six segments of cash flow, in the pyramid format, might be illustrated as shown in Figure 2–3.

The pyramid, as you've seen, eases the process of relating the present to the desired future. Identifying and measuring the hurdles that exist between what your client is like now and what he or she wants to be must come before choosing strategies for getting there. Recognizing the extent to which the client's current segments of capital are aligned with his or her goals is an important part of diagnosing financial problems. Studying cash flow and how it's being used is even more crucial for those who are in the accumulation of wealth phase of financial planning. Finally, checking the current versus needed levels of risk management, considering the impact of inflation, and factoring in the erosive effects of progressive income and estate taxation are all integral aspects of what comes next in the financial planning process. The chapters throughout Section II deal with all of these issues in great detail.

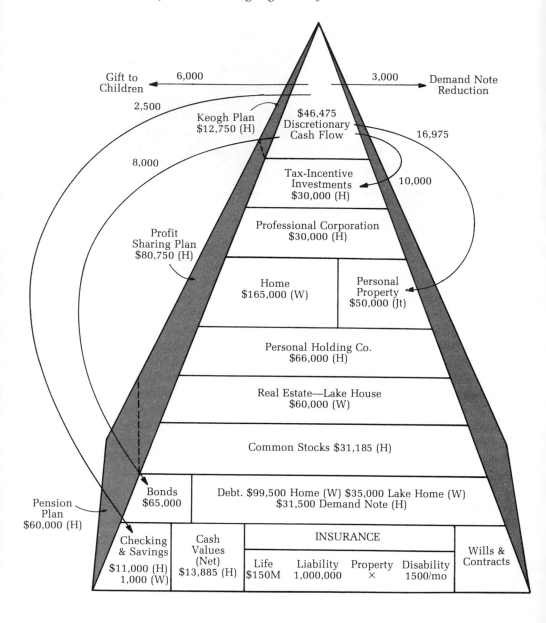

FIGURE 2–3
The Financial Pyramid: Directing Segments of Cash Flow

II

HOW TO
DIAGNOSE
OBSTACLES
TO YOUR
CLIENT'S
INTENDED
FINANCIAL
DESTINY

3

How to
Redirect
Misguided
Objectives

Delving into the interface of today's pyramid and tomorrow's needs is crucial in the diagnostic phase of the financial planning process. In Section I, the examination phase, it is almost automatic that you at least begin to see what some of the problems look like. But harder, more penetrating diagnosis than that is required. Section II now shows you how to dig deeper for the important obstacles that lie between today and your client's intended financial destiny.

It is unimaginable, for example, that a physician would recommend a prescription drug before determining if and exactly what type of illness exists. And so it must also be in our developing world of financial planning. Yet millions of affluent American households today use somewhere in the area of 25 to 45 different "financial medications"—products and services—without first measuring their financial needs.

In Chapter 2 the principle of *segmentation* was

introduced. I stressed the significance of thinking in terms of segments of assets and cash flow. Doing so enables you to relate each segment to a purpose or responsibility during your client's financial journey. That purpose then defines the risk level that can be attached to each segment and, because risk and reward are directly related, the financial speed at which that segment can travel. This chapter will first help you to understand and define overall goals. It will then demonstrate how a Rate of Return Matrix Study can be used to determine the right financial speed and risk level for each segment of capital so that your clients will safely reach their financial objectives in time.

Choosing from among the three types of financial objectives

It is a good bet that you already know whether your client wants to emphasize:

1. building more capital for the future,
2. preserving the wealth that has already been accumulated, or
3. distributing some financial achievements to heirs and/or chosen charities.

One of the following three financial directions, usually measured in terms of asset or income levels, must therefore be established as a clear goal before the key financial problems can be diagnosed:

1. *Accumulation:* acquiring a given amount of wealth by means of either positioning current assets for appreciation, converting discretionary cash flow into assets, or both.
2. *Preservation:* conserving the buying power of, or the income produced by, the wealth you have already accumulated.
3. *Distribution:* sharing existing or accumulating wealth with potential heirs or charities.

It is most difficult to conceive of a person whose every asset and segment of cash flow is dedicated to only one of the three objectives. We can safely state, however, that unless your client is on the deathbed, he or she will feel a deep underlying need to lean toward one of these three major goals. Even with that recognition, we frequently see a financial pyramid whose segments of assets and cash flow are totally misguided toward alien objectives.

It is not uncommon to find older, retired individuals with nearly all of their assets in fixed income positions when they are already strapped for current spendable income—not to mention the bind they will find themselves in after a period of severe inflation. One cannot possibly have resources dedicated to the important middle or upper sections of the pyramid of financial wherewithal if all of the financial building materials are spent on the foundation.

Conversely, it is not at all uncommon to find younger executives and professionals directing their first financial energies toward the upper end of the pyramid before creating a solid base upon which to build for the future. In Chapter 2, we talked about what inevitably happens to a pyramid that tries to stand on its apex. Resurrecting a crumbled pyramid can be avoided through a combination of the proper diversified allocation of resources and risk management.

Those who are in the giant middle ground, where accumulation and preservation combine, are also not without tempting distractions. There is frequently the desire to give away too much too soon or to shy away from gifting when it could simultaneously facilitate both lifetime and estate planning.

There is also the tendency to get either over-liquid or too frozen. Those who are totally liquid must frequently ask themselves, "What price liquidity?"—especially in an inflationary environment. Hardly anyone *needs* total liquidity. On the other hand, everything has its price. Inadequate liquidity can place great stress upon the lifetime planning process by not providing enough general flexibility and specific reserves for emergencies, tax liabilities, and/or future investment opportunities. The total lack of liquidity or procedural provisions for creating it upon death can play havoc with the orderly payment of estate settlement costs or income to heirs.

Diagnosing obstacles to either living or estate objectives requires measuring, sometimes with mathematical exactitude, your client's future asset, income, and liquidity needs. Early recognition of the misalignment of these financial resources and goals will ease the journey to financial independence.

How to graphically display financial objectives

Just as the pyramid graphically displays what your clients are and what they would like to be, a similar method for displaying their broad overall objective can be used. Such an illustration is best accomplished by varying the use of the following basic income-asset flow chart:

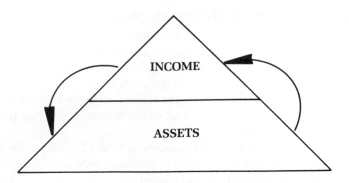

A BETTER WAY TO ILLUSTRATE ACCUMULATION

To depict the three major goals of financial life, let's now alter the complexion of the pyramid. Accumulation has been defined as the process of acquiring further assets via (1) converting cash flow to assets and (2) positioning those assets for further growth or capital enhancement. Our flow chart in this instance might be given the following emphasis:

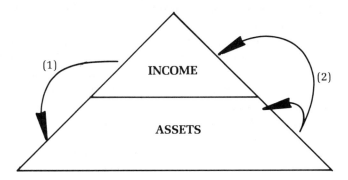

The key here is that discretionary income must exist. It must then be converted to assets for capital growth, and any income that results from these assets must be integrated into the investable cash flow stream. It perhaps, but not necessarily, is reinvested for future compounding into the asset that produced it.

HOW TO PORTRAY PRESERVATION

Preserving wealth has been described as the conserving of the buying power of and/or the income produced by the wealth that has already been accumulated. While Chapter 5, "Inflation, How to Capture the Silent Embezzler," will expand on this subject, suffice it to say now that preservation is no longer achieved if provisions are made for only the guaranteed return of fixed dollars and the fixed income they produce. Attention must be refocused on tryng to assure a return of fixed buying power. That means two things:

1. The "preserving assets" themselves must be positioned in variable or managed fashion to create *increasing* income . . . or
2. some or all of the hopefully tax-benefited cash flow that is produced by fixed assets is reinvested.

The chart therefore reverses itself, as follows:

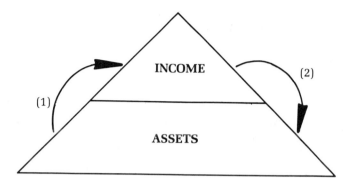

The key to successful problem identification here lies in realizing that assets and income maintain their usefulness only when they maintain or increase their buying power. Whenever the major segments of assets must be preserved and are not positioned in ways that have the potential to return level buying power, a classic but perhaps hidden case of misguided objectives exists. The client is guaranteed to lose.

A METHOD FOR DEPICTING DISTRIBUTION

We have defined lifetime or testamentary distribution as the orderly gifting or sharing of assets and/or income with family members, friends, or charities. Measuring the extent to which the emotional, tax, or financial ramifications of lifetime gifting programs are overriding is a significant aspect of comprehensive and objective financial diagnosis. That eventual measurement can be facilitated by portraying distribution in the following flow chart:

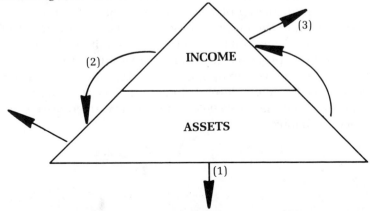

The choices among lifetime gifting programs are more varied than meets the uninitiated planning eye. Each creates its own problems and opportunities. After having identified that it is wise to share acquired or developing wealth, a detailed diagnosis will suggest one of the following routes. One can:

1. gift appreciated assets,
2. create assets by disposing of pretax cash flow and then gift those assets, or
3. gift the income that accumulated assets produce.

How much is gifted in what way, and to whom will determine the potential risks and rewards of any one of these three routes. These alternatives are discussed in detail in Chapter 10, under the section on gifting strategies.

Using the rate of return matrix study to properly align assets

During the initial *examination* of your client's current financial condition and its relationship to his or her goals, it is impossible not to begin seeing some of the hurdles that lie ahead. One of the most common problems uncovered by diagnosis arises when the majority of the specific segments of investment assets are not properly aligned with the client's financial goals. To quantify this type of problem, let's look at a simple example.

A 40-year-old executive, Mr. Richard Valentine, has investment assets of $100,000. His discretionary "investable" cash flow is currently $5,000 per year, and his new employer will be contributing $5,000 per year to a profit sharing plan. Mr. Valentine has no control over the 9% rate of return the profit sharing plan will earn. This $5,000 of annual discretionary cash flow is currently committed to building an equity portfolio projected to average a 12% total annual rate of return. He is in the 48% marginal tax bracket, and he desires a $36,000 spendable income level in today's dollars at a retirement age of 65. Mr. Valentine's $100,000 of current investment assets are positioned as follows:

Credit Union @ 6%	$ 5,000
8½% Certificate of Deposit	20,000
Deferred Annuity @ 8½%	25,000
Municipal Bonds @ 6½%	25,000
Growth Stocks—Estimated Average 12% Total Return	10,000
Real Estate Limited Partnership—Estimated Average 15% Total Return	15,000
	$100,000

HOW THE RATE OF RETURN MATRIX WORKS

Our purpose now is to illustrate a succinct method for determining whether Mr. Valentine's segments of investment assets are properly aligned with his overall long-term retirement goal. The Rate of Return Matrix Study in Table 3–1 explains why he must better position his existing investment assets and/or better direct his discretionary cash flow. Because he is not properly segmented and aligned, this study will also help determine the precise financial speed at which he should travel to get "there."

Obviously, none of the assumptions used in the prior analysis can be carved in stone. That is the greatest argument in support of the need for constant, usually annual, financial plan updating. Using those assumptions, however, and the resulting calculations, we conclude that Mr. Valentine will have a capital shortage of $986,721. This *is* the overall problem. We must now arrive at a more specific definition of what Mr. Valentine must later work toward in the "therapy" phase of the financial planning process.

FOUR ALTERNATIVES FOR ALLEVIATING A CAPITAL SHORTAGE

1. Increase the Rate of Return Matrix of Existing Investment Assets. For Mr. Valentine to accummulate the projected $904,816, plus the $986,721 shortage with his existing $100,000 of investment assets, a rate of return matrix of at least 12.47% must be achieved. Stated differently, $100,000 compounded at an after-tax rate of 12.47% for 25 years produces the $1,891,537 ($904,816 plus $986,721) of needed capital. That matrix could be achieved by lifting the risk levels and hence the projected returns of several segments of current investment assets, perhaps as shown in Table 3–2.

For sake of simplicity, we have not changed the amount of Mr. Valentine's taxable income and discretionary cash flow. The rate of return matrix study therefore serves to mathematically measure the financial speed at which the matrix of Mr. Valentine's various segments of repositioned investment assets must travel for him to reach his overall goal.

TABLE 3–1
Mr. Richard Valentine's Current Rate of Return Matrix

Asset	Current Amount	Estimated Average Return on Investment	Percent of Total	Estimated Weighted Avg. ROI**
Credit Union	$ 5,000	6.00%*	5%	.30%
C.D.	20,000	8.50%*	20%	1.70%
Deferred Annuity	25,000	8.50%	25%	2.13%
Municipal Bonds	25,000	6.50%	25%	1.63%
Common Stocks	10,000	12.00%*	10%	1.20%
Real Estate	15,000	15.00%*	15%	2.25%
	$100,000		100%	9.21%

Computation of Mr. Valentine's Capital Shortage
Using Existing Rate of Return Matrix on Assets and Cash Flow

1. Current Income Needs (in today's dollars) at age 65 (25 years)	$ 36,000
2. Less Approximate Currently Legislated Social Security Tax-Free Income	(12,000)
3. Income Needed after Social Security (in today's dollars)	24,000
4. Retirement Income Needs Inflated at 12% for 25 Years	408,002
5. Capital Needed Assuming 10% After-Tax Income	4,080,020
LESS: Current Investment Assets of $100,000	
Compounded at 9.21% (matrix study)	(904,816)
$5,000 Discretionary Cash Flow***	
Compounded at 12% After-Tax	(666,669)
$5,000 Annual Profit Sharing Contribution	
Increased 12% per Year Compounded at 9%	(1,521,814)
6. Capital Shortage (Surplus)	$ 986,721

*Remember that, as per the Joe Shearer example at the beginning of Chapter 2, the total return must be compounded since the tax liability thereon reduced the discretionary cash flow to the indicated $5,000.

**Simple compounded annual rate of return on investment. This is computed by multiplying the "Estimated Average Return on Investment" times the "Percent of Total."

***Discretionary Cash Flow is not increased for inflation for two reasons. The increased cost of living (see Chapter 5) and graduated tax brackets (see Chapter 6) act in concert to make increasing discretionary cash flow very difficult.

That then dictates, to a major extent, what risk levels need to be attached to what sized segments of capital.

2. Increase the Rate of Return Matrix of Discretionary Cash Flow.
Let us now assume that Mr. Valentine's temperament or other considerations prevent him from altering his $100,000 of investments. He currently has $5,000 of savable or investable cash flow and is committed to building his small equity portfolio, which was projected to grow at a 12% after-tax

TABLE 3–2
Mr. Richard Valentine's Revised Rate of Return Matrix

Asset	Current Amount	Estimated Average Annual Return on Investment	Percent of Total	Estimated Weighted Average ROI
Money Market Fund	$ 10,000	12.0%	10%	1.20%
Deferred Annuity	10,000	8.5% tax-deferred	10%	.85%
Municipal Bonds	5,000	6.5% tax-free	5%	.33%
Common Stocks	35,000	12.0%	35%	4.20%
Real Estate	40,000	15%	40%	6.00%
	$100,000	Revised Rate of Return Matrix		12.58%

return on investment. We can now reconstruct the Rate of Return Matrix Study to determine how fast that $5,000 would have to travel to reach the retirement or financial independence goal of $36,000 of after-tax income in today's dollars. (See Table 3–3.)

It may well be, for reasons of risk tolerance limitations, tax considerations, liquidity needs, or current economics, that it would not be appropriate for Mr. Valentine to subject his $5,000 per year to the level of risk associated with an investment program projecting a return on investment (ROI) of 17.78%. Conversely, many of the investment areas that are often recommended, such as tax-incentive investment areas of energy and real estate projects under construction, should certainly not be considered unless they *are* projected to compound capital at least at 17% or higher.

The key question here, as will be discussed in detail in Section III, involves the degree of probability of getting a return *of* your investment before getting too wild-eyed about projecting a 17+% after-tax return *on*

TABLE 3–3
Computation Redirecting Mr. Valentine's Discretionary Cash Flow

1. Current Income Needs (in today's dollars) At Age 65	$ 36,000
2. Less Currently Legislated Social Security Tax Free Income	$ (12,000)
3. Income Needed After Social Security (in today's dollars)	$ 24,000
4. Retirement Needs Inflated at 12% for 25 years	408,002
Capital Needed Assuming 10% After-Tax Income Rate	$ 4,080,020
LESS: Current Investment Assets of $100,000 Compounded at 9.21%	(904,816)
Annual Profit Sharing Plan Contribution Increased 12% per year Compounded at 9%	(1,521,814)
Capital Shortage	$ 1,653,390
Rate of Return Matrix Needed to Compound $5,000/Year into $1,653,390 in 25 years	17.78%

investment. The fact still remains that shifting the $5,000 per year away from equities toward tax shelters could be a viable alternative.

As we discuss the redirecting of Mr. Valentine's discretionary cash flow, there is still another distinct possibility. After reviewing the various alternatives discussed thus far, Mr. Valentine could decide that he would rather forsake some of today's luxuries in exchange for tomorrow's income needs. That would require creating more than $5,000 of annual discretionary cash flow.

For example, if the Valentine family were able to reduce their annual expenditures for personal expenses, travel, clothing, and entertainment through more careful budgeting, it may be that another $5,000 could be made available for their future. In such a case, the total $10,000 of excess cash flow would have to be compounded at a lesser matrix return of 13.39% to accumulate the capital shortage of $1,653,390. Or, it might mean continuing to direct $5,000 per year toward his equity portfolio projected to return 12% and directing the other $5,000 toward more conservative tax-incentive investments projected to return 14.52%.

$5,000/year compounded at 12% year for 25 years	$ 666,669
5,000/year compounded at 14.52%/year for 25 years	986,721
Total	$ 1,653,390

3. Increase Rate of Return Matrix on Both Existing Investment Assets and Discretionary Cash Flow. For many conceivable reasons, including temperament or liquidity needs, perhaps Mr. Valentine can neither reach a 12.47% ROI on his $100,000 of existing investment assets, increase the ROI on his $5,000 of discretionary cash flow to 17.78%, nor increase the $5,000 of excess cash flow to $10,000. The third alternative would be to seek some combination of the first two alternatives.

For example, in order to have the $100,000 of investments and $5,000 per year of investable cash flow create the needed $2,558,206 ($986,721 capital shortage plus $904,816 current investment assets projection plus $666,669 current cash flow investment projection), the rate of return matrix objectives could be changed as shown in Table 3–4.

TABLE 3–4
Computation Combining Mr. Valentine's Investment Assets and Discretionary Cash Flow

Resources	Objective	Rate of Return Matrix Needed
$100,000 of Current Investment Assets	$1,279,103	10.73%
$5,000/year of Investable Cash Flow	$1,279,103	16.17%
Total	$2,558,206	

Even though you can imagine an almost infinite number of combinations, depending upon what you aim for with each resource, the Rate of Return Matrix Study serves to better delineate what hurdles need to be jumped, if any, for the Valentines to reach their financial finish line.

4. Other Alternatives. Mr. Valentine's alternatives for (1) repositioning existing investment capital, (2) redirecting or increasing discretionary cash flow, and (3) a combination of alternatives one and two, serve well to illustrate the use of the Rate of Return Matrix Study. We would, however, be remiss by not suggesting the possibility of still other meaningful alternatives.

While using up capital is not a particularly popular source of cash flow during one's later years, particularly with those who have high goals in the "conservation of assets for heirs" category, it can be a very attractive alternative. It is especially applicable to those who are risk-averse.

As an example, assume that we resign ourselves to the Valentine family's original projected capital shortage of $986,721 and that they were to actually end up with total investment assets of only $3,093,299 at age 65. Assuming, too, that those assets could all be converted to a current after-tax income of 10%, Mr. Valentine could go on for almost 15 years withdrawing $408,002 every year before he would run out of money. That, of course, assumes that inflation stopped the day he reached 65 and that the investment assets stopped growing and produced only 10% after-tax cash flow.

It could be argued very successfully that none of this is realistic. Alternatively, if inflation continues at anything near today's rate, and the Valentine's capital is positioned to produce increasing tax-advantaged income, they should be in good stead. All of these types of questions and assumptions again serve to stress the need for constant updating of your every projection. It is interesting, however, that changes in your assumptions about inflation then affect your assumptions about interest rates and other rates of return. Experience with the Rate of Return Matrix Study shows that changes in inflation and projected rates of return compensate for each other. For example, if rapid inflation does not continue, the Valentines will need far less income in 25 years. In that case, it will have been less necessary and more difficult to earn the types of returns we have projected. Conversely, if inflation remains a problem, earning 6% taxable in a credit union, 6.5% in municipal bonds, and 8.5% in deferred annuity contracts will all indeed constitute dismal performance. That would almost be like sitting still with those segments of capital on a conveyor belt that is moving backwards. But certain common stocks (mainly asset plays), collectibles, real estate and certain tax-incentive in-

TABLE 3–5
Dr. Wright's Rate of Return Matrix

Assets	January 1, 1983 Amount	Assumed Average ROI	Percent of Total	Weighted Average ROI
Savings	$ 8,000	5.25%[1]	2%	.10%
Cash Values	13,885	4.00%	3%	.12%
Tax Exempt Bonds	65,000	6.46%[2]	15%	.97%
Common Stock Fund	31,185	9.00 [3]	7%	.63%
Real Estate				
(Lake House)	60,000	10.00%	13%	1.30%
Personal Holding Co.				
Note	31,500	6.00%[4]	7%	.42%
Utility Stocks	34,500	12.00%[5]	8%	.96%
Professional Corp.	30,000	0%[6]	7%	.00%
Tax-Incentive Investments				
Gas/Oil	10,000[7]	20.00%[8]	2%	.40%
Real Estate	10,000	15.00%[9]	2%	.30%
Keogh Plan	12,750	10.00%[10]	3%	.30%
Pension Plan	60,000	9.50%[11]	13%	1.24%
Profit Sharing Plan	80,750	9.00%[12]	18%	1.62%
Totals	$447,570		100%	8.36%

[1]Passbook Savings rate of 5¼%.

[2]5.6% of $75,000 face amount = 6.46% of current market value.

[3]Average stock market performance of 9% is also assumed to be Dr. Wright's average performance of a conservatively run tax-managed trust.

[4]$31,500 note earns 6% interest annually.

[5]$34,500 utility stocks produce $4,140 dividend.

[6]Assumes that assets of Professional Corp. will not appreciate.

[7]$20,000 present value of gas/oil drilling investments is reduced by contemplated gift to children of his $10,000 present value of the 1981 investment.

[8]An internal rate of return of 20% is assumed as a compounding rate. It is therefore assumed that all tax savings and cash flow which result from this investment will be reinvested into an investment whose performance will be identical to the investment which creates it.

[9]15% return is assumed for these two existing, income-oriented commercial real estate portfolios.

[10]Keogh Plan consists of a quality corporate bond fund currently paying a 10.00% compounded annual rate of return tax-sheltered by the plan's qualified status.

[11]The mixture of CDs at 10% and Bank Common Funds at 9% is assumed to produce an average tax-sheltered return of 9.5%.

[12]The tax-sheltered rate of return on the combination of common stocks selected by Dr. Wright and his broker and the equity mutual funds is assumed to average 9%.

vestments should perform extremely well for Mr. Valentine—perhaps better than we may even dream of projecting today.

It must also be emphasized that, if inflation does proceed at anywhere near the assumed 12% rate, Mr. Valentine's discretionary income could rise, though not nearly at as high a rate as inflation itself. This phenomenona is due to the dramatic way in which inflation and taxation act in concert to hinder the maintenance of purchasing power and is discussed in Chapters 5 and 6. It is why we have purposely not factored an increase in the discretionary cash flow of $5,000 into these examples.

USING THE RATE OF RETURN MATRIX TO DIAGNOSE PROBLEMS

Let us now look at our original case through the financial planning eyes of Dr. Wright. We have already determined in Chapter 2 that Dr. and Mrs. Wright have $294,070 of personal investment assets, plus the $153,500 in the various qualified retirement plans. Let us segment all of these various assets into various pyramid and subpyramid components, and then make assumptions as to their average return on investment (ROI) and weighted average return on investment (ROI). (See Table 3–5.)

WHAT THE RATE OF RETURN MATRIX STUDY ACCOMPLISHES

The sum total of this analysis for planning purposes is that we are to project an average rate of return of 8.36% on Dr. Wright's $447,570 of available investment assets. This will become an important assumption in developing the rate of return matrix that will help to guide Dr. Wright's discretionary cash flow during the year or two between financial planning updates.

Try now to place yourself into the shoes of Dr. Wright. Try, too, to keep in mind *what* we are trying to get the Rate of Return Matrix Study to accomplish. Remember that we have continued to stress the significance of determining how fast financially this client must travel in order to reach *his* financial destiny in time.

If the overriding goal is to increase investment income while preserving assets, the task is more precise. You simply consider all of the available income sources and diversification strategies on an after-tax basis and decide what risks can be taken with which segments of capital in order to produce the desired level of increasing, spendable cash flow. If you are like Dr. Wright, however, and accumulation is your overall direction, you simply have to determine which risks can or must be taken to accumulate the desired levels of assets and income. Table 3–6 demonstrates how it works.

What Are Dr. Wright's Alternatives? Unlike Mr. Richard Valentine, Dr. Wright's Rate of Return Matrix Study concludes that he really does not have very much of a problem at all. Quite importantly, it tells Dr.

TABLE 3–6
Computation of Dr. Wright's Required Rate of Return Matrix on Discretionary Cash Flow

1. Current Income Needs (in Today's dollars) At Age 65	$ 55,000
2. Less Approximate $1,000/month Social Security Tax-Free Income	(12,000)
3. Income Needed after Social Security	43,000
4. Current Income Needs Inflated at 10% for 19 Years	262,984
5. Capital Needed Assuming 8% After-Tax Income Rate	3,287,300
Less: Current Investment Assets	
($447,570) Compounded At Current Projected ROI Matrix of 8.36% for 19 Years	(2,057,652)
Current Annual Qualified Retirement Plan Contribution of $10,000/year Increased 12% per year Compounded at 9.21%/year	(1,283,731)
Capital Shortage (Surplus)	(54,083)
Rate of Return Matrix Needed to Compound $23,500 */year of Investable Cash Flow into capital shortage in 19 years	0

*While Dr. Wright has $46,475 of discretionary cash flow, after considering his typical $6,000/year gifts to children and $16,975 of personal property purchases, only $23,500 was available for investments and/or debt reductions.

Wright that, as is often the case, he does not have to travel as fast financially as he would expect. Investing his assets or investable cash flow at risk levels any higher than necessary subjects his principal to perils not required for him to reach financial independence at a reasonable age.

The specific conclusion of the reasonable zero rate of return needed on Dr. Wright's available cash flow indicates that:

1. He can easily reach financial independence by age 65 or earlier without upping the overall risk level of his current investment assets and without taking any consequential risk with his cash flow.

2. He can increase expenditures on current luxuries without sacrificing income for tomorrow's needs. He in fact does not have to save or invest any of the $23,500 of discretionary cash flow.

3. He can reduce the risk posture of his current assets of $447,570 if he becomes so inclined without taking undue risk with the assumed level of $23,500 annual investable cash flow.

4. He can sizably increase his lifetime gifting to charity or to family members instead of waiting until too far into the future or upon his death.

5. He can easily increase his contributions to the qualified retirement plans, including an IRA for himself and Mrs. Wright, to provide

greater benefits to his employees and his family, but he does not have to do so.

Other conclusions with regard to both lifetime and estate planning can, of course, be reached, but that would carry us too far too prematurely into the "therapy" phase of mapping out Dr. Wright's several desired financial destinations.

It is important to further understand that none of the assumed rates of inflation or return on investment are to be considered gospel or current. Reasonable and differing rates were projected here only for purposes of illustrating the usefulness of the Rate of Return Matrix Study in diagnosing problems. In real life, annual plan updating along with systemic compensating factors will keep your clients and their financial journeys on course.

In the Joe Shearer case at the beginning of Chapter 2 and in the Valentine and Wright examples in this chapter, you were reminded of one of the few cardinal rules of financial planning: *You have two principal tools that can be used to build a financial pyramid—assets and cash flow.* The precise delineation of the total cash flow and the isolation of the part of it that is "savable or investable" is central to performing a complete Rate of Return Matrix Study. The next chapter will show you, in eight easy steps, exactly how to create discretionary income as well as demonstrate the significance of the role it plays in planning your client's financial future.

4

How to
Create
Discretionary
Cash Flow

With today's high and steeply graduated income tax rates, many people believe that we cannot create substantial wealth from earned income. It is also argued that only the entrepreneur has a fighting chance of becoming rich and that, even then, the odds are slim because the stakes are high.

This chapter espouses a very different viewpoint. Granted, the height and steepness of the tax scale *is* a huge "bear market" in the journey toward success. Also granted, business owners *do* have access to more tools with which to create capital. Yet clients whose main "asset" is relatively high earned income can and do accumulate enormous financial wherewithal. Those who have the ability to interject an extra dose of discipline and a healthy measure of contrarian thinking into their financial planning can be among that number. They can not only achieve great net worth, but they can do it more predictably than those who start out with a lump sum but no annual investable cash flow.

In this chapter we illustrate a practical method for precisely measuring this key element in creating wealth—discretionary cash flow. We then show through systematic, short-, and intermediate-term budgeting and/or tax sheltering how the amount of annual cash flow can be increased. And finally, you will become familiar with how your clients' cash flow can be converted into assets for their future financial independence.

The rate of investing is more crucial than the rate of return

Think for a moment of the vast sums of money that travel through your clients' bank accounts during the most productive years of their lives. It probably amounts to hundreds of thousands of dollars or more for each client. Cannot the accumulation of wealth, then, be simply a matter of converting some of that cash flow into capital?

Practically speaking, clients must pay themselves regular and preferably tax-free amounts, instead of just paying the bills for today's perceived needs and luxuries. This means that an even greater emphasis must be placed upon the rate of investing than upon the rate of return on investments.

Note: The purpose here is not so much to diminish the importance of achieving the appropriate overall rate of return that we discussed in Chapter 3. It is, however, meant to stress that, for the majority of clients who are still emphasizing accumulation, the rate at which cash flow is set aside for investment is probably more crucial to financial success than stretching too far toward the maximum rate of return on investment. ROI on very little money produces too little wealth. Conversely, substantial capital invested systematically can provide handsomely for the future, as long as you avoid chasing the most popular investments of the moment. This principle of contrarian thinking is discussed more fully in Chapter 11.

Why It's Done This Way. Let us assume that, due to a change in your projections about inflation, you judge that your client will need an extra $100,000 at retirement in 15 years to achieve his or her capital and income aims. A $10,000 investment compounded at 16.59% annually after taxes will grow to exactly $100,000 in 15 years. On the other hand, only $153.58 invested each month at 16.59% over that same period will achieve the same end. The point is that an add-on goal to any financial plan is achieved more easily by creating and investing a relatively small incremental increase in discretionary cash than by either "finding" a lump sum of investable cash or dramatically increasing the rate of return on an existing segment of capital. But it takes discipline!

THE RELATIONSHIP BETWEEN THE RATIO OF DISCRETIONARY CASH FLOW TO INITIAL CAPITAL VERSUS THE TIME TO FINANCIAL INDEPENDENCE

EXAMPLE 1

Mr. Richard Valentine has $100,000 of current investment assets, $5,000 of discretionary cash flow, and $5,000 of annual profit sharing plan contributions. To both simplify the case and not overstate it, we will assume that the profit sharing contribution and discretionary cash flow do not increase with inflation. We will also assume that everything compounds at an even 10% after taxes, so that the results are not distorted by taking differing risks with different segments of capital. Remember, too, that Mr. Valentine is age 40 and therefore has 25 years until he reaches his principal objective, retirement in dignity, by age 65.

Compounding the $100,000 at 10% after taxes for 25 years creates $1,083,470 of future capital. Making investments of $10,000 per year for 25 years at the same 10% after-tax rate of return produces $983,470 of future capital. The key point is that, with time and discipline, creating and then carefully directing investable cash flow amounting to $10,000 (only 10% of Mr. Valentine's current investment assets) produces ultimate capital almost as much as that produced by the much larger initial $100,000 of investment assets.

EXAMPLE 2

Now look at Dr. Tom Wright who has a larger $447,500 of current investment assets, $10,000 of cash flow going into qualified retirement plans, and $29,500 going to other outside investments. He has 19 years to achieve his desired level of financial independence. Again for simplicity sake, we will assume an even 10% after-tax rate of return on all investments.

To determine the relative importance of each of his two major sources of future wealth in his future financial picture, the figures look like this:

$447,500 (current investment assets) compounded at 10% for 19 years	$2,737,869
$39,500 ($10,000 in a qualified retirement plan plus $29,500 in other investments) for 19 years at 10% grows to:	2.020,784
For an impressive 42.5% of the total of:	$4,758,653

Even though Dr. Wright's cash flow does not produce the larger portion of his future net worth, the purpose here is to point out its crucial nature even when planning begins a long 19 years ahead of his goal with almost a half a million dollars of capital for starters.

EXAMPLE 3

Finally, consider a much younger 30-year-old Bob Jones. He was discouraged to learn that the $10,000 he had saved during his first few years out of college would grow to only $527,996 in 35 years. And that was no where near the millionaire status to which he aspired.

$10,000 (current investment assets) compounded at 12% for 35 years	$527,996

Bob Jones was then pleasantly surprised to later learn that it would take relatively little in additional monthly investments to make up the difference.

$91.12 per month ($1,093.45 annually) compounded at 12% annually for 35 years	472,004
For a significant 47.2% of the total of	$1,000,000

The Significance of Discretionary Cash Flow to Investment Assets with Time. The chart in Figure 4–1 illustrates this relationship. If you begin the design of a financial road map with $50,000 of investment capital and budgeted annual savings and investments of $5,000, the ratio (discretionary cash flow divided by initial investment capital) is 10%. Assume your client is 40 and wants to retire in 15 years at age 55 and all of her investments average a 10% after-tax compounded rate of return. The chart indicates that the portion of her future pyramid that results from the cash flow will be about .9 times as large as the part that results from the investment of her initial capital.

However, if through astute cash flow analysis and careful budgeting, you are able to lift her annual investments (including contributions to retirement plans) to $10,000, the ratio of cash flow to initial investment as-

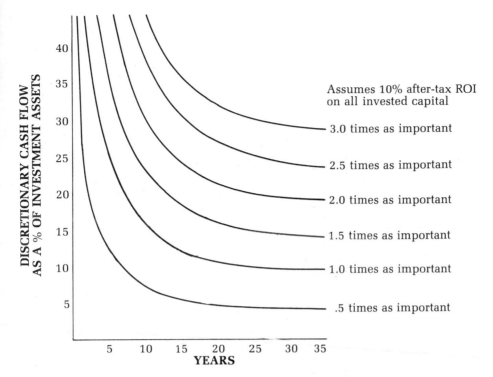

FIGURE 4–1
Chart Showing Significance of Discretionary Cash Flow to Investment Assets with Time

sets becomes 20%. The chart now indicates that the future capital that results from her discretionary cash flow will be about 1.7 times as large as the nest egg that results from her initial capital. Note that, if you double the ratio, you just about double the importance of the discretionary cash flow. Also, an increase in the time allowed to achieve the objective does not have as dramatic an effect as increasing the ratio itself.

The Affect of Risk on Needed Cash Flow. Although the chart in Figure 4–1 does not show the affect of increasing or decreasing the assumed overall rate of return, it is a mathematical fact that, the lower the assumed rate of return, the more important the cash flow becomes relative to the initial capital in determining financial success. Stated differently, if the current overall risk tolerance level suggests taking less risk than the average weighted 10% rate of return implies, the affect of cash flow on future net worth will be even more dramatic than the chart implies. *Risk-averse clients must therefore place even greater emphasis on forsaking some of today's luxuries for tomorrow's necessities.* Conversely, if capital and cash flow can be subjected to an even higher than 10% projected average after-tax annual rate of return, the effect of the amount of cash flow invested is still dramatic but less so than the chart indicates.

In any case, there can be no "rate of investing" if there is no discretionary cash flow to invest. We will now demonstrate, how you should determine what your client's discretionary cash flow actually is. We will also discuss, philosophically, two major, divergent approaches to improving it.

An eight-step method for measuring your client's available cash flow for saving/investing

It is often said that one does not plan to fail, one simply fails to plan. Particularly with accumulation cases, a chief downfall in lifetime and estate accumulation planning—other than not planning at all—is the failure to rigidly measure and then carefully direct a predetermined level of annual cash flow toward appropriate investments. The process of achieving that end begins with a detailed cash flow analysis. The ideal cash flow analysis is one that simultaneously:

1. indicates all sources of income,

2. extracts all tax liabilities and living expenses, and

3. defines the remaining discretionary cash flow surplus or deficit.

As a starting point, you need to analyze your client's present cash flow situation for accomplishing these three desired ends. We're going to use Dr. Tom Wright's cash flow analysis, as it appeared in Chapter 2, to illustrate how the eight-step method works. Later on you'll see how we used Dr. Wright's analysis to improve his discretionary cash flow.

STEP ONE:
ENTER PERSONAL SERVICE AND NONPERSONAL SERVICE INCOME

The cash flow analysis begins with a listing of all the items that appear on the federal income tax form "1040" prior to Adjusted Gross Income. See an example of a filled-out 1040 tax form in Figure 4–2. First, list personal service income items (earned income) such as salary, bonus, fees, commissions, tips, director fees, and the like. This figure must be the net of any contributions to any type of qualified retirement plan (Corporate, Keogh, IRA, etc.). Then include the nonpersonal service income

TABLE 4–1
Dr. Tom Wright—Current Cash Flow Analysis

Step One:	Income:	
	Salary	$110,000
	Interest	1,250
	Dividends from Professional Corporation*	4,560
	Personal Holding Company (Sub S Corporation)	6,000
Step Two:	40% of Net Long-Term Gains	4,000
Step Three:	Business Deductions	(3,500)
	Tax-Incentive Investment Deductions	(10,000)
	Adjusted Gross Income	$112,310
Step Four:	Less: Excess Itemized Deductions	(21,600)
	(25,000 − 3,400)	
	Personal Exemptions	(4,000)
Step Five:	Taxable Income	86,710
	Federal Income Tax Liability	27,811
		$ 58,899
Step Six:	Add: Tax-Incentive Investment Deductions	10,000
	Dividend Exclusion	200
	Personal Exemptions	4,000
	Tax-Free Income	4,200
	Excess Itemized Deductions	21,600
		$ 98,899
Step Seven:	Less: Taxable Gain	(4,000)
	Living Expenses	(48,424)
	Discretionary Cash Flow	$ 46,475
	Less: Tax-Incentive Investment Commitments	(10,000)
Step Eight:	Remaining Discretionary Cash Flow	$ 36,475

*After the $200 dividend exclusion

items, such as rents, dividends (less the $100 or $200 dividend exclusion), and interest income.

STEP TWO:
FIGURE GAINS/LOSSES

The details of any net capital gains or losses appear next. That figure, for example, would be 40% of your net long-term capital gains. Or, if you have a combination of large short-term gains and small long-term losses, 100% of the net short-term gain figure would appear here. If you have a net long-term loss or carry-forward loss, you simply put 50% of a maximum of $6,000 or a negative $3,000 (−$3,000) here. If there is ever a question as to what figure appears under *gains/losses*, your best bet is to

FIGURE 4–2 *Dr. Wright's Tax Forms*

Form **1040** Department of the Treasury—Internal Revenue Service **U.S. Individual Income Tax Return** 1981 (O)

For the year January 1–December 31, 1981, or other tax year beginning	, 1981, ending	, 19	OMB No. 1545-0074

Use IRS label. Other-wise, please print or type.	Your first name and initial (if joint return, also give spouse's name and initial) Last name	Your social security number
	Thomas J. & Mary G. Wright	123 ¦ 45 ¦6789
	Present home address (Number and street, including apartment number, or rural route)	Spouse's social security no.
	1385 Medical Hall Rd., NE	101 ¦ 11 ¦2131
	City, town or post office, State and ZIP code	Your occupation ▶ Medical Doctor
	Atlanta, Georgia 30319	Spouse's occupation ▶ Housewife

Presidential Election Campaign ▶ Do you want $1 to go to this fund? . . . . X Yes ▨ No **Note:** Checking "Yes" will not increase your tax or reduce your refund.
If joint return, does your spouse want $1 to go to this fund? . . . X Yes ▨ No

Filing Status

Check only one box.

1		Single	For Privacy Act and Paperwork Reduction Act Notice, see Instructions.
2	X	Married filing joint return (even if only one had income)	
3		Married filing separate return. Enter spouse's social security no. above and full name here ▶	
4		Head of household (with qualifying person). (See page 6 of Instructions.) If he or she is your unmarried child, enter child's name ▶	
5		Qualifying widow(er) with dependent child (Year spouse died ▶ 19). (See page 6 of Instructions.)	

Exemptions

Always check the box labeled Yourself.
Check other boxes if they apply.

6a	X	Yourself		65 or over		Blind	Enter number of boxes checked on 6a and b ▶	2
b	X	Spouse		65 or over		Blind		

c First names of your dependent children who lived with you ▶ .... Enter number of children listed on 6c ▶ 2
.... Jean & David ....▲

d Other dependents:		(3) Number of	(4) Did dependent	(5) Did you provide	
(1) Name	(2) Relationship	months lived in your home	have income of $1,000 or more?	more than one-half of dependent's support?	Enter number of other dependents ▶

Add numbers entered in boxes above ▶ 4

e Total number of exemptions claimed . . . .

Income

Please attach Copy B of your Forms W–2 here.

If you do not have a W–2, see page 5 of Instructions.

7	Wages, salaries, tips, etc.			7	110,000	00
8a	Interest income (attach Schedule B if over $400 or you have any All-Savers interest). . . .	8a	1,250 00			
b	Dividends (attach Schedule B if over $400)	8b	10,760 00			
c	Total. Add lines 8a and 8b	8c	12,010 00			
d	Exclusion (See page 9 of Instructions)	8d	200 00			
e	Subtract line 8d from line 8c (but not less than zero)			8e	11,810	00
9	Refunds of State and local income taxes (do not enter an amount unless you deducted those taxes in an earlier year—see page 9 of Instructions)			9	–	–
10	Alimony received			10	–	–
11	Business income or (loss) (attach Schedule C) . . . . ▶			11	–	–
12	Capital gain or (loss) (attach Schedule D)			12	4,000	00
13	40% of capital gain distributions not reported on line 12 (See page 9 of Instructions) .			13	–	–
14	Supplemental gains or (losses) (attach Form 4797)			14	–	–
15	Fully taxable pensions and annuities not reported on line 16			15	–	–
16a	Other pensions and annuities. Total received	16a				
b	Taxable amount, if any, from worksheet on page 10 of Instructions			16b	–	–
17	Rents, royalties, partnerships, estates, trusts, etc. (attach Schedule E)			17	(10,000	00)
18	Farm income or (loss) (attach Schedule F) . . . . ▶			18	–	–
19a	Unemployment compensation (insurance). Total received	19a				
b	Taxable amount, if any, from worksheet on page 10 of Instructions			19b	–	–
20	Other income (state nature and source—see page 11 of Instructions) ▶			20	–	–
21	**Total income.** Add amounts in column for lines 7 through 20 . . . . ▶			21	115,810	00

Adjustments to Income

(See Instructions on page 11)

22	Moving expense (attach Form 3903 or 3903F)	22	–	–			
23	Employee business expenses (attach Form 2106) . . .	23	3,500	00			
24	Payments to an IRA (enter code from page 11 ....) .	24	–	–			
25	Payments to a Keogh (H.R. 10) retirement plan	25	–	–			
26	Interest penalty on early withdrawal of savings	26	–	–			
27	Alimony paid	27	–	–			
28	Disability income exclusion (attach Form 2440)	28	–	–			
29	Other adjustments—see page 12 ▶	29	–	–			
30	**Total adjustments.** Add lines 22 through 29 . . . . ▶				30	3,500	00

Adjusted Gross Income

31	**Adjusted gross income.** Subtract line 30 from line 21. *If this line is less than $10,000, see "Earned Income Credit" (line 57) on page 15 of Instructions.* *If you want IRS to figure your tax, see page 3 of Instructions* . . . . ▶	31	112,310	00

☆ U.S. GOVERNMENT PRINTING OFFICE: 1981—O-343-402 58-040-1110

FIGURE 4–2 *(cont.)*

Form 1040 (1981)   Page **2**

Tax Compu-tation (See Instructions on page 12)	32a Amount from line 31 *(adjusted gross income)*	**32a**	112,310	00
	32b If you do not itemize deductions, enter zero	**32b**	21,600	00
	If you itemize, complete Schedule A (Form 1040) and enter the amount from Schedule A, line 41 . . .			
	Caution: If you have unearned income and can be claimed as a dependent on your parent's return, check here ▶ ☐ and see page 12 of the Instructions. Also see page 12 of the Instructions if:			
	• *You are married filing a separate return and your spouse itemizes deductions, OR*			
	• *You file Form 4563, OR*			
	• *You are a dual-status alien.*			
	32c Subtract line 32b from line 32a	**32c**	90,710	00
	33 Multiply $1,000 by the total number of exemptions claimed on Form 1040, line 6e . .	**33**	4,000	00
	34 Taxable Income. Subtract line 33 from line 32c	**34**	86,710	00
	35 Tax. Enter tax here and check if from ☐ Tax Table, ☒ Tax Rate Schedule X, Y, or Z, ☐ Schedule D, ☐ Schedule G, or ☐ Form 4726	**35**	27,810	00
	36 Additional Taxes. (See page 13 of Instructions.) Enter here and check if from ☐ Form 4970, ☐ Form 4972, ☐ Form 5544, or ☐ Section 72(m)(5) penalty tax	**36**	–	–
	37 **Total.** Add lines 35 and 36 . . . . ▶	**37**	27,810	00

Credits (See Instructions on page 13)	38 Credit for contributions to candidates for public office . . . **38**			
	39 Credit for the elderly *(attach Schedules R&RP)* **39**			
	40 Credit for child and dependent care expenses (*attach Form 2441*). **40**			
	41 Investment credit *(attach Form 3468)* **41**			
	42 Foreign tax credit *(attach Form 1116)* **42**			
	43 Work incentive (WIN) credit *(attach Form 4874)* **43**			
	44 Jobs credit *(attach Form 5884)* **44**			
	45 Residential energy credit *(attach Form 5695)* **45**			
	46 **Total credits.** Add lines 38 through 45	**46**	–	–
	47 **Balance.** Subtract line 46 from line 37 and enter difference (but not less than zero) . ▶	**47**	27,810	00

Other Taxes (Including Advance EIC Payments)	48 Self-employment tax *(attach Schedule SE)*	**48**	–	–
	49a Minimum tax. Attach Form 4625 and check here ▶ ☐	**49a**	0	–
	49b Alternative minimum tax. Attach Form 6251 and check here ▶ ☐	**49b**	–	–
	50 Tax from recomputing prior-year investment credit *(attach Form 4255)*	**50**	–	–
	51a Social security (FICA) tax on tip income not reported to employer *(attach Form 4137)* . .	**51a**	–	–
	51b Uncollected employee FICA and RRTA tax on tips *(from Form W–2)*	**51b**	–	–
	52 Tax on an IRA *(attach Form 5329)*	**52**	–	–
06	53 Advance earned income credit (EIC) payments received *(from Form W–2)*	**53**	–	–
	54 **Total tax.** Add lines 47 through 53 . . . . ▶	**54**	27,810	00

Payments Attach Forms W–2, W–2G, and W–2P to front.	55 Total Federal income tax withheld **55** 27,077 10			
	56 1981 estimated tax payments and amount applied from 1980 return . **56** – –			
	57 Earned income credit. If line 32a is under $10,000, see page 15 of Instructions . . . . **57** – –			
	58 Amount paid with Form 4868 . . . . **58** – –			
	59 Excess FICA and RRTA tax withheld (two or more employers) **59** – –			
	60 Credit for Federal tax on special fuels and oils *(attach Form 4136 or 4136–T)* . . . . **60** – –			
	61 Regulated Investment Company credit *(attach Form 2439)* **61** – –			
	62 **Total.** Add lines 55 through 61 . . . . ▶	**62**	27,077	10

Refund or Balance Due	63 If line 62 is larger than line 54, enter amount **OVERPAID** . . . . ▶	**63**		
	64 Amount of line 63 to be **REFUNDED TO YOU** . . . . ▶	**64**		
	65 Amount of line 63 to be applied to your 1982 estimated tax . . . ▶ **65**			
	66 If line 54 is larger than line 62, enter **BALANCE DUE.** Attach check or money order for full amount payable to "Internal Revenue Service." Write your social security number and "1981 Form 1040" on it. ▶ (Check ▶ ☐ if Form 2210 (2210F) is attached. See page 16 of Instructions.) ▶ $	**66**	732	90

Please Sign Here	Under penalties of perjury, I declare that I have examined this return, including accompanying schedules and statements, and to the best of my knowledge and belief, it is true, correct, and complete. Declaration of preparer (other than taxpayer) is based on all information of which preparer has any knowledge.
	▶ *Thomas J. Wright* 4/15/83 ▶ *Mary D. Wright*
	Your signature Date Spouse's signature (if filing jointly, BOTH must sign even if only one had income)

Paid Preparer's Use Only	Preparer's signature ▶ *Bill Green*	Date 4-15-83	Check if self-employed ▶ ☐	Preparer's social security no. 234 : 56 : 7891
	Firm's name (or yours, if self-employed) and address ▶ Martin, Budd & Sands, Inc. 123 Konzin Way, Trinity, Ga		E.I. No. ▶ 12 : 3456789 ZIP code ▶ 30303	

FIGURE 4–2 (cont.)

Schedules A&B (Form 1040)

Department of the Treasury
Internal Revenue Service   (0)

Schedule A—Itemized Deductions

(Schedule B is on back)

▶ Attach to Form 1040.   ▶ See Instructions for Schedules A and B (Form 1040).

OMB No. 1545–0074

1981
07

Name(s) as shown on Form 1040
Thomas J. & Mary G. Wright

Your social security number
123 45 6789

Medical and Dental Expenses (Do not include expenses reimbursed or paid by others.) (See page 17 of Instructions.)

1 One-half (but not more than $150) of insurance premiums you paid for medical care. (Be sure to include in line 10 below.) . ▶	0	
2 Medicine and drugs .		
3 Enter 1% of Form 1040, line 31 . . .		
4 Subtract line 3 from line 2. If line 3 is more than line 2, enter zero.		
5 Balance of insurance premiums for medical care not entered on line 1		
6 Other medical and dental expenses:		
a Doctors, dentists, nurses, etc. . . .		
b Hospitals		
c Transportation		
d Other (itemize—include hearing aids, dentures, eyeglasses, etc.) ▶		
7 Total (add lines 4 through 6d)		
8 Enter 3% of Form 1040, line 31 . . .		
9 Subtract line 8 from line 7. If line 8 is more than line 7, enter zero.		
10 Total medical and dental expenses (add lines 1 and 9). Enter here and on line 33 . ▶	0	

Taxes (See page 18 of Instructions.)

11 State and local income	5,488	00
12 Real estate.	2,000	00
13 a General sales (see sales tax tables) .	512	00
b General sales on motor vehicles . .		
14 Personal property		
15 Other (itemize) ▶		
16 Total taxes (add lines 11 through 15). Enter here and on line 34 . . . . ▶	8,000	00

Interest Expense (See page 18 of Instructions.)

17 Home mortgage	10,876	00
18 Credit and charge cards		
19 Other (itemize) ▶	4,124	00
20 Total interest expense (add lines 17 through 19). Enter here and on line 35 ▶	15,000	00

Contributions (See page 19 of Instructions.)

21 a Cash contributions (If you gave $3,000 or more to any one organization, report those contributions on line 21b) .	2,000	00
b Cash contributions totaling $3,000 or more to any one organization (show to whom you gave and how much you gave) ▶		
22 Other than cash (see page 19 of Instructions for required statement)	–	
23 Carryover from prior years	–	
24 Total contributions (add lines 21a through 23). Enter here and on line 36 ▶	2,000	00

Casualty or Theft Loss(es) (You must attach Form 4684 if line 29 is $1,000 or more, OR if certain other situations apply.) (See page 19 of Instructions.)

25 Loss before reimbursement		
26 Insurance or other reimbursement you received or expect to receive		
27 Subtract line 26 from line 25. If line 26 is more than line 25, enter zero. . . .		
28 Enter $100 or amount from line 27, whichever is smaller		
29 Total casualty or theft loss(es) (subtract line 28 from line 27). Enter here and on line 37 ▶	–	–

Miscellaneous Deductions (See page 19 of Instructions.)

30 a Union dues		
b Tax return preparation fee		
31 Other (itemize) ▶		
32 Total miscellaneous deductions (add lines 30a through 31). Enter here and on line 38 . . . . ▶	–	–

Summary of Itemized Deductions   A
(See page 20 of Instructions.)

33 Total medical and dental—from line 10 .	–	–
34 Total taxes—from line 16	8,000	00
35 Total interest—from line 20	15,000	00
36 Total contributions—from line 24 . . .	2,000	00
37 Total casualty or theft loss(es)—from line 29 .	–	–
38 Total miscellaneous—from line 32 . .	–	–
39 Add lines 33 through 38	2,500	00
40 If you checked Form 1040, Filing Status box: 2 or 5, enter $3,400 . . . . } 1 or 4, enter $2,300 . . . . } . . 3, enter $1,700 . . . . . }	3,400	00
41 Subtract line 40 from line 39. Enter here and on Form 1040, line 32b. (If line 40 is more than line 39, see the Instructions for line 41 on page 20.) . . . . . ▶	21,600	00

For Paperwork Reduction Act Notice, see Form 1040 Instructions.

FIGURE 4–2 *(cont.)*

Schedule B—Interest and Dividend Income   OMB No. 1545-0074   Page **2**

Name(s) as shown on Form 1040 (Do not enter name and social security number if shown on other side) | Your social security number

Thomas J. & Mary G. Wright   123 45 6789

Part I Interest Income		**Part II** Dividend Income	

Part I — Interest Income

If you received more than $400 in interest or you received any interest from an All-Savers Certificate, you must complete Part I and list ALL interest received. Also complete Part III if you received more than $400 in interest. See page 8 of the Instructions to find out what interest to report. Then answer the questions in Part III, below. If you received interest as a nominee for another, or you received or paid accrued interest on securities transferred between interest payment dates, please see page 20 of the Instructions.

Name of payer	Amount
1a Interest income (other than qualifying interest from All-Savers Certificates).	
Saunders Bank & Trust Co.	1,250 00
1b Total. Add above amounts	1,250 00
1c Qualifying interest from All-Savers Certificates. (List payers and amounts even if $400 or less.) See page 20 of Instructions.	
1d Total	
1e Exclusion (See page 20 of Instructions) .	
1f Subtract line 1e from line 1d.	
Caution: *No part of the amount on line 1f may be excluded on Form 1040, line 8d .*	— —
2 Total interest income (add lines 1b and 1f). Enter here and on Form 1040, line 8a	1,250 00

Part II — Dividend Income

If you received more than $400 in gross dividends (including capital gain distributions) and other distributions on stock, complete Part II and Part III. Please see page 9 of the Instructions. Then answer the questions in Part III, below. If you received dividends as a nominee for another, please see page 21 of the Instructions.

	Name of payer	Amount
3	Wright Radiology Professional Corp.	4,760 00
	Wright Personal Holding Co. Inc.	6,000 00
4	Total. Add above amounts	10,760 00

5 Capital gain distributions. Enter here and on line 13, Schedule D. See Note below . . .	—	—	
6 Nontaxable distributions (See Instructions for adjustment to basis)	—	—	**B**
7 Total (add lines 5 and 6)			— —
8 Total dividend income (subtract line 7 from line 4). Enter here and on Form 1040, line 8b			10,760 00

Note: *If you received capital gain distributions for the year and you do not need Schedule D to report any other gains or losses or to compute the alternative tax, do not file that schedule. Instead, enter 40% of your capital gain distributions on Form 1040, line 13.*

Part III Foreign Accounts and Foreign Trusts		

If you received more than $400 of interest or dividends, OR if you had a foreign account or were a grantor of, or a transferor to, a foreign trust, you must answer both questions in Part III. Please see page 21 of the Instructions.

	Yes	No
9 At any time during the tax year, did you have an interest in or a signature or other authority over a bank account, securities account, or other financial account in a foreign country?		
10 Were you the grantor of, or transferor to, a foreign trust which existed during the current tax year, whether or not you have any beneficial interest in it? . . . . If "Yes," you may have to file Forms 3520, 3520-A, or 926.		

For Paperwork Reduction Act Notice, see Form 1040 Instructions.

FIGURE 4–2 (cont.)

| SCHEDULE E
(Form 1040)
Department of the Treasury
Internal Revenue Service (0) | **Supplemental Income Schedule**
(From rents and royalties, partnerships, estates and trusts, etc.)
▶ Attach to Form 1040. ▶ See Instructions for Schedule E (Form 1040). | OMB No. 1545–0074
1981
15 |

Name(s) as shown on Form 1040	Your social security number
Thomas J. & Mary G. Wright	123 : 45 : 6789

Part I   Rent and Royalty Income or Loss.

1 Are any of the expenses listed below for a vacation home or similar dwelling rented to others (see Instructions)? . ☐ Yes ☐ No

2 If you checked "Yes" to question 1, did you or a member of your family occupy the vacation home or similar dwelling for more than 14 days during the tax year? . . . . ☐ Yes ☐ No

Rental and Royalty Income (describe property in Part V)		Properties			Totals
		A	B	C	
3 a Rents received					3
b Royalties received					
Rental and Royalty Expenses					
4 Advertising	4				
5 Auto and travel	5				
6 Cleaning and maintenance . . .	6				
7 Commissions	7				
8 Insurance	8				
9 Interest	9				
10 Legal and other professional fees . .	10				
11 Repairs	11				
12 Supplies	12				
13 Taxes (do NOT include Windfall Profit Tax, see Part III, line 35)	13				
14 Utilities	14				
15 Wages and salaries	15				
16 Other (list) ▶					
17 Total deductions (add lines 4 through 16)	17				17
18 Depreciation expense (see Instructions), or Depletion (attach computation)	18				18
19 Total (add lines 17 and 18)	19				
20 Income or (loss) from rental or royalty properties (subtract line 19 from line 3a (rents) or 3b (royalties))	20				E

21 Add properties with profits on line 20, and enter total profits here . . . . | 21 |

22 Add properties with losses on line 20, and enter total (losses) here . . . . | 22 ( )

23 Combine amounts on lines 21 and 22, and enter net profit or (loss) here . . . . | 23 |

24 Net farm rental profit or (loss) from Form 4835, line 50 . . . . | 24 |

25 Total rental or royalty income or (loss). Combine amounts on lines 23 and 24. Enter here and include in line 37 on page 2 . . . . | 25 |

For Paperwork Reduction Act Notice, see Form 1040 Instructions.

FIGURE 4–2 *(cont.)*

Part II **Income or Losses from Partnerships, Estates or Trusts, or Small Business Corporations**

If you report a loss below, do you have amounts invested in that activity for which you are not "at risk" (see Instructions)? ☐ Yes ☐ No
If "Yes," and your loss exceeded your amount "at risk," did you limit your loss to your amount "at risk"? . . . . ☐ Yes ☐ No

(a) Name	(b) Employer identification number	(c) Net loss (see instructions for "at risk" limitations)	(d) Net income
Gas & Oil Drilling 1981	89–1234567	2,000 00	
Gas & Oil Drilling 1982	91–2345678	8,000 00	

Partnerships

26 Add amounts in columns (c) and (d) and enter here . . . . **26** (10,000 00 |

27 Combine amounts in columns (c) and (d), line 26, and enter net income or (loss) **27** (10,000 00)

28 Additional first-year depreciation from 1980/1981 fiscal-year partnerships. Enter amount from Form 1065, Schedule K–1, line 2, but not more than $2,000 ($4,000 if a joint return) . . . **28** ( )

29 Total partnership income or (loss). Combine lines 27 and 28. Enter here and include in line 37 . **29** (10,000 00)

Estates or Trusts

30 Add amounts in columns (c) and (d) and enter here . . . . **30** ( )

31 Total estate or trust income or (loss). Combine amounts in columns (c) and (d), line 30. Enter here and include in line 37 . . . . **31**

Small Business Corporations

32 Add amounts in columns (c) and (d) and enter here . . . . **32** ( )

33 Total small business corporation income or (loss). Combine amounts in columns (c) and (d), line 32. Enter here and include in line 37 . . . . **33**

Part III **Windfall Profit Tax Summary**

34 Windfall Profit Tax Credit or Refund received in 1981 (see Instructions) **34**

35 Windfall Profit Tax withheld in 1981 (see Instructions) . . . . **35** ( )

36 Combine amounts on lines 34 and 35. Enter here and include in line 37 . . . . **36**

Part IV **Summary**

37 TOTAL income or (loss). Combine lines 25, 29, 31, 33, and 36. Enter here and on Form 1040, line 17 . ► **37**

38 Farmers and fishermen: Enter your share of gross farming and fishing income applicable to Parts I and II **38**

Part V **Depreciation Claimed in Part I.**—Complete only if property was placed in service before January 1, 1981. For more space, use Form 4562. If you placed any property in service after December 31, 1980, use Form 4562 for all property; do NOT complete Part V.

(a) Description and location of property	(b) Date acquired	(c) Cost or other basis	(d) Depreciation allowed or allowable in prior years	(e) Depreciation method	(f) Life or rate	(g) Depreciation for this year
Property A						
Totals (Property A)			. . . .			
Property B						
Totals (Property B)			. . . .			
Property C						
Totals (Property C)			. . . .			

☆ U.S. GOVERNMENT PRINTING OFFICE: 1981—O-343-417 58-040-1110

FIGURE 4–2 *(cont.)*

SCHEDULE D (FORM 1040) Department of the Treasury Internal Revenue Service (O)	**Capital Gains and Losses** (Examples of property to be reported on this Schedule are gains and losses on stocks, bonds, and similar investments, and gains (but not losses) on personal assets such as a home or jewelry.) ▶ Attach to Form 1040. ▶ See Instructions for Schedule D (Form 1040).	OMB No. 1545-0074 19**81** 14

Name(s) as shown on Form 1040 Thomas J. & Mary G. Wright	Your social security number 123 : 45 : 6789

Part I   Short-term Capital Gains and Losses—Assets Held One Year or Less   **D**

a. Kind of property and description (Example, 100 shares 7% preferred of ''Z'' Co.)	b. Date acquired (Mo., day, yr.)	c. Date sold (Mo., day, yr.)	d. Gross sales price less expense of sale	e. Cost or other basis, as adjusted (see instructions page 23)	f. LOSS If column (e) is more than (d) subtract (d) from (e)	g. GAIN If column (d) is more than (e) subtract (e) from (d)
1						

2a Gain from sale or exchange of a principal residence held one year or less, from Form 2119, lines 7 or 11 . . . .

b Short-term capital gain from installment sales from Form 6252, line 19 or 27 . . .

3 Enter your share of net short-term gain or (loss) from partnerships and fiduciaries .

4 Add lines 1 through 3 in column f and column g . . . . ( )

5 Combine line 4, column f and line 4, column g and enter the net gain or (loss) . . . .

6 Short-term capital loss carryover from years beginning after 1969 . . . . ( )

7 Net short-term gain or (loss), combine lines 5 and 6 . . . .

Part II   Long-term Capital Gains and Losses—Assets Held More Than One Year

8						

9a Gain from sale or exchange of a principal residence held more than one year, from Form 2119, lines 7, 11, 16 or 18 . . . .

b Long-term capital gain from installment sales from Form 6252, line 19 or 27 . . . .

10 Enter your share of net long-term gain or (loss) from partnerships and fiduciaries .

11 Add lines 8 through 10 in column f and column g . . . . ( )

12 Combine line 11, column f and line 11, column g and enter the net gain or (loss) . . . .

13 Capital gain distributions . . . .

14 Enter gain from Form 4797, line 5(a)(1) . . . .

15 Enter your share of net long-term gain from small business corporations (Subchapter S) . . . . . .   10,000 | 00

16 Combine lines 12 through 15 . . . .   10,000 | 00

17 Long-term capital loss carryover from years beginning after 1969 . . . . (—)

18 Net long-term gain or (loss), combine lines 16 and 17 . . . .   10,000 | 00

Note: Complete this form on reverse. However, if you have capital loss carryovers from years beginning before 1970, do not complete Parts III or V. See Form 4798 instead.

For Paperwork Reduction Act Notice, see Form 1040 instructions

FIGURE 4–2 (cont.)

Schedule D (Form 1040) 1981

Page 2

Part III Summary of Parts I and II

19 Combine lines 7 and 18, and enter the net gain or (loss) here	10,000	00

NOTE: *If line 19 is a gain complete lines 20 through 22. If line 19 is a loss complete lines 23 and 24.*

20 If line 19 shows a gain, enter the smaller of line 18 or line 19. Enter zero if there is a loss or no entry on line 18   10,000   00

21 Enter 60% of line 20	6,000	00

If line 21 is more than zero, you may be liable for the alternative minimum tax. See Form 6251.

22 Subtract line 21 from line 19. Enter here and on Form 1040, line 12	4,000	00

23 If line 19 shows a loss, enter one of the following amounts:
   (i)   If line 7 is zero or a net gain, enter 50% of line 19,
   (ii) If line 18 is zero or a net gain, enter line 19; or,
   (iii) If line 7 and line 18 are net losses, enter amount on line 7 added to 50% of the amount on line 18 . .

24 Enter here and as a loss on Form 1040, line 12, the smallest of:
   (i)   The amount on line 23;
   (ii) $3,000 ($1,500 if married and filing a separate return); or,
   (iii) Taxable income, as adjusted . . . .

Computation of Alternative Tax

Part IV *(Complete this part if line 20 (or Form 4798, line 8) shows a gain and your tax rate is above 50%. See instructions page 23.)*

25 Net short-term gain or (loss) from line 5, from sales or exchanges after June 9, 1981 . . . .
26 Net long-term gain or (loss) from line 16, from sales or exchanges after June 9, 1981 . . . .
27 If line 26 shows a gain, combine line 25 and line 26. If line 26 or this line shows a loss or zero, enter zero and do not complete rest of this part . . . .
28 Enter the smaller of line 26 or line 27 . . . .
29 Enter the smaller of line 20 (or Form 4798, line 8) or line 28 . . . . . .
30 Enter your Taxable Income from Form 1040, line 34 . . . .
31 Enter 40% of line 29 . . . .
32 Subtract line 31 from line 30. If line 31 is more than line 30, enter zero . . . .
33 Tax on amount on line 32. ☐ Tax Rate Schedule X, Y, or Z; ☐ Schedule G. (See instructions page 23) . .
34 Enter 20% of line 29 . . . .
35 Add lines 33 and 34. If the result is less than your tax using other methods, enter this amount on Form 1040, line 35 and check Schedule D box . . . .

Part V **Computation of Post-1969 Capital Loss Carryovers from 1981 to 1982**
(Complete this part if the loss on line 23 is more than the loss on line 24)

Section A.—Short-term Capital Loss Carryover

36 Enter loss shown on line 7; if none, enter zero and skip lines 37 through 41—then go to line 42 . . . .
37 Enter gain shown on line 18. If that line is blank or shows a loss, enter zero . . . .
38 Reduce any loss on line 36 to the extent of any gain on line 37 . . . .
39 Enter amount shown on line 24 . . . .
40 Enter smaller of line 38 or 39 . . . .

41 Subtract line 40 from line 38. This is your short-term capital loss carryover from 1981 to 1982 . . . . .

Section B.—Long-term Capital Loss Carryover

42 Subtract line 40 from line 39 (Note: *If you skipped lines 37 through 41, enter amount from line 24)* . . .
43 Enter loss from line 18; if none, enter zero and skip lines 44 through 47 . . . .
44 Enter gain shown on line 7. If that line is blank or shows a loss, enter zero . . . .
45 Reduce any loss on line 43 to the extent of any gain on line 44 . . . .
46 Multiply amount on line 42 by 2 . . . .

47 Subtract line 46 from line 45. This is your long-term capital loss carryover from 1981 to 1982 . . . . .

Part VI Complete this Part Only if You are Electing Out of the Installment Method And are Reporting a Note or Other Obligation at Less Than Full Face Value

☐ Check here if you elect out of the installment method.

   Enter the face amount of the note or other obligation ▶ ....
   Enter the percentage of valuation of the note or other obligation ▶

☆ U.S. GOVERNMENT PRINTING OFFICE: 1981—O-343-414 58-040-1110

FIGURE 4-2 (cont.)

Form **2106**

Department of the Treasury
Internal Revenue Service (O)

Employee Business Expenses

(Please use Form 3903 to figure moving expense deduction.)
▶ Attach to Form 1040.

OMB No. 1545-0139

1981

Your name Thomas J. Wright	Social security number 123 : 45 : 6789	Occupation in which expenses were incurred Medical Doctor
Employer's name Wright Radiology Professional Corp.	Employer's address 3333 Financial Rd., Atlanta, Ga 30026	

Paperwork Reduction Act Notice.—The Paperwork Reduction Act of 1980 says we must tell you why we are collecting this information, how we will use it, and whether you have to give it to us. We ask for the information to carry out the Internal Revenue laws of the United States. We need it to ensure that you are complying with these laws and to allow us to figure and collect the right amount of tax. You are required to give us this information.

Instructions

Use this form to show your business expenses as an employee during 1981. Include amounts:

● You paid as an employee;
● You charged to your employer (such as by credit card);
● You received as an advance, allowance, or repayment.

Several publications available from IRS give more information about business expenses:
Publication 463, Travel, Entertainment, and Gift Expenses.
Publication 529, Miscellaneous Deductions.
Publication 587, Business Use of Your Home.
Publication 508, Educational Expenses.

Part I.—You can deduct some business expenses even if you do not itemize your deductions on Schedule A (Form 1040). Examples are expenses for travel (except commuting to and from work), meals, or lodging. List these expenses in Part I and use them in figuring your adjusted gross income on Form 1040, line 31.

Line 2.—You can deduct meals and lodging costs if you were on a business trip away from your main place of work. Do not deduct the cost of meals that are on one-day trips when you did not need sleep or rest.

Line 3.—If you use a car you own in your work, you can deduct the cost of the business use. Enter the cost here after figuring it in Part IV. You can take either the cost of your actual

expenses (such as gas, oil, repairs, depreciation, etc.) or you can use the standard mileage rate.

The mileage rate is 20 cents a mile up to 15,000 miles. After that, or for all business mileage on a fully depreciated car, the rate is 11 cents a mile. If you use the standard mileage rate to figure the cost of business use, the car is considered to have a useful life of 60,000 miles of business use at the maximum standard mileage rate. After 60,000 miles of business use at the maximum rate, the car is considered to be fully depreciated. (For details, see **Publication 463.**)

Caution: You cannot use the mileage rate for a leased vehicle.

Figure your mileage rate amount and add it to the business part of what you spent on the car for parking fees, tolls, interest, and State and local taxes (except gasoline tax).

Line 4.—If you were an outside salesperson with other business expenses, list them on line 4. Examples are selling expenses or expenses for stationery and stamps. An outside salesperson does all selling outside the employer's place of business. A driver-salesperson whose main duties are service and delivery, such as delivering bread or milk, is not an outside salesperson. (For details, see **Publication 463.**)

Line 5.—Show other business expenses on line 5 if your employer repaid you for them. If you were repaid for part of them, show here the amount you were repaid. Show the rest in Part II.

Part II.—You can deduct other business expenses only if (a) your employer did not repay you, and (b) you itemize your deductions on Schedule A (Form 1040). Report these expenses here and under Miscellaneous Deductions on Schedule A. (For details, see **Publication 529.**)

You can deduct expenses for business use of the part of your home that you exclusively and consistently use for your work. If you are not self-employed, your working at home must be for your employer's convenience. (For business use of home, see **Publication 587.**)

If you show education expenses in Part I or Part II, you must fill out Part III.

Part III.—You can deduct the cost of education that helps you keep or improve your skills for the job you have now. This includes education that your employer, the law, or regulations require you to get in order to keep your job or your salary. Do not deduct the cost of study that helps you meet the basic requirements for your job or helps you get a new job. (For education expenses, see **Publication 508.**)

Part IV, line 8—Depreciation

Cars placed in service **before 1/1/81:**
You must continue to use either the standard mileage rate or the method of depreciation you used in earlier years. You cannot change to either of the new methods available in 1981.

Cars placed in service **after 12/31/80:**
If you placed a car in service in 1981 and you do not use the standard mileage rate, you must use the new Accelerated Cost Recovery System (ACRS). One method lets you deduct the following percentages of your cost basis regardless of what month you placed the car in service:

1981—25%
1982—38%
1983—37%

Example: You bought a new car, without a trade-in, for $10,000 in September 1981, and used it 60% for business. Your basis for depreciation is $6,000 ($10,000 × 60%). For 1981 your depreciation deduction is $1,500 ($6,000 × 25%). If your percentage of business use changes in 1982, you must refigure your basis for depreciation.

There is also an alternate ACRS method under which you may use a straight-line method over a recovery period of 3, 5, or 12 years.

Note: If you use the mileage rate, you are considered to have made an election to exclude this vehicle from ACRS.

You do not have to consider salvage value in either of these methods. Please see **Publication 463** for details on how to figure the deduction under either method.

PART I.—Employee Business Expenses Deductible in Figuring Adjusted Gross Income on Form 1040, Line 31

1 Fares for airplane, boat, bus, taxicab, train, etc.		
2 Meals and lodging		
3 Car expenses (from Part IV, line 21)		
4 Outside salesperson's expenses (see Part I instructions above) ▶		
5 Other (see Part I instructions above) ▶ Entertainment		3,500.00
6 Add lines 1 through 5		3,500.00
7 Employer's payments for these expenses if not included on Form W-2		−
8 Deductible business expenses (subtract line 7 from line 6). Enter here and include on Form 1040, line 23 .		3,500.00
9 Income from excess business expense payments (subtract line 6 from line 7). Enter here and include on Form 1040, line 20		0

PART II.—Employee Business Expenses that are Deductible Only if You Itemize Deductions on Schedule A (Form 1040)

1 Business expenses not included above (list expense and amount) ▶		
2 Total. Deduct under Miscellaneous Deductions, Schedule A (Form 1040)		

Form **2106** (1981)

FIGURE 4–2 (*cont.*)

PART III.—Information About Education Expenses Shown in Part I or Part II

1 Name of educational institution or activity ▶--
2 Address ▶--
3 Did you need this education to meet the basic requirements for your job? . . . . ☐ Yes   ☐ No
4 Will this study program qualify you for a new job? . . . . ☐ Yes   ☐ No
5 If your answer to question 3 or 4 is Yes, you cannot deduct these expenses. If No, explain (1) why you are getting the education, and
  (2) what the relationship was between the courses you took and your job. (If you need more space, attach a statement.) ▶----------
  ----
6 List your main subjects, or describe your educational activity ▶---
----

PART IV.—Car Expenses (Use either your actual expenses or the mileage rate.)

	Car 1	Car 2	Car 3
A. Number of months you used car for business during 1981 . .	_____ months	_____ months	_____ months
B. Total mileage for months in line A	_____ miles	_____ miles	_____ miles
C. Business part of line B mileage	_____ miles	_____ miles	_____ miles

Actual Expenses (Include expenses on lines 1–5 for only the months shown in line A, above.)

	Car 1	Car 2	Car 3
1 Gasoline, oil, lubrication, etc.			
2 Repairs			
3 Tires, supplies, etc.			
4 Other: **(a)** Insurance			
(b) Taxes			
(c) Tags and licenses			
(d) Interest			
(e) Miscellaneous			
5 Total (add lines 1 through 4(e))			
6 Business percentage of car use (divide line C by line B, above)	%	%	%
7 Business part of car expense (multiply line 5 by line 6) . . .			
8 Depreciation (see instructions on front) . . . . **Caution:** If you use ACRS, skip line 9 and enter the amount from line 8 on line 10.			
9 Divide line 8 by 12 months			
10 Multiply line 9 by line A, above			
11 Total (add line 7 and line 10; then skip to line 19)			

Mileage Rate

12 Enter the smaller of (a) 15,000 miles or (b) the combined mileages from line C, above . . . . _____ miles
13 Multiply line 12 by 20¢ (11¢ if car is fully depreciated) and enter here . . . .
14 Enter any combined mileage from line C that is over 15,000 miles . . . . . . | _____ miles |////////|
15 Multiply line 14 by 11¢ and enter here . . . .
16 Total mileage expense (add lines 13 and 15) . . . .
17 Business part of car interest and State and local taxes (except gasoline tax) . . . .
18 Total (add lines 16 and 17) . . . .

Summary

19 Enter amount from line 11 or line 18, whichever you used . . . .
20 Parking fees and tolls . . . .
21 Total (add lines 19 and 20). Enter here and in Part I, line 3 . . . .

complete a Schedule D with anticipated short-term and long-term gains and losses. The final line will give you the appropriate figure to use.

STEP THREE:
DETERMINE BUSINESS DEDUCTIONS AND TAX-INCENTIVE
INVESTMENT DEDUCTIONS

Usually the principal items to follow gains/losses would be the deductions or income that result from Schedules C and E of the federal tax form 1040.

Schedule C provides all of the information you need at this point with regard to income or deductions from business or professional activities that occur in the sole proprietorship format. For instance, if the professional practice is a sole proprietorship, this Schedule C would arrive at the net profit or loss, after subtracting all deductions (cash and noncash) from total income. Employed executives of incorporated businesses, as well as professionals practicing in the professional corporation or association format, may incur expenses for which they are not reimbursed. Such deductions appear in this section of the cash flow analysis and are easily lifted from Schedule C.

Schedule E, the Supplemental Income Schedule, is the great provider of a record of all of the tax deductions that result from investment tax sheltering. Exercise extra caution here to make certain that information is extracted from Schedule E in a way that will facilitate the correct cash flow analysis.

For instance, it is easy to have the multiple tax and economic aspects of real estate investments distort the analysis of cash flow. Part II of Schedule E breaks down a real estate investment into rental income, depreciation, and "other" expenses. For the purposes of a meaningful cash flow analysis, the rental income net of "other" expenses should be shown in the previous Income section under nonpersonal service income. Only the depreciation expense (noncash expense) should be shown in step three under tax-incentive investments so that it can be added back, after taxes are computed, in a later section of this analysis.

Another example of the proper breakdown of Schedule E information would involve gas/oil drilling limited partnership investments. If you have such drilling investments, the net loss that results from intangible drilling expenses, depreciation, and depletion allowances will be shown here, but distributions from gas and oil sales are included earlier in the Income section. It is quite important that you do all of these things properly, particularly as they relate to tax-incentive investments, or you will not end up with the correct discretionary income figure.

STEP FOUR:
LESS EXCESS ITEMIZED DEDUCTIONS AND PERSONAL EXEMPTIONS

The addition of all of the taxable income items net of any business and investment deductions results in a major item that the federal government calls *Adjusted Gross Income*. Note that all business and investment deductions come before Adjusted Gross Income and that itemized personal deductions and exemptions will come after AGI.

It is also important here to use only the *Excess* Itemized Deductions, that is, the deductions that exceed $3,400 ($2,300 for a single return) since the current tax tables now tax the first $3,400 at the "0" bracket. The Personal Exemption is now $1,000 for each individual taxpayer and each qualified dependent.

STEP FIVE:
CALCULATE TAXABLE INCOME AND FEDERAL INCOME TAX LIABILITY

You are now at the part of the Cash Flow Analysis that not only deserves but requires a full discussion. We could be totally useless and just refer you to the appropriate sections of the Internal Revenue Code or to the tax section of an accounting firm. Instead, we have chosen to devise a practical and understandable approach to measuring and illustrating your income tax picture. It is all in Chapter 6.

STEP SIX:
ADD ADJUSTMENTS TO CASH FLOW

After deducting the Federal Income Tax Liability from Taxable Income, a number of significant adjustments must be made. These adjustments will transform what has thus far been an income tax analysis to a true cash flow analysis. Yet it was necessary to go through the taxable income scenario in order to first define Taxable Income, to arrive at the federal tax liability, and then to extract it—before proceeding to determine the true available cash flow after taxation.

Now several important items must be added back to net income after taxes. First, and typically most significant, are the tax-incentive investment deductions. They were deducted in order to arrive at the correct level of Taxable Income but do not necessarily represent the actual amount of cash flow, paid in and taken out. They must therefore be added back into the developing total. The business deductions from Schedule C are not normally added back because they do represent a true extraction from cash flow.

Next the dividend exclusion is added, to reflect the true level of dividend income. Likewise, the personal exemptions are added back since these were an exclusion for tax computation purposes only; the same is true for the Excess Itemized Deductions.

You must also include certain totally tax-free income, such as Social Security payments and municipal bond interest income, as well as distributions from tax-incentive investments that are net of the tax-incentive investment deductions reported in that section. You must also add back any capital losses reported above unless they were truly extracted from this year's cash flow. Also, if 40% of a net long-term capital gain is included, the cost basis and the 60% tax-free portion of the gain must be added to cash flow if, in fact, receipt of the proceeds of the sale that produced the gain was part of this year's cash flow and therefore available for redirection.

STEP SEVEN:
SUBTRACT TAXABLE GAIN AND LIVING EXPENSES FROM CASH FLOW

Conversely, if a taxable gain was reported but was not actually received during the year in question, it must now be extracted.

Example: Dr. Tom Wright took a $10,000 long-term gain in his stock portfolio held at a brokerage firm, reported a $4,000 (40%) taxable gain, but never actually received the cash proceeds of the sale. It would therefore be misleading to include it in his cash flow analysis other than for tax computation purposes.

The same would be true for a capital gains distribution in a mutual fund where gains are automatically reinvested or where taxable items flowed through from a family partnership or subchapter S corporation or personal holding company for tax reporting purposes only.

Now, finally, Living Expenses (which usually include all itemized deductions) must be extracted. Identifying the proper and correct level of Living Expenses is *the* single most difficult aspect of cash flow analysis. Yet nothing is more crucial if you are to achieve the real purpose of this entire exercise. As a result, the Expense Worksheet in Figure 4–3 becomes useful if your clients have to adjust their lifestyles to create discretionary cash flow when it does not exist or needs to be increased. Conversely, if they have excess discretionary cash flow, they may return to the Expense Worksheet to see where they might best increase today's standard of living. Most of us hardly need a worksheet to make that determination.

STEP EIGHT:
TOTAL FOR DISCRETIONARY CASH FLOW

We finally have arrived at our ultimate goal: identifying cash flow surplus or deficit after weighing all income and all expenses. If your client is closer to the beginning than the end of the process of accumulating

FIGURE 4–3 *Expense Worksheet (State Whether Annual or Monthly)*

Expense Worksheet
(State whether annual or monthly)

	CURRENT MONTHLY	IN EVENT OF DISABILITY	IN EVENT OF DEATH
LIVING EXPENSES:			
Food, Household Supplies			
Allowances, Subscriptions			
Household or Yard Help, Pool Maintenance			
Clothes, Cleaning			
Miscellaneous Cash Expenses			
Auto Expenses (Gas, OVIL, Tires Repairs)			
Utilities (Phone, Electricity, Gas, Water)			
Commuting (Other Than Use of Auto)			
Vacations			
Recreation, Club Dues			
Entertainment			
Hobbies			
Family Gifts			
Boat, Airplane, etc., Maintenance			
Other			
SUBTOTAL (LIVING EXPENSES)			
DURABLES (PURCHASES)			
Autos			
Boats, Airplanes			
Furniture, Appliances			
Other			
SUBTOTAL (DURABLES)			
INSURANCE			
Life			
Health			
Home			
Auto			
Liability			
SUBTOTAL (INSURANCE)			

	CURRENT MONTHLY	IN EVENT OF DISABILITY	IN EVENT OF DEATH
OTHER			
Medical and Dental			
Education			
Mortgage (Excludes Taxes and Insurance)			
Rent			
Debts (Other Than Mortgage			
Charitable Contributions			
Professional Advice (Lawyer, Accountant)			
Alimony			
Child Support			
Political Contributions			
Unreimbursed Business Expense			
Property Taxes			
Intangibles Tax			
Ad Valorem Tax			
State Income Tax			
Miscellaneous			
SUBTOTAL (OTHER)			
GRAND TOTAL OF EXPENSES			

a desired level of wealth, and if you arrive at only a small or negative discretionary cash flow, major financial surgery is probably required.

Alternatively, while it is usually anathema to those who are in their later years to use up some capital to live in the lifestyle to which they aspire or have become accustomed, today's inflationary scenario may make it appropriate and advisable.

Two ways for improving discretionary cash flow

The principal concern now, however, is for those clients who are still building their financial pyramid but who are having difficulty making ends meet. That condition, negative cash flow, can aptly be called financial chaos. And it seems to occur regularly in all sections of the financial net worth spectrum. Frequently we see executives and professionals alike at least double their expenditures as their income doubles. The graduated income tax scale, however, *prevents* after-tax spendable income from doubling. A cash flow deficit easily becomes the result.

My experience is that uncontrolled and nonprogrammed spending—not planned expenditures—creates the havoc. And the havoc arises to some extent with everyone even where there still is positive net cash flow. The answer to the problem is easy if you apply the following system for budgeting major irregular expenditures.

AN EASY WAY TO PROGRAM EXPENSES

Just about every client needs a programmed expense account, and here is how this *first* system for creating more discretionary cash flow works. Your clients must first identify all the expenses that always seem to come at the wrong time or in the wrong amount. Panic ensues and they run to the bank for a loan, charge it, cancel a vacation or planned investment, delay the purchase of something they or the family need, or otherwise react instead of act. These expenses are almost always ones that do not come up monthly but can still be programmed.

Table 4–2 shows a typical list for Dr. Tom Wright. Dr. Wright's $2,208 per month or $26,500 per year of regular expenses (from Current Income and Expenses section of the financial questionnaire appearing in Chapter 1), plus this $21,924, adds up to his total of $48,424. Should he experience expenses other than those already factored, he will usually dip into his emergency reserves. If need be, some of his discretionary cash flow can be used in the future to replenish cash reserves. But let's get back to the Programmed Expense Account.

TABLE 4–2
Programmed Expense Account

Items	Comment	Annual Assumed Budget
Clothes and Personal Property	Decide how much will be spent this year and stick to it.	$ 3,400
Home/Lake House Maintenance	Be generous here and carry over to the next year whatever is not spent this year.	1,200
Auto Taxes	Put in little items, too.	200
Club Dues/Bills	Business and personal	4,000
Real Estate Taxes	Factor in possible increases.	2,000
Tuition	This is always too much too soon.	3,900
Interest	The bank must be paid.	4,124
Vacations	At least $200 a day.	2,100
Holiday, Wedding, and Birthday Gifts	Don't ever forget this one! Your client has more friends and relatives than he thinks.	1,000
		$21,924

One Way to Earn Interest While Programming Expenses. Dr. Wright must divide the $21,924 by 12 and then religiously deposit $1,827 each and every month into his Programmed Expense Account. He should open a special checking account, making certain that checks for *only* Programmed Expenses are written on this account. Excess cash contained in this account can be journaled over into a money market fund so that temporarily idle funds will at least earn interest. When budgeting the following year's Programmed Expense Account, a return to this special checking account will provide a perfect record of the real world of irregular expenses. Modern day brokerage house financial management accounts are also ideal Programmed Expense Accounts.

The creation of the Programmed Expense Account system for controlling moderate to major annual expenses is highly recommended. It, like so much else in financial planning that makes sense, is not at all complicated but does require discipline. Using and monitoring such a program over the months and years will save most clients a lot of headaches at the very least. More importantly, it is a no-cost way to guarantee the creation and improvement of your client's discretionary cash flow.

OPTIONS FOR CONVERTING TAX LIABILITY INTO INVESTMENT ASSETS

The *second* major system for creating discretionary cash flow for investments is tax sheltering. Basically we can divide tax shelters of all types into two major categories:

1. Some tax shelters enable you to deduct from taxation an amount equal to most if not all of the capital that goes into the investment. We

often say that these investments create tax deductions (or tax credits) that can be used to shelter "unrelated" income from income taxation, that is, income other than the income produced by the investment itself.

An excellent example would be a qualified retirement plan. This type of nearly perfect shelter takes an appropriate level of otherwise taxable personal service income and shelters 100% of it from current taxation.

Another good example of this type of tax shelter would be investments in well structured diversified limited partnerships that drill for gas and oil reserves. These investments will usually produce tax deductions of close or equal to 100% of investment over the first one to four years of operation. Cash flow resulting from gas/oil sales is then partially sheltered by depletion and other business expenses.

2. The second category of tax shelters provides tax deductions that partly or totally offset the income that the shelter itself produces. Investment examples would be municipal bonds, annuities, income-producing real estate, or existing oil and gas properties.

In the municipal bond example, interest income is, by law, free of federal taxation. In real estate, depreciation and interest deductions offset rental income. Investments in existing gas/oil income-producing properties provide deductions, such as depletion and depreciation, which offset at least part of the income from gas and oil sales. Again the qualified retirement plan is also a perfect example of this type of shelter, inasmuch as it shelters 100% of the income produced in the plan. A deferred annuity contract is another good example of a very low-risk procedural method of sheltering interest income from current taxes.

What You Must Watch Out For. Obviously, any legal method that can be used to divert taxes away from a one-way trip to Washington, D.C. and toward your client's investment pyramid is advantageous. An equally important axiom is that decreasing liquidity and/or taking some level of risk is necessary in order to achieve increased investable cash flow through tax reduction. As with all financial planning decisions, you must weigh the pros and cons, the risks and the rewards, and then make an intelligent decision about the direction or allocation of that specific segment of your client's capital or annual cash flow.

Since tax sheltering either eliminates, reduces, or delays the taxation of the income it offsets, future anticipated tax bracket levels may determine which sheltering method is most applicable for which client. Using sheltering to increase the discretionary cash flow available for investments therefore requires far greater analysis and care than is illustrated at this point. Chapters 9 through 12 on problem solving will treat this subject more generously.

My experience has been that most clients and planners alike place more emphasis on "money doctoring" existing investment assets than on creating and then regularly directing a stipulated amount of annual discretionary cash flow. Given the relative importance of the latter, I see this phenomenon as an important obstacle to maximum financial success. This chapter has therefore shown that, given a fixed level of income, spending less via (1) intelligent budgeting of expenses and (2) the reduction of excessive taxation are two key ways to increase discretionary cash flow. Nothing is kept if it is either all spent or sent on to Washington, D.C.

Controlled spending is the lowest-risk way to increase what is available for savings or investments. But it is the most difficult because it is not "pizzazzy." It is also painful for those whose expenses are out of control. It may, however, become more popular as today's socio-political climate returns us to some semblance of supply side economics in the 1980s and its attendant emphasis on investment versus consumption.

Tax sheltering is usually the easiest way to increase what is left. It is also the most glamorous—which is why it must be approached in such a guarded fashion. In fact, it contains so much snarl power that it often leads to putting the tax caboose before the economic locomotive. Tax sheltering can, however, be very effective when you balance your client's involvement with both procedural and investment shelters. You must learn, too, to select carefully between the two major types of investment shelters described in this chapter and later in Chapter 11.

This chapter has placed a good deal of emphasis on tax sheltering. The implication is that income taxation is a key obstacle to accumulating wealth. Considerable attention will therefore be devoted to a total understanding of income taxation in Chapter 6. But it is actually *inflation*, acting in concert with taxation, that can greatly diminish the financial muscle of both existing assets and discretionary cash flow. That is why, once accumulation-oriented clients are committed to the creation of increased and increasing investable cash flow, they must also dedicate themselves to hedging against the thievery of inflation. The next chapter will shed light on today's inflation and its dire consequences for tomorrow. Chapter 5 will also guide you toward ways in which you can use inflation to your client's distinct advantage.

5

Inflation:
How to
Capture the
Silent Embezzler

How to best position assets and direct discretionary income in today's inflationary economy is on just about everyone's mind. But it wasn't always that way. In the 1950s and '60s, we spoke of a Robin Hood who stole from the rich and gave to the poor. Today we read about a different Robin Hood, one who is really the antithesis of yesteryear's. In the guise of inflation, he steals from those who are economically ignorant and gives to those who are financially savvy. Factoring this silent embezzler of inflation into your client's future financial goals has therefore become crucial to setting your sights on a meaningful planning destination.

Why factor today's inflation into tomorrow's needs?

Concern for the effect of inflation upon your client's financial future cannot be overstated. The assets that you now think will be required to produce the after-tax income your client wants or will need may not at all be sufficient. For those who are in the early to middle stages of accumulating wealth, there is time to combat the insidious nature of today's most legal thief. For those who have, for all practical purposes, already traversed the accumulation stage of life, it's a different story. A more delicate financial surgery will be required. For those who have already begun the process of distributing assets and income to family members or charity, a closer look may be very revealing. It could well be that they are giving away the future buying power that will be needed to replace what is now being stolen. A complete reversal of their gifting direction may well be in order.

WHY CONTRARIAN THINKING IS A KEY TO REAL GROWTH OF CAPITAL

An inflationary economy dictates that, when capital is devoted to growth, you must continue to direct it, in *contrarian* fashion: (1) toward only those areas that would appear to provide unusual profit potential *and* (2) in ways that will provide appropriate current and future tax benefits without taking undue risk.

Inflation, coupled with graduated taxes, puts a big enough dent in your client's financial pyramid. Not limiting losses through contrarian thinking will make a wreck of it.

For example, *when looking at an investment tax shelter as a "growth of capital" vehicle, you must always look for an investment area that offers the greatest economic or investment potential aside from any front end tax benefits.* Only then should you consider the attendant tax deductions and/or credits and how they may help your clients reach their objectives. The resulting tax savings must be viewed as interest-free leverage, rather than an object in itself. That is because you effectively borrow the tax savings from Uncle Sam, don't have to pay interest on it, but do have to pay back at least part of the original tax savings at some point in the future. Like Will Rogers, do not lose sight of the importance of first seeking the return *of* your client's principal before chasing too wild-eyed a return *on* that principal. When seeking maximum growth of capital through tax sheltering, emphasize this fundamental though *contrarian* guideline. Your clients will find themselves moving more steadily forward instead of playing catch-up football. Embodying this type of contrarian investment attitude is therefore a key to causing capital to grow at a speed that exceeds inflation. On *any* risk level, it will cause you to miss an occasional opportunity. But, more than anything else, it will severely limit your investment disasters during a period when inflation is already more of a setback than any of us have bargained for.

WHY YOU MUST SEEK "INCREASING" INCOME

When resources are at work to provide investment income, you need to place more emphasis than ever upon that income's ability to

TABLE 5–1
$25,000 of After-Tax Income Adjusted for Time and Inflation

	7% Inflation	10% Inflation	13% Inflation
5 Years	$35,064	$ 40,263	$ 46,061
10 Years	49,179	64,844	84,864
15 Years	68,976	104,431	156,357
20 Years	96,742	168,188	288,077

grow, preferably in a tax-benefited manner. Keeping *more* of the *increasing* income that investments produce is the essence of modern income planning.

To demonstrate inflation's powerful erosion of buying power, examine the effect of it and time upon $25,000 of after-tax spendable investment income, as shown in Table 5–1. Shocking, isn't it! After only five short years of 10% price increases, $40,263 of spendable income will be needed to buy what $25,000 of after-tax cash flow buys today. This vicious treadmill of having to move fast financially in order to stand still makes planning today more important than ever before. Yet not a day goes by without hearing someone mention that they just do not understand where their money is going. Actually it's easy. Today all of us are paying the price of the mistakes our government made yesterday—and continues to make. To understand it more fully is to begin to be able to halt its weakening effect upon your clients' financial pyramids.

In the final analysis, with any particular segment of your client's financial structure, getting ahead in absolute net worth or spendable income may not be stepping forward at all. You may be creating another immaculate deception, falling behind in real terms while only seeming to move forward. It is, of course, all relative to the rate at which the cost of living is rising.

How inflation became energized

The follies of Fort Fumble in Washington, D.C. started today's inflationary ball rolling in the 1960s through fiscal and monetary mismanagement. The dramatic upward trend in petroleum pricing, however, begun in the 1970s, has kicked it higher and farther than the most sophisticated econometric models predicted. And the fumbling of energy policy, currently represented by the so-called windfall profits tax on oil and by continuing natural gas price controls, continues to turn the entire exercise into a losing ballgame for the modern Robin Hood's victims.

Periods of rapidly advancing prices on the gasoline pump meters and of climbing utility and heating fuel bills are a very obvious but relatively small part of the overall problem. The price of oil and natural gas, as raw materials or production costs, also affects the price of everything else for which we spend money. What we pay for food, clothes, housing, transportation, education, and entertainment—as well as for products like chemicals, plastics, drugs, paper, metals, and packaging—is all rising far more rapidly than it otherwise would due to continually rising energy costs.

Most people will agree with this scenario as long as petroleum prices increase every month or so. But when prices temporarily level off or even drop, as all commodities inevitably do, we tend to perceive our hearts' desire—*the end of the storm instead of the eye of the hurricane.* Don't be misled by emotion into believing that moderating inflation rates won't be jolted by sporadic jumps in the cost of energy. Price lulls only represent temporary excesses in supplies *above* the ground, not *below*.

How energy is priced in a world of depleting resources

If you were to compact into one day all of the time it took to produce all of this earth's oil and gas reserves, it would be as though it rained but once on a meadow, creating just one great crop of beautiful wild flowers. The day following, with puddles of water still around, you went out to pick the flowers you knew you could sell. You selected the most beautiful ones from the most accessible areas of the meadow. You received a fair profit margin in a rather stable market, in exchange for the easy work and beauty of your first harvest. Because of the easy-to-pick, bountiful supply relative to early demand, wild flowers sold cheaply. Gradually your buyers began to waste them with almost wild abandon. That whole scene continued for some time until each day's harvest gradually became a noticably larger and larger part of what was left. The remaining flowers became less accessible and therefore harder and more expensive to gather. You then watched without surprise as the price you would get for your flowers rose exponentially.

What do flowers have to do with inflation and financial planning? The wild flower analogy is but a reflection of what is essentially happening in the world of oil and gas pricing, even without Fort Fumble's help. It is, as a matter of mathematical fact, what must eventually happen to the price of any nonreplaceable commodity in a free market environment. And to add insult to injury, abnormal and wasteful US demand, stimulated by a policy of artificially low, government-controlled prices has helped push the world market even higher and faster than is dictated by the wild flower scenario. Ironically, US policy was intended to placate voters by keeping energy cheap. One shocking result of it all is that the exporting nations have intermittently threatened to cut production unless we develop a sane national energy policy, including the production of synthetic fuels and the development of replaceable, solar-related energy sources. But now and then, even the Arabs, the smartest barterers the world has ever known, lose control of petroluem pricing with spot quotes having at times reached levels much higher than contract prices. Simultaneously, interest rates occupied record or near-record levels in 1979–82 to reportedly slow demand for goods and services and therefore slow inflation. But dramatically higher interest rates, even if we in the US were in total control of them, do not seem to put much of a dent in the wasteful use of oil and natural gas, which seems to be almost inelastic, at least under current domestic pricing policy. Only a sudden return to the free and natural market place in natural gas, as well as in oil, will accomplish the natural and proper resolution—*ensition*, an orderly *energy* source trans*ition* to replaceable energy sources such as the sun, wind, water, tide, alcohol, and methane gas produced from biomass.

How inflation and taxation act in concert to lift the tax rate

In the past, even when your income rose, inflation complicated the problem of providing level or increasing buying power by pushing your taxable income into higher unindexed and graduated income tax brackets. In more traditional times it may have been supportable to argue that increases in earned income (such as wages, salaries, bonuses, fees, commissions) often precede price increases. Even today, in the eyes of this financial planner, it would appear that the whole matter has become something of a vicious cycle.

But the wild flower analogy gives strong support to the argument that increased income today is more a follower of the increased cost of living than it is the initiator of it. The real crippling blow has been that the increases in personal service income climbed upward into loftier tax brackets even when they did not represent increases in real income. To be more precise, with a joint return, the 1981 brackets climbed rapidly from 14% to 50% in eleven easy steps. The top bracket on personal service income, you were told by countless articles, never went higher than 50%. But that was just one more deception. While the higher wages and salaries did not themselves get taxed at more than 50% rate, they had the effect of pushing your investment or nonpersonal service income into higher and higher tax brackets until you conceivably reached the pre-1982 peak rate of 70%. The whole process was so gradual and mired in a maze of income tax forms, ranging from Schedule G to form 4726, that it was almost immoral. Now, under President Reagan's policies and the Economic Recovery Tax Act of 1981, the maximum tax rate on *all* ordinary income is 50%, and rates beyond 1984 are indexed to inflation. Chapter 6 will go into great detail on how to measure your feverish tax temperature, after literally years of severe bracket creep, even with the recent tax reform.

Putting yourself into the right frame of mind to fight inflation

Before you can develop a strategy for whipping inflation your attitude must be in concert with reality. First, for planning purposes, assume that inflation will stay at just about the rate it is right now. Trying to forecast how much more or less it will be for the next month, year, or decade is foolish. If you ask a hundred different economists that question, you will get a hundred different answers. So why should you expect to come up with the precise answer that would outfox the masses. That would be like gambling, and gambling has no place in financial planning since its results lack predictability. Instead, you should assume that today's average annual rate will continue. Go along with what the trend has been for the last several months. After all, the rates of return you predict for the investment strategies you choose for your clients will generally be aligned with today's inflationary environment. If inflation becomes worse than you assume, upping your future needs, it is likely that equity-oriented investments will eventually outperform your expectations. If inflation is not as onerous as at present, the investment performance you assumed will not be needed. There is, you see, a sort of built-in compensation.

Second, evolving an overall strategy must precede deciding on specifics. My experience in the financial services industry over the past twenty years indicates that people react more positively toward solving problems when they have developed an overall plan of action or strategy before they are called upon to make specific decisions. If you don't have a goal, any road will get you there! But if you want to beat inflation, you must put on the right thinking cap. The remainder of this chapter guides you toward overall strategies that have been successfully used to fight inflation. Chapter 11 will then delve more specifically into investment areas for hedging against inflation *in tax-favored fashion.*

Two strategic inflation fighters

There are but two general strategies for winning the battle against inflation. The first, *ownership,* is primary and should at least keep your client from being *beat by inflation.* The second, *financial leverage,* is secondary and must usually be employed when *your client wants to beat inflation.* It appears in the two forms of *debt leverage* and *tax leverage.*

WHY OWNING MORE AND LOANING LESS ATTACKS INFLATION

Philosophically speaking, only two things can be done with investable cash. It can be used to purchase and therefore own something, or it can be loaned out to someone else.

1. *Owning* provides the opportunity for growth of capital and/or increasing income. Ownership involves two negatives. Often you do not know exactly what you own is worth. Second, it is not always liquid. One may therefore have to sell for an amount less than the original investment if liquidity becomes a problem at the wrong time.

2. *Loaning* pays usually fixed interest, and then eventually returns, in fixed dollars, the exact amount in existence in the beginning.

Loaning also has two distinct negatives in an inflationary environment. First, your client is guaranteed to lose—to be returned less in terms of purchasing power than was invested. Second, one cannot generally depend upon interest payments increasing over the period in question. More importantly, no known guaranteed interest rate will, on an after-tax basis, average as high as the inflationary rate over any extended period of time.

As an example of the difference between owning and loaning, let's look at owning a home versus renting.

EXAMPLE: OWNING VERSUS LENDING

For the sake of demonstrating the affect of ownership exclusive of the benefits of debt financing, let's unrealistically assume that inherited cash is used to purchase a $75,000 home. A young executive earning about $35,000 in a 33% marginal tax bracket invests the $75,000 in a home instead of renting and "lending" the $75,000 at interest. The $75,000 home would increase in value to a staggering

$2,246,994 in 30 years with 12% constant annual inflation. That may sound outlandish, but remember that homes that cost $5,000 to $10,000 30 years ago are worth over $50,000 to $100,000 today. And that's after a period that averaged far less than the recent 12% average inflation rate.

Now, let's instead assume that our young executive placed his $75,000 inheritance at 13% interest, 1% above the assumed inflation, over the 30 years and rented instead of buying. The $75,000 would grow, on an after-33%-tax-bracket basis, to $918,641.66. There was, of course, the probably increasing rent that he would also had to pay for housing. But for the sake of being very fair and conservative, we will assume that, had he purchased the home instead of renting, he would have spent that same amount on repairs and maintenance over the 30 years in question.

The difference between owning and loaning in the case of a 12% inflationary scenario made at least the following difference:

Value of "Home Ownerhsip" in 30 Years	$2,246,994
Value of "Cash Loaning" in 30 Years	$ 918,642
Cost of "Loaning" Versus "Owning"	$1,328,352
Average Cost per Year of "Loaning" Versus "Owning"	$ 44,278

This discussion is not meant to imply that you should position all of your client's capital in the position of owning assets. It does mean to demonstrate that you positively should *not* have all of your client's assets loaned out at fixed income rates during an expected prolonged period of even mild inflation. It also means that a closer look has to be taken to make certain that enough assets are hedged against rising costs. That is the crux of the problem that this chapter insists you examine.

On the one extreme, you must be reminded that the segments of your client's net worth that are guaranteed against loss of principal are also guaranteed to lose purchasing power. Conversely, it profits one little to seek protection against inflation if in doing so, principal is forfeited.

HOW TO USE FINANCIAL LEVERAGE TO BUILD REAL WEALTH

The second strategic inflation fighter is financial leverage. There are actually two types of financial leverage that can be used to build wealth at a rate that exceeds inflation. The *first* results from the borrowing of cash, and it is frequently called *debt financing*. The *second* results from the "borrowing" of cash from Uncle Sam, and it is most commonly called *tax sheltering*. Both have pros and cons.

Debt financing involves the borrowing of part or all of the original cost of owning an asset. It is the exact opposite of loaning in that interest is paid to someone else for the temporary use of their cash. If the asset purchased goes up in value at only the inflation rate, and if the after-tax cost of the interest is less than the inflation rate, you beat inflation. In other words, that segment of capital will grow at a faster pace than inflation and therefore build real wealth. On the other hand, if the asset purchased with borrowed funds appreciates at a slower rate than the after-tax cost of the debt, negative return results. You will be losing ground at a faster pace than would be inflicted by inflation alone.

EXAMPLE: LEVERAGING OWNERSHIP VIA DEBT FINANCING

We will again use the example of a young married executive earning about $35,000 in a constant 33% marginal tax bracket. This time, he inherits $25,000, which he uses as a down payment on a $75,000 home. A $50,000 mortgage at 13% is secured for 30 years. Assume, again, that inflation remains at 12%. His monthly payments are $553. With the 12% inflation rate, the home increases from $75,000 to $2,246,994 in 30 years. Essentially, his $25,000 down payment is compounded on an after-tax rate of 16.2% versus the 12% rate at which the home was appreciating. In other words, the use of debt financing upped his rate of return by 35%. An even higher figure would result if you factored in the benefit of (1) being able to deduct the interest and (2) locking in a fixed housing cost versus a rising rental bill.

HOW TO HAVE YOUR INFLATIONARY CAKE AND EAT IT TOO

It is also quite possible through partial leveraging to hedge your client's entire net worth against inflation without forsaking the most conservative segments of capital. This concept, too, can best be explained by actual example.

EXAMPLE:

Your client's overall financial plan is in a preservation mode.

She is extremely conservative and determined to have at least two-thirds of her pyramid positioned in fixed income assets. You may be automatically assuming that it is impossible for her to be adequately hedged against inflation. Not so—if she is willing to use leverage.

Her assets total $600,000, and she is not comfortable unless she has $400,000 "loaned out" in the form of liquid cash, cash equivalents, and bonds. Here's the strategy you should consider:

Invest the remaining $200,000 in an investment asset or in a combination thereof that can traditionally be leveraged internally on a two-to-one debt to equity ratio. The following breakdown illustrates the point:

Investment	Equity	Debt Leverage	Market Value
Cash and Bonds	$400,000	$ 0	$ 400,000
Real Estate	100,000	200,000	300,000
Cable TV Properties	100,000	200,000	300,000
	$600,000	$400,000	$1,000,000

Note that $600,000 of the total $1,000,000 of market value is in a position to fight inflation. That is also her exact net worth. The result is that, via debt leverage, she is able to rest well with $400,000 of fixed income assets and still have her entire net worth protected against inflation.

Tax sheltering is the second type of financial leverage that can be used to build wealth in real terms. It involves the investment of a segment of capital or cash flow into economic areas that provide certain legal tax advantages. These tax benefits or incentives most often appear in the form of tax deductions. Common examples of these tax deductions are:

1. the ability to quickly depreciate or write off the cost of an apartment complex or cable television system, even when it is probably appreciating and
2. the ability to deduct the cost of drilling an oil or gas well entirely in the year during which it is drilled.

Note that, in both instances, the incentives were clearly provided by the law. The purpose of the law is to lure investor capital toward areas of investment intended to better the economic or social well-being of the nation. A red flag must be raised in advance of using tax sheltering as a type of financial leverage. You must make certain that there is a very high probability of at least getting your client's money—and hopefully much more—back within a reasonable period of time. While a lengthy discussion of tax-incentive investments can be found in Chapter 11, suffice it to say here that the major tax-favored investment opportunities are found within the acronym REACT: *r*eal estate, *e*nergy, *a*griculture, *c*ommunications, and *t*ransportation. You must identify one or more of these areas that not only historically provides an inflation hedge but that *currently* appears to offer unusually attractive reward versus risk. That will almost always be the case where the investment opportunity appears opposite the risk side of a coin of current economic crisis (such as the US' current energy, housing, and communications crises).

EXAMPLE: LEVERAGING OWNERSHIP VIA TAX SHELTERING

Let's consider a successful married professional, Mr. Saunders, whose income has risen to the $100,000+ level. After itemized deductions and personal exemptions, he still usually has substantial income on a joint return taxed at 48%.

He has the option of receiving his last $10,000 or so of income, paying $4,800 in federal taxes and, investing the remaining $5,200 in a nontax-favored investment area, which grows at the inflation rate of 12%. In 10 years, that $5,200 is worth $16,150 or $14,048 after long-term capital gain taxes (10.45% after-tax annual compounded rate of return).

If Mr. Nunn, with similar financial circumstances, invests in a tax-incentive investment area that provides 100% deductibility in the year of investment, he is in effect able to invest the entire $10,000 of pretax income as follows:

Investment	$10,000	Investment	$10,000
Deduction	10,000	Federal Tax Savings	4,800
Federal Taxes	–0–		
Net Available for Investment	$10,000	Actual Out-of-Pocket Cost or Money at Risk	$ 5,200

If this $10,000 investment also grows at 12% per year, it will be worth $31,058 in 10 years. Even if Mr. Nunn must recapture the $10,000 of deductions and pay an ordinary income tax rate of 48% on all of the proceeds, the after-tax proceeds of $16,150 is 15% better than the $14,048 achieved without tax sheltering by Mr. Saunders.

This is admittedly an over-simplified and over-generalized example. But it does serve to illustrate the benefit of using Uncle Sam's money (without paying interest) to work for your clients, even if it is only a deferral and they have to pay a lot of it back later. Of course, if they can so arrange their affairs or those of their families in such a way as to transform future taxation to a lower level or eliminate it altogether, an even greater advantage results.

For example, assume that the above-$10,000 tax-incentive investment ($5,200 of Nunn's money and $4,800 of tax liability) was donated to children or grandchildren. As the investment is liquidated in the nonexistent to lower income tax brackets of the minors, little or no tax erosion occurs. In this instance, the investment did over twice as well as the after-tax example of Mr. Saunders.

Pretax Income Available for Investment	$10,000
Deductions (100%) from Investment	10,000
Federal Taxes	0
Net Available for Investment	$10,000
Investment Value in 10 years at 12%	$31,058
Ordinary Income Taxes Due upon Liquidation in "Lower" Tax Brackets of Children	0
Net After-Tax Proceeds to Family Unit (2.21 times the $14,048 of proceeds for Mr. Saunders)	$31,058
Actual Money at Risk	5,200
After-Tax Profit	$25,858
After-Tax Annual Compounded Rate of Return to Family Unit (versus 12% inflation)	17%

The same is true if your client had kept the investment but had selected one that is taxed as a capital gain upon liquidation.

Investment	$10,000
Federal Tax Savings	(4,800)
Actual Money at Risk	$ 5,200
Investment Proceeds upon Liquidation (10 years at 12%)	$31,058
Long-Term Capital Gains Tax (zero basis)	5,963
After-Tax Proceeds	$ 25,095
Less: Actual Money at Risk	(5,200)
After-Tax Profit	$ 19,859
After-Tax Annual Compounded Rate of Return	14.36%

Note that only a 3.91% difference in after-tax rate of return (14.36%–10.45%) changes the end result from $14,048 to $19,895. That's a 42% improvement. Over a lifetime, that makes an enormous difference. For example, $1 grows at 10.45% over 30 years to $19.72. That same $1 grows at 14.36% to $56 in 30 years. That is almost three times as much "financial future." And that is what *financial leverage* via tax sheltering is all about.

Why updating for inflation is crucial

All that has been said thus far about inflation should, in itself, be enough to support an argument for frequently updating your clients' financial plans. Both the lifetime and estate planning sections of their plans will be dramatically affected by changes you make in the assumptions about inflation. Inflation rate estimates affect every conceivable category of their future financial needs. Yet, it is amazing how many affluent Americans have not yet factored inflation into their projections of future asset and income needs if, in actuality, they have made any projections at all.

Not planning is the first big mistake. Not updating a plan for inflation is the second great error—one that could result in spending retirement on the back of a boat fishing for food instead of on the back of a yacht for pleasure.

Yet inflation alone is not the most formidable problem. Actually, the greatest obstacle to one's intended financial destination is the manner in which inflation reacts with graduated income tax rates. "Bracket creep", as it has been aptly described, can be appreciated only when income taxation itself is thoroughly understood. Section II continues with the next chapter's unique but practical approach to determining and displaying your client's income tax picture.

6

Step-by-Step Guide to Measuring Your Client's Income Tax Temperature

Some people find it difficult to remember and then to apply the most fundamental financial management rule of them all: *It is not what you earn that counts in the accumulation and preservation of wealth; it is what you keep.* This seemingly obvious rule says so much more than it appears to say.

Nothing is preserved or accumulated if it is spent. We have already discussed in Chapter 4 the significance of discretionary cash flow. Its importance is magnified by the fact that it is virtually impossible to properly shelter an appropriate level of income from tax erosion unless some of it is directed toward the creation of tax deductions or tax credits. Investable cash flow is therefore the premier cornerstone for building wealth in stable periods and of maintaining it in inflationary times. Its merits are best expressed in our previous deliberations on the relative importance of the rate of investing versus the rate of return on investment.

Dispelling the pretax rate of return myth

That leads us to the second fundamental guideline for keeping more of what you earn. Pretax rate of return is perfectly meaningless. Many do not realize it. Fewer practice it. Giving it just lip service is simply not enough. You have to learn to think that way. For instance, it is generally regarded as gospel by investors that 6% tax-free is the same as 12% in a 50% marginal tax bracket. That is not really right, mainly because it is as practical as an anchor on a sinking ship. It is like telling an American child that "red" means *rouge* in French. Instead, we tell the student that *rouge* is a French word that means "red."

Similarly, what the financial services industry ought to be telling investing adults is that an unsheltered 12% taxable return is actually a true 6% return in a 50% or a 10.32% return in a 14% bracket. The conclusion must be that the standard tables that compare taxable returns and tax-free yields are structured in reverse. You simply have to learn to think in terms of after-tax return. It is a lot like learning a foreign language. You don't really know it until you *think* in it.

Another major myth about income taxation, as it relates to investment return and financial planning, is the confusion between the *aggregate* tax rate and the *marginal* tax bracket. I recently met with an exceptionally wealthy professional who indicated that he was not considering any further tax savings techniques or investment strategies because his family's oil and gas drilling activities had him down to a projected 25% tax bracket. I asked for his current federal income tax liability, and he mentioned a figure of over $100,000. I then remarked that I must have misunderstood because I could not envision someone with that high a tax liability, even after tax sheltering, with so low a tax bracket. He curtly offered that I obviously didn't understand his situation because about $100,000 in taxes divided by his $400,000 or so of total professional fees and investment income meant that he was paying only 25% of his income in taxes—and that was that!

To make a long story short, it took the greatest diplomacy and some time to explain several things. One was why his aggregate tax rate was not of significance in tax planning. Another was that the marginal tax bracket affected the last dollar of income that was added or deducted from his taxable income. Finally, he was surprised to learn that *his* marginal bracket was actually a lofty 50%.

At issue here is the fact that everyone except tax-exempt entities, such as qualified retirement plans and charitable institutions, is subjected to a multitude of tax brackets beginning with the zero bracket and ending at the top with the marginal bracket. This marginal bracket is what eats into the last dollar of income that our investments create—but then only to the extent to which we allow it to happen. *Converting some of those top tax dollars into assets and/or spendable income, without taking undue risk, is what modern tax plannning is all about.*

Now, a critical point is that it is just as important in some cases to note how *low* the marginal bracket is! A low or nonexisting top tax bracket enables one to take advantage of opportunities that higher-bracketed investors cannot. For instance, a child can perhaps accumulate capital at a true after-tax 12–14+% rate in a diversified portfolio of corporate bonds on a relatively low risk level. A higher-bracketed parent, however, may do best by investing that risk level of capital in tax-exempt bonds at a 8–10+% rate of return. So having a low bracket, as in the case of a child, or a nonexistent bracket, as in the case of a pension plan, sometimes opens up investment vistas at lower financial speeds not otherwise available to those who share a larger burden of the one-way pipeline to the Potomac.

Back to the more prevalent problem of high and steeply graduated tax rates. There is almost always some way to position capital in a tax-benefited way for either the preservation or the accumulation of wealth. But before we can review those techniques and strategies in detail in future chapters, you must gain a greater understanding of exactly how your clients are taxed and how taxation changes with changing tax planning tactics. This chapter is designed to accomplish that exact end.

How to determine your client's tax temperature

Ever since 1913, when the first Form 1040 appeared, measuring the personal tax ramifications of all that is done financially has simultaneously become important *and* complex. In fact, *everything* you can do with existing assets and/or annual discretionary cash flow is directly or indirectly affected by taxation of one type or another.

In an effort to simplify both the measurement and graphic portrayal of your client's income tax picture, a device known as the Taxation Thermometer has been developed. In Figure 6–1, we have chosen an example of where one's taxable income always exceeds $24,600 on a joint return and $18,200 on a single return.

As will be amply demonstrated, part of the significance of the Tax Thermometer lies in its ability to rapidly compute the estimated income tax liability itself, whether you would otherwise use the tax tables or income averaging. More practically, it graphically identifies the various segments of Taxable Income and the federal tax rates to which each segment is subjected.

FIGURE 6–1a

Taxation Thermometer for Joint Returns – 1983

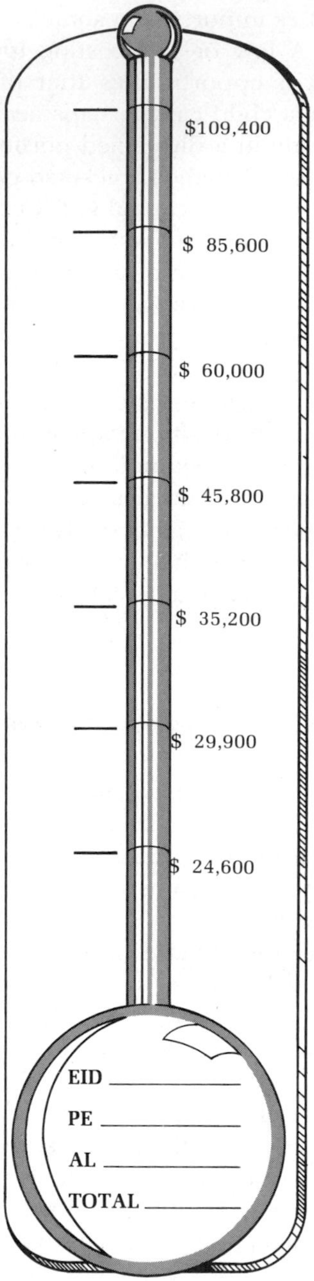

TAXABLE INCOME	TAX BRACKET	TAXABLE INCOME	INCOME TAX
	50% ×		
$109,400			
	48% ×		
$ 85,600			
	44% ×		
$ 60,000			
	40% ×		
$ 45,800			
	35% ×		
$ 35,200			
	30% ×		
$ 29,900			
	26% ×		
$ 24,600			
	23% × to 0%	24,600	3,656

EID _____

PE _____

AL _____

TOTAL _____

TOTALS

TAX CREDITS ( )

TOTAL TAX

FIGURE 6–1b

Taxation Thermometer for Single Returns–1983

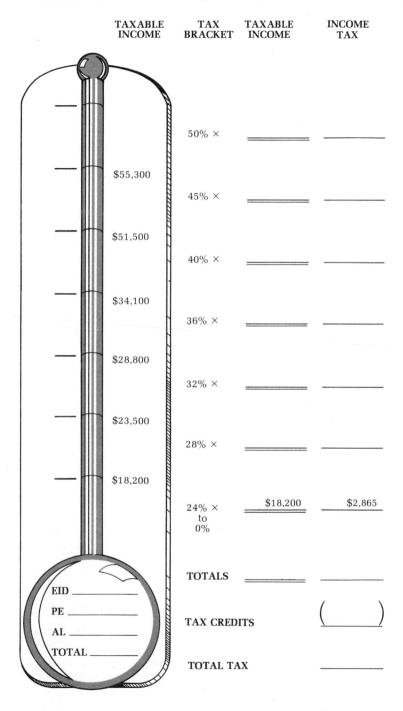

TAXABLE INCOME	TAX BRACKET	TAXABLE INCOME	INCOME TAX
	50% ×		
$55,300			
	45% ×		
$51,500			
	40% ×		
$34,100			
	36% ×		
$28,800			
	32% ×		
$23,500			
	28% ×		
$18,200			
	24% × to 0%	$18,200	$2,865

EID _____

PE _____

AL _____

TOTAL _____

TOTALS _____

TAX CREDITS (_____)

TOTAL TAX _____

How to identify the components of taxable income

The very first step in this total process of measuring tax temperature is to identify the various major segments of income and deductions and finally arrive at a figure for Taxable Income. The form in Table 6–1 is easily used to do exactly that. Note that we have filled in the form with data extracted from Dr. Tom Wright's Cash Flow Analysis appearing in Chapter 2, repeated in Table 6–2 for the sake of convenience.

Category I: PSI consists of all of the personal service income or earned income net of any business deductions connected with the production of such income. In Dr. Wright's case, only the $110,000 salary from the professional corporation is considered personal service income. That, less his $3,500 of business entertainment deductions, gives him $106,500 of PSI. With your client, it may include a bonus, professional fees, installment distributions from qualified retirement plans, and director's fees, *less* any contributions to a Keogh Plan or individual retirement account (IRA). In general, it is the net income produced by your client's expertise.

Category II. NPSI represents all of the taxable nonpersonal service or investment income. With Dr. Wright, that means $1,250 of interest, $4,560 ($4,760−$200) of dividends, and $6,000 of Personal Holding Co. income for a total of $11,810.

Category III. GAINS include the total of the net short-term gains plus 40% of the net long-term gains. For a detailed explanation of this category, including how to net out losses, refer to Chapter 4. Dr. Wright's only gain or loss was a $10,000 long-term gain, and 40% of that or $4,000 is included in *Category III, GAINS.*

TABLE 6–1
Major Categories of Taxable Income

Category	
I. PSI	$106,500
II. NPSI	11,810
III. GAINS	4,000
IV. A+ALs	(10,000)
V. AGI	$112,310
VI. EID	(21,600)
VII. PE	(4,000)
VIII. TI	$ 86,710

TABLE 6–2
Cash Flow Analysis for Dr. Tom Wright

Income:	
Salary	$110,000
Interest	1,250
Dividends from Professional Corporation*	4,560
40% of Net Long-Term Gains	4,000
Personal Holding Company	6,000
Business Deductions	(3,500)
Tax-Incentive Investment Deductions	(10,000)
Adjusted Gross Income	$112,310
Less: Excess Itemized Deductions ($25,000 − $3,400)	(21,600)
Personal Exemptions	(4,000)
Taxable Income	$ 86,710
Less: Federal Income Tax Liability	(27,811)
	$ 58,899
Add: Tax-Incentive Investment Deductions	10,000
Dividend Exclusion	200
Personal Exemptions	4,000
Tax-Free Income	4,200
Excess Itemized Deductions	21,600
	$ 98,899
Less: Taxable Gain	(4,000)
Living Expenses**	(48,424)
Discretionary Cash Flow	$ 46,475
Less: Tax-Incentive Investment Committments	(10,000)
Remaining Discretionary Cash Flow	$ 36,475

*After the $200 dividend exclusion.
**Includes Social Security Taxes, plus all itemized deductions, such as state income taxes.

Category IV. A+ALs included all adjustments and accounting losses such as alimony, business deductions not connected with the production of PSI, and tax-incentive investment deductions. In Dr. Wright's case, there are only the $10,000 of estimated deductible expenses from his tax incentive investment participations.

Category V. AGI is the adjusted gross income. It is derived by totaling all of the previous categories. Dr. Wright's AGI is $112,310. From adjusted gross income, you must subtract the Excess Itemized Deductions. Dr. Wright's total itemized deductions are $25,000. Since the current federal tax schedules include a "zero" bracket amount of $3,400 for joint returns and $2,300 for single returns, this amount must be subtracted from the itemized deductions in order to arrive at the excess itemized deductions (EID). This figure is, in essence, the deductions that are over and above the standard amount that is already allowed in the current tax schedules.

Category VI. EID for Dr. Wright is therefore $25,000 less $3,400, or $21,600.

Category VII. PE contains the personal exemptions. The Wright family consists of Dr. and Mrs. Wright and two dependents for a total of four exemptions. The personal exemption is now $1,000 per individual, and so PE for Dr. Wright is $4,000.

Category VIII. TI is, of course, taxable income. Subtract the excess itemized deductions (EID) and the personal exemptions (PE) from adjusted gross income (AGI), and you now have the all important definition of taxable income (TI). Dr. Wright's TI is therefore $86,710.

How to use the tax thermometer

Now that the taxable income (TI), $86,710, has been appropriately defined, you can place it onto the right side of the Thermometer as indicated. This process will automatically compute the tax liability and simultaneously identify the various segments of taxable income and their applicable tax rates. Dr. Wright's thermometer is shown in Figure 6–2. The first task is to place the estimated TI in the middle of the thermometer in handwriting to act as the crucial stopping point.

Next, this total $86,710 is divided up in the appropriate double-lined blanks on the right side of the thermometer from the bottom up. The tax on the first segment of $24,600 is always taxed at rates ranging from 0% to 23% for a total tax of $3,656. The next double-lined blank holds its maximum allowable of $5,300 for a total tax of $1,378, and so on. The final double-lined blank theoretically could hold a total of $23,800 ($109,400−85,600), but that would take the cumulative total TI far beyond Dr. Wright's $86,710. So that line will only hold $1,110.

Having placed all of the taxable income segments on the double-lined blanks of the thermometer, multiply the applicable tax bracket percentages by the segments, placing the results on the respective single-lined blanks. Total up the various brackets. The total equals the *tentative* regular income tax liability. From this you must subtract the investment tax credits to arrive at the total tax.

The tax thermometer and two key conclusions

A couple of key financial planning considerations have been mentioned, and they are illustrated by the very physical nature of the Tax Thermometer.

FIGURE 6–2

Taxation Thermometer for Joint Returns–1983

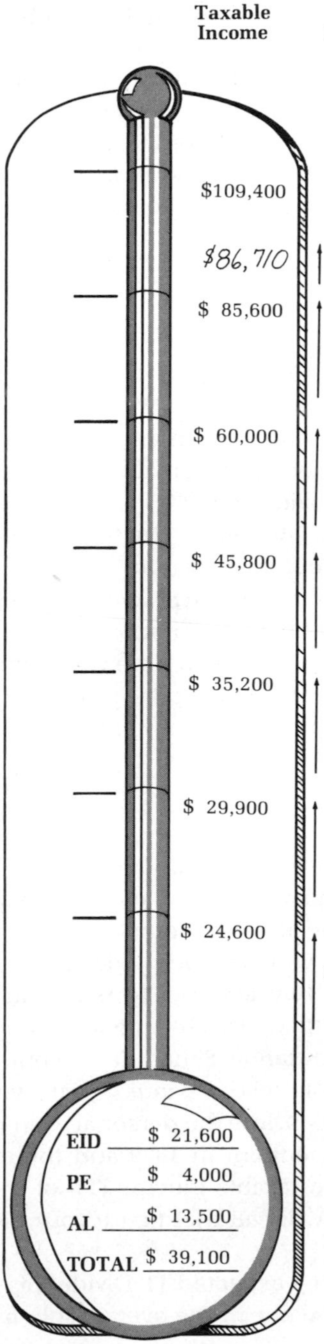

	Taxable Income	TAX BRACKET	TAXABLE INCOME	INCOME TAX
		50% ×		
	$109,400			
	$86,710	48% ×	$ 1,110	$ 533
	$ 85,600			
		44% ×	25,600	11,264
	$ 60,000			
		40% ×	14,200	5,680
	$ 45,800			
		35% ×	10,600	3,710
	$ 35,200			
		30% ×	5,300	1,590
	$ 29,900			
		26% ×	5,300	1,378
	$ 24,600			
		23% × to 0%	$24,600	3,656
		TOTALS	86,710	27,811

EID $ 21,600
PE $ 4,000
AL $ 13,500
TOTAL $ 39,100

TAX CREDITS $\left(\qquad 0 \qquad\right)$

TOTAL TAX   27,811

First, your client is not in *a* tax bracket, but rather in a multitude of tax brackets, beginning with "0" and ending with possibly as high as 50%. The highest or top bracket is call the *marginal* bracket.

Second, the marginal tax bracket is more significant than the aggregate tax rate. The marginal tax bracket is actually the rate affecting the last dollar of income that is added or subtracted from taxable income via real cash or accounting adjustments. It, not the overall tax rate, is what must be considered when making all investment decisions.

How to check on the applicability of alternate tax computation methods

We have thus far assumed that the tax thermometer method, as illustrated by Dr. Wright's current situation, is universally applicable. And certainly it can be applied to the vast majority of clients. The methodology may not, however, be suited to two situations. The first is when the average taxable income of the four previous years was lower than the estimate for this year. That could mean that *income averaging* may produce the lower and therefore applicable tax computation. The second alternate computation method may exist when you have very high items of tax preference including large net long-term capital gains. Then, the *alternative minimum tax* may be relevant. Here is how you test for these two situations.

HOW AND WHEN TO USE INCOME AVERAGING

If 30% of the sum of the appropriate taxable income figures of the four previous years is $3,000 less than this year's taxable income, you had better check it out. Here is how you do that very quickly.

First, you must make certain that you are adding up the right figures for each of the four previous years. In years prior to 1981, that figure should be the one found on the line entitled "Taxable Income" (normally line 3) on Schedule TC, the Tax Computation Schedule. If your client didn't use Schedule TC in one or more of those previous 4 years, you will have to use the figure on line 34 of the 1040, less the personal exemptions for the year in question ($1,000 per dependent in 1979 and thereafter).

Now that you have the sum of the taxable income (TI) of the four previous years, multiply it by 30%. We will call that figure your *base income level* (BIL).

Now subtract the BIL from this year's expected TI. Divide this difference by 5, and you have a number we will call the *averageable income layer* (AIL).

Using a blank Thermometer, determine the tax on the BIL. Then, place the AIL on top of the BIL and tax it. Multiply the tax on the AIL by 5 and add it to the tax on the BIL. *The total is the income averaging tax.*

If the income averaging method produces a lower tax than the regular Tax Thermometer, it is the applicable tax liability, less any investment tax credit. Note what actually takes place under the income averaging method. Simply put, the AIL portion of your income is allowed to be taxed horizontally instead of vertically up the thermometer or tax schedule.

EXAMPLE

Dr. Wright's TI for this year is expected to be $86,710, and our original "Wright" computation showed a regular tax liability of $27,811. Let us assume that his four previous years of TI were $60,000, $50,000, $40,000, and $10,000 for a total of $160,000. His BIL is therefore 30% of $160,000 or $48,000.

The difference between this year's estimated TI of $86,710 and the BIL of $48,000 is $38,710. That divided by 5 is the AIL of $7,742. It, plus the BIL of $48,000, equals *$55,742.* These two figures of *$55,742* and *$48,000* are the two stopping points on our Thermometer illustration. The tax on the BIL of $48,000 is, as illustrated on the Taxation Thermometer adapted for income averaging, $11,214. The AIL of $7,742 falls entirely within the 40% bracket as shown, and its tax is therefore $3,097 ($7,742 × 40%).

The total tax is the tax on the BIL plus 5 times the tax on the AIL. The total income averaging tax is therefore $11,214 + (5) × ($3,097) or $26,669 versus the $27,811 via the regular thermometer way. While averaging saves Dr. Wright only $1,142, there are instances with higher income (such as in a year of very large gains) where it is a substantial advantage.

Table 6–3 contains a useful format, completed for Dr. Wright, that can be used to summarize and record your simplified income averaging computations. Note that you must subtract any investment tax credits (ITCs) to arrive at the total tax liability as summarized above and on the adapted Tax Thermometer for Dr. Wright.

HOW AND WHEN TO USE THE ALTERNATIVE MINIMUM TAX (AMT)

The alternative minimum tax (AMT) is a relatively new (since January 1, 1979) overall tax computation method designed by Congress to make certain that at least a certain level of tax liability exists under most circumstances. It was then expanded under the Tax Equity and Fiscal Responsibility Act of 1982, enacted on August 19, 1982.

TABLE 6–3
Income Averaging Worksheet

a. Sum of TI of 4 Previous Years	$160,000
b. Base Income Level, BIL (30% × a)	48,000
c. TI for Current Year	86,710
d. Averageable Income (c − b)	38,710
e. Averageable Income Layer (d ÷ 5)	7,742
f. Tax on BIL	11,214
g. Tax on AIL (×5)	15,485
h. Total Income Averaging Tax (f + g)	26,699
i. Investment Tax Credits	(0)
j. Total Tax Liability	26,699

The alternative minimum tax is easy to understand and is computed as shown in Table 6–4.

TABLE 6–4
Abbreviated Alternative Minimum Tax Worksheet

1. Adjusted Gross Income   _____
2. Add: Tax-Preference Items   _____
3. Subtotal   _____
4. Subtract: Certain Itemized Deductions   (_____)
5. Alternative Minimum Tax Base Before Exemption   _____
6. Subtract: Exemption*   (_____)
7. Alternative Minimum Tax Base   _____
8. Alternative Minimum Tax (AMT): (line 7.) × 20%   _____

*$40,000 for joint returns, $30,000 for single returns, and $20,000 for married individuals filing separate returns.

Here is a complete list of those preference items which must be considered:

1. accelerated depreciation on real property in excess of straight line;
2. accelerated depreciation on leased personal property;
3. amortization of certified pollution control facilities;
4. bargain element on exercise of incentive stock options;
5. excluded 60% of net long-term capital gains;
6. percentage depletion in excess of adjusted basis of the property;
7. excess intangible drilling costs of oil and gas wells;

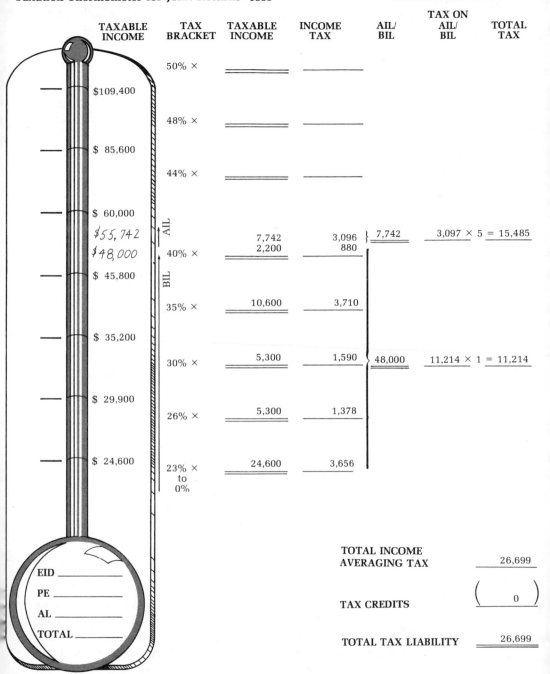

FIGURE 6–3

Taxation Thermometer for Joint Returns – 1983   **INCOME AVERAGING**

TAXABLE INCOME	TAX BRACKET	TAXABLE INCOME	INCOME TAX	AIL/ BIL	TAX ON AIL/ BIL	TOTAL TAX
	50% ×					
$109,400						
	48% ×					
$ 85,600						
	44% ×					
$ 60,000						
$55,742		7,742	3,096 }	7,742	3,097 × 5 =	15,485
$48,000	40% ×	2,200	880			
$ 45,800						
	35% ×	10,600	3,710			
$ 35,200						
	30% ×	5,300	1,590 }	48,000	11,214 × 1 =	11,214
$ 29,900						
	26% ×	5,300	1,378			
$ 24,600	23% × to 0%	24,600	3,656			

EID _____

PE _____

AL _____

TOTAL _____

TOTAL INCOME AVERAGING TAX _____ 26,699

TAX CREDITS (0)

TOTAL TAX LIABILITY _____ 26,699

103

8. excess of expensing over 10-year amortization for the following:

   a. mining exploration costs,

   b. development expenditures,

   c. magazine circulation expenditures, and

   d. research and experimental expenditures;

9. excluded interest (all-savers, and future net interest exclusion), and

10. the dividend exclusion.

The "certain" itemized deductions referred to on line 4. of the abbreviated alternative minimum tax worksheet are as follows:

1. medical expenses in excess of 10% of AGI,

2. casualty losses in excess of 10% of AGI,

3. charitable contributions,

4. housing interest (generally home mortgage interest),

5. other interest to the extent of net investment income, including net capital gains, and

6. federal estate tax attributable to after-death income.

The total federal tax liability is the *greater* of the alternative minimum tax or the previously computed applicable tax (Tax Thermometer or income averaging, whichever was less).

Raising a red flag on the sheltering of net long-term capital gains

The major result of the interaction of the traditional tax methods and the new alternative minimum tax is that, even if it is in fact not yet the applicable tax, there can be an unforeseen limitation on the amount of *any type* of additional deductions you may want to create in a year of a very large net long-term capital gain or any large amount of other preference item.

In general, if your client has *no other taxable income* and takes a net long-term gain, very little, if any, of the taxable portion of it should be sheltered. When this scenario arises, the alternative minimum tax quickly becomes the required tax computation method. Very significantly, *whenever the alternative minimum tax comes into play, each additional dollar of tax shelter produces a maximum of only 20¢ of tax savings.*

For example, if your client has zero *taxable* income and a $300,000 net LTCG is taken, the traditional tax on $120,000 on a joint return would be $44,002. The alternative minimum tax, however, is $52,000. The tax liability is therefore the larger or $52,000. If $10,000 of deductions are then created, only $2,000 in tax savings results.

Whenever the AMT is already applicable, an appropriate tax tactic may be to somehow create more taxable income so that it can be taxed now at 20% instead of the next year at a higher normal rate.

On the other hand, if you are already into the higher income tax brackets with other ordinary income, you can appropriately shelter at least part of the gain. In 1983, *if that gain is $147,350 or less*, there are *no restrictions* on the amount of the gain you should shelter other than the conventional 48% to 50% bracket limitation (lowering taxable income to no less than $85,600 for joint returns). However, when the gain exceeds $147,350, and when taxable income other than that created by the gain is in the $50,000 area or above, Table 6–5 will be helpful in determining the approximate *maximum* amount of additional deductions that should be considered for joint returns in 1983.

EXAMPLE

An investor has $100,000 of taxable income and then takes a $250,000 long-term gain. The maximum amount of appropriate shelter would be $73,340. The reasoning is as follows: $100,000 of taxable income plus $100,000 of taxable gain (40% of $250,000) totals $200,000 of total taxable income. The regular-way tax on $200,000 on a joint return is $84,002. The alternative minimum tax is $62,000. After $73,340 of shelter, taxable income is reduced to $126,660. The

TABLE 6–5
Approximate Maximum Recommended Shelter (1983)

| Net | | | | TOI* | | | |
LTCG**	50m	100m	150m	200m	300m	400m	500m
0	0	14,400	64,400	114,400	214,400	314,400	414,000
50,000	0	34,400	84,400	134,400	234,400	334,400	434,400
100,000	4,400	54,400	104,400	154,400	254,400	354,400	454,400
147,350	23,340	73,340	123,340	173,340	273,340	373,340	473,340
150,000	23,340	73,340	123,340	173,340	273,340	373,340	473,340
200,000	23,340	73,340	123,340	173,340	273,340	373,340	473,340
250,000	23,340	73,340	123,340	173,340	273,340	373,340	473,340

*TOI = anticipated taxable ordinary income prior to taking the gain.
**Long-term capital gain.

regular-way tax on $126,660 is $47,332. The alternative minimum tax is also $47,332. Since the alternative minimum tax is equal to the regular tax liability, $47,332 is the tax liability. An additional $1 of any type of deduction that is also a deduction beyond the $73,340 would then produce only 20¢ in incremental tax savings. Therefore, $73,340 is the limit the investor should create of any type of additional deductions. Note that taking any further deductions *not* listed among the "certain" deductions allowed in the minimum tax computation *would produce no tax savings at all.* That is so because nonallowed itemized deductions such as the prepayment of state income taxes, reduces the regular tax liability, but not the alternative minimum tax. Note, too, that if such deductions were used as part of the original goal of the $73,340 of maximum recommended shelter, it would have the effect of reducing the total to below $73,340. In effect, using nonallowed itemized deductions to shelter all or part of a gain reduces the amount of the gain that should be sheltered.

It should also be strongly emphasized that if the client's regular-way income tax on the ordinary income is reduced via income averaging or investment tax credits, or if the creation of deductions results in increased preference items, the "maximum shelter amount" is reduced and *individualized tax computations should be accomplished.*

A good way for you to compute the precise *maximum* amount of additional deductions of any type that can be created in a year of sizable net long-term capital gains is to follow these few quick steps:

1. After taking the GAIN into consideration in both tax computations, subtract the lower alternative minimum tax from the higher total regular tax.

2. Subtract the marginal alternative minimum tax bracket of 20% from the regular marginal tax bracket (usually 50%).

3. Divide 1 by 2, and you have the amount of additional deductions that must be created in order for both tax computations to be in balance. Whenever you have a desire to create the maximum level of appropriate deductibility, this computation gives you the precise prescription as long as all of the deductions created would shelter against the beginning marginal tax bracket.

A major tax planning objective should be to avoid causing the AMT to take effect. Otherwise, you would want to have your client create more taxable income or delay some deductions so as to get out of that tax computation method. Using any existing deductions against the AMT's maximum 20% bracket is probably a waste.

Putting the tax cart before the economic horse is a major error frequently made by clients and planners alike. Taxation creates such snarl power that it sometimes drives us to ridiculous if not scandalous ends. Those who would rush into year-end decisions for tax reasons alone are usually yet to experience the emptiness that can be felt after April 15. This is precisely when your clients usually begin to wonder what they got themselves into.

Conversely, an equally great mistake is to not understand and then weigh all of the current, ongoing, and future tax benefits that can be derived from both alternative investment directions and from simply varying certain investments' ownership structures. As a matter of fact, tax leverage can be a most powerful tool in helping your clients to reach their intended financial destinations in time, especially if you are careful to coordinate it with other considerations, such as liquidity needs and risk tolerance limitations.

7

How to Reduce
or Avoid
Estate and
Gift Taxes

You can do absolutely nothing, financially, that does not affect the amount of taxes that will or will not eventually be paid. While Chapter 6 showed how income taxes can act as a substantial hurdle to keeping what is earned, this chapter illustrates the tax effects of transferring wealth to heirs and how to reduce or avoid them. We seem to be the victim of a giant bear market of taxation, both coming and going across the financial stage of life—unless we hedge against it. Understanding the basics of today's "unified" approach to taxing gifts and estates, as well as the options to consider for coping with it, is crucial in total financial planning.

The unified transfer tax is a significant part of what has become a whole new set of rules for gift and estate planning. The crux of the matter is that all of the old rules must be discarded. You can no longer consider the tax ramifications of large lifetime gifting and future estate settlement as being even remotely independent of each other. In fact, the government's purpose in integrating gift and estate taxes is to levy a tax on larger gifts that approximates the estate tax that would be payable had the gift not been made but instead been part of the taxable estate.

What is done in gifting may therefore dramatically affect future estate settlement costs. And what can be done to reduce gift and estate taxes is now, after the Economic Recovery Tax Act of 1981 (ERTA), probably much more than you think possible. If reducing estate taxes and conserving assets for heirs is a major financial goal, understanding this part of the tax law and its affect upon the need for *early* and *continual* planning is more important than ever before.

How the unified transfer tax schedule taxes both gifts and estates

The first step in understanding how the unified gift and estate tax law is interwoven is to review the structure of the schedule itself. A quick glance at the unified rates for 1983 (Table 7–1) will indicate that the schedule begins at 18% on the first $10,000 and is graduated upward to 60% for taxable transfers of over $3,500,000. The Economic Recovery Tax Act of 1981 (ERTA) reduces the 1983 maximum rate of 60% as follows:

In Year	Maximum Rate of	Applies to Taxable Transfers of Over
1984	55%	$3,000,000
1985	50%	2,500,000

To update the current unified tax rate schedule for 1984, simply blank out the last figure in each column of Table 7-1, Unified Gift and Estate Tax Rate Schedule, and change the 57% to 55%. For 1985, do exactly the same except that you change the 53% to 50%. There are no changes in the tax rates on taxable transfers below $2,500,000.

A basic point of emphasis is that this single tax schedule relates to the "tentative" tax liability on *cumulative* lifetime *taxable gifts and* then upon the *net taxable estate*. These terms will be defined later as we proceed in our discussion of gift and estate taxation.

The second point is that the unified transfer tax system provides for a $79,300 tax credit toward the *tentative tax* computed by the 1983 unified transfer tax schedule. It is called a *tentative tax* because you subtract from it part or all of that credit of $79,300, plus possibly other credits, be-

TABLE 7-1
Unified Gift and Estate Tax Rate Schedule (1983)

Taxable Transfers		Tentative	Plus	Of Excess
From	To	Tax =	Percent	Over
$ 0	$ 10,000	$ 0	18	$ 0
10,000	20,000	1,800	20	10,000
20,000	40,000	3,800	22	20,000
40,000	60,000	8,200	24	40,000
60,000	80,000	13,200	26	60,000
80,000	100,000	18,200	28	80,000
100,000	150,000	23,800	30	100,000
150,000	250,000	38,800	32	150,000
250,000	500,000	70,800	34	250,000
500,000	750,000	155,800	37	500,000
750,000	1,000,000	248,300	39	750,000
1,000,000	1,250,000	345,800	41	1,000,000
1,250,000	1,500,000	448,300	43	1,250,000
1,500,000	2,000,000	555,800	45	1,500,000
2,000,000	2,500,000	780,800	49	2,000,000
2,500,000	3,000,000	1,025,800	53	2,500,000
3,000,000	3,500,000	1,290,800	57	3,000,000
3,500,000+		1,575,800	60	3,500,000

fore arriving at the final tax liability. In essence, in 1983, the first $79,300 of taxes computed by the schedule is never paid.

Under ERTA this unified credit and therefore the amounts of taxable transfer exempt from unified taxation are increased as follows:

Year of Gift or Death	Amount of Estate and Gift Tax Credit	Amount of Transfer Exempt from Tax	Lowest Applicable Tax Bracket
1983	$ 79,300	$275,000	34%
1984	96,300	325,000	34%
1985	121,800	400,000	34%
1986	155,800	500,000	37%
1987 and thereafter	192,800	600,000	37%

Now that you understand (1) how the maximum tax rate declines to 50% by 1985 *and* (2) how the amount exempted from taxation gradually increases to $600,000 by 1987, an important observation can be made. In effect, the then remaining rates for taxable gifts and/or estates are not significantly less than the eventual maximum 50% rate. For example, when the $600,000 exemption is operative in 1987, the effective tax rates will be as follows:

Amount of Taxable Transfer	Applicable Rate
Under $600,000	0%
600,000–750,000	37%
750,000–1,000,000	39%
1,000,000–1,250,000	41%
1,250,000–1,500,000	43%
1,500,000–2,000,000	45%
2,000,000–2,500,000	49%
2,500,000 and over	50%

Interestingly, beginning in 1987, there is only a spread of 13% (50% − 37%) on *all* taxable transfers (gifts or estates). This is very close to being a "flat" tax rate.

What is a taxable gift and how is it taxed

A taxable gift is an absolute transfer of property to another. To be a completed gift, a donor may not retain control or rights in the gifted property. An exclusion of $10,000 per donor per donee per year is allowed for gifts in which the donee has an immediate right to the enjoyment of the property, that is, a present interest. Now let's look at how this exclusion interacts with the taxable gifts and the applicable transfer credit.

EXAMPLE

If by 1987 someone makes cumulative lifetime transfers (gifts) of $600,000 *over and above* the $10,000 exclusion, the unified transfer tax schedule computes a tentative tax of $192,800. Since there is an available credit of $192,800, it is gradually applied against the tentative tax of $192,800. No tax liability results even though the law requires that gift tax returns be filed annually by April 15. However, since the $192,800 credit has been used up during life, it is, in effect, not allowed upon the settlement of the estate at death. Uncle Sam sees to that by making us add the lifetime *taxable* gifts to the *taxable estate* and then reallows the use of the $192,800 unified tax credit.

A WORD OF CAUTION BEFORE MAKING LARGER THAN $10,000 GIFTS

Once taxable gifts cumulatively exceed the applicable credit, gift taxes must be paid via the annual gift tax return, since the cumulative unified tax exceeds the credit. At that point we actually begin the process of paying these taxes at the lowest applicable gift tax bracket (34% in 1983, 1984, and 1985; 37% in 1986 and thereafter).

Even though this tax is paid, it is very important to remember that all of the *taxable* gifts must be added to the taxable estate.

USING GIFTS TO REMOVE CURRENT INCOME
AND FUTURE APPRECIATION FROM THE ESTATE

When death occurs, only the taxable gift value of the property (not its appreciation and the taxes previously paid) is added to the net taxable estate. It is therefore possible to remove the future appreciation of a gifted asset from the estate after making a *taxable* gift, but the present value of the gifted asset can never be removed. Also removed from the estate is the income produced by the gift from the moment of the gift. For planning purposes, note that ERTA essentially removed the three-year contemplation of death rule for all gifts except life insurance and certain other transfers with retained powers. *This essentially means that death bed transfers could produce meaningful estate tax savings.*

We can now conclude that except for (1) the $10,000 exclusion allowance, (2) gifts within the equivalent of the applicable unified transfer tax credit, and (3) gifts to the spouse that are described later, making larger taxable gifts is generally not appropriate unless the primary goal is to remove the current income and/or future appreciation from the estate.

HOW TO DOUBLE THE $10,000 EXCLUSION

We have already noted that gifts up to $10,000 per year may be made to as many donees, family or not, as is desirable without even having to look at the unified rate schedule or reporting the gift on a gift tax return. To some, $10,000 may seem small. Remember, however, the value of the future income produced by, and the future appreciation of, this $10,000 annual exclusion allowance are also removed permanently from the estate. In addition, through a gift-splitting provision of the law, if the spouse consents to the gift, a minimum annual exclusion of $20,000 per donee is allowed. However, the use of this $20,000 gift-splitting provision requires the filing of a gift tax return. If death occurs within the old three-year waiting period, neither gift value nor the present value of the split gift must be included in the gross estate.

The ability to make tax-free gifts is, of course, greatly increased due to this provision of ERTA. Because a married couple can now gift up to $20,000 of assets to each donee without paying gift taxes or even using up any of their unified transfer credit, significant reductions in the size of that couple's estate can be achieved.

EXAMPLE

A couple with two married children and four grandchildren could make annual tax-free gifts of $160,000 ($20,000 × 8) if gifts are also made to the children-in-law. If that gifting program is continued over a three-year period, $480,000 plus appreciation and income would be permanently removed from the couple's respective estates. If all of the gifts are being made from one spouse, all that is necessary is that the other spouse consent to one-half of each gift being made by the other spouse.

The income tax savings due to such a gifting program deserves more than just a passing note. Assume that the $480,000 produces a taxable income of 10% each year and that the donors are in the maximum 50% bracket. Of the $48,000 earned, only $24,000 is kept. By gifting the $480,000 to other lower-tax-paying family members, big savings result. If the average marginal tax bracket of the donees is 22%, for example, $37,440 of the $48,000 is kept within the family unit—a giant 56% increase. More practically speaking, $13,440 per year is transformed from income tax liability to family wealth.

HOW TO USE THE LARGEST GIFT TAX EXCLUSION OF ALL

One of the most significant estate tax changes under ERTA relates to the new unlimited gift and estate *marital* deduction. If your client predeceases a spouse, estate taxes upon the client's death can essentially be totally eliminated. This can be achieved by leaving all of the estate that is in excess of the remaining exemption ($275,000 in 1983 and on up to $600,000 after 1986) to the spouse. Before 1982, this marital deduction was limited to 50% of the estate or $250,000, whichever was greater. Wills executed prior to September 12, 1981 that provide for the maximum marital deduction will be interpreted as being limited to the old 50% or $250,000 maximum rule unless a state law is enacted that would construe the prior language as compatible with the new unlimited marital deduction. Using this unlimited marital deduction (the total estate less applicable exemption) is, however, not desirable for everyone, and it will be addressed in greater detail later in this chapter.

The central point now is that ultimate estate taxes can be reduced if a couple maximizes the use of their respective exemptions. This objective is clearly not achieved if (1) the estate of only one spouse exceeds the exemption *and* (2) the other spouse dies first. To maximize the exemption, one spouse can gift to the other the exempt amount so that, if the other spouse dies first, an exemption is not lost.

Year	1983
Husband's Estate	$500,000
Wife's Estate	$ 50,000

If Husband transfers $225,000 of assets of property to Wife, Wife's estate will be increased to $275,000, the 1983 exemption. If Wife were to die first, the use of the unified credit rather than the marital deduction would eliminate federal estate taxes. Husband's estate, at his subsequent death, would also be $275,000 and therefore estate tax-free. This assumes Wife's property could pass to a residuary trust for Husband's benefit.

Since all transfers between spouses are totally exempt from gift taxes, gifts may now be made back and forth between spouses without fear of adverse tax consequences. Two clear warning signals must, however, be sounded. First, all such gifting causes the donor to lose control over the assets gifted. While this may not be of concern in many family situations, it will have been most undesirable if there is a subsequent separation or divorce. Second, attention should be paid to the potential negative of gifting low cost basis property. Property acquired by a gift takes on the donor's basis, while property inherited receives a "stepped-up" basis. This means that the new cost basis of inherited property becomes the estate tax value.

WHEN AND HOW THE UNLIMITED GIFT TAX MARITAL DEDUCTION PRESERVES WEALTH

We have shown how estate taxes can be totally eliminated by leaving all of your client's estate in excess of the estate tax exemption outright or in trust to the spouse. Because this exemption, or the amount of the estate sheltered by the unified credit, gradually increases each year through 1987, the unlimited marital deduction will not always be larger than the old 50% marital deduction. The following table indicates the size that the estate must be before this happens:

Year	Estate Size Needed Before the Unlimited Marital Deduction Exceeds the 50% Marital Deducation
1983	$ 550,000
1984	600,000
1985	800,000
1986	1,000,000
1987	1,200,000

If an estate is smaller than the indicated amount, don't disregard the need to consider the implications of the unlimited marital deduction. Inflation of only 7.2% per year would compound an estate to double its current value in only 10 years.

Clearly, use of the unlimited marital deduction eliminates any estate taxes upon the first spouse's death. Undiminished by estate tax erosion, the total estate of the first spouse is available for the support of the surviving spouse. In this instance, the whole estate is also available for the remaining family's needs during the entire life of the surviving

TABLE 7–2
Unlimited Marital Deducation
Summary of Advantages and Disadvantages

Advantages	Disadvantages
1. The entire estate, without reduction for any estate tax, will be available for the surviving spouse's needs, thereby providing greater security for the surviving spouse.	1. During the surviving spouse's lifetime, less will be available for the family's needs (emergency or otherwise) *unless* the surviving spouse is given the right (not available under a QTI trust) to gift the marital deduction property during his/her lifetime and he/she is *willing and able* to do so.
2. During the surviving spouse's lifetime, a greater amount will be available for the family's needs (emergency or otherwise) if the surviving spouse is given the right (not available in the QTI trust) to gift the marital deduction property during his/her lifetime and he/she is willing and able to make such gifts.	2. In some cases, a higher total estate tax may result. Consequently, a lesser amount would be ultimately available for the couple's children and beneficiaries after both spouses' deaths. This will apply where the surviving spouse's estate has a higher effective estate tax rate than the estate of the first spouse to die (if the unlimited marital deduction had not been provided for). This may result where the earnings on the estate tax deferral are accumulated (and not spent or gifted) or where the marital deduction property appreciates in value between the deaths of the spouses.
3. In some cases, estate tax on a couple's estates may be completely eliminated.	
4. The estate tax deferral and the earnings thereon may result in a greater amount being ultimately available for the couple's children and beneficiaries after both spouses' deaths. This will apply where the surviving spouse's estate does not have a higher effective estate tax rate than the estate of the first spouse to die (if the unlimited marital deduction had not been provided for). The favorable tax result may depend upon the surviving spouse's consumption or gifting of the earnings on the deferred estate taxes, which he/she may be unable or unwilling to do.	3. Higher income taxes will likely result since more income will be taxed to the surviving spouse at a higher income tax rate rather than to a lower-bracket trust for the entire family.
	4. The first spouse to die loses control over the ultimate disposition, after the surviving spouse's death, of the additional marital deduction property (the excess of the unlimited marital deduction over what would have otherwise been provided for the spouse).

spouse. Also, the death of the first spouse forces no assets to be sold for the payment of estate taxes.

As already mentioned, use of the unlimited marital deduction will not be desirable in all cases. In some instances, a higher total estate tax upon the deaths of both spouses will result. This will happen whenever the surviving spouse's estate will have a higher effective estate tax rate than the estate of the first spouse to die. The larger the estate, the greater will be the excess estate tax caused by the use of the unlimited marital deduction. The problem is even more acute when the assets left to the surviving spouse appreciate substantially. Conversely, there is sometimes a benefit to deferring estate taxes even if they will ultimately be larger than if paid upon the first spouse's death. In some situations the increased estate taxes will be more than offset by the income produced by the deferred tax liability.

There is another significant drawback to the unlimited marital deduction. The first spouse to die loses control, in more ways than one, over the assets left to the surviving spouse. When marital deduction property is bequeathed to a surviving spouse, it is left for his or her benefit to the exclusion of all other family members. Less may therefore be available for the needs of other family members *unless* the surviving spouse is both willing and able to share. The surviving spouse may have remarried and had additional children. So, under the unlimited marital deduction, to the extent the first spouse's estate exceeds the estate tax exemption amount, the deceased spouse will have upped the surviving spouse's nest egg while decreasing the rest of the family's residuary trust.

There are clearly both pros and cons to the unlimited estate marital deduction. All estates must be thoroughly analyzed in light of these multiple considerations. Table 7–2 summarizes the advantages and disadvantages of using the unlimited marital deduction.

How the qualified terminable interest trust can keep your client in control

One of the less attractive aspects of leaving the total estate minus the applicable exemption to the spouse is the loss of control. Prior to 1982, such a bequest to the spouse via a trust would qualify for the marital deduction only if the spouse had total control over the ultimate disposition of the trust's assets in life or at death. Now, a new type of trust called the qualified terminable interest Trust (QTI) can also contain assets left for the spouse's use under the marital deduction *and* still maintain control over their future disposition.

Under the QTI, the *first* spouse to die decides whether the couple's children or possibly others will receive the trust assets after the death of the surviving spouse. The surviving spouse has no power to gift any portion of the QTI assets. All income from the trust must be paid to the surviving spouse during his lifetime.

A disadvantage of the QTI is that no one else, including the ultimate trust beneficiaries, can receive any QTI assets or income until the death of the surviving spouse. As a result, the QTI may be appropriately used either in place of the more traditional marital deduction trust or in combination with it, where you do not wish to "freeze" too large a portion of the assets left under the unlimited marital deduction to your spouse. Table 7–3 presents a comparison of the two types of marital trusts:

TABLE 7–3
Traditional Power of Appointment Marital Trust
Vs.
Qualified Terminable Interest (QTI) Trust
Since 1982, an individual may choose to utilize (1) the traditional power of appointment marital trust, (2) the "qualified terminable interest" trust, or (3) a combination of these two trusts.

Description	Traditional Marital Trust	QTI Trust

1. Ability of decedent to control disposition of marital trust property after surviving spouse's death:
   a. Traditional—No
   b. QTI—Yes
	1. Surviving spouse has sole right to determine who will receive the marital trust property after their death. This may be undesirable where the surviving spouse has children from a prior marriage or where the surviving spouse remarries and could leave the trust property to new spouse.	1. Decedent can establish who will receive QTI trust property after the surviving spouse's death. The ultimate beneficiaries to receive the property after the surviving spouse's death are unchangeable by the surviving spouse.

2. Ability of surviving spouse during their lifetime to gift marital trust property for children's needs:
   a. Traditional—Yes
   b. QTI—No
	2. The trust may provide surviving spouse with right to gift portions of the trust property to family members.	2. No portion of the QTI property can be distributed to anyone other than the surviving spouse during their lifetime.

3. Ability of surviving spouse to gift to family members marital trust	3. Tax-free gifts from the marital trust property of $10,000/year/donee can be	3. The marital trust property included in the surviving spouse's estate can only be re-

TABLE 7–3 (*continued*)

Description	Traditional Marital Trust	QTI Trust

property to reduce their taxable estate:
  a. Traditional—Yes
  b. QTI—No
	made by surviving spouse to reduce marital trust property included in their taxable estate.	duced if it is first distributed to the surviving spouse or if it is consumed by the surviving spouse's living expenses.

4. All income of marital trust distributable to surviving spouse:
  a. Traditional—Yes
  b. QTI—Yes
	All marital trust income must be distributed annually or more frequently to the surviving spouse.	4. Same.

HOW TO COMPUTE GIFT TAXES

The computation of gift taxes is the simplest part of the whole matter of unified transfer taxes. The tax for a given period is computed by:

1. combining the value of all prior taxable gifts with current taxable gifts,
2. using the unified rate schedule to compute the tentative tax on this total,
3. subtracting the actual tax liability under the unified rate schedule for all prior taxable gifts, and
4. subtracting the applicable unified credit from the difference between (2) and (3).

TABLE 7–4
What Gifts are Included in the Estate

Gift	Death Within Three Years	Death After Three Years
Gifts within the $10,000 exclusion	Not included in the estate	Not included in the estate
$10,000 exclusion, qualifying as a split gift	Not included in the estate	Not included in the estate
Gifts that produce a tentative unified transfer tax	The taxable gift value is added to the taxable estate	The taxable gift value is added to the taxable estate
Gifts of life insurance	Included in the gross estate at the value at date of death	Not included in the estate

EXAMPLE A: HOW TO COMPUTE THE TAXES ON GIFTS TO A CHILD

Your client is, in 1983, making a $200,000 gift to a child, he has previously made and reported $200,000 of such taxable gifts to his child, and his spouse is consenting to the current $200,000 gift. The gift tax computation would be as follows:

Previous Taxable Gifts 1981	$ 200,000
Tentative Tax from Unified Schedule on Previous Taxable Gifts	54,800
LESS: Unified Credit Applicable In 1981	(47,000)
Gift Taxes Paid (1981)	$ 7,800
Gross Amount of Current Gift (1983)	$ 200,000
Less: Annual Exclusion	(20,000)
Current Taxable Gift	180,000
Previous Taxable Gift	200,000
Total Taxable Gifts	$ 380,000
Tentative Tax on Total Taxable Gifts	115,000
Less: Previous Taxes Paid	(7,800)
Current Unified Credit	(79,300)
Gift Tax Due on Current Gift	$ 27,900

WHEN SHOULD APPRECIATED ASSETS BE GIFTED

It is frequently more advantageous to gift appreciated assets to family members or charity rather than cash.

EXAMPLE

If your client is in a 50% marginal income tax bracket and is contemplating gifting to a child in a low to zero marginal tax bracket, gifting $3,000 of cash causes no immediate income or gift tax ramification. If instead, she held a $3,000 asset with a cost basis of $1,500 and gifted it instead of cash, the asset could be liquidated with the resulting $600 taxable income ($1,500 long-term gain times 40%), causing little or no income taxes to the child and therefore the family unit. She would have also forever removed the possibility of having to pay taxes on those gains.

On the other hand, had she in error liquidated the asset prior to the gift, the after-tax proceeds would be $2,700 [$3,000 − $1,500 (40%) (50%)]. It would take that $2,700 of proceeds plus $300 of other cash to create the total $3,000 gift to the child or grandchild or, for that matter, charity. If, in fact, she did not want to part with that particular security, she could simply gift it instead of cash and then buy the asset anew with the cash she didn't gift *and* thereby establish a higher cost basis.

Again, care must be taken when gifting appreciated assets to one's spouse that might have to be sold prior to death. A donor could be giving up the great benefit of a stepped-up cost basis upon death. This is so because the receiver of a gift upon which no gift tax is due assumes the donor's tax basis. If the donee is not the spouse and a gift tax is paid, the increase in basis to the donee is limited to the portion of the gift tax that is a result of the appreciated part of the gift.

EXAMPLE

A $20,000 gift has a cost basis of $10,000, and it resulted in gift taxes paid of $3,900. The cost basis for the donee increases by $1,950 to $11,950. The $11,950 is derived as follows:

$10,000 Appreciation ÷ $20,000 Fair Market Value =	50%
50% × $3,900 Gift Tax	= $1,950
Plus: Prior Cost Basis	+ $10,000
New Cost Basis	$11,950

What is the "estate"?

Before going into precise estate tax computations, you must first understand the meaning of certain estate tax law terminology such as gross taxable estate, adjusted gross estate, net taxable estate, tentative tax base, and total tax liability. And those meanings are clarified by taking a look at the format used in Dr. Tom Wright's estate at death analysis, in Table 7–5.

WHAT MAKES UP THE GROSS TAXABLE ESTATE?

Gross taxable estate includes all of the assets, tangible and intangible, that are owned by the deceased. For example, stocks, bonds, real estate, powers of appointment in trusts, certain jointly held interests, life insurance proceeds, and qualified retirement plan assets, under certain circumstances, are all included in the gross estate. Certain of these broad categories of assets are further detailed as follows:

Life Insurance. The proceeds of life insurance contracts are included in the gross taxable estate when the deceased is *both the insured and the owner* of the policies. Alternatives to the erosion of these proceeds by current estate taxation, such as ownership by family members or by an irrevocable life insurance trust, are often quite desirable. By

TABLE 7–5
Dr. Wright's Estate at Death Analysis

Estate Assets:		
Checking Accounts		$ 3,000
Savings Account		8,000
Municipal Bonds and Corporate Bonds		65,000
Proceeds Life Insurance		0
Common Stocks		31,185
Keogh Plan		0*
Pension Plan		0*
Profit Sharing Plan		53,500*
Personal Holding Company		66,000
Wright Radiology Professional Corporation		30,000
Tax Incentive Investments		30,000
Personal Property		25,000
Prior Taxable Gifts (Split gift made to children		26,000
within 3 years of death)		
Gross Taxable Estate:		337,685
Administration and Probate (4½%)	$(15,196)	
Estimated Final Expenses	(5,000)	
Liabilities	(31,500)	
Adjusted Gross Estate:		$285,989
Marital Deduction	$(78,500)	
Net Taxable Estate:		$207,489
Prior Taxable gifts	–0–	
Tentative Tax Base:		$207,489
Tentative Federal Estate Tax	$ 57,196	
Unified Transfer Credit	(79,300)	
State Death Tax Credit	–0–	
Net Federal Estate Tax	–0–	
State Death Tax	–0–	
Total Taxes		$ –0–
Add: Administration and Probate	$ 15,196	
Estimated Final Expenses	5,000	
Liabilities	31,500	
Total Estate Settlement Costs		$51,696

*First $100,000 of proceeds excluded from taxable estate if left to a named beneficiary (other than "estate") and not paid in a lump sum. $100,000 of proceeds paid in a lump sum can be excluded if beneficiary elects not to use special income tax provisions such as capital gains or ten-year averaging.

transferring all ownership rights in insurance policies to an irrevocable trust, the proceeds can be excluded not only from the estate but also from the surviving spouse's estate at his subsequent death. The trustee would receive the proceeds at death and would pay the income from the trust to the surviving spouse during his or her lifetime.

At the subsequent death of the surviving spouse, the assets would pass to whoever is or are named as beneficiary, presumably the children. The trustee can be given the right, but not the obligation, to purchase assets from the estate or to lend money to the estate. This would provide the executor with cash for estate settlement costs. A qualified attorney must, of course, be employed to draw up the actual irrevocable insurance trust instrument.

Charitable Gifts. If a charitable gift were previously made via a charitable remainder trust, the value of the remainder at the time of death is added in at this point, just as though it had not yet been implemented, and then later deducted before arriving at the Net Taxable Estate.

Qualified Retirement Plans. The first $100,000 if the value of qualified retirement plans, such as Dr. Wright's Keogh, pension, and profit sharing plans are not included in gross taxable estate if they are left to a beneficiary other than the estate *and* if the proceeds are not left in lump sum. The proceeds can be left in lump sum and the first $100,000 excluded from the taxable estate if the beneficiary does not elect special income tax treatment such as ten-year averaging or capital gains. There are important decisions that must be made as to the advisability of having the proceeds of such plans taken in lump sum or installment. The pros and cons will vary in each instance, and therefore no generalizations can be made.

WHAT MAKES UP THE ADJUSTED GROSS ESTATE?

From the gross taxable estate, you subtract administrative and probate costs, final expenses, and estate liabilities in order to arrive at the adjusted gross estate. Probate and administration costs will usually vary between 2% and 7%, depending on the size and complexity of the estate.

How to Arrive At the Net Taxable Estate. Two major deductions appear below the adjusted gross estate prior to arriving at the net taxable estate. The first is the marital deduction, and the second involves certain charitable gifts.

The Marital Deduction. In the previously mentioned estate marital deduction, current law allows the legally married an unlimited deduction against the adjusted gross estate.

How much of the marital deduction should be used? Maximum use of the marital deduction can create sizable estate tax savings in the estate of the first spouse to die, when a prime concern is to increase the amount left to produce income or assets for the use of heirs.

On the other hand, it is sometimes best to reduce or eliminate the use of the marital deduction when it is not needed to lower estate taxes or when maximum use of it would so increase the future estate taxes of the remaining spouse and therefore dramatically increase the total ultimate estate taxes of both spouses. Please refer to the previous table summarizing the advantages and disadvantages of using the unlimited marital deduction.

What is right for Dr. Wright? In Dr. Wright's case, only $78,500 of his maximum marital deduction should be used since more is not needed to reduce his tentative tax to $79,300 or lower. The more important implication is that assets transferred to the spouse or the spouse's trust cannot be less than the amount of the marital deduction that you use. The remainder, depending upon what the will stipulates, also flows to the surviving spouse or to a residuary trust, whose income can be the surving spouse's for life but whose principal will not be taxed in the subsequent estate.

On the other hand, had Dr. Wright's adjusted gross estate been upped by $1,000,000 to $1,285,989, a marital deduction of $1,010,989 may have been used in this case to minimize estate taxes and thereby to maximize assets available for income production for his wife and children.

How does the marital deduction affect the will? The marital deduction has nothing to do with whether all or a greater portion of the estate goes to the surviving spouse. Therein, however, lies a major factor in the proper structuring of the will. It is necessary that the property qualifying for the marital deduction be in the deceased spouse's gross taxable estate and that these assets pass to the surviving spouse or to the spouse's trust. It is, however, not necessary for all *other* assets to be so directed. In fact, if overall estate preservation is to be optimized, it is important for all assets not to flow to the remaining spouse. This will prevent these other assets from being taxed upon the deaths of both husband and wife. Under most circumstances it will be beneficial to avoid this undesirable result by having the will stipulate that the part of the estate that is not sheltered from estate taxation by the marital deduction, and after all settlement costs, pass into a separate residual trust. This trust should be designed to provide benefits to the surviving spouse and children in a manner that will not require the trust fund to be included in the surviving spouse's estate. The benefits that the surviving spouse may receive include all of the annual trust income, up to the greater of $5,000 or 5% of the trust's principal each year, and whatever amounts of principal that the trustee deems necessary. To further avoid estate taxes upon the surviving spouse's death, it is a common practice to place the more stable assets in the marital deduction trust and the faster growing assets in the residual trust.

Charitable Bequests and Trusts. At this point, *after* computing and subtracting the marital deduction, charitable bequests via the will or the current value of charitable remainder trusts are deducted in order to arrive at the net taxable estate.

ARRIVING AT THE TENTATIVE TAX BASE

To the net taxable estate, you must add prior taxable gifts to arrive at the tentative tax base. That is the figure with which you approach the unified transfer tax schedule.

HOW TO COMPUTE THE ESTATE TAX

Now that you have a clearer picture of how to arrive at what must be taxed upon death, let us revert to our gifting example A at the beginning of the chapter. That will allow us to provide a more coordinated and complete example of how estate taxes are computed. It will simultaneously demonstrate how gift and estate taxation is unified in an attempt to impose taxes that are about the same for wealthier individuals, whether that wealth is transferred now or upon death.

EXAMPLE B ESTATE TAXES

Assume that your client is the individual in Example A, the same individual who made previous taxable gifts of $200,000 to a child during 1981 and a $200,000 gross gift in 1983. Assume too, that he had assets of $2,500,000 prior to the gifts with no liabilities and that he dies early in 1987. Under his will, he leaves all that remains after estate settlement costs to his spouse via a simple "I love you" will.

Estate Assets Prior to Gifts	$ 2,500,000
Less: Gifts to Children	(400,000)
Taxes Paid on Gifts	(35,700)
Gross Taxable Estate:	$ 2,064,300
Administration and Probate Costs (4½%)	92,893
Final Expenses	5,000
Liabilities	–0–
Adjusted Gross Estate:	$ 1,966,407
Marital Deduction	$(1,966,407)
Net Taxable Estate	0
Plus: Adjusted Taxable Gifts	380,000
Tentative Tax Base	$ 380,000
Tentative Tax	115,000
Less: State Death Taxes Paid	(0)
Federal Gift Taxes Paid	35,700
Unified Credit	192,800
Federal Estate Tax	0

EXAMPLE C ESTATE TAXES—WILLS

As mentioned, there are demonstratable benefits to the use of the marital deduction trust and residual trust arrangements. Clearly— not just as an alternative consideration—most married couples of means who have children only of this marriage should have not only a will, but also what is commonly called a marital deduction will with a residuary trust. There are situations, however, where one or two of the spouses have been married before with children. In such cases, especially where both spouses are affluent in their own rights, it may be that wealth should pass directly to their separate children.

What the will should say

Upon the death of the individual in Example B, the will should divide the assets that remain, after specific bequests and expenses, into two parts. Part one is the marital deduction, and part two is the residual trust (previously detailed). To prevent an over-funding of the marital part, provisions should be included to compensate for direct bequests made in the will to the surviving spouse (C) such as home or personal property and lifetime gifts. Consideration as previously suggested, should also be given to adjusting the marital deduction so that the residual trust is funded with an amount of property equivalent to the applicable unified credit. Provisions can be detailed in the will to allow the marital part to be held in trust for the surviving spouse (C) unless he or she elects within a reasonable period to take the property outright. This provision would serve to protect the surviving spouse should he be disabled at or upon the other spouse's death.

In Example B, the deceased's will left all property to the surviving spouse C. As things stand under that arrangement, surviving spouse C now has the following:

Total Assets of Deceased Spouse's Estate	$2,064,300
Less: Administration and Probate Costs	(92,893)
Final Expenses	(5,000)
Federal Estate Taxes	–0–
Net Assets from Spouse	1,966,407
Plus: Other Assets	100,000
Total Net Worth	$2,066,407

Upon the subsequent death, spouse C has the following estate at death:

Gross Taxable Estate:	$2,066,407
Administration and Probate Costs (4½%)	(92,988)
Final Expenses	(5,000)
Adjusted Gross Estate:	$1,968,419
Marital Deduction	–0–
Net Taxable Estate	$1,968,419
Tentative Tax Base	1,968,419
Tentative Tax	766,589
Less: Unified Credit	$ 192,800
Federal Estate Tax	$ 573,789
Previous Spouse B's Estate Tax	–0–
Total Estate Shrinkage Due to Federal Estate Taxes	$ 573,789

Let us now see how the numbers change if the first spouse to die, B, had provided for a residuary trust in the will:

Proceeds of B's Estate	$1,966,407
Amount to Marital Deduction Trust for Surviving Spouse C (Adjusted Gross Estate less 1987 exemption)	1,366,407
Amount to Residual Trust	600,000

Upon the subsequent death, C has the following estate at death:

Marital Deduction Trust	$ 1,366,407
Plus: Other Assets	100,000
Gross Taxable Estate:	$1,466,407
Administration and Probate (4½%)	(65,988)
Final Expenses	(5,000)
Adjusted Gross Estate:	$ 1,399,919
Marital Deduction	–0–
Net Taxable Estate	$ 1,399,919
Tentative Tax Base	512,765
Less: Unified Credit	192,800
Federal State Tax	$ 319,965
Spouse B's Estate Tax	–0–
Total Estate Shrinkage due to Federal Estate Taxes	$ 319,965
Taxes Saved for Heirs via Two-Trust Marital Deduction Will ($573,789 – $319,965)	$ 253,824

Note that no mention has been made regarding the gift and estate taxation of property in the eight community property states—Arizona, California, Idaho, Louisiana, Nevada, New Mexico, Texas, and Washington. In general, property acquired during marriage is considered to be owned equally by each spouse in these states. Because of community property laws, adjustments must be made to the marital deduction to equalize the federal estate taxation for persons in both common law and community property states. Due to the complexity of these adjustments and the variance of community property law from state to state, you should consult with competent legal counsel if your client is so affected.

As has been emphasized earlier, comprehensive objective financial planning must consist of and coordinate both "living" and "estate at death" plans. Neither can be properly accomplished in a vacuum without the high probability of creating as many, if not more, problems than are being solved.

Because unified transfer taxation, like income taxation, has such enormous snarl power, extreme care must be taken by financial planners not to let the lure of transfer tax savings place a blinder over their view of lifetime needs. Conversely, ignoring the potential erosion of the estate by transfer taxation, especially during these inflationary times, may mean that much of your client's wealth-building efforts will have been in vain.

8

How To
Make Risk
Management
Work

If life is long and healthy, and if the rate of investing and rate of return on investment equals or exceeds projections, your client's financial pyramid will be in fine shape. But if death occurs before the client has built the pyramid that the dependents require for the future, life insurance can fill the gap. In this sense, the purchase of life insurance is the repurchase of stolen time. The essential purpose of life insurance is to bridge the important gap of capital, plus possibly to provide for an appropriate portion of estate settlement costs and/or liquidity at death.

This chapter provides an approach to capital needs analysis—telling if life insurance *is* needed and precisely how much. It will key in on the usefulness of and the extent of the need for protecting against the loss of earned income through accident or illness. Managing rising health care costs, covering the risks of property ownership, and general liability are all shown to be part of a total method for protecting the financial ground that has already been gained.

Insuring one's pyramid

Substantial financial risks are associated with owning assets, producing income, and, for that matter, mere existence, particularly when dependents are involved. Managing these substantial risks becomes a fundamental planning need.

Having already examined your client's financial picture, you are now in a perfect position to identify exactly what is at risk. And what is at risk *that cannot easily or economically be replaced or reproduced must somehow be protected against loss or damage.* For instance, losing the ability to earn due to disability or premature death, before building the financial structure that dependents want or need, would mean financial defeat—unless those two possibilities have been insured against. Or, if the property, business interests, and investment securities that have already been acquired are lost through fire, theft, lawsuit or the like, it could call for a financially draining type of catch-up football—unless protection against these financial hazards and hurdles has been secured.

Risk management therefore implies hiring one or more insurance companies for a fee (premium) to carry the burden of only those potential losses (risks) that would create financial hardship. *This means that, with all types of insurance coverage, your client must spend money only to buy protection against the loss of something of measurable value or need.* More specifically, it must be *something that the client either has or is aiming to acquire in time. It should not be something the client would like to have that is otherwise unobtainable.*

This is absolutely fundamental to proper risk management. Any recommendation to do otherwise is a pure marketing ploy, a temptation that must be resisted with vigor. Paying for excess coverage of any type automatically saps the current budget of cash flow that could otherwise be used to build assets more quickly and less expensively, assets that are needed to provide for the present or to create a *living* future. It may just be that *your client is not disabled or does not die earlier than the life expectancy tables would predict.* He or she has to prepare for that contingency, too.

On the other hand, directing all discretionary cash flow to extra living expenses and investments and none to insurance policies assumes that the client will never sustain a loss of property, lose good health, become disabled, or die before life expectancy. That is an invalid assumption for everyone. For instance, with regard to mere existence, the odds are about 50% that a person will not live to life expectancy. You should not bet very much of your financial future against those odds.

You are probably already gaining some appreciation for the likelihood that there is no aspect of financial planning that stirs more emotion and creates more controversy than the area of risk management. We must frequently choose between those who totally ignore the immensely important health insurance and disability income protection and those who preach that you cannot possibly buy enough. We are frequently confused by the constant battle between the monied and powerful "permanent or whole" life insurance forces versus the evangelical disciples of "buy term and invest the difference."

Conversely, a high percentage of us, at one time or another, have accurately determined the level of fire, theft, and liability protection that is needed on business assets, investments, cars, home, and personal property. And yet, we have done it with little or no argument or confrontation. In fact, if anything, advisors in these particular areas of risk management have probably undersold their wares by not having levels of protection updated as inflation increased the values of the items that need protection. The main reason for the lack of controversy surrounding protecting property versus life is that the former has not been made more complicated, confusing and expensive by packaging pure risk protection for "today" with the build-up of contingency funds to pay for "tomorrow's" ill defined needs.

The result of all of these conflicting considerations, philosophies, and advice is that too many spend too much time wallowing in indecision about what levels of what types of what protection is needed for what reasons. The fallout is that cash flow is either being robbed or falsely ballooned by over- or under-insuring. Too much of the crucial annual discretionary cash flow we discussed in Chapter 3 is being spent on costly protection that is not really needed. Or, too much of the discretionary cash flow is being directed to building new capital without protecting against the loss of existing assets.

Deciding among the different life insurance products

We must make certain that we really understand what life insurance is— not what far too many well intentioned people on all sides of the issues have been taught. Pure life insurance is nothing but a contract with a life insurance company to pay a specified amount of money upon death. The major cost of the contract is based upon pure mortality statistics, that is, on how many of 1,000 people your age are expected to die this year.

Let's assume that, of all of the people your age, 5% (50 out of 1,000) are expected to die this year. For every $100,000 that a life insurance company is expected to pay out to the beneficiary of each insured person of your age, it must collect $100,000 in premiums plus interest and expense factors plus profits.

Because our statistics show that $500,000 will be paid out on the five of your age group who expire each year, the group of 1,000 must pay $500,000 (plus costs and profits) in premiums. The true death protection cost would therefore be $500 plus per person in your age group per $100,000 of coverage. Obviously, the cost of this protection must go up each year as the statistical odds of dying go up.

What has just been described *is* pure life insurance. In the industry, it is called *term* because, like other types of insurance, it covers you for a specific term, usually one year at a time. Once the term expires, you have no more insurance unless you renew it. In other words, you insure against the financial hardship caused by a premature death, one year at a time, and only to the degree to which it is needed. Term insurance is very cheap when one is young. That is precisely when you are apt to have the largest gap between what you have and what your dependents would need in your absence. That is when life insurance is usually needed the most, especially if you factor the need for future estate settlement costs and liquidity into the financial plan, as recommended later in this chapter.

Any variation from this description of pure insurance is most often an expensive and sophisticated attempt to spread the increasing cost of *long-term* death protection evenly over a long period of time. That is not to imply that all deviations from term insurance are totally bad; a few hybrid life insurance products—that is, variations of pure term protection—may be useful in some financial planning cases.

Here in descending order—from highly recommended to the least recommended—are the types of insurance policies you can choose from.

ANNUAL RENEWABLE TERM

This improvement on pure term life insurance is the most recommendable. It corrects the weakest aspect of pure term, that is, the inability to automatically repurchase protection every year even if you become uninsurable. Annual renewable term:

1. remains level each year unless you decide that the amount of protection needed has decreased,

2. the cost per $1,000 of protection automatically goes up each year as you get older, and

3. you are allowed to renew the policy each year until age 75 or 100, depending upon the specific policy and state of domicile.

After you have digested this chapter's approach to "capital needs analysis," you will clearly understand why annual renewable term is the type of life insurance contract that the vast majority of clients should purchase.

DEPOSIT TERM

One of the greatest expenses of the life insurance industry results from the early cancellation of as much as one-third of all policies written within three years. The costs of sales commissions, underwriting, administration, and medical examinations are all nonrecoverable. These costs of lapsed policies must be born by all policy holders. To increase the cost of term insurance to those who "lapse" and to decrease the cost for those who "stay," many companies offer "deposit" term policies. Policyholders deposit lump sums at the beginning of their terms of the policy over and above a reduced annual premium. If they stay with the policy, they are returned the lump sum (plus tax-free interest) at the end of the term. If they cancel the policy, the insurance company keeps the lump sum to recapture its start-up costs.

On the surface, this may seem quite attractive. For it to be so, however, the decrease in premium cost must be greater than a combination of the (1) loss in earnings of the money deposited and (2) inconvenience of not being able to otherwise use it during the term of the contract. More often than not, after considering the increased sales commissions and administrative costs on deposit term policies, this concept solves more problems for the insurance company than for the client.

DECREASING TERM

A decreasing term contract is in two ways just the opposite of annual renewable term. With this variation of term insurance the amount of the:

1. insurance protection automatically decreases over the period of years in question, and,
2. premium remains level as the amount of protection decreases.

Beneath the surface, however, it is exactly the same as annual renewable term. You are, each year, paying about the same per $1,000 of protection for your age. This is further evidence of the fact that all insurance increases in cost with age, that is, as mortality rates increase.

I see no advantage to decreasing term whatsoever. No one, in the financial planning context, knows exactly how much protection will be needed into the distant future. Everyone should be able to decide, through a periodic capital needs analysis, to what extent, if any, his other insurance must decrease each period.

Some cite mortgage insurance as a perfect application of decreasing term. Yet a long-term, relatively low-interest rate mortgage is the last debt you would want paid off upon your death. Further, an underlying principle of the capital needs analysis, discussed later in this chapter, is that the problems solved by life insurance should be measured as a whole instead of in bits and pieces.

Conversely, if buying mortgage insurance is the only way your client can get a mortgage or insurance for that matter, fine. Yet the insured gets over-charged when young. Older clients could be getting a bargain, and they should check that out.

LEVEL TERM

The face amount of a level-term policy stays the same over the period in question, and so does the annual premium. Since we know that the cost of a level amount of pure insurance must rise each year, we can conclude that the insurance company "levels" out your cost over the term of the contract. For instance, if a five-year level-term policy is bought, the insurance company adds up the premium cost for the five years and divides that total by five in order to come up with the average "level" cost. Hence, the name. You should object to this effective front loading of the premium, especially during inflationary times. When you consider the time value of money, paying too much during the beginning and too little later simply does not make sense for anyone—except the insurance company.

WHOLE LIFE

The most popular hybrid life insurance policy is whole life, alternatively called "permanent" or "cash value" life insurance. It really is too simplistic to say that whole life is term insurance plus a savings plan. The chart in Figure 8–1 describes whole life versus term.

Line A represents the annual premium cost of a given level of annual renewable term insurance. Note that its cost rises more gradually during the earlier years and then very dramatically in the later years. Curve B represents the level cost of that same amount of protection, assuming that you keep it for life and that you live to 100. At age 40, B is usually around five to seven times as large as A. At age 62, they are about the same. After age 62, the opposite relationship develops assuming that each type of policy was purchased at about age 40. This crossover point will vary with original age of purchase and from company to company.

The key is that B remains level because it represents the average

FIGURE 8–1   *The Cost of Term Versus Whole Life*

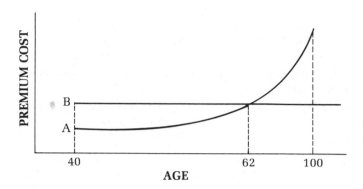

cost of owning that level of protection for the *whole* of your life. It is related to the average mortality that is expected for all of the years between the age of purchase and your life expectancy. It also factors in some of the interest earned on reserves and the company's expense factors.

A, on the other hand, is related to the specific mortality that is expected for your age in only the one year at hand. The difference between B and A, after extracting costs and adding interest, produces a cash reserve or cash value that the insurance company sets aside to reduce its risk to less than the face amount of the contract.

The net amount at risk to the insurance company is the difference between the face amount and accumulated cash reserve. That cash value is returned to the owner if the contract is canceled. It can also be borrowed without discontinuing the protection. However, if death occurs before life expectancy, it effectively stays with the life insurance company. We know that to be the case because far more premium was being paid than was necessary to buy the level of protection that equals the face amount of the contract. Conversely, if your client lives beyond life expectancy and still needs coverage, that cash reserve goes toward funding pure death protection that would have otherwise been prohibitively expensive.

The problem with a permanent program of a set level of protection, in my opinion, is that there is no way for anyone to know how much life insurance will be needed, if any, that many years in advance. Why then set up a contingency fund with the insurance company to pay for something your client may not be around to need or may not need if around? It clearly amounts to a case of *misguided objectives and misappropriation of capital.* And I do not see how so-called "universal life" solves this over-all problem.

My lesser problem with whole or permanent life relates to the probability that insurance companies do not in general credit the "cash value account" with enough of the interest they earn on those funds. That is why every period of tight money and high interest rates produces such a drain on the life insurance industry—and for good reason.

My carefully considered opinion is that whole life insurance is the worst example in the world of the saying, "You get what you pay for". More specifically, you pay a lot for what on the surface looks like a poor savings plan at a life insurance company. On the other hand, if an individual would not otherwise put aside any money for the future, a life insurance policy that builds up a cash reserve is probably worth more than its high cost.

How much life insurance is really needed?

Contrary to widespread opinion, not everyone needs life insurance. In fact, the coordination of lifetime and estate planning reaches perfection when it aims for that point in time when no life insurance at all is needed. In the meantime, life insurance should be more properly viewed as either "asset accumulation" insurance or "estate liquidity" insurance. These are the two great problems that life insurance is meant to solve.

Conversely if your client's plans do not call for the gradual accumulation of wealth or gradually acquiring the needed level of asset liquidity, a fixed or increasing level of life insurance will be needed. Coordinated financial planning, however, purposely avoids devoting larger and larger percentages of cash flow toward death planning problem solvers, such as life insurance. It is always more efficient to direct the maximum amount of cash flow toward problem solvers that are of benefit during *both* life and at death.

Since most financial planners and clients reading this book will be primarily interested in planning for the accumulation of further wealth, the most critical use of life insurance—financially replacing the time for building wealth that today's death would take away—will be discussed first. The process for measuring precisely the extent of this gap between what one now has and what one now needs is called *capital needs analysis.*

The great benefit of the following ten-step method for determining current life insurance needs is its simplicity. Using this method, you will be killing several birds with one stone. You do not have to address the need for insurance separately for potential college education costs, to cover the mortgage or demand note at the bank, to make sure there is enough capital to produce day-to-day income for the dependent's ordinary living expenses, or for estate settlement costs. Instead, all of this is addressed as a whole. You assess the family's financial needs at your client's death, determine what assets are available to provide for those needs, and then use life insurance to provide the difference. It is just that simple.

To demonstrate the process, we will consider the case of a 35-year-old couple, Cheryl and Mel Coleman, and their two children, Gary and Kathy, ages 11 and 13. Inflation will be intentionally ignored for the moment.

STEP ONE:
CAPITAL NEEDS FOR FAMILY INCOME

Most families will maintain their standard of living with about 75% of the budget used prior to the breadwinner's death. That, then, can be used as a rough guideline for this step. An exact amount can, however, be arrived at by using the Expense Worksheet in Chapter 4. That worksheet is ideally suited for measuring and then updating income needs in the event of death. (Note that page 9 of the questionnaire in Chapter 1 also addresses this same question.)

The Colemans have determined that, if Mel dies now, Cheryl and the two children would require 75% of their current expenses of $32,000 or *$24,000* per year. From this income requirement, you must subtract Social Security income benefits, which will, of course, vary in each case. For the family as a whole, as of first half of 1982, the maximum benefit for the surviving parent and two or more children is $1,079 per month. The surviving parent and one child would receive $925. One surviving child would receive $460. This is tax-free income, and it must be subtracted from the after-tax income needs.

The Colemans would initially receive the maximum amount of $12,950 but then drop as the children leave home for college. In discussing this problem, Cheryl decided that, were it not for the extra expenses for the children, she would not actually need the Social Security income. The Colemans must therefore subtract the initial $12,950 benefit from the annual after-tax need of $24,000. They must also subtract any private pension income, computed on an estimated after-tax basis, that the dependents would receive. They will also sometimes have a choice of receiving a lump sum or installment payment from such a qualified plan. That decision will depend on their relative income and estate tax brackets. In most instances, except where the estate tax bracket is relatively high, they will want to take a lump sum distribution and show its estimated amount in Step Seven.

The Colemans do not expect a regular pension income from their employer but do anticipate a lump sum distribution from a profit sharing plan.

The Colemans' income need from investment capital is therefore $11,050 ($24,000—$12,950). Assuming an after-tax return of 8%, $138,125 of capital is needed for family income.

STEP TWO:
CAPITAL NEEDS FOR DEBT REPAYMENTS

Typical debts include the home mortgage, charge cards, and bank notes. Mel Coleman has factored this monthly payment into his survivor's income needs and therefore makes no provision for it in this step. In general, this same recommendation applies to everyone. Paying off long-term debt related to as reliable as inflation hedge as one's home is unwarranted in today's inflationary environment. This is, however, not the wisest advice with regard to larger short-term liabilities, such as credit card debt, bank demand notes, or auto loans.

The Colemans, with an auto note of *$7,000,* have decided that it, plus *$500* of credit card debt or a total of *$7,500,* should be paid off if he died.

STEP THREE:
OTHER SIDE FUNDS

Two particular lump sum needs appear in most financial plans. There is the ever present need for emergency cash reserves. The income produced by these reserves must be automatically reinvested so as to at least partially repair the inflation damage being inflicted upon their emergency buying power. This is why these reserves are set up as a separate category and not included in the capital needed for family income. Most families will need emergency reserves of between 50% and 100% of their annual after-tax income needs.

The Colemans are very conservative and indicate a need for *$48,000* of emergency cash reserves.

In addition, Cheryl and Mel have estimated that their children will each need $25,000 in today's dollars for college education at State University. Assuming that a side fund for that purpose could be invested to grow with rising costs, they decide on an educational side fund of *$50,000,* or a total of *$98,000* for "other side funds."

STEP FOUR:
ESTATE SETTLEMENT COSTS

The average funeral expense of middle- to upper-middle-class Americans is estimated to be *$5,000*. The Colemans agree. Administration and probate is approximately 4½% of gross taxable estate, which, as you saw in Chapter 7, should not include the proceeds of life insurance. The Coleman's gross taxable estate is $100,000, and they therefore allot $4,500 for this expense.

Mel Coleman has no federal estate tax liability. Chapter 7 covered the subject of the unified transfer tax in detail.

Because state death taxes vary so greatly, it is assumed here that Mel Coleman has none. You should, however, check each situation with regard to state taxes. Just about every state is different in that regard.

Uninsured medical expenses are impossible to predict. If your client dies of an illness, the estate will be billed for any medical costs not covered by hospital and medical policies. Health coverage should be checked very carefully. Even with a very comprehensive plan, such as Blue Cross/Blue Shield, you will still want to factor in about $1,000 here. If it is not such a comprehensive plan, a much larger amount of about $5,000 is warranted. The Coleman's health coverage is adequate, and *$1,000* is set aside for this eventuality.

Estate settlement cost needs therefore total *$10,500*.

STEP FIVE:
TOTAL CAPITAL NEEDS

Total capital needs are determined by adding the bottom line figures derived in Steps One through Four. The Colemans have estimated needs for family income of $138,125, needs for debt repayment of $7,500, side fund needs of $98,000, and estate settlement cost needs of $10,500—for total capital needs of $254,125.

STEP SIX:
CURRENT ASSETS AVAILABLE FOR INCOME PRODUCTION

Step six must total up all investment assets currently available for income production or convertible to income producing investments. At this time, the Colemans find their current assets consisting of $3,500 of cash in a savings account plus $16,800 they have accumulated in growth mutual fund shares. This total of $20,300 is all of the "living" assets that they personally have that could easily be used to create income or to provide the side funds they would need.

STEP SEVEN:
LUMP SUM DISTRIBUTIONS FROM QUALIFIED RETIREMENT PLANS

Next, the lump sum distributions expected from all of the qualified retirement plans must be totaled. Inasmuch as decisions are not usually made in advance as to how and when such assets will be distributed, the total is shown here, as opposed to appearing as a regular income in Step One.

Mel Coleman has built up *$12,000* of capital in his current employer's profit sharing plan over the past 11 years. He expects his estate to accept it as a lump sum void of any income or estate taxation since he has named his wife as the beneficiary.

STEP EIGHT:
CURRENT LIFE INSURANCE

Now you must total up all of the proceeds the immediate family or the insurance trust is expected to receive for life policies. Note again, that the proceeds of any policies that are owned by the spouse, children, or trusts or that were gifted to others three years before death are not included in the estate. These proceeds should, however, be available for the dependents' capital needs.

Mel Coleman's group insurance policy totals twice his annual $50,000 salary, or *$100,000*. It was assigned to his wife and was therefore not included in his estate. Even had it been, after his transfer credit and/or the marital deduction, it would not have produced any estate taxes. In addition, he owns a *$25,000* whole life policy with $6,080 of cash value. His family's life insurance proceeds therefore total $125,000.

STEP NINE:
TOTAL CAPITAL AVAILABLE

The total capital available is determined by adding the bottom line figures in Steps Six, Seven, and Eight. The Colemans have $20,300 of "living" assets available for producing income, $12,000 from a profit sharing plan, and $125,000 of current life insurance. This total of $157,300 would be available to offset their capital needs.

STEP TEN:
NET CAPITAL NEEDS (SURPLUS)

You now determine the crucial number that tells whether one is under- or over-insured. Subtract the total from Step Nine (Capital Available) from the total from Step Five (Capital Needs), and you have the answer. The Colemans have capital needs of $254,125 (Step Five) and capital

TABLE 8–1
Capital Needs Worksheet

1.	*Capital Needs family Income:*	
	After-Tax Income Needs	$ 24,000
	Less: Estimated Social Security Benefits	(12,950)
	Pension Income	–0–
	Income Needs from Investment Capital	11,050
	Capital Needed Assuming 8% After Tax Return.	$138,125
2.	*Capital Needs for Debt Repayment*	
	Home Mortgage	$ –0–
	Charge Cards	500
	Bank Notes	7,000
	Other	–0–
	Total Debts	$ 7,500
3.	*Other Side Funds:*	
	Emergency Reserces	$ 48,000
	College Education Funds	50,000
	Other	—
	Total	$ 98,000
4.	*Estate Settlement Costs:*	
	Funeral Expenses	$ 5,000
	Administration and Probate	4,500
	Federal Estate Taxes	–0–
	State Death Taxes	–0–
	Uninsured Medical Costs	1,000
	Other	
	Total	$ 10,500
5.	Total Capital Needs	$254,125

(handwritten notes in margin: "may not want to pay off—may be incl'd in #1 above)", "Not in pa")

available of $157,300 (Step Nine) for a Net Capital Need of exactly $96,825. They should round upward to the nearest $5,000 and therefore immediately purchase $100,000 of annual renewable term.

The Capital Needs Worksheet in Table 8–1 is completed for the Colemans as a summary of our Ten-Step method of diagnosing Mel's life insurance needs.

It must again be emphasized that the two chief causes of a capital gap are:

TABLE 8–1 *(cont.)*

6.	*Current Assets Available or Convertible to Income-Producing Investments*	$ 20,300	
7.	*Lump Sum Distributions from Qualified Retirement Plans:*		
	IRA	–0–	
	Keogh	–0–	
	Pension	–0–	
	Profit Sharing	12,000	
	Other	–0–	
8.	*Current Life Insurance*	$125,000	
9.	Total Capital Available		$157,300
10.	Net Capital Needs (Surplus)—Capital Needs Less Capital Available		$ 96,825

1. insufficient investment assets, or
2. severe erosion of the assets already accumulated by estate settlement costs.

There can, of course, be a combination of the two.

In the case of the Colemans, the gap of $96,825 is clearly a result of a lack of current assets available or convertible into income-producing investments. Time should allow the Coleman's financial plan to increase these assets and thereby reduce their capital gap. This then reduces their need for life insurance.

For others, the major problem is often the erosion of assets caused by estate settlement costs. With passing time, investment success and inflation, it is conceivable that the problem could get worse. This would be especially true if capital needs for family income, debt repayment, and other side funds grew as rapidly as did the available capital.

This brings up a central point of contention. Your best advice is to ignore inflation and, in fact, anything but the current picture for the purpose of computing the capital gap or surplus. In other words, future insurance needs should be determined only through computing a new capital needs analysis at least once a year. That alone is what should then determine the proper level of life insurance.

As the estate grows, and as the capital needs analysis points toward increasing estate settlement costs, new objectives often develop. In addition to filling the gap, if indeed one exists, one may decide to pay an insurance company in advance, through increased life insurance coverage, to allow the estate to pass without shrinkage.

There is, of course, no way for an objective financial planner to recommend that life insurance be purchased years in advance to cover projected future estate settlement costs that do not exist today. (That would almost be analagous to recommending prepaying the cost of marine insurance today because your client might buy a boat somewhere off into the indefinite future.) Such a financial strategy would excessively rob today's cash flow of part of the means to develop the assets needed just in case the client is among the 50% or more who do live to or beyond life expectancy.

Please realize that the two arguments usually presented conflict with these recommendations, relative to covering possible future estate settlement costs. The first is that clients should buy all they can now while they are younger and it is cheaper. That statement, in my opinion, is a perfect example of false economy. Historically the cost of life insurance has gone down as medical advances cause life expectancy to rise. Obviously, the premiums paid for insurance that is not needed now could at least be put aside at interest to cover the future increased cost of any further insurance need. Moreover, if your client possesses successful financial planning's greatest ingredient, *tenacity*, he or she will be buying pure (annual renewable term) insurance. While there can be no guarantee for the future, term rates have declined, and should continue to decline, as and if life expectancy continues to increase.

The second argument for buying too much insurance in advance is that the client may not be healthy enough to get it at standard rates in the future. Admittedly, that is a remote possibility. However, it is far more economical to build estate settlement costs into future capital needs by determining the investment dollar amounts and risk levels needed to match that total goal than to pay an insurance company years in advance to do it. But again, that takes planning at its very best.

How to increase wealth through life insurance: interesting ways to structure insurance and pass on tax-free proceeds

One of the most glaring errors seen in estate planning is the ownership of one's own life insurance policies. When your client is both the insured and the owner of life insurance, the proceeds upon death are included in the gross taxable estate (as shown in Chapter 7). Conversely, if life insurance is owned by someone else with an insurable interest, the proceeds are *not* included in the estate at all. It is just about that simple. Yet few know it, and even fewer do anything about it.

KEEPING LIFE INSURANCE PROCEEDS OUT OF THE ESTATE

Here's a typical case of what can happen. Assume that Mrs. Sands is a widow with one son. Wishing to leave her entire estate *intact* to Son, she measures her current potential estate settlement costs to be $100,000 and then purchases a life insurance policy for that exact amount in her name. Upon her death, the proceeds of $100,000 are included in her estate and taxed at her top estate tax bracket. The entire $100,000 is therefore not available to cover the $100,000 of estate settlement costs. Her objective is unfortunately not met.

Instead, Mrs. Sands could have Son purchase the policy, pay the premium with annual tax-free gifts of $10,000 or less. The entire $100,000 would be available to reduce estate shrinkage to zero.

SKIPPING ONE GENERATION OF
ESTATE TAXES VIA THE LIFE INSURANCE TRUST

Had Mrs. Sands been married instead of widowed, she may have desired to leave the use of the maximum estate intact to her husband. In that case, it would not have been necessary for her husband to purchase the policy. She could have allowed the proceeds to be included in her estate and then use the unlimited marital deduction to have them pass to her husband without shrinkage. Note, however, that the principal would be included in Mr. Sands' subsequent estate, assuming it was not spent or gifted prior to his death.

The way to avoid that potential problem is for Mrs. Sands to have her insurance trust purchase the policy. As such, the proceeds would be excluded not only from her estate but from Mr. Sands' as well—an entire generation. The trustee would receive the $100,000 of life insurance proceeds upon Mrs. Sands' death and pay the income from the trust to Mr. Sands during his lifetime. Upon his death the assets would pass to Son, the named beneficiary of the trust's principal, void of estate taxes. The trustee would normally be given the right to purchase assets from Mrs. Sands' estate or to lend money to the estate, should liquidity be needed to meet her estate settlement costs.

AVOIDING TWO GENERATIONS OF ESTATE TAXES
ON INSURANCE PROCEEDS VIA THE GENERATION SKIPPING TRUST

Assume now that Mrs. Sands has a grandson as well. She wishes to avoid the estate taxes on the $100,000 of insurance upon her death and also when her son dies. The generation skipping trust provides an easy answer.

Suppose Mrs. Sands creates such a trust, naming Son as income beneficiary for life and stipulating that Grandson is to receive the principal upon Son's death. In this case, the trust would be given $10,000 or less annually gift tax free to pay the premium resulting from the trust's purchase of the policy on Mrs. Sands' life. Upon her death, the proceeds are available to provide income from the trust to Son. Then, upon Son's death, the remaining principal would pass to Grandson without estate taxes having been paid by the estates of either his grandmother or his father. Two generations of estate taxes are therefore avoided. But it is more valuable than just that. Further wealth is created and preserved through the decades of increased family income and growth produced by the investment of the deferred taxes.

Building wealth by not paying for protection that is not needed

Much has already been writtren about how over-insuring siphons off too much of what is needed to construct the living pyramid. Every dollar directed toward insurance coverage that is in excess of the mathematically measured current need is a dollar that will not be used to create wealth. It's actually worse than paying a dollar too much in taxes. The taxes might be at least partially used to fund a few worthy projects.

The area of "spouse" insurance and "child" insurance is fraught with examples of such abuse. You can never replace the love of a deceased spouse or child with money. It's, of course, a different story if the spouse is a breadwinner or houseworker *and* the spouse's death would create a capital gap. The same is true if the assets owned by the spouse are so large or illiquid as to require such coverage—but not just to replace his or her life. In that sense, "life insurance" is a misnomer. It should instead be called "capital gap" or "liquidity" insurance.

Likewise for a child or grandchild. You can't replace that loss with dollars. Unless your child is a famous actor or model and the source of "adult support," forget life insurance. A life insurance policy on a child's life is never even close to being the best alternative investment consideration. Instead, use the cash flow that would otherwise go toward premiums to fortify your client's own pyramid or the child's.

How and when to buy liquidity when the estate needs it most

Liquidity becomes the major estate problem whenever otherwise plentiful assets are not sufficiently convertible into cash to pay estate settlement costs. The problem can also surface when forced liquidation would cause realized proceeds to be far less than the expected fair market value.

These two liquidity problems are obviously not very well measured by the capital needs analysis and must therefore be dealt with quite separately.

When the liquidity problem results from the ownership of a farm or closely held business, the Economic Recovery Tax Act of 1981 helps out a great deal. Before 1982, the value of such a business had to make up over 65% of your estate before it would qualify for an installment payout of estate taxes. Now, such a closely held business must only constitute more than 35% of your estate for favorable estate tax deferral. Interest-only payments (only 4% interest on the estate taxes owed on up to $1,000,000 of such business interests) must be made for the first five years, and principal and interest payments must be made over years six through 15.

Of course, in some cases the illiquidity problem arises from the sale of one's business via an installment sale without a prepayment provision or from having spectacular success with less liquid investments, such as real estate or gas/oil properties. Your client may have been overextended in less liquid investment areas right from the outset. It is in these instances that the estate needs to acquire liquidity most. The only way to get is is thourgh the purchase of life insurance, *if* the client is insurable and *if* his or her cash flow can support the premium expense. If not, the estate will have to borrow to meet Uncle's call for his due.

Even if, in time, the problem of excessive illiquidity is automatically ameliorated or corrected by restructuring your client's financial affairs temporary coverage is warranted. No one would consider letting the home go uninsured for a year. Why, then, under the described conditions, would anyone risk a year of not being protected against illiquidity. If the person is not insurable, there is even greater reason to rapidly evolve strategies for meeting the potential liability—before it is too late.

How and when to buy income in the event of disability

With many financial plans, all is adequately prepared for in healthy life or at death—but not in the event of disability. Thus far in this chapter, we have talked about some of what Mel Coleman must do to provide financially for himself and/or his family in the event of a normal healthy life or premature death. What we have not yet done is to prepare for the third possibility, disability.

For purposes of planning, disability can be defined as the temporary or permanent loss of *earned* income due to illness or accident. The key questions here relate to how much protection is needed and when it should begin. Both have everything to do with how much discretionary income must be used to buy that needed protection if, in fact, it is not provided by one's employer. Let's first address the dollar level of the current need for disability income insurance and how it can best be adjusted in advance for inflation.

Referring again to the case of the Colemans, we find that he and his family have current after-tax income needs of $32,000. Remember that the expense worksheet in Chapter 4 is quite useful in making this type of determination.

For purposes of computing disability income needs, the *first* adjustment to this $32,000 is a reduction due to expenses that would be eliminated or reduced due to the disability. For instance, adjustments might be made for Mel Coleman's normal daily transportation and business-oriented expenses, for which he is not being reimbursed. That, plus reduced entertainment expenses, may call for a $5,000-per-year reduction in normal living expenses. That brings the Colmans' needs down to $27,000.

Next, an adjustment for Social Security must be made. Current benefit tables indicate that the Colemans would be entitled to the maximum of $895 of disability income per month as long as they have children under age 18. When they no longer have children under age 18, the figure would drop to $600. When Cheryl Coleman reaches age 62, an additional benefit again becomes available. Also, to receive Social Security, Mel Coleman must be unable to engage in any gainful employment and the disability is expected to last for 12 months or more. The best news is that the payments are tax-free. (What you are not told is that it is tax-free because you paid for the coverage with after-tax dollars.) Subtracting that $895 per month or $10,740 annually from the previous $27,000 results in a subtotal of $16,260.

The third step is to adjust for any possible after-tax income that Cheryl Coleman earns. Inasmuch as she could earn about $2,500 per year writing articles on childcare for local magazines during her husband's disability, that adjustment must be made. Because this, plus the Coleman's investment income, will result in little or no income taxation during the period of disability, the entire pretax $2,500 is subtracted to produce a new subtotal of $13,760.

Fourth, an adjustment must be made for any investment income that would be derived from their current, existing investment assets. According to our earlier assumptions, the Coleman's could expect $1,624 of current spendable income from $20,300 of assets. Again, due to a combination of the $4,000 of personal exemptions and $3,400 of zero bracket income, no income taxes need to be deducted. Subtracting the $1,624 from the previous subtotal of $13,760 leaves a preinflation adjusted disability income need of $12,136.

We have now arrived at Step 5, the point where some adjustment must be made for inflation. Assuming that all prior adjustments (investment income, Mrs. Coleman's income, and Social Security disability income payments) will keep pace with inflation, we can adjust only this remaining $12,136 for cost of living increases. Here is a simple way of doing that. Compound the $12,136 at the assumed inflation rate of 5%, and you will arrive at an annual figure of $77,494 for 38 years, when Mel Coleman is at his life expectancy of 73. Averaging this $77,494 and the $12,136, you get $44,815 or $3,734 per month. The usual maximum possible payment for long-term disability from an insurance company per month is now $4,000 but then only if your earned income is over $190,000.

A review of recent guidelines issued by insurance companies specializing in disability insurance indicates the following participation limits (for long-term coverage) for different income levels:

Earned Income		Participation
Annual	*Monthly*	*Limit—Monthly*
$ 25,000	$ 2,100	$1,000
36,000	3,000	1,500
48,000	4,000	2,000
63,000	5,300	2,500
90,000	7,500	3,000
105,000	8,750	3,500
190,000+	15,833	4,000

Mel Coleman's salary is $50,000, and therefore the $2,000 limitation applies. He should therefore purchase the maximum allowable or about $2,000/month of coverage. If the disability were long-term, the family would then have to annuitize some of the principal part of the investment assets or further lower their standard of living during the last half of the period of disability. If the disability period were short, the permissable coverage would prove to be more than adequate.

The worksheet in Table 8–2 can be used as a guide for determining the desired level of disability coverage. It has been completed for Mel Coleman in order to put his long-term disability needs into perspective.

How to reduce the cost of disability coverage

If you delve very deeply into a businessperson's, executive's, or professional's true financial objectives, you will discover something revealing. Most such successful individuals don't want to (1) retire at the normal retirement age or (2) aim for reaching financial independence at the normal retirement age. What they really want is to reach financial independ-

TABLE 8–2
Long-Term Disability Income Needs Worksheet
(Completed for Dr. Tom Wright)

After-Tax Income Needs	$32,000
Reduction (Reduced business, entertainment and other expenditures during disability period)	(5,000)
Social Security (monthly benefit × 12)	(10,740)
Spouse's After-Tax Income	(2,500)
Aftertax Investment Income	(1,624)
Preinflation-Adjusted Disability Income Needs	$12,136
Adjustment for Inflation: Long-term Inflation Rate Assumption	5%
Preinflation-Adjusted Disability Income Needs Compounded at 5% for Life Expectancy (38 years)	$77,494
Add: Preinflation-Adjusted Disability Income Needs	12,136
Total	$89,630
Average Annual Need (Total ÷ 2)	$44,815
Inflation-Adjusted Average Monthly Disability Income Need (Annual Need ÷ 12)	$ 3,734

ence *as soon as practical* so that they can work *because they want to rather than because they have to*. And that relates very much to the cost of disability insurance.

Disability protection is only needed as long as your clients *have* to work. After they have reached financial independence—usually later in life when disability insurance is most expensive—they don't need it! This is but one more argument for all that has been espoused in this book about planning. The earlier your clients begin accumulating the assets they need to produce the income they desire, the sooner some of their most expensive risk management costs become non-needs. That is also the point when more financial muscle can be used on today's luxuries and less on tomorrow's needs.

Of course, many employers provide disability insurance throughout employment via the company's group long-term disability plan. In fact, some companies provide disability coverage of up to one-half to two-thirds of salary. That may not be enough, particularly during the earlier years well before the point of financial independence. Those early earning years could turn into yearning years if disability protection is not sufficient. The Disability Worksheet should therefore be used to see if the company's benefits should be supplemented with a personal policy.

There is even a legitimate way to acquire total disability coverage in excess of the amounts shown in the previous table on participation limits *and* simultaneously lower cost. First, your client must acquire a given level personally and *then* have his or her company or employer adopt group coverage. For instance, suppose a physician or business owner has purchased the maximum personal coverage, and it is not enough. The client can subsequently incorporate the practice or business, acquire lower cost group coverage for himself/herself and the employees, and thereby make up the coverage gap. Actually, the business should provide the larger part of the total needed, because the group coverage is a deductible expense. Even though the disability income from such a policy would be taxable income, it is better to receive the tax benefit on the front end for two reasons. First, the tax savings rate is probably higher when the owner is buying the coverage than will be the tax paying rate when the benefits are received. Second, since the odds are against the owner becoming disabled, it is better to take the tax benefit now for sure rather than holding out for a benefit that will hopefully never have to be used.

To further reduce the cost of disability insurance, there is, as with most types of insurance, some type of deductible. With disability insurance, the deductible is expressed in terms of *time*. Benefits usually begin after a waiting period of between one month and two years. (Social Security has a five-month waiting period.) As a result, some amount of self-insurance is necessary. The longer the waiting period, the less expensive the coverage becomes. Most employers provide short-term disability benefits, such as a certain number of sick leave days. There may also be some form of salary continuation plan, which is designed to bridge the gap between the onset of long-term disability and the start-up of insurance benefits. *For those who are self-employed, even more significance must be attached to determining the proper level of emergency cash reserves.* The larger the reserves are, the longer the disability insurance waiting period can be and therefore the lower the cost of the coverage. For this reason alone, those who are not adequately covered by employer-sponsored sick leave and salary continuation plans should maintain cash reserves of *at least six months* of budgeted living expenses.

Finally, the chances for disability are reduced significantly when your client is healthy, alert, and energetic. Good health results from the best possible health care. All of us enjoy "going to the doctor" for both real and imagined ills, when insurance at least partially covers our costs. For these reasons—plus the even more important overall financial ones—there is a necessity to protect against the high cost of health care. Expenses for hospital care, medications, surgery, and other aspects of health care have risen even faster than the general cost of living. While a certain amount of self-insuring is warranted (again through the maintenance of adequate cash reserves), the total lack of predictability of possible future health care needs and costs dictate that much of that risk be transferred to an insurance company. Your clients must ascertain whether their employers provide adequate coverage, or otherwise obtain it directly for themselves and their families.

How to protect what has already been accumulated

A multitude of other types of insurance protection must be considered to avoid the potential burden of replacing existing assets. The home and personal property, for instance, probably represent an important percentage of your client's asset base. While used to provide shelter and pleasure instead of current or future income, those two insurable asset categories usually represent the past positioning and directing of a consequential amount of assets and/or cash flow. Having to replace them in the event of loss, theft, or destruction would probably drain all or a large part of one's discretionary cash flow from its proper current direction.

Here again, the risk can be properly managed only by transfering all or part of it to others. And as already implied, the insurance industry can be relied upon to recommend the adequate level of coverage. Your major responsibility will be to ensure that the coverage has been or will be adjusted upward as inflation increases values and as asset accumulation dictates.

The final but certainly not the least important aspect of risk management is liability. Your client must go beyond the legal requirement that you or your property not adversely affect others' rights. The legally aware world of today is fraught with those who would recommend or use a lawsuit to create their own financial pyramids. In dollar amounts, the size of court settlements for injury caused by activities or by work engaged in by your client or employees through the negligent use of the client's property, are staggering. The threat of exorbitant malpractice suits is a risk that professionals simply must transfer to the insurance industry. In some states, substantial cash reserves can also be positioned in ways that prevent loss due to lawsuit, such as in single premium deferred annuities and qualified retirement plans.

A client who is sued and then found guilty in a court of law may lose a lot—if not everything. Liability insurance—not self-insuring—is therefore a necessity since there is no way to adequately measure or totally self-prepare for such potentially huge eventualities. Except for some contracts for medical malpractice insurance, which is a major expense of many medical doctors and therefore a part of your medical bill, liability insurance is generally very affordable for everyone.

In addition to *minimum* liability insurance of $100,000 per person and $300,000 per accident on your automobile, *just about everyone should have an umbrella liability insurance policy of at least $1,000,000 at a cost of less than $75 per year.* Again, most insurance companies can be relied upon to provide honest, intelligent, and objective advice on the amount of liability insurance that, preceding the umbrella policy, should be a part of automobile and homeowner's coverage. If there is any doubt in your mind, check on the coverage currently being recommended for a similar situation by the United States Auto Association (USAA). Their standards are fair, up-to-date, and reasonably priced. Although only current and past military personnel and their dependents can actually purchase insurance through USAA, the Association's recommendations and rates can be used by all as useful guidelines.

Having now discussed all of Section II's formidable obstacles to realizing future financial aims, we are now prepared to begin the third phase of designing your client's overall financial plan. You will now be shown how to select from among the myriad alternative strategies and solutions for getting your clients from where they are today, to where they would like to be tomorrow.

III

Financial Therapy Via Alternative Solutions

9

Step-by-Step Guide to Selecting the Proper Solutions to Financial Problems

Section III keys in on the problem-solving part of financial planning. Chapter 9 tells how to select among the major *alternative choices* for solving financial problems. Chapter 10 delves into the *procedural strategies* for solving many of your client's most important financial problems. Chapter 11 illustrates with bottom-line conviction the most usable tax-advantaged investment strategies for positioning assets on every possible risk level. The section then concludes with Chapter 12's tried and proven guidelines for selecting the professional management assistance that will be needed in the implementation of every client's plan.

Solving financial problems through the eyes of the financial planner

It should be no surprise by now that I believe that the proper practice of financial planning is similar to the practice of general medicine. The thoroughly profes-

TABLE 9–1
Financial Problem Solvers Table

Procedural Tools	Investment Strategies
	Indirect Investment Strategies:
Qualified Retirement Plans:	Cash Reserves:
Individual Retirement Accounts	Checking Accounts
Keogh Plans	Money Market Funds
Corporate Plans	Deferred Annuities
	Fixed
	Variable
	US Government Savings Bonds
Wills:	Debt Securities:
Simple	Municipal Bonds
Marital Deduction Will	Corporate Bonds
with Residuary Trust	
Trusts:	Equity Securities:
Revocable	Common Stocks and Mutual Funds
Living Trust	Tax-Managed Trusts
Irrevocable	
Insurance Trust	
Charitable Remainder Trust	*Direct Investment Strategies:*
Short-Term Reversionary Trust	
Generation Skipping Trust	Collectables and Precious Metals:
Interest-Free Loans	
	Tax-Incentive Investments:
Gifting Strategies:	Real Estate
Intrafamily	Existing Properties
Intrafamily Annuity	To-Be-Built Properties
Charitable	Wrap-Around Mortgages
Charitable Remainder Trust	
	Energy
Ownership Structures:	Gas/Oil Income Properties
Custodianship	Gas/Oil Drilling
Joint Ownership	Royalty Interests
Corporate Recapitalization	Equipment Financings
The Installment Sale	Communications
	Cable Television Systems
Insurance	
Life	
Disability	
Health	
Property and Casualty	
Liability	

(Handwritten annotations: "Liquid, →" and "dbl tax also" near Cash Reserves; "More illiquid, elimin. dbl. tax problem" near Direct Investment Strategies)

sional *medical* doctor always concentrates on an overall goal—the patient's best possible physical and mental health. The top-notch *money* doctor is concerned, likewise, with achieving the client's desired level of financial wealth. Similarly, *medical* doctors seek remedies from two categories: medical procedures and medications. They weigh the pros and cons of medication versus surgery. The *money* doctor's practice of financial problem solving must proceed along those same lines. You must therefore face the absolute financial law of nature: *there is always both a procedural tool and an investment strategy for solving every conceivable financial problem.*

Financial planners are best guided toward the most appropriate solution or combination of solutions to a given financial problem when they neatly categorize their alternatives. We therefore divide all of the possible choices into two categories: (1) procedural tools and (2) investment strategies.

The first step in the process of selecting the best solution to a given financial problem is to departmentalize these two categories of solutions via the Financial Problem Solvers Table (Table 9–1).

How to select from among the alternative problem solvers

To select a solution on either side of the Financial Problem Solvers Table, we'll now explore the major questions that arise when creating a comprehensive financial plan. Not surprisingly, they are the issues that are usually uppermost in the minds of the rich as well as of those who would like to be.

PROVIDING FOR FAMILY INCOME
IN THE EVENT OF DISABILITY OR PREMATURE DEATH

There are but two mechanisms for reaching any financial goal: better positioning what your clients already have and properly directing what they are getting.

Providing for family income, should earned income cease for one reason or another, is initially a matter of properly directing discretionary cash flow. That can be accomplished via procedural tools and/or investment strategies. In either case, current luxuries must sometimes be sacrificed for possible future necessities.

On the left side of the problem solver's table, risk management techniques can be employed to shift certain risks to an insurance company. A proper level of disability insurance will replace some or all of your client's earned income in the event of disability. Life insurance fills the gap between what he or she has and what the heirs will *need* in the event of premature death. In fact, some risk managers advocate buying as much as you can afford. That would mean using up a lot if not all of the discretionary cash flow.

Alternatively, your client could purchase a bare minimum of insurance. This choice calls for the sacrifice of all of today's luxuries and the devotion of almost all—or a large amount of—discretionary cash flow to build a mighty financial pyramid as soon as possible. That would be the poor but pure investment answer.

The pure procedural choice would probably be better than relying solely on the investment strategy. But in this case, a mixture of the two would actually be the best answer. One should buy only enough insurance to provide the *proper* level of protection as measured by the tools, techniques, and forms presented in Chapter 8. Then build the pyramid at the prescribed "financial speed" with what remains of a sane level of total discretionary income. Sooner than later, the greatest part of the risk of providing future family income will gradually be transferred from the insurance companies to a well constructed financial pyramid. The farther along you go, the easier it will become, as a greater and greater percentage of cash flow is made available for both today's luxuries and tomorrow's necessities. It is then not wasted on paying for protection your client no longer needs.

PROVIDING FOR FAMILY EDUCATION NEEDS

This multifaceted problem involves decisions related to when, how, and how much. For the purposes of illustration, let's wear the shoes of a business executive, Mr. Jim Smith, who has accumulated diversified wealth on schedule. Jim Smith suddenly realizes that he has not prepared in advance for the much higher-than-expected college education costs of his teenage daughter.

Procedurally, 50% tax-bracketed Jim Smith can plan to lend $50,000 of serious emergency cash reserves to his daughter's trust on an interest-free demand note basis. Her trustee then positions it in a taxable money market fund at 12%, which earns $6,000 per year practically tax-free. The college education costs are paid by the trustee in a state that does not consider that cost the parent's responsibility, and Jim Smith can call on his cash in the case of emergency.

From the standpoint of investment strategy, Jim could instead invest in a series of gas/oil drilling partnerships, deduct the investment, and then gift the future net revenues to his daughter as soon as taxable income is forecast to begin. Such a strategy, when successful, can reduce the cost of college education to a quarter of the normal cost. But it requires more risk taking, assumes that Jim Smith can afford to part with the assets, and presumes Miss Smith will use the gifted assets properly. A trust format of ownership can, of course, better assure the latter assumption at least to a point.

In practice, if Jim Smith's daughter is near 18, the procedural answer is best. If she is much younger, say less than 14 years of age, a tax-incentive investment strategy is often recommendable, especially when Jim Smith has the procedural answer to fall back on in an emergency.

Other variables, such as Jim Smith's liquidity, his tax bracket, his risk tolerance level, and his current discretionary cash flow, will sway the decision toward one side or the other of the problem solver's table.

As is almost always the case, *the procedural answer is the lower risk solution, while the investment strategy provides the greater opportunity.* Often, the sheer temperament of the "patient" will dictate whether we use one or the other of the alternative solutions.

TRANSFORMING TAX LIABILITY INTO INCREASED FINANCIAL RESOURCES FOR THE FUTURE

Chapter 4 devoted significant attention to creating discretionary cash flow. We have also discussed budgeting expenditures in a way that is neither restrictive nor wasteful, relative to your client's intended financial destiny. Cash flow, over and above necessary living expenses, quite naturally accumulates for future needs more rapidly if it can do so on a pretax basis. Setting it aside via procedural or investment strategies that produce tax deductions approximately equal to that cash flow dramatically increases its potential future value.

Procedurally, taxation of personal service income can be deferred by committing it on a pretax basis to a qualified corporate or individual retirement plan, such as a pension, profit sharing, Keogh or IRA (Individual Retirement Account) plan or to a deferred compensation plan. Individual, vastly varying circumstances will dictate which plan or set of plans is possible or right.

In the investment area, certain economically viable tax-incentive involvements can be successfully employed. Investments in real estate under construction, gas/oil drilling participations, and cable television system ownership will easily provide immediate or eventual deductibility of close to 100% of the capital committed. These deductions can be used to offset the amount of personal service income that should be sheltered.

Again, the investment solutions usually involve more risk and are sometimes analagous to the more aggressive "brain surgery" type solution to a financial headache! But, while the tax-incentive investment is more aggressive and relatively illiquid, it has compensations. For instance, it is usually self-liquidating. It typically has low, legally acceptable valuations for intrafamily gifting or estate valuation purposes, and it may even produce tax-benefited cash flow.

Conversely, the qualified retirement plan, or procedural "aspirin"-type answer, involves no risk whatsoever until a decision is made with regard to the investment of the cash. A salient point is that the 100% deductibility of this type of procedural solution results from the mere repositioning of cash, not from the level of risk taken as in the case of tax-incentive investments. We must remember that assets held in qualified plans are not generally available until vesting and/or retirement and, in the meantime, cannot be collateralized. The earnings, however, always accumulate tax-sheltered.

Using this method for choosing between alternative *procedural* and/or *investment* strategies, or combinations thereof, provides a clear means of weighing the pluses and minuses of each possible direction. As in all areas of the life of business and the business of life, you must give up something to get something. You must decide what is of greater importance to your clients and their desired financial end, the safer and more controlled procedural, qualified retirement plan answer or the more aggressive, more flexible, tax-incentive investment direction.

In either case, we must constantly remind ourselves that "saving taxes" is not an end in itself. The *real objective is the conversion of taxes to assets* for the future or increased cash flow for today.

As is usually the case, wherever the lower risk procedural solution answers the need, it should be employed first. Sometimes, as is the case with qualified retirement planning, there is a legal limit to its use. After exhausting all possible appropriate uses of such a technical tool, one can then go on to fulfill the total objective with the investment strategy side of the equation. Again, some balancing of the strengths and weaknesses of both categories of problem solvers will most often meet the specific needs.

PROTECTING EMERGENCY CASH RESERVES
WHILE MAXIMIZING RELATED INCOME

Maintaining adequate cash reserves for emergencies, estate liquidity, and/or anticipated future investment opportunities is a must in financial planning. For that segment of the pyramid, sanctity of principal is paramount in spite of inflationary expectations. Inasmuch as the principal can therefore not be hedged against rising costs, the income that these reserves produce should be accumulated as part of the reserves to at least partially restore the loss of buying power. That objective is facilitated when tax erosion of the interest earned on the reserves is minimized via sheltering without risking principal.

Here again, there are clear alternatives. Investment-wise, cash can be moved from taxable cash equivalents to tax-exempt project notes or short-term municipal bonds or bond funds. With such a move comes the slightly increased risk of principal but absolutely tax-free income. An even safer strategy would be to shift the cash to the storehouse of a legal reserve life insurance company's deferred annuity contract, have the principal guaranteed, and receive a high pretax interest rate, which is tax-deferred but not tax-free. Ultimately, taxes will be paid on the accumulated interest when it is withdrawn, but *the mere deferral of the income tax* on that interest *is of considerable value in itself.*

Procedurally, where it is not important to further build up assets in the name of the owner of the cash reserves, two prominent tools can be profitably employed. First, the interest-free loan is close to being financial poetry in motion. It has already been discussed as a technique for meeting college education costs without sacrificing financial independence. Additionally, the cash could be shifted to a short-term reversionary trust (Clifford trust), shifting the income and its attendant tax liability to a lower-bracketed income beneficiary. Such a trust has estate planning considerations that are discussed in the next chapter. Where the cash reserves are for estate liquidity purposes as opposed to emergency needs, the reversionary trust may be a very worthy consideration.

I believe that the deferred annuity and the interest-free demand loan tie for honors in this category. Where the "financial patient" needs the income build-up, the annuity is obviously better. Where there is no such need, or where it is obviously better to shift the tax burden and the after-tax income to a different entity for income tax and/or future estate tax purposes, the interest-free loan gets the nod. Our "patients" frequently use both. The real point in this discussion is that *there are alternatives*. Having the clear choice between both categories of problem solvers presents you with a forced consideration of all of the issues at hand.

MAKING CURRENT INVESTMENTS PRODUCE MORE AFTER-TAX RETURN

Chapter 6 emphasized the importance of keeping more of what your client's investments make via income tax avoidance. If there is any reservation whatsoever about *avoiding* taxes, it is probably because of a misunderstanding of terminology. There is nothing sinister or unethical at all about paying less taxes. Much of the tax law, as we have already indicated by example, is designed to help convert tax liability to assets for the future or increased spendable cash flow for today. And as we would have it, the law provides both procedural *and* investment strategies for doing just that.

First, here are some examples of procedural answers: Appreciated assets can sometimes be made to produce dramatically increased spendable income via the "financial trinity" of (1) the installment sale, (2) the private intrafamily annuity and/or (3) the charitable remainder trust. (All are discussed in detail in Chapter 10.)

Where charity must begin at home, the installment sale enables one to sell an appreciated asset more orderly over a long period. That then spreads the capital gain over lower future brackets (much as income averaging spreads income over past lower brackets) and increases cash flow. Because the after-tax interest paid is either larger than the asset's after-tax income, or because your client chooses to spend principal, the cash flow increases.

Don't be misled into thinking that it is automatically offensive for a client to spend some principal. It is sometimes a worthy design. The installment sale can be a good way to structure such an answer to the need for increased cash flow.

As with all such ready answers, certain red flags arise. Inflation causes the level stream of payments to decrease in purchasing power. If life extends beyond the term of the sale, cash flow ceases, and one could be faced with a sudden drop in spendable cash flow. That, of course, must all be factored into the planning process. For instance, not spending the principal, reinvesting it wisely, and later replacing the interest income with tax-benefited cash flow from the reinvested principal can be easily achieved with discipline.

In the final analysis, a decision to use the installment sale should not be made, especially in inflationary times, just to save taxes. Like the private annuity and charitable trusts discussed in the next chapter, use of the installment sale should be motivated by a desire to achieve some *combination* of increased cash flow, reduced or deferred capital gains taxes, and increased estate liquidity.

Another procedural answer to the problem of increasing spendable income for the family unit might involve shifting its ownership temporarily to a lower-tax paying entity within or for the family's benefit. Corporate bonds or high-dividend paying stocks, for example, might be transferred to the same type of reversionary, ten year-and-one day Clifford trust (mentioned in the previous section on protecting cash reserves). This technique is particularly applicable when some of the after-tax income produced by investments is being used to help fund expenses of elderly dependents or prep school or college age children. In such a case, the lower-tax-paying entity receives the income produced by the investments held in the trust.

The trust is called "reversionary" because the capital legally reverts to the donor no sooner than ten years and one day unless the income beneficiary dies before the specified period ends. Care must be taken, so that more problems are not created than are solved. For example, about 44% of the current value of the assets transferred to a ten-year Clifford trust are considered a gift for the purpose of the unified transfer tax discussed in Chapter 7. The result is that, if 44% of the assets involved exceeds the gift exclusion of $10,000 or $20,000 per donee per year, the resulting tentative tax, reduced by the amount of unused unified credit, is payable. That cost, plus the future effective loss of part or all of the unified credit, must be weighed against the current income tax savings (as well as other alternatives) before creating such a trust.

Another procedural alternative to the reversionary trust is the interest-free demand loan, discussed in the section related to maximizing earnings produced by cash reserves. The interest, dividends, or other cash flow produced by the investment of the loan proceeds is obviously increased in spending power as it falls, at little cost, onto the "1040" of a child or other lower-tax-paying entity. Extreme care must be taken to comply with all of the legal provisions that will sustain the validity of this procedure. It has greater power to help reduce the after-tax cost of financing certain living costs of a family member for which your client is not legally obligated. It can also serve to remove income build-up in an estate without increasing gift taxes.

Outright intrafamily gifting of appreciated, taxable, income-producing assets almost always produces a reduction in taxes paid by the family unit and a corresponding increase in spendable or reinvestable income. But heirs lose the later stepped-up basis. Again, the tax cart cannot be placed before the economic horse. In other words, gifting has to be an important objective in the first place.

Tax-incentive investments that have begun to produce taxable income, where a negative cost basis has not been created, can be gifted to children or trusts in lower or nonexistent marginal tax brackets with a dramatic effect upon the overall after-tax rate of return. Also, instead of gifting cash in fulfilling pledges and obligations to charities, appreciated assets should be gifted. The deductions created can then be used to shelter otherwise taxable income while potentially avoiding the future capital gains tax on the gifted asset.

Besides all of these procedural solutions, a multitude of investment strategies can be used, where appropriate, to achieve an increase in after-tax return.

One can shift from taxable, interest-paying debt securities to tax-exempt bonds, or convert from taxable, dividend-paying individual stocks to tax-managed trusts (trusts, taxed as corporations, that receive the dividends of other US corporations 85% tax-free).

Capital from any taxable, income-producing investment can be re-positioned into incentive investments, such as existing real estate properties whose income is sheltered by depreciation, existing gas and oil wells whose income is partially sheltered by cost depletion allowances, depreciation, and other business and operating expenses, or tax-managed trusts as indicated. If capital gains result from the repositioning of assets and the resulting capital erosion is not palatable, and if the alternative minimum tax allows for it, the taxable portion of the gain can be sheltered with the front-end deductions provided by carefully selected tax-incentive investments.

That leads to our final overall investment strategy alternative for keeping more of what your client's investments earn. For increasing the after-tax results of investment assets whose income can be reinvested for the future rather than being spent, give strong consideration to directing that very income towards a diversified portfolio of tax-incentive investments. The beneficial tax ramifications of sheltering highly taxed income should become quite obvious after reading Chapter 11—if it is not already clear. More importantly, there are several very attractive alternatives due to today's energy source transition scenario, the effect it has had upon inflation and interest rates, and the resulting burst of technology in communications.

Tax-advantaged participations in energy, real estate, and cable television are today more appropriate than ever. These direct participations can all be neatly structured to accomplish the tax deductibility and/or investment tax credits that are needed to delay today's tax liability and/or partly transform it to a lower overall tax rate in the future. Don't ever forget the benefit of not paying the taxes today that can be delayed until tomorrow. Because your client can at least earn interest on the money that he would have otherwise sent to his silent partner on Capitol Hill, tax deferral is a powerful way to increase the income produced by investment capital. There is no greater proof of this than the ease with which capital could accumulate prior to the enactment of the first income tax law in 1913.

UNLOCKING FROZEN APPRECIATED ASSETS
WITHOUT PAYING CAPITAL GAINS TAXES

The potential or existing problem of a large long-term capital gain is very close to being the most mathematically intriguing and, for many, a most difficult problem to fully evaluate. Herein lies the perfect example of how options increase dramatically when you identify a problem months, if not years, in advance. Addressing the issue ahead of time produces alternatives and advantages that are manifold. After the fact, you are more limited. If your client has already taken a large gain and hopefully no capital losses with which to offset it, you are practically limited to investment solutions. Considered early, however, you may first find an "aspirin" solution in one of these lower-risk procedures. Here are the alternatives, depending on the nature of the appreciated asset.

Real Estate. Highly appreciated real estate properties whose net rental income exceeds depreciation may be exchanged on a tax-free basis for a like property. That is the *procedural* alternative. The *investment* solution is to sell the property and reinvest the proceeds, partially in tax-incentive investments that shelter the appropriate portion of the gain and the balance in other income and/or growth investments that meet the client's multiple objectives.

Highly Appreciated Stock The problems associated with seemingly locked-in gains are many. Highly appreciated securities with close to a zero basis, paying too little after-tax income, and/or occupying too large a portion of your client's total financial wherewithal also provide you with intriguing and creative opportunities—and onerous pitfalls. Let us consider a few of the major alternatives that you might consider.

We have previously discussed the possibility of using the installment sale to spread out and hopefully reduce the tax impact. Prior to 1979, the installment sale was easily actuated with a close family member. Since that is no longer permitted by law, you must search for an investment firm or company that will buy the appreciated security on an installment basis if, in fact, that suits your client's needs. Such a strategy can be particularly useful when you wish to tax shelter all of the taxable portion of the gain. But doing it all in one year would sometimes trigger the alternative minimum tax. It is relatively easy to determine how much of a gain you can take in any one year and still shelter all of the taxable portion of it. If your client then limits the portion of the total gain in any one year to that amount, via an installment sale, he or she can effectively exit the appreciated security without any tax erosion at all.

Combining the installment sale and tax incentive investments obviously involves using a procedural tool *and* an investment strategy simultaneously. It is certainly a useful ploy when the amount of the liquidation is unusually large.

Whenever the capital gain is relatively small compared to the ordinary taxable income, an investment strategy alone can be used to your client's best advantage. Tax-incentive investment deductions equal to 40% of the gain will accomplish the goal of eliminating the gains tax. The portion of the sales proceeds not used to create the deductions can be positioned in ways that will create far more after-tax income than the original appreciated asset produced.

On the pure procedural side of the table, highly appreciated securities are ideally suited to funding private intrafamily annuities and charitable remainder trusts. Both procedures effectively spread out and hopefully reduce the taxes on the gain. Both can remove the asset from the estate. The annuity moves it over to the generation of the obligor, usually children or a trust with them as beneficiaries, but in any case a very trusted payor. The charitable remainder trust, like an immediate annuity, provides income for life but transfers the corpus to the designated charity upon the income beneficiaries' death.

Procedure . . . investment . . . it is always yours for the choosing.

Closely Held Businesses. Where the owner wants to be divested of such an asset, the choice is usually one of exchanging tax-free for the securities of an existing corporate entity, selling for cash now, or selling for cash on an installment basis. Due to the birth of the alternative minimum tax on January 1, 1980, it is clearly preferable to procedurally exchange the company tax-free for the liquid shares of a financially strong company *if the goal is to shelter all of the gain*. One can then gradually ease out of such a usually heavy position in one equity security into a combination of tax-incentive investments and other investment strategies that meet your client's objectives for the present and the future.

Conversely, your client will frequently get advice to sell for cash, paying a top capital gain tax rate of only 20%. That 20% is a myth. Long-term gains, even if you are in the 50% marginal bracket, are *not* taxed at 20%. The truth of the matter is that only a percentage of your long-term gains (now 40%) are taxed at a maximum of 50% unless some of them, via the alternative minimum tax, are taxed at 20%. Assuming that the alternative minimum tax does not apply, you must look at gains under current law as being 60% tax-free and 40% taxable. It is that 40% that you want to try to remove from your client's taxable income without taking undue or unknown risks.

Naturally, in some instances you have no choice in how to get out of such a closely held asset. Perhaps the choice must be whether to get out at all. Go back to why your client wants out. If it is just for liquidity, maybe there are other alternatives, such as life insurance. If it is just to get cash, maybe some form of corporate recapitalization—which is a complex corporate planning subject of its own—should be considered. Obviously very astute tax counsel should always be used in making these decisions. Avoiding legal fees in this instance, can hardly be viewed as saving.

Finally, on the subject of gains and the alternative minimum tax, you may experience the unfortunate event of finding this computation method already applicable. Suppose that due to the charitable gifts or tax-incentive investments your client made prior to the event of a forced or economically dictated sale of the business, the alternative minimum tax has already been triggered. Even though it is a larger tax than the regular tax, the *top* tax bracket will have probably dropped from 50% or so to 20%. That obviously changes the whole tax and investment perspective for the year in question.

For example, it may be advantageous to swap part or all of your client's tax-benefited income for the year for taxable income. Succinctly stated, 12% taxable in the 20% bracket is a true return of 9.6% and therefore better than 6% tax-free in a 50% bracket. Certainly a taxable money market fund for storehousing the tax liability on the gain would be better than the normal route of a tax free fund of short-term tax-free project notes. And, too, you may want to *not* prepay *all* state income tax liability but instead delay it until the next year when it may be usable against a bracket much higher than 20%. The client will have the use of those funds for a little longer as well.

MAKING THE ESTATE LIQUID
WHEN IT NEEDS LIQUIDITY MOST

Let's assume that your client's estate is relatively illiquid for estate settlement purposes but more than adequate in size to sustain the heirs after estate settlement costs are paid. The problem becomes one of creating the needed liquidity through *procedural* or *investment* strategies.

A procedural answer to the immediate problem is life insurance on the client's life, preferably owned by members of the family or an insurance trust. Thereafter, gradual intrafamily and/or charitable gifting might lower the estate settlement costs and therefore the liquidity needs. The private annuity and the charitable remainder trust, both explained in detail in Chapter 10, are also good examples of procedural solutions to this problem.

On the other hand, the client could immediately proceed with the liquidation or tax-free exchange of the least liquid holdings, such as closely held businesses, real estate, or restricted stock, and in so doing convert them into more liquid investment holdings.

It is impossible to say in advance which approach is best for whom. Age, temperament, income necds, the economy, market conditions, and tax circumstances will all pay crucial roles in determining the proper direction. But knowing that there are alternatives, and selecting from neatly categorized procedural or investment strategies, will better guide you to more successful conclusions.

Crucial factors to consider when finalizing a financial decision

This chapter has shown, via examples of major financial planning problems, how both *procedural* and *investment* strategies can be employed to attain somewhat similar ends. We began by illustrating the proper categorization of the alternative problem solvers. The second step involved demonstrating the selection of the right procedure(s) and/or investment(s) for your client's specific problem. The third step now involves a final check of the very basic factors that must be considered before any specific solution is implemented.

1. Be it a procedure, such as a gifting strategy or an investment of any sort, it is necessary to have a good fix on its economic merit versus the risk that is taken to achieve it. The days are gone when anyone can say whether this or that procedure or investment is "good" or "bad"! *A solution's economic potential must be related to risk before its relative merits can be determined.*

2. For each and every potential solution, know the estimated current, ongoing and future income tax and unified transfer tax ramifications. Keep surprises to a minimum. They are usually not pleasant.

3. Identify your client's risk tolerance level for that particular segment of his/her pyramid. The perfect mathematical solution may be the one that will also keep a person awake at night or destroy a family. No amount of wealth is worth that.

4. Don't forget the solution's potential effect upon estate liquidity needs. Here is where it is easy to create more problems for the future than are being solved for today.

As noted, the profession of financial planning is very properly rising from the synergism of law, tax accounting, investments, and risk management. My professional friends in law, accounting, and insurance—with their specialized training, educational backgrounds, and professional bias—typically rely more heavily upon the procedural category of financial problem solvers. Conversely, in the investment milieu in which I grew up, securities brokers and investment advisors alike typically lean heavily toward investment solutions. No wonder so many individuals are dissatisfied with the planning experiences they have had with financial advisors who traffic without objectivity in one side or the other of the Problem Solvers Table. Only when the expertise of all of these disciplines are combined are your clients most apt to reach their financial destiny via the combination of both procedural *and* investment vehicles.

Throughout this chapter, we have repeatedly demonstrated how every possible financial question has both procedural tools and/or investment strategies as potential answers. In so doing, it was often necessary to mention perhaps new and relatively complex planning strategies in somewhat abbreviated fashion.

Now, in the next two chapters, we will pursue in much greater detail this provocative, innovative, and money-making world of the two major categories of financial problem solvers. You will learn all about the procedural tools in Chapter 10, then Chapter 11 will guide you to the most attractive tax-advantaged investment strategies.

10

Financial Planning Procedures for Building and Managing Wealth

Before Chapter 11 discusses the enticing world of tax-benefited *investment strategies*, this chapter will serve as a very practical guide to all of the intriguing *procedures* for positioning assets and directing discretionary cash flow. For your convenience, Table 10–1 lists again of page 170 the major categories of procedural tools and investment problem solvers. Each procedure on the left side of the table will now be discussed in detail.

Your clients can build wealth with qualified plans—whether they retire or not

Tax-deductible individual and/or corporate retirement plans offer everyone who has any earned income unique opportunities for wealth building. Qualified plans are, in fact, perfect tax shelters.

One type of plan or another is available for anyone who:

1. has some earned income, and

TABLE 10–1
Financial Problem Solvers Table

Procedural Tools	Investment Strategies
	Indirect Investment Strategies:
Qualified Retirement Plans:	Cash Reserves:
Individual Retirement Accounts	Checking Accounts
Keogh Plans	Money Market Funds
Corporate Plans	Deferred Annuities
	Fixed
	Variable
	US Government Savings Bonds
Wills:	Debt Securities:
Simple	Municipal Bonds
Marital Deduction Will	Corporate Bonds
with Residuary Trust	
Trusts:	Equity Securities:
Revocable	Common Stocks and Mutual Funds
Living Trust	Tax-Managed Trusts
Irrevocable	
Insurance Trust	
Charitable Remainder Trust	*Direct Investment Strategies:*
Short-Term Reversionary Trust	
Generation Skipping Trust	Collectables and Precious Metals:
Interest-Free Loans	
	Tax-Incentive Investments:
Gifting Strategies:	Real Estate
Intrafamily	Existing Properties
Intrafamily Annuity	To-Be-Built Properties
Charitable	Wrap-Around Mortgages
Charitable Remainder Trust	
	Energy
Ownership Structures:	Gas/Oil Income Properties
Custodianship	Gas/Oil Drilling
Joint Ownership	Royalty Interests
Corporate Recapitalization	Equipment Financings
The Installment Sale	Communications
	Cable Television Systems
Insurance	
Life	
Disability	
Health	
Property and Casualty	
Liability	

2. wants to build assets and income for the future in tax-assisted fashion.

This fact alone suggests that this major procedural tool for building
a financial pyramid be placed at the top of any list of financial problem
solvers.

HOW THE TAX BENEFITS WORK

If the last dollar of earned income is eroded by, say, a 50% marginal tax bracket, only 50¢ remains to produce an assumed 10% taxable yield of 5¢ per year. That 5¢ of taxable income is then taxed at a 50% rate, leaving only 2.5¢. In summary, one year after that $1 of income was earned, the net result is an increase in net worth of 52.5¢.

On the other hand, assume the $1 of earnings is not currently made available. Instead, let's say that your client or the client's employer places the dollar in the appropriate qualified retirement plan. The dollar will have accumulated to $1.10, again assuming a tax-sheltered rate of return of 10%. Just one year later, he would have exactly twice as much principal potentially available and four times as much in earnings. If you then compound this double-barreled benefit of being able to invest pretax income and tax shelter the earnings for several years, the results are amazing.

From the standpoint of a risk-to-reward ratio, what has just been described is probably the most powerful, predictable wealth builder allowed by the law. Even so, that's not the total picture. When the proceeds of the plan are distributed upon eligibility, they are apt to be collected at reduced tax rates. The proceeds of any qualified plan can be received in tax-advantaged style either through special accounting methods or through legal deductions created via the tax incentive investment strategies discussed in the next chapter. Even the client who is taxed at ordinary income tax rates upon withdrawal will often be in a lower tax bracket than during the highest earning years—especially now that brackets are expected to be indexed to inflation after 1984.

Furthermore, the first $100,000 of value of qualified retirement plans are not included in the gross taxable estate if they are left to a beneficiary other than the estate *and* if the proceeds are not left to the beneficiary in lump sum. These proceeds can be left in lump sum and excluded from the taxable estate if the beneficiary does not elect special income tax treatment, such as ten-year forward averaging or capital gains.

The suitable type (or types of) qualified retirement plans depends on the employer and the nature of the client's work. Fortunately, the options are many and varied.

HOW IRAs WORK

Everyone who has earned income—whether covered by any other existing retirement plan or plans or not—can establish an individual retirement account in literally less than fifteen minutes. An IRA offers an easy and efficient way to create a retirement fund by allowing your client to put up to $2,000 or 100% of earned income, if less, in such a plan per year. In total, $2,250 is allowed if the spouse doesn't have earned income, and the person puts no more than $2,000 in the IRA and the rest in the spousal IRA. An employed spouse can also invest up to $2,000 in an IRA. The amount invested in an IRA can then be deducted from taxable income. The earnings in the account accumulate, tax-sheltered, until they are withdrawn.

Contributions can be made up to age 70½. Withdrawals to supplement income, however, cannot be made without penalty—except in the case of death or permanent disability—until age 59½ or later. Withdrawals from IRAs, unlike options available with many other types of plans, must be taxed at ordinary income tax rates. In any case, the benefits of simply deferring income are plenty worthwhile. This is especially so if one's retirement years are expected to provide lower tax brackets.

How the Money in an IRA Can Be Invested. From an investment viewpoint, IRAs are generally set up in three ways. First, some company employers allow employees to contribute, through payroll deduction plans, to a *group IRA* that is either a part of or separate from the company's regular retirement plan. Investments are then handled just like the funds in the regular plan. Alternatively, the investments may be handled differently, such as offering participants various investment selections among mutual funds, annuities, thrift accounts, or individual securities of their choice.

Second, with a *self-directed IRA* with a trust company, a person makes his or her own investment decisions—savings accounts, bonds, stocks, Treasury bills, mutual funds, or certain limited partnerships. Only collectibles are not allowed by law.

Third, and usually most attractive from a standpoint of cost-to-benefit ratio, is a *product IRA*. At virtually little or no cost, such prepackaged IRAs are offered by many respected institutions, such as the major mutual fund groups, insurance companies, banks, and thrift institutions.

HOW KEOGH PLANS CAN PUT MORE TO WORK FOR THE SELF-EMPLOYED

Keogh plans, unlike IRAs, are available only for certain individuals. To create a Keogh plan, your clients must be self-employed or operate an unincorporated full- or part-time business and their earned income must be derived from personal service. Also unlike an IRA, the plan must be established by the employer. The client who runs the business alone is, of course, his or her own employer, and therefore may set up a Keogh plan.

The regular contribution limits in 1983 are 15% of self-employed earned income or $20,000, whichever is less. The dollar limit rises to

$25,000 in 1984 and $30,000 in 1985. If adjusted gross income does not exceed $15,000 and self-employed earned income is less than $5,000, your client may be eligible for a mini-Keogh. Under this arrangement a contribution and tax deduction of up to $750 or 100% of earned income, whichever is less, is allowed.

The tax consequences at retirement depend on whether distributions are received in installments or lump sum. Periodic distributions are taxed as ordinary income. Even while withdrawals are being made, the remaining assets continue to compound tax-sheltered. Installments may be received over any period of time, as long as they do not exceed the greater of (a) life expectancy or (b) the joint life expectancy of the participant and the spouse.

If, instead, the participant opts for a lump sum distribution, it gets a little more complicated, but it could be better from an income tax point of view. The portion of the distribution allocated to years of participation in the plan prior to January 1, 1974 receives long-term capital gain treatment. The balance is ordinary income but taxed by a special ten-year forward averaging method. Alternatively, one can elect to treat the entire lump sum as ordinary income and utilize the special ten-year averaging method.

Just as with IRAs, one can start receiving plan payments anytime after age 59½ or upon becoming permanently disabled, but in no case later than 70½.

HOW TO MAXIMIZE
RETIREMENT PLANNING WITH CORPORATE RETIREMENT PLANS

Chances are an employee won't have much of a choice among the corporate profit sharing or pension plans. Either clients are blessed with corporate employers who contribute to retirement funds in their behalf, or they aren't. Typically, corporate plans allow for larger contributions per individual than are permissable via the individual plans, such as IRA and Keogh. In fact, the chief motivation toward incorporation by the owner–employee of a business may be to take advantage of these more liberal benefits. Here is how the three principal kinds of corporate plans work.

A Defined Benefit Pension Plan. This type of plan allows the employer to contribute as much as is necessary to fund whatever it defines as the future annual pension at retirement—within limits. Current law limits the defined retirement benefit to a maximum of $136,425 in 1983. For existing plans, this annual benefit drops from $136,425 to $90,000 for plan years ending after December 31, 1983. For plans not in existence on August 19, 1982, the $90,000 applies immediately. A two-year freeze on the cost of living adjustments to the $90,000 limit is imposed by the Tax Equity and Fiscal Responsibility Act of 1982.

A Defined Contribution Pension Plan. This plan stipulates what amount will be contributed to the employee's retirement fund. The defined contribution is usually expressed as some percentage of compensation. The upper limit on what the employer could contribute to such a plan on the employee's behalf was $45,475 for 1982. This maximum annual contribution limit drops from $45,475 to $30,000 (subject to the two-year freeze) for plan years ending after December 31, 1983. The Tax Equity and Fiscal Responsibility Act of 1982 provided transitional rules to insure that a participant's previously accrued benefit is not reduced due to the law's reduced overall limits on contributions and benefits.

One can maximize the benefits of corporate retirement plans by using in combination a defined contribution and a defined benefit plan. When benefits are so maximized, the sum of the ratios of each plan's actual contribution to maximum allowable contribution must not exceed 1.25.

Profit Sharing Plans. These plans are the simplest and most flexible corporate plans by far. The company is, however, limited to contributions of no greater than 15% of compensation. Unlike corporate pension plans, the employer is not obligated to contribute to the plan if company profits are lower than a stipulated level. When one or both types of pension plans are provided in conjunction with profit sharing, the total contributions to the plans cannot exceed 25% of compensation unless minimum funding requirements are not met.

It should quickly become obvious that corporate plans can provide far greater benefits for business owners *and* employees. That's usually the single greatest advantage to incorporation. A perfect example is the typical professional corporation. Like a fine-tuned orchestra, a professional corporation can balance salaries, bonuses, expenses, and contributions to a combination of corporate qualified retirement plans so as to maximize wealth creation like no other stroke of a legal pen. It is sheer financial beauty—and easy to implement as long as the right advisors are involved.

The disadvantages of corporate plans mainly surround the legal requirements for including the eligible employees. Under the necessary close scrutiny, clients may well determine that the increased benefit to themselves is greatly diminished by the cost of funding such attractive benefits for their employees. Conversely, they may not be able to attract and keep worthwhile employees without attractive retirement benefits.

The tax consequences of distributions from corporate plans are exactly as they were previously described for Keogh plans. There are, however, important technical differences in vesting schedules and eligibility requirements that must be considered before moving ahead with a corporate plan.

THREE KEY DISADVANTAGES WITH QUALIFIED PLANS

In total, qualified retirement plans are ideal techniques for setting aside assets on a pretax and tax-sheltered basis. The tax incentives and potential economic benefits are so attractive that it is easy to overlook the negatives. The crux of the matter is that you must always balance the pyramid building that is accomplished inside and outside of qualified plans for the following main reasons:

First, the assets held in a qualified plan may not be available until one has been with the employer for a stipulated period of years. That is what the plan's *vesting schedule* is all about.

Second, one may find it necessary to supplement regular income prior to retirement. Qualified plan assets are not generally available—without penalty—for such use. It varies greatly from plan to plan and is something one must consider before putting all the wealth-accumulation eggs into one basket, however tax-benefitted it is.

Third, plan assets are not collaterable. Some of the most attractive investment opportunities seem to knock when the door with money behind it is the friendly banker's vault. That vault usually has a sign on it saying, "No Exit Without Collateral." And qualified plan assets don't qualify for that! On the other hand, many plans permit participants, or certain categories thereof, to borrow a certain percentage of the vested portion of their accounts. The Tax Equity and Fiscal Responsibility Act of 1982 places a limit on outstanding loans to plan participants at any one time under all qualified plans. Essentially, this provision limits loans to the lesser of $50,000 or one-half the vested interest, but in no case can that limit be less than $10,000.

How to maximize the ultimate distribution of your client's estate

While it is easy enough for clients to manage their estates while they are around, it is more difficult after they are gone—unless their estate plan does it for them. A properly drafted will, as the main estate planning document, is, therefore, the cornerstone of all estate planning programs. The purpose of a will is to have created, in advance, an initial financial plan for your client's dependents and/or heirs upon death. More specifically, it is the legal vehicle that transfers property to them in the way the client wants and that simultaneously minimizes estate settlement costs. With the will properly conceived and implemented, what your client wants to happen to his or her property will happen. Without it, much of the capital may be dissipated needlessly. Because of the many facets of a will, it, like the footings of the lifetime financial plan, must be reviewed at least every few years not by just *any* attorney, but by an attorney who is experienced in estate planning and who can assure that the provisions of the will conform to the laws of your client's state.

WHAT SHOULD A WILL ACCOMPLISH?

Wills must address several major issues. First, the will should assign certain legal responsibilities to an *executor* and, if trusts are involved, to *trustees* of the trusts that the will creates. The executor of the estate must assemble the assets and liabilities. The balance sheet in the most recent written financial plan is a great starting point. The executor must:

1. manage these assets and the resulting cash flow while the estate is being administered,

2. pay all estate settlement costs such as debts, expenses, and taxes, and

3. distribute what remains to the beneficaries as dictated by the will.

The trustee then receives property from the executor, as is legally spelled out by the will, and manages such property on behalf of the beneficiaries of the trust or trusts in question. After the executor has fulfilled all responsibilities, such as the payment of appropriate debts and expenses, and filed an estate tax return, distributions can begin in accordance with the deceased's instructions. It is often recommended to name a corporate trustee, such as a trust company or bank, either as executor and/or trustee or as Successor–Executor and/or Trustee, and to appoint an individual as co-executor and/or trustee. As a corporate entity, it is at least theoretically "forever" and, in the case of the inability or lack of desire to perform on the part of the will's designee, continuity would result.

The will should also provide that the executor begin immediate income payments to the family. Since the period of administering the estate necessarily includes the time taken by the IRS to process and finally review the estate tax returns, sometimes as much as two or three years, waiting for income to begin after assets are distributed could prove very burdensome. Distributions during administration should be accounted for the executor as though they had been distributed from the parts provided in the will.

Second, the will should then stipulate who is to receive *personal and household effects*. Any interest in a personal residence is most frequently given to the surviving spouse. If a spouse does not survive, it should go outright, or via a residual trust, to the children.

Third, any *life insurance* owned on the spouse's life should be gifted to the surviving children in order to implement the estate's original planning intentions.

Fourth, assuming that one is married, the will, as previously recommended in Chapter 7, should usually divide the remaining estate into two parts. Part I is the marital deduction amount, and Part II becomes the residual trust. We have already discussed the marital deduction in detail. The part that goes to the residual trust is designed to provide the spouse and children with benefits in such a way as to prevent the assets of this trust from being taxed again in the spouse's estate.

WHO NEEDS A WILL?

Everyone! Always remember that the state legislature has already written a will for your clients—if they don't take the time to have proper wills professionally prepared for themselves and for their spouses. *Everyone* therefore needs a will, however simple it needs to be.

If wills are dated prior to September 12, 1981, they should be reviewed immediately if this has not already been accomplished. If such a will provides for the "maximum marital deduction," it will be interpreted as being limited to the old pre-ERTA 1981 50% or $250,000 maximum rule unless state law contains provisions parallel to ERTA's. Many wills drafted prior to 1982 also contain provisions for the orphan's deduction and for an orphan's deduction trust. ERTA 1981 eliminated this provision totally.

How to use trusts to provide tax-benefited wealth management

In general, most planners make trusts unnecessarily complicated. A trust is simply a legal entity—just as is an individual, a corporation, or a legal partnership—into whose name assets can be held for the purposes of convenience, control, management, or tax benefit.

WHEN SHOULD REVOCABLE TRUSTS BE USED TO CONTAIN ASSETS?

A revocable trust is one that can be discontinued or changed by the grantor at any time. This usually causes the assets to revert to the name of the grantor of the trust.

Most revocable trusts are established simply to contain assets more *conveniently.* For instance, a *living trust* (created during life) could be set up to contain some or all of your client's investment assets under terms that will provide for him or her in life and for the heirs thereafter. The income or estate tax results of such an arrangement would be no different from outright ownership. The will can direct that other assets not prepositioned in the living trust would be added to such a trust upon death. In such a way, the client could make arrangements for another trustee, such as a bank trust department, to take over the management of the trust in the client's absence. This could relieve surviving family members of making some of the hard investment decisions that they may be incapable of handling. Also, assets properly held in a living revocable trust at the time of death avoid probate costs, delays, and publicity.

If your client (a) has assets that are subject to intensive management, (b) has not already selected professional asset managers, and (c) is seriously concerned about their fate in the event of his or her untimely demise, then a *revocable* living trust may be the answer.

HOW TO USE AN IRREVOCABLE
INSURANCE TRUST TO SAVE ESTATE TAXES

The *insurance trust* discussed in Chapter 7 is a perfect example of a trust entity that must be made permanent and irrevocable in order to provide the benefits desired. Under this arrangement, your client transfers the ownership rights to insurance policies, particularly those with little or no present value, to an irrevocable insurance trust. Upon death, the proceeds flow estate-tax-free and income-tax-free to the trust. This avoids unified transfer tax erosion upon both the client's death and the spouse's subsequent passing. The principal and income produced by it will serve in its entirety to produce benefits for the named beneficiaries.

If your client and spouse own insurance on themselves or on each other, *and* if estate taxes would be due upon the death of either or both, the client should definitely consider having an insurance trust own the policies. Remember, however, that it is an *irrevocable* gift!

WHEN TO USE A SHORT-TERM TRUST
TO SHIFT INCOME TO LOWER BRACKETS

A *short term reversionary trust* (or Clifford Trust) is another popular example of the use of an *irrevocable* trust. In this example, one transfers assets that produce taxable income to such a trust, which stipulates that the income flows to and is taxed either to the trust itself or to the named income beneficiary or beneficiaries at hopefully lower tax brackets. This arrangement has the benefit of either increasing the after-tax cash flow to the family unit or slowing the accumulation of income in a larger estate or both. The negatives are twofold. The trust must last for at least ten years and one day before the assets can revert to the grantor. Also, since about 44% of the fair market value of the assets so positioned is considered a gift, there are important additional estate planning considerations.

Extreme care must be taken to ensure that the income tax savings are greater than the potential increase in estate taxes. Remember that the gifted income interest over and above the gift exclusion will always be included in the grantor's estate. In many instances, some application of the "interest-free demand loan" will better solve the problem of transferring income.

In some cases, on the other hand, the Clifford trust can be a most useful tool. When clients own highly appreciated assets producing meaningful taxable income that should be shifted to a child's lower bracket, *and* they do not want to divest themselves of the asset, this trust is ideal.

HOW TO INCREASE TODAY'S INCOME AND DECREASE TOMORROW'S ESTATE TAXES WITH A CHARITABLE REMAINDER TRUST

"Asset-rich and income-poor" is how many well-to-do clients describe themselves to planners. The typical large shareholder of yesterday's perfect growth company faces too low a dividend rate, particularly after tax, and feels locked in due to too high a potential long-term gain. If these clients also have a real desire to leave some or all of these highly appreciated holdings to charity, the charitable remainder trust was designed with them in mind.

The charitable remainder trust is an *irrevocable* trust created to hold assets that your clients desire to pass to an established charity upon death or upon the death of any other designated income beneficiary. As long as they or any other designated income beneficiaries live, a specified amount of annual income from the trust property is reserved for the beneficiary's use. In addition to ultimately benefiting their favorite charity or charities, as well as keeping the income produced by the gifted assets for life, there can be other attractions.

HOW TO USE THE CHARITABLE REMAINDER TRUST TO CREATE ADDED TAX DEDUCTIONS

If your client leaves assets to charity via a will, they pass *estate-tax-free*. The clients who set them aside now, via a charitable remainder trust, also gets an *income tax* deduction that would otherwise be lost. More specifically, the deduction is equal to the contribution of the "remainder interest." The exact amount of the tax deduction depends on the current fair market value of the assets involved, the amount of income that the income beneficiary is to receive, *and* which of the *two* types of trusts—annuity or unitrust—is used.

Annuity Trust. This type of trust provides for a set, fixed amount to be paid to the income beneficiary. It must be at least 5% of the fair market value of the property donated, and it must be paid by the trustee at least annually. Assume that, at age 64, just prior to retirement, your client gifts appreciated securities worth $100,000 to a charitable remainder annuity trust. The trust stipulates that he, a male, is to receive $6,000 a year. Table 10–2, which can be found under the estate and gift tax regulations of the Internal Revenue Code, provides that the annuity factor for a male age 64 is 8.2642. This factor must be multiplied by the amount of the annual income in order to find the life interest: 8.2642 times $6,000 equals $49,585. The present value, and therefore the current charitable deduction, equals the original market value of the gift, $100,000, less the life interest, $49,585, or $50,415. Recall that, if this figure exceeds 30% of the adjusted gross income for the year in question, the overage can be carried forward for up to five years.

Unitrust. If instead of choosing a fixed $6,000 of annual income, your client prefers to have his or her income fluctuate annually with the value of the trust assets, a 6% unitrust might be set up. As such, the assets would be valued by the trustee at the end of each year, and the income payment for the next year is determined by multiplying 6% times that valuation. Table 10–3, the charitable remainder trust table, which can be found in the Treasury regulations under the Internal Revenue Code, shows the present value of the remainder interest in a charitable remainder unitrust with a 6% payout for a male age 64 to be .48626. This factor is then multiplied by the original value of the trust's assets in order to give the value of the charitable remainder, that is, the amount of the tax deduction. In this example, the deduction would be .48626 times $100,000 or $48,626. Note that if your client wanted a higher percentage of income, the tax deduction would go down. Also, if the spouse is included as an income beneficiary, the deduction would also decline. In any case, the deduction is an added benefit that the client would not have gotten had he or she simply designated the assets to pass on to the charity upon death via a will.

HOW TO FORCE THE
CHARITABLE REMAINDER TRUST TO UP YOUR CLIENT'S INCOME

First, highly appreciated assets may be donated to the trust and sold by the trustee. The entire proceeds—with no erosion due to capital gains taxes—is then reinvested for maximum income production. Payments of trust income are first ordinary income to the extent the trust creates either ordinary income for the year in question or undistributed ordinary income for previous years. Next, the payments are capital gains to the extent to which the trust has undistributed capital gains for the current or prior years, with short-term gains preceding long-term gains. The payments are then other income and finally tax-free return of the principal. The Internal Revenue Service prohibits the receipt of tax-free income from municipal bonds in a charitable remainder trust unless there was absolutely no knowledge or discussion of the contemplation of their use between the donor and trustee. This trust, like any qualified retirement trust, is tax-free provided it does not realize unrelated business income of over $1,000 per year.

The entire cash flow to the income beneficiary may be considered capital gains until such time as the paper gain taken by the trust is exceeded by cumulative income payments. The proceeds must be reinvested, however, in ways that produce no income that is normally considered taxable income to individuals (such as real estate income sheltered by depreciation; oil income sheltered by depletion and by other deductible business expenses; or cash flow from a withdrawal plan from a tax-managed open-end investment company or from any mutual fund that does not produce much if any income other than capital gains). Thereafter, the cash flow would either be tax-free or capital gains to the extent the trust created additional capital gains. You can now see how the CRT can be used to substantially increase the spendable income produced by what might otherwise be viewed as a frozen or locked-in asset.

PITFALLS TO WATCH FOR

The trust must be irrevocable. The charitable beneficiary can, however, be changed if the donor's inclinations change as life goes on. Principal cannot be invaded except to satisfy the income stipulations of either the annuity (fixed income) trust or the unitrust (variable income). Payment of the entire remainder interest must be made to or for the use of the charity upon the death of the income beneficiary or beneficiaries. All income beneficiaries named must be living upon creation of the trust. For example, a yet unborn child or grandchild cannot be included. Care should also be taken to ensure that charitable trusts created in one's will meet all legal requirements.

KEEPING FAMILY WEALTH INTACT
VIA THE GENERATION SKIPPING TRUST

Chapter 8 has already shed some light on an important use of the generation skipping trust. This type of trust makes it possible to bypass estate taxes on a considerable amount of money in one subsequent generation. Suppose your client creates such a trust by gifting up to $250,000 to it over a period of several years in a way that avoids gift taxes as well as

TABLE 10–2
For Use with Annuity Trusts

Male Age	Annuity	Life Estate	Remainder
34	13.8758	.83255	.16745
40	13.1538	.78923	.21077
45	12.3013	.73808	.26192
50	11.3329	.67997	.32003
51	11.1308	.66785	.32215
52	10.9267	.65560	.34440
53	10.7200	.64320	.35680
54	10.5100	.63060	.36940
55	10.2960	.61776	.38224
56	10.0777	.60466	.39534
57	9.8552	.59131	.40869
58	9.6297	.57778	.42222
59	9.4028	.56417	.43583
60	9.1753	.55052	.44948
61	8.9478	.53687	.46313
62	8.7202	.52321	.47679
63	8.4924	.50954	.49046
64	8.2642	.49585	.50415
65	8.0353	.48212	.51788
66	7.8060	.46836	.53164
67	7.5763	.45458	.54542
68	7.3462	.44077	.55923
69	7.1149	.42689	.57311
70	6.8823	.41294	.58706
71	6.6481	.39889	.60111
72	6.4123	.38474	.61526
73	6.1752	.37051	.62949
74	5.9373	.35624	.64376
75	5.6990	.34194	.65806
76	5.4602	.32761	.67239
77	5.2211	.31327	.68673
78	4.9825	.29895	.70105
79	4.7469	.28481	.71519
80	4.5164	.27098	.72902
85	3.5117	.21070	.78930
90	2.6536	.15922	.84078

*Estate and Gift Tax Regulation Section 20.2031–10.

TABLE 10–3
*For Use with Unitrusts**

Male Age	5%	6%	7%	8%	9%
34	.20056	.15309	.11900	.09419	.07587
40	.24666	.19491	.15638	.12735	.10522
45	.29993	.24481	.20235	.16931	.14334
50	.35929	.30206	.25654	.22003	.19050
51	.37156	.31406	.26804	.23092	.20073
52	.38392	.32620	.27973	.24202	.21119
53	.39639	.33851	.29162	.25336	.22192
54	.40903	.35104	.30379	.26502	.23298
55	.42186	.36383	.31627	.27703	.24444
56	.43486	.37690	.32910	.28944	.25632
57	.44813	.39025	.34226	.30223	.26864
58	.46150	.40380	.35569	.31534	.28131
59	.47492	.41746	.36928	.32867	.29424
60	.48833	.43117	.38298	.34214	.30736
61	.50170	.44489	.39675	.35574	.32064
62	.51505	.45865	.41059	.36945	.33407
63	.52837	.47243	.42452	.38330	.34768
64	.54168	.48626	.43855	.39730	.36149
65	.55499	.50015	.45269	.41146	.37550
66	.56828	.51408	.46693	.42577	.38971
67	.58156	.52806	.48128	.45025	.40413
68	.59483	.54208	.49573	.45488	.41876
69	.60813	.55619	.51933	.46972	.43365
70	.62146	.57041	.52511	.48480	.44884
71	.63485	.58474	.54007	.50014	.46435
72	.64828	.59920	.55522	.51573	.48019
73	.66175	.61375	.57055	.53158	.49634
74	.67522	.62839	.58603	.54764	.51279
75	.68867	.64306	.60162	.56390	.52949
76	.70211	.65779	.61734	.58035	.54648
77	.71553	.67256	.63317	.59701	.56375
78	.72888	.68732	.64907	.61379	.58122
79	.74202	.70192	.66485	.63054	.59873
80	.75484	.71622	.68038	.64707	.61607
85	.81043	.77873	.74877	.72044	.69361
90	.85741	.83241	.80844	.78544	.76337

*Treasury Regulation—Section 1.664–4

the use of the unified credit. The client stipulates that the principal is to go to the grandchildren upon the daughter's death. The client could not avoid potential estate taxation in his or her estate had the gifts to the trust been taxable gifts. But in this example, since they were not taxable gifts, taxation upon death is completely avoided. Then, when the daughter dies, the assets contained in the trust, up to $250,000, will not be included in the daughter's estate since she was only an income beneficiary. The principal would, in fact, not be taxed in an estate until the grandchildren die.

Key Points with Generation Skipping Trusts. Uncle Sam is only so generous, and so there are limits to what can be done. Current law allows your client to pass up to $250,000 tax-free through the estate of each of the children to their children (the client's grandchildren) through generation skipping trusts.

Another key point is that the client must limit the usefulness of the trust to the child to its income to avoid the taxation of its principal in the child's estate.

Generation skipping trusts can be created either while living or via the will.

How to cut the cost of college education in half with the interest-free demand loan

If one of the technical tools for solving lifetime and/or estate planning problems listed in the Problem Solver's Table is an infant, this is it. Being the newest on your list, it is also probably the one that is the least known. Yet, it is by far the most easily understood, and, if continually upheld by our courts and the law, one of the most beneficial.

The essence of the interest-free loan is the legal ability, under current court decisions, to lend cash to a family member interest-free under a demand note arrangement. The theory is that anyone has the right to lend anyone the use of property without the legal requirement that interest be charged or that the uncharged interest be considered a gift. As you can already imagine, the IRS disagrees and hopes to intimidate us into inaction by shaking its head sideways. The courts have ruled otherwise, fortunately, and you should take their cue.

EXAMPLE: CUT THE COST OF AN EXPENSE SUCH AS COLLEGE TUITION

Father and Mother have $50,000 of long-term cash reserves currently producing taxable interest at 8% for reasons of temperament or at a bank whose deposits they feel a need to support for one reason or another. They are simultaneously providing a child with $4,000 of college expenses. Instead of paying for that expense with $7,692 or more of pretax earnings because they are in the 48% marginal tax bracket, they lend the cash to the child who is paying little or no taxes. The $4,000 of interest earned by investing the $50,000 at 8% now takes care of the assumed expense, saving Father and Mother $1,920 in income taxes on that interest without incurring a dime of risk. If an emergency requires the use of the $50,000 of cash, it reverts to them upon demand. In any case, the child's education now costs them the $4,000 of pretax interest (after-tax for the child) instead of the $7,692 of pretax earnings—a net savings of $3,692 pretax or the $1,920 after-tax already mentioned. You can readily see that the interest-free demand loan is a near perfect way to gift interest income pretax and gift tax free.

What to Watch Out for with Interest-Free Demand Loans. The interest-free loan seems almost too good to be true. It can obviously create increased after-tax wealth for a family unit by increasing after-tax discretionary income. It can also serve to remove income accumulations from the estate that are in excess of anticipated needs without increased gift taxes or the premature and unnecessary use of the unified transfer tax credit.

Because the interest-free loan can solve so many problems all at one time, every precaution must be exercised to use it correctly. Care must clearly be taken that legal counsel both agrees with and drafts the interest-free loan in a manner that complies with current law and court guidelines. You must also make certain that it has been loaned to someone whose credit is beyond reproach—like a dependent and dependable relative. One must be able to prove that the earnings on the money loaned were not used to cover expenses for which the client is legally obligated—like private preparatory school or college tuition in certain states. Otherwise, the IRS could rightfully insist that the earnings are taxable income to the lender. That would defeat the whole purpose.

How to use gifting strategies to preserve wealth

The income tax and estate tax ramifications of gifting depends a lot on how much, when, and to whom the gifts are made. To clarify your appreciation of these variables, gifting will be divided into first intrafamily and then charitable gifting strategies.

HOW TO REDUCE INCOME
AND ESTATE TAXES WITH GIFTS TO INDIVIDUALS

Insofar as lifetime gifting is concerned, we have already discussed that a present interest gift worth up to $10,000 may be made each year to as many individuals, family or not, as is desirable. It is not necessary even to look at the unified rate schedule or to report the gift on a gift tax return. The value of gifts made within this $10,000 annual exclusion allowance are removed permanently from the estate. Through a gift-splitting provision of the law, if the spouse consents to a gift, a maximum $20,000 per donee exclusion is available. The use of this $20,000 gift-splitting exclusion, however, requires the filing of a gift tax return.

Gifts above these exclusion allowances are subject to the unified rate schedule. Remember that the schedule produces what is called a tentative tax. That is because each individual has what we have already referred to as a unified credit. The 1983 credit of $79,300 is the equivalent of an exemption of $275,000 of gifts or net taxable estate. If your client has made taxable gifts during 1983 (gifts above the $10,000 or $20,000 exclusion allowances) of exactly $275,000, he or she does not have to pay the first $79,300 of tentative gift taxes due to the availability of the unified credit of $79,300. However, upon death later in 1983, the $275,000 of taxable gifts would have to be included in the net taxable estate. The tentative estate tax would then be computed via the unified rate schedule, the unified credit of $79,300 would be applied, and the net federal estate tax results.

Several clear conclusions regarding the reduction of gift and estate taxes can be drawn at this point. For tax liability considerations only, making annual gifts within the $10,000 and $20,000 exclusion allowances out of net taxable estates of $275,000 (1983) or more is definitely advisable. Where estates are considerably larger, making even larger gifts could also be advantageous after careful considerations of their total tax implications. For instance, while making appropriate intrafamily taxable gifts may effectively result in first using up the unified credit and then possibly the payment of some unified transfer taxes now, this disadvantage may be more than offset due to:

1. The reduction of income taxes on the taxable income produced by assets that are gifted to lower-income bracketed individuals, and

2. the elimination of one generation of estate taxes on the accumulated income produced by the asset and/or the appreciation of the asset's value that occurs between the time of the gift and the estate of the donor's death.

DISADVANTAGE OF LIFETIME GIFTING TO INDIVIDUALS

There are, however, several major reasons why lifetime gifting, tax-free or taxable, may prove disadvantageous to the donor. As pointed out in Chapter 1, over-gifting to family or charity may deplete the financial pyramid of the ability to provide the increasing income necessitated by the current rate of inflation. From a different view, attaching too much financial power to too young or immature an heir may serve to reduce or eliminate the incentive that is so central to economic success in a free enterprise system. (Enough has already been done to weaken the work ethic that originally made our nation so economically vibrant.) Finally, gifting appreciated assets, while frequently quite advantageous when received and subsequently sold by lower-bracketed donees or charities, may rob heirs of the valuable step-up in basis.

HOW TO GET GREATER INCOME
FROM THE ESTATE WITH A PRIVATE ANNUITY

One major alternative to substantial gifting of appreciated assets to family members is often overlooked when planning for the very wealthy. The private intrafamily annuity is probably one of the most underused financial planning tools ever legislated. Under annuity laws, an individual (annuitant) can exchange cash for lifetime income with an insurance company (obligor) under an arrangement called an immediate annuity. In exchange for a lump sum of cash, the insurance company agrees to pay a fixed annual cash flow to the annuitant for as long as he or she lives. The amount of the annual payment is determined by the amount of cash exchanged, the life expectancy of the annuitant, and an interest factor. The annuitant receiving the annual cash flow pays income taxes on the portion of the cash flow that is considered income and does not pay taxes on the portion that is considered return of principal. This is also commonly referred to as a *commercial* annuity.

Similarly, a *private* annuity is an arrangement between two individuals where one (the annuitant) exchanges an appreciated asset for the other's (obligor's) agreement to pay a specified sum of cash, usually in annual payments, to the annuitant for life. If there is more than one annuitant, as in the case of a father exchanging an asset with a son or daughter, then payments must be made to *both* parents and then continuing to the surviving parent after the first dies.

WHEN TO USE A PRIVATE ANNUITY

Several aspects of the private intrafamily annuity make it equal or preferable to a commercial annuity:

1. The property exchanged may be appreciated assets. The annuity payments are then considered a mixture of return of principal, capital gain, and income. As such, the taxable part of the capital gain is spread over the annuitant's life expectancy rather than in the year in which the property might have otherwise been sold to create cash for a commercial annuity. More importantly, a much larger amount of capital will be at work for the entire family unit over a longer span of time than would have otherwise been the case.

2. Estate taxes are reduced to the extent to which the exchanged asset is in excess of any accumulated cash payments that are not spent and therefore included in the estate of the annuitant.

The extent of these accumulated payments at the time of the death of the annuitant has another tax ramification. Here is how that works. Sometimes, the obligor has to record a paper gain by repositioning the appreciated exchanged asset into an investment that provides greater *cash flow at least equal to the required* annuity payments. If the annuitant lives until such time as the annuity payments equal the unadjusted basis (payments actually made plus present worth of future payments) that existed at the time of the sale, no gain will have to be reported by the obligor at the time of the annuitant's death. Should the annuitant's death occur prior to the cumulative payments equaling the unadjusted basis, the difference would have to be reported as a gain at the time of the last annuitant's death. If the cumulative payments are greater, the obligor would report a loss. With a *commercial* immediate annuity, estate taxes are also avoided. But in that case, the family unit keeps none of the annuity's residual value. Now back to the benefits of the private annuity.

3. Gift taxes are avoided. No gift has been consummated if the present value of annuity payments are equal to the fair value of the appreciated asset that is exchanged. Again, versus the commercial annuity, family wealth is kept whole.

4. Finally, and perhaps most importantly, the annuitant's income can be increased by exchanging an appreciated, low-income-producing asset for a higher stream of tax-benefited cash flow. Should the father and/or mother annuitant not need the cash flow, $10,000 or $20,000 of it can be gifted back to the obligor under the gift tax exclusion allowance.

A Red Flag with the Private Annuity. Extreme care must be exercised in using the private annuity arrangement with individuals other than the closest family members. The promise to pay is totally unsecured and therefore only as good as the full faith and credit of the obligor. Like the interest-free loan, it would be well not to venture beyond the immediate family with the private annuity and then only if they are currently or eventually expecting something worth more than the obligation of the annuity from the estate.

EXAMPLE: USING A PRIVATE ANNUITY PROPERLY AND PROFITABLY

David Brandy is 63, and his spouse is 60. His daughter is 35 and is to inherit his estate currently valued at $1,000,000. Because you know that the unified transfer taxes and state inheritance taxes will take a substantial bite out of their estate, you would prefer to recommend the removal of $100,000 of assets from the estate now, but they cannot afford to give up the $6,000 of pretax and $3,060 of after-tax income they produce in their 50% marginal bracket. You know, too, that if they liquidate a highly appreciated $100,000 holding with a cost basis of $20,000, a capital gains tax erosion will reduce both assets available to produce income and assets that can be left to their daughter with a stepped-up basis.

The solution may be to execute a private annuity contract with the daughter. This contract would provide that they transfer the $100,000 holding to their daughter. In return, she promises to pay $8,581.11 a year to him and his spouse, and then to whomever survives the other. The $8,581.11 is determined by:

1. The fair market value of the property involved, and
2. The life expectancy of the annuitants.

In fact, in this specific case, the payout rate is determined by dividing $100,000 by 11.6535, the annuity factor for a male 63 and female 60 as published in federal gift and estate tax tables.

After the transfer is made, if the asset is not suitable to the daughter's income tax bracket, cash flow situation, or temperament, she can sell the asset and reinvest the proceeds appropriately so as to achieve her multiple objectives. (see the section on tax-incentive investment types in Chapter 11.)

The tax consequences to the daughter would be dictated only by the tax ramifications of the income produced by the asset she holds. The Brandys receive $8,581.11 annually. Of that, $796.81 ($20,000 of cost basis divided by 25.1 years of combined life expectancies) is considered tax-free. Of the balance, $3,187.25 is considered capital gain ($80,000 of paper gain ÷ 25.1), and the remainder $4,597.05 ($8,581.11 - $796.81 - $3,187.25) is ordinary income.

The result is that, even in as high as a 50% marginal tax bracket, the spendable cash flow would increase 84% from the current $3,060 to $5,645 as follows:

Pretax Payment		After-Tax Income
$ 796.81	Tax-Free Income	$ 796,81
3,187.25	Long-Term Capital Gain	2,549.80
4,597.05	Ordinary Income	2,298.53
$8,581.11		$5,645.14

Had David Brandy instead liquidated the $100,000, the tax liability would have been at least $16,000, leaving $84,000 for reinvestment at an after-tax rate of at least 7% in order to equal the $5,880 of after-tax income. That may easily be achieved but not while simultaneously (1) keeping it whole and (2) removing the asset plus its appreciation potential from the net taxable estate. Of course, it may be that he really does not need the income and can gift up to $10,000 per year back to the daughter. In that case, $100,000 and its future appreciation and income may have permanently exited the $1,000,000 estate *totally void of gift and estate taxes.*

WHEN AND HOW MUCH TO GIFT TO CHARITY

Since charity usually begins at home, our gifting discussions have thus far principally centered on intrafamily gifting. *The entire realm of charitable gifting, however, provides myriad opportunities for fulfilling personal, religious, and tax planning objectives.*

The tax law allows one to gift cash and deduct against income an amount equal to the gift or 50% of the adjusted gross income, whichever is lower. If the gift is an appreciated asset, the restriction as to deductibility is 30% of adjusted gross income. If the gift is to a private foundation, the deduction is limited to 20%. Deductions resulting from gifts to other than private foundations in excess of these limitations may be carried forward for five years.

The key in making charitable gifting decisions is that the motivation must be a desire to have the charity own and use the gift instead of the donor. The gain due to tax savings that results from the outright gift of an asset obviously never equals the asset loss, not to speak of the future stream of income that the asset may be producing. Conversely, very wealthy individuals, at times, can transfer wealth to a worthy charity without losing very much at all.

TWO SPECIAL OPPORTUNITIES FOR CHARITABLE GIFTING

The first such opportunity is created in advance of the buy-out of or the economically dictated sale of a highly appreciated asset with close to a zero basis.

EXAMPLE

> Jean Slater owns $1,000,000 of XYZ Corporation, which is being sold. Her cost basis is, for all practical purposes, zero. She has a charity that she would like to help now if it would not subtract substantially from her ability to provide for her own family's needs. If she gifts $10,000 of the holding in advance of its sale, and, if the deductions go against income in the 50% marginal tax bracket, she will, of course, be out of the $10,000 asset less the capital gains tax liability of $2,000 ($10,000 × 40% × 50%) that she would have otherwise incurred. Her net *outflow* would so far be $8,000 *less* any state income taxes. However, the donation of the $10,000 of property creates a $10,000 deduction, which reduces her income tax liability by $5,000 *plus* any state tax savings. She is therefore out of pocket no more than $3,000 per $10,000. On the other hand, the charity has $10,000 that it otherwise would not have had, and it cost Jean Slater only $3,000 to gift it. The only red flag that must again be raised here for normally high-bracketed taxpayers is the important limitation on all deductions imposed by the alternative minimum tax.

The second great opportunity for double-edged charitable gifting advantages exists when your client simultaneously owns an appreciated asset, can use a current tax deduction and more after-tax income, would like to benefit a charity in the future, and would like to reduce the future estate tax liability. The answer may be the charitable remainder trust, already discussed.

FUNDAMENTAL PRINCIPLES TO GUIDE YOUR CLIENT'S GIFTING PROGRAM

Sharing the economic fruits of one's life may, in fact, develop into one of life's great pleasures. Even when the preservation of wealth for heirs, or its current or future distribution to family or charities, is high in terms of one's overall objectives, safeguards must be taken. Gifting programs can create more problems than they solve if the prime purpose for gifting is ill conceived.

Gifting to anyone before being confident of providing for one's own financial well-being is a potentially grave error. Gifting to minors without safeguards for the proper and controlled use of the capital has high odds for negative overall results. Conversely, carefully conceived intrafamily gifting can multiply the benefits of the well employed use of expertise and capital.

Once your client's intrafamily gifting objectives have either begun or been achieved, consequential charitable gifting programs can be employed to fulfill personal, religious or pure financial needs. Innovative gifting strategies can leverage the usefulness of sharing wealth with worthy charities.

There are two keys to successful gifting:

1. be certain that your client is primarily motivated by the total economic impact of the contemplated action, and

2. the current, continuing, and ultimate income and unified transfer tax impact must be understood before acting.

Only then is the client apt to select the gifting strategy to best achieve the multiple possible goals of distributing wealth via lifetime gifting.

How ownership structures can be used to enhance family wealth

What is owned by which entity in a family unit can very positively enhance overall family wealth. It plays a crucial role in all phases of the accumulation, preservation, and distribution of wealth. The perfect example of this involves the proper ownership of life insurance policies, already discussed in this chapter and in the chapter on risk management. Now we will look at a few other procedural tools that can be used to preserve wealth by altering ownership structure.

USING GIFTS TO MINORS TO LOWER INCOME AND ESTATE TAXES

The use of the state's Uniform Gift to Minors Act is probably one of the most popular tactics for shifting income to lower brackets and for reducing estate taxes. It is most often employed to set up a college education fund for a minor dependent. Once the gift is made within the exclusion allowance, it is usually out of the donor's estate. It also now produces more after-tax results due to the lower bracket of the donee. Those are the two great benefits.

After these state laws were originally passed years ago, many states have declared that minors become majors at age 18. The point of contention here is that such family gifting may place control of these assets directly into the hands of an 18-year-old in certain states, just as the child makes a decision to pursue lesser objectives than the capital was intended to fund. Even if a custodian format is preferred over a more controlled trust arrangement, care must be taken that the donor and custodian are different individuals. Otherwise, the assets, unused, will be taxed in the estate of the donor upon death. In the final analysis, my advice would be to forsake use of "gift to minors" where substantial gifts are involved and instead, use a trust as the receptacle for such gifts.

HOW TO PUT A LID ON RISING ESTATE TAXES

Freezing or capping the value of a substantial estate is frequently listed as a top objective among the wealthy. In addition to the use of intrafamily and charitable gifting programs, of private annuities, and of interest-free loans to reduce future estate tax erosion, incorporation or recapitalization of part or all of an estate can prove quite useful.

EXAMPLE

Glen Jeffares' growth-oriented, $1,000,000 equity portfolio is paying a 3% dividend rate or $30,000. His marginal tax bracket is 50%, and his tentative tax base will be in excess of $5,000,000 when he dies. (By the way, if 10% inflation were to be fairly permanent, and he has a net worth of $1,000,000 today, he will be worth $5,000,000 in 16 years and 11 months unless he loses financial ground!) You now incorporate his $1,000,000 portfolio, creating a capitalization that consists of two shares of preferred voting stock with a par value of $497,000 each and a dividend of $15,000 per share and two shares of nonvoting common with a par value of $3,000 each. Capitalization is therefore valued at $994,000 for the preferred plus $6,000 for the common shares for a total of $1,000,000.

Now Mr. Jeffares continues to own the two shares of voting preferred stock for control purposes and to retain all the income that he wants for himself. He gifts the two $3,000 shares of common to his two children, Jan and Tori.

After 5 years, the dividend rate has doubled to $60,000. If he still owned the stock outright, the increase in income to the family unit would be the $30,000 of increased dividends less his individual tax rate of 50% or $15,000 for a total increase of only $15,000 in spendable income. And after his assumed 1983 death, Uncle Sam would get 60% of that $15,000, leaving the heirs with only $6,000 of the $30,000 of increased annual dividend. That dividend increase would have been a super deal for Uncle and an immaculate deception for Glen Jeffares. Instead, what really happened was that the $30,000 in increased dividends was paid out to Jan and Tori as dividends on the common and presumably kept more intact *now* because of reduced income taxes and for the *future* because it will no longer be in his estate.

Even more dramatically, assume that the portfolio rises to $5,000,000 in value before he goes on to the great stock market in the sky. His preferred shares stay at a $1,000,000 value, and Jan's and Tori's common shares go from $3,000 each in value to $2,003,000. He has just reduced the government's take upon his death (and upon the 1983 death of his surviving spouse) by $2,400,000 (60% of $4,000,000). Incorporating and/or properly recapitalizing your client's portfolio of appreciating nontax-sheltered assets could prove to be financial poetry in motion. It is, however, a very complex legal technique (sometimes a family partnership is used in place of a corporation). It should therefore be pursued only with the expert assistance of a very qualified tax specialist.

How to use the installment sale to shelter large capital gains

If a highly appreciated asset were to be sold outright, a large capital gain, of course, would all be reported in one year. If the gain is extremely large relative to ordinary income, there may be a severe limitation upon the degree to which it can be appropriately sheltered because of the interaction of the alternative minimum tax (see Chapter 6). If, instead, the asset were sold on an installment sale basis, the buyer would agree to pay for an appropriate part of it in the year of sale and the rest plus interest in installments over a period of one or more additional years. That way, the gain can effectively be spread over at least two years. Since the relationship between the amount of the gain and each year's level of taxable ordinary income makes or breaks one's ability to properly shelter the taxable portion of a gain, merely spreading the gain could be an answer. In fact, you can design the installment sale around the desire to use tax-incentive investments to shelter the 40% taxable portion of the gain and thereby effectively exit the appreciated asset tax-free.

The installment sale, like the private intrafamily annuity and the charitable remainder trust, can also have the effect of dramatically increasing current spendable cash flow. The installment payments from the buyer, usually well in excess of the income produced by the asset sold, fortifies cash flow without the immediate erosion of large capital gains taxes. The offsetting negative is that the taxable interest earned on the extended use of the future tax liability may be less valuable than the loss in purchasing power of the note received in exchange for the appreciating asset. That is a real problem in a milieu of heavy inflation. But it can be turned into a benefit if the installment sale is made to a family member or trust for the purpose of capping the estate. Again, every coin has two sides. You must weigh having your client pay any capital gains taxes at all versus providing heirs with a step-up in basis. You must also watch very carefully current laws governing installment sales to family members.

How to build, protect, and share one's financial pyramind with insurance

The concluding set of procedural tools in the Financial Problem Solvers Table involves the many and varied uses of insurance contracts to create, maintain, and distribute wealth. Chapter 8 on risk management told us how to use life insurance to provide needed capital when death robs us of the time we need to build and shape our financial destiny. We talked about how disability insurance can be used to replace the earned income that accidents and illnesses sometimes take away. Health insurance, along with property and casualty insurance, was shown to be necessary tools in transferring real risks to someone else. And liability coverage was spelled out to be something almost all of us need to avoid playing the game of major league catch-up football.

In this chapter, the mere listing of the insurance category of procedural tools serves to remind us of another basic tenet of financial planning: *Everything we do financially should be designed to produce a specific reward without taking undue risk or to remove a specific risk without excessive cost.* The ratio of cost to benefit must in all cases be carefully weighed when comparing *all* of the alternative solutions and potential directions.

This chapter served to highlight the major procedural tools for solving the problems of personal finance. But now we must again be reminded of the absolute law of financial nature: *For every single procedure we have discussed, there is a rival answer in the world of investments.* The following Chapter 11 will therefore delve into the intriguing world of investment strategies for building and managing wealth.

11

Tax Advantaged Investment Strategies for Repositioning Capital and Redirecting Discretionary Cash Flow

The best laid plans for your clients' future will sooner or later be in disarray if ill conceived investment strategies lead their capital astray. Directed by only a few fundamental investment rules, however, a portfolio can easily be aligned with a client's multiple objectives and thus properly positioned for maximum success. This chapter will first provide you with clear guidelines for positive investment results. It then walks you through an intriguing path of investment opportunities and applications for clients of every financial size and overall objective.

Four crises to key in on

Four major economic crises must be scrutinized before structuring an investment portfolio:

1. *inflation* and its resulting low P-E ratios and high interest rates,

2. *ensition* (energy source transition) and its affect on future petroleum prices,

3. The coming *housing crisis* and its affect on the level of future rents,
   and

4. The *transformation* of *transportation* into *communications*.

Using these guideposts, we'll travel through the specific profit-
making ideas listed in the Financial Problem Solvers Table that follows.
These investment strategies are unusually attractive from both an economic and taxation viewpoint. You will be told how each investment
works, what the advantages and disadvantages are, which are the prime
financial planning applications, for whom they are suitable, and what
you should watch out for in certain cases.

First, consider carefully the most important guideline for consistent, positive investment results: *When investing in the mid- to high-risk
economic opportunities, invest only in those that lie opposite the risk side
of a coin of economic crisis.*

The Chinese symbol for "crisis" consists of the two separate sym-
bols for opportunity and danger. Likewise, your vision of investment reward must be flanked by the risk that, together with the potential reward,
defines a significant economic crisis. Such a strategy will dramatically increase the likelihood that you will only be involved in unusually attractive
investment opportunities. This is especially meaningful when selecting
from among the mid- to higher-risk investment areas. It may also mean
missing an unpredictable bonanza from time to time. But it will always
help you avoid the the unmitigated investment disasters that cause your
clients to play financial catch-up. It will automatically insure that you do
not diversify a portfolio into mediocrity.

How investment choices are categorized

All investments must clearly attach an asset and/or cash flow stream to
the investor to achieve a specific financial objective. Whether the goal is
to build, preserve, or distribute capital, how your client gains access to
the asset and/or cash flow becomes the overriding question.

Broadly speaking, one can acquire investments *directly* or *indirectly*. Real estate, for example, can be owned directly either via outright
ownership or partnership arrangements. Alternatively, real estate can be
acquired through the purchase of the stock of a corporation whose principal asset is real property. Which direction you choose for your client
with real estate or any other asset depends on the characteristics of each

TABLE 11–1
Financial Problem Solvers Table

Procedural Tools	Investment Strategies
	Indirect Investment Strategies:
Qualified Retirement Plans:	Cash Reserves:
Individual Retirement Accounts	Checking Accounts
Keogh Plans	Money Market Funds
Corporate Plans	Deferred Annuities
	Fixed
	Variable
	US Government Savings Bonds
Wills:	Debt Securities:
Simple	Municipal Bonds
Marital Deduction Will	Corporate Bonds
with Residuary Trust	
Trusts:	Equity Securities:
Revocable	Common Stocks and Mutual Funds
Living Trust	Tax-Managed Trusts
Irrevocable	
Insurance Trust	
Charitable Remainder Trust	*Direct Investment Strategies:*
Short-Term Reversionary Trust	
Generation Skipping Trust	Collectables and Precious Metals
Interest-Free Loans	
	Tax-Incentive Investments:
Gifting Strategies:	Real Estate
Intrafamily	Existing Properties
Intrafamily Annuity	To-Be-Built Properties
Charitable	Wrap-Around Mortgages
Charitable Remainder Trust	
	Energy:
Ownership Structures:	Gas/Oil Income Properties
Custodianship	Gas/Oil Drilling
Joint Ownership	Royalty Interests
Corporate Recapitalization	Equipment Financings
The Installment Sale	Communications:
	Cable Television Systems
Insurance:	
Life	
Disability	
Health	
Property and Casualty	
Liability	

method of ownership and how they best meet the objectives of a particular segment of the client's capital. Let's study how that might work in today's universe of investment alternatives.

HOW DIRECT INVESTMENTS GO TO WORK FOR YOUR CLIENTS

Direct investments are designed to attach assets, cash flow streams, or both, more directly to the client. Using outright ownership, Subchapter S, or a general/limited partnership you avoid double taxation of investment profits (corporate and then individual). The flow-through, and resulting deductibility of start-up business expenses, is also provided to the individual. This is very important in certain areas of economic endeavor, such as real estate, energy, and agriculture.

As with everything else, you must give up something to get something. In this case, you usually gain tax advantages by giving up liquidity. The market for direct investments, much like one's home, is not extremely liquid. Values are less certain. Careful balancing of the liquid and less liquid sections of the overall investment portfolio is therefore essential.

Ironically, the preponderance of investments owned by individuals in the United States is heavily weighted toward direct ones. Yet until the nationwide financial planning movement injected increased objectivity when selecting investments, many sectors of the investment advisory community virtually ignored the total needs and inclinations of the majority of investors. Even today, the largest segment by far of the securities industry's budgeted expenses is directed toward the more traditional *indirect* investment sector. Ever since 1913 when income taxation entered the picture and until the late 1970s, investment advice became increasingly out of kilter with reality.

WHAT INDIRECT INVESTMENTS CAN DO FOR YOUR CLIENTS

Indirect investments are those the world of securities firms and banks would typically call "traditional." They consist mainly of thrift accounts, stocks and bonds, annuities, and mutual funds. Indirect investments have liquidity as their premier quality. Obviously, a measured amount of liquidity in one's portfolio is essential. Otherwise, a perfect example arises of creating more problems for the future than are being solved for today.

A second major advantage of many indirect investments, such as stocks and bonds, is the opportunity for psychological leverage. When assets and/or cash flow streams are owned via the bond or corporate stock format, prices fluctuate from day to day. Their value in the marketplace reflects both the underlying economic value *and* the temperament or mood of buyers and sellers.

When purchases of stocks are made while both earnings and price-to-earnings ratios are rising, assets grow in price much more rapidly than underlying economic values. When bonds are acquired prior to or during a period of declining interest rates, prices increase even as cash flow stays level. These are perfect examples of successful psychological leverage. Of course, the opposite can happen when judgments regarding the directions of interest rates, corporate earnings, and P-E ratios are wrong. Hence timing, as well as selection, is crucial for successful performance with indirect investments. One must be right twice. When you are, the profits are handsome. When you aren't, you had better be very diversified in every sense.

WHY COMBINATIONS OF INVESTMENTS ARE IMPORTANT

By combining both categories of investments into one financial portfolio, two common methods for reducing investment risk, without necessarily reducing upside potential, work in your client's behalf.

The first is tax leverage. The one common ingredient through all tax-advantaged investing is the ability to reduce risk due to Uncle Sam's putting up part of the cost and/or part of the return. Combinations of taxable and tax-advantaged investments often enable one to maximize tax benefits while providing needed liquidity. (See Chapter 4, "Options for Converting Tax Liability into Investment Assets," and Chapter 5, "How to Use Financial Leverage to Build Real Wealth.")

The second, and probably most common and accepted risk-reduction technique, is specific investment diversification. A proven key to consistent success involves selecting from among all of the available direct and indirect investment media, *and* then broadly diversifying within each carefully chosen area.

These two crucial ways to reduce risk are best employed via portfolio combinations of both direct and indirect investment strategies. The world abounds in examples of unusual investment opportunities in both investment categories. Having the ability to choose from *both* possible alternatives for investment problem solving opens up a world of opportunity. Yet such a level of objectivity and impartiality in structuring investment portfolios is not *yet* characteristic of most investment advisors and planners in the last quarter of the twentieth century. Too often the recommendation is what is traditional to the vendor, what is more popular in the marketplace, or whatever is available on the shelf at the moment. Reaching your client's financial destiny is not made easier by simply buying the "deal du jour." Instead, what must be considered is a very diversified portfolio of a combination of direct *and* and indirect investments that:

1. provides the highest total after-tax return consistent with income and asset growth needs.

2. furnishes the proper balance of liquidity dictated by coordinated lifetime and estate planning, and

3. matches risk tolerance and temperament requirements.

Your client must pursue a course of *total investment planning* instead of a more narrow, popular, join-the-ranks, pack approach. He, like Bernard Baruch, must buy his straw hats in the fall, when he knows that they will be popular again in the spring.

INDIRECT INVESTMENT STRATEGIES

How to protect cash reserves against economic fluctuations

Everyone should maintain adequate cash reserves for emergencies, specific forthcoming purchases and investment opportunities, and estate liquidity. How to best position these reserves in today's economic climate is a fundamental question that must be addressed before the rest of the investment pyramid can be properly structured. As with any construction project, the foundation has to come first. The cash reserves for emergencies alone should be equal to at least 50% of annual budgeted living expenses.

WHERE SHORT-TERM RESERVES SHOULD BE

The very *short-term reserves* for day-to-day needs of $500 or less should be contained in an *interest bearing checking account*. For most clients, $1,000 to $2,000 or about 5% of the emergency cash reserves should be the maximum checking account balance.

HOW TO BEST HOLD INTERMEDIATE CASH RESERVES

Intermediate reserves needed for week-to-week and month-to-month household operations—replenished from each month's income—should be held in a money market fund. These might average $5,000 or about 20% of the emergency reserves. In recent years, it has rightfully become popular to "beat the bank" by investing billions of dollars of cash reserves in *money market funds*. These pooled investments, usually in open-end investment trusts, buy short-term, high-interest money market instruments such as US Treasury bills and notes, US government agency securities, bank Certificates of Deposit, commercial paper, and other corporate notes and repurchase agreements. Money market funds provide an attractive but taxable short-term yield. Even so, the after-tax results are usually better than the yields on the few available tax-free short-term municipal bond funds.

Most money market funds allow investors to write checks of $500 or more through an agent bank against the cash held in their accounts. Since such funds earn interest at rates close to short-term government securities, they will typically provide a better short-term rate than the 5% + interest-bearing checking accounts.

Even so, you should not place as much emphasis upon the interest rate as you do upon sanctity of principal where cash reserves are concerned. The number one objective must be the absolute availability of what is storehoused if and when an emergency—such as short-term disability—arises. The interest earned should be automatically reinvested or plowed back in order to repair the damages inflicted by inflation upon the purchasing power of these cash reserves.

How to Invest Longer-Term Cash Reserves and Earn High Tax-Sheltered Interest

The longer-term reserves—or about 75% of your total cash reserves for emergencies, which you hope never to have to touch—should be held in a *single premium deferred annuity*. Deferred annuities occupy a unique position in our body of tax law. Due to Section 72 of the Internal Revenue Code, it is possible to simply move cash from the safe depository of one financial institution (the bank or money market fund) to another (a legal reserve life insurance company) without cost and, in so doing, gain a tax-sheltering umbrella over the interest.

The annuity concept is not new to investors. Annuities have been available for accumulating tax-sheltered interest for retirement income since the late 1800s. Offered by most of the largest life insurance companies in the country, annuities have become synonymous with safety, guarantees, and tax benefits.

The modern-day annuity still incorporates all of these features while providing increased rates of return and investor flexibility. Today's annuities offer the following benefits:

1. safety of principal,
2. tax-deferred accumulation of interest,
3. guarantees of interest,
4. contract flexibility and liquidity,
5. collateral value,
6. guaranteed lifetime retirement income (if elected),

7. avoidance of probate upon death, and

8. possible estate tax benefits.

Now you can see why the annuity can be a valuable cornerstone in most investors' financial planning pyramids.

HOW DOES AN ANNUITY WORK FOR PROTECTING AND BUILDING CASH?

An annuity is a financial contract between the policy owner and a life insurance company. In return for a cash premium contribution, the life insurance company makes certain guarantees as to principal, interest, and an additional annuitization guarantee, only if elected, of a monthly income that could never be outlived.

In the past, *immediate annuities* have been used principally by people who have already reached retirement and who, in less inflationary periods, desire or require fixed monthly income and lifetime guarantees. The deferred annuity products *now* being offered include these traditional benefits as well as the all-important tax-deferred compounding and accrual of interest during all the years prior to retirement. The combination of these benefits provide an increased annuity value for the future.

HOW THE DEFERRED ANNUITY GUARANTEES PRINCIPAL AND INCOME

Annuity income payments from deferred annuities commence at some point in the future. During the interim deferral period, the value of the annuity grows. Both the principal and a stated rate of interest are guaranteed and accumulate, tax deferred, until:

1. the contract value is withdrawn, or

2. income payments begin.

The interest rate credited will usually reflect the life insurance company's earnings on short- and or long-term debt obligations. Depending on the contract, current interest guarantees can range from one calendar quarter to one to ten years.

HOW TO USE THE DEFERRED ANNUITY TO CREATE INCOME IN LATER LIFE

It's as easy as the stroke of a pen if in fact your client wants regular payments for life instead of irregular withdrawals at will. The client simply elects to transform the contract into the older immediate type of contract. Annuity income payments from immediate annuities begin shortly after the election is made. When annuity payments begin, they are guaranteed by the life insurance company. This monthly income is treated favorably for tax purposes. A portion of each payment, considered a return of your original principal, is therefore not taxable. The remaining portion represents accumulated interest and is taxable. The exact breakdown of the principal and interest portions depend on the annuitant's life expectancy when the annuity payments begin. In many instances the interest portion of each payment could be taxed in a lower tax bracket, especially if received during retirement years.

HOW DO INSURANCE COMPANIES INVEST YOUR CLIENT'S CASH RESERVES?

If the deferred annuity is of the *fixed* type, the funds are invested by the insurance company usually in high-rated fixed-income investments that, by their nature, are income-producing and contain specific guarantees. These guarantees allow the life insurance company to provide the following contractual guarantees:

- Principal is always 100% guaranteed.

- Annuity interest is guaranteed two ways:

    1. A guaranteed minimum interest rate is included in the contract.

    2. In addition to the guaranteed minimum interest, there is a current (usually higher) interest rate declared for specific periods of time such as one quarter, one year, or more.

- Annuity income is guaranteed for the lifetime of the annuitant when the immediate annuity feature is elected.

If the deferred annuity is a *variable* type, the contribution will be invested in other than fixed-income investments. Typically, contributions will be professionally invested and managed in equity investments. The value of the variable annuity account will vary depending on the performance of the underlying investment. Unlike the fixed annuity, the variable annuity has no guarantee of principal.

Many contracts available today combine both fixed and variable annuities in one plan, thereby allowing the selection of one or both accumulation vehicles as economic circumstances dictate. The intent of the variable annuity is to provide a hedge against inflation through equity investments. When annuity payments commence, the choice of either a variable or fixed settlement option may be elected.

WHAT TO WATCH FOR WITH VARIABLE ANNUITIES

A serious word of caution about variable annuities: There is no big problem with using a variable annuity to house relatively stable income-producing assets, such as bonds or bond funds, *if* the value of income deferral exceeds the insurance company's annual charge *and if* it then produces greater net income accumulation than a fixed annuity. But then you have essentially created a fixed annuity. So why not just recommend that in the first place?

Guard against using a variable annuity for appreciating assets. There are two taxes on the capital gains taken within an annuity. First, they must be taxed at the insurance company's capital gains rate. Then the resulting after-tax proceeds are taxed again, as ordinary income, when they are withdrawn or upon the death of the owner–annuitant. The event that has just been described is the antithesis of tax sheltering—the transformation of capital gains into ordinary income. A financial FDA should stamp POTENTIALLY DANGEROUS TO YOUR WEALTH on most variable annuity contracts. It's a typical immaculate deception—a financial product with more sizzle than steak.

EXTRA BENEFITS OF ANNUITIES

In addition to the fixed annuity's guarantee of principal and interest, one can decide when to withdraw the interest and therefore when to report it as taxable income. For example, you can wait to withdraw the interest from your annuity contract during a year when your other taxable income is low.

Obviously, by being able to compound interest on a tax-deferred basis, the annuity value will be greater. The annuity therefore provides an excellent way to conservatively accumulate cash reserves for emergencies, education, business investment purposes, income for retirement, and estate liquidity, particularly during periods when the guaranteed rate exceeds the core inflation rate.

The annuity provides security and peace of mind in anticipation of those years when clients or their survivors' cash needs become greater. Also, the concern expressed by many people over the amount of retirement income that will be available from retirement plans and Social Security is genuine and cannot be ignored.

In planning for the future, the deferred annuity can be an invaluable, yet conservative complement to properly positioning the rest of your client's entire financial pyramid. Tax-deferred accumulation, liquidity, safety, and the latent, supplemental cash flow are among the many inherent benefits of this financial planning vehicle.

HOW TAX DEFERRAL BUILDS WEALTH

To show how tax deferral can benefit your client, we have compared the tax-deferred annuity with a taxable investment. Our example assumes that both investors are in the 40% combined state and federal income marginal tax bracket:

	Deferred Annuity $15,000	Taxable Investment $15,000
Interest	@ 12%	@ 12%
(end of one year)	$1,800	$1,800
Taxes	0	720
Net Income	1,800	1,080
Effective Accumulation Rate	12.0%	7.2%

Notice that both investments earned a like amount of interest in one year. However, since the interest on the annuity is not taxed, our investor has increased the effective yield on the investment by 67%. The effect of tax deferral is meaningful even after one year: The tax-deferred annuity is valued at $16,800, while the Certificate of Deposit's net value is $16,080. If we go on to assume the same rate of interest compounding tax-deferred versus taxable for 5, 10, and 15 years, the values would be more dramatic, as follows:

	Deferred Annuity	Taxable Investment
5 Years	$26,435.13	$21,335.63
10 Years	$46,587.72	$30,063.47
15 Years	$82,103.49	$42,561.12

WHAT TO WATCH FOR WHEN EXITING A DEFERRED ANNUITY

Obviously, tax-deferred compounding creates a larger annuity value without forcing capital to "travel" at a faster "financial speed." Many policy owners defer taxation until after retirement when they anticipate being in a lower tax bracket with increased personal tax exemptions. A lump sum surrender of the annuity is therefore not usually recommended as it could create a heavy tax burden in the year of receipt. Caution must also be exercised not to lock too great a segment of capital into the production of a future stream of cash flow that cannot possibly rise with increasing living costs. Also, our latest tax "deform" legislation levies a 5% tax penalty on all withdrawals of accumulated interest prior to age 59½ or within ten years, whichever period occurs first.

How the annuity can be used to meet multiple goals

Under present tax legislation, the only income tax liability the policy owner has is on the accumulated tax-deferred interest; so the interest earned in our previous illustration ($67,103.49 in fifteen years) must be withdrawn for an emergency *on a last-in-first-out basis as taxable income.* The difference that represents the original $15,000 of principal could be left to compound further, tax-deferred, or withdrawn tax-free. Or, as permitted by most annuity contracts, isolated partial withdrawals could be made.

HOW THE IMMEDIATE ANNUITY OPTION
CAN BE USED TO SUPPLEMENT RETIREMENT INCOME

Some people contemplating the purchase of annuities are interested in supplemental retirement income and will choose to receive annuity payments upon retirement. With this objective in mind, a couple contemplating retirement might elect to receive either annuity income over the next 15 years or a monthly income guaranteed for life with or without benefits to survivors. Using our previous illustration, the original annuity purchase of $15,000 grew tax-deferred over 15 years to $82,103.49. An annuity payout would provide the following monthly income, annual income, and total expected return. In addition, since part of each payment represents a return of principal, a certain percentage of each payment would be tax-free.

Accumulated Annuity Value	$ 82,103.49
Monthly Income	717.59*
Annual Income	8,611.09
Annual Income Tax-Free As a Return of Principal	1,000.00
Total Expected Return	$129,166.29

*Annuity income figures are based on the current rates for a life annuity for a male age 65 with a 15-year certain factor.

As you can see from this illustration, when both the accumulation phase and the annuity or payout phase are combined, the investor benefits not only from the initial period of tax deferral, but from continued tax-deferred accumulation during the payout period.

Additionally, when one of the annuity options has been selected at retirement, the monthly income payments will be guaranteed either for the life of the annuitant with survivor guarantees or for designated periods of time. The choice of available annuity options is your client's to make . . . not now when he or she purchases the annuity but at retirement. The annuity option selected will usually be predicated upon age, family situation, and economic needs.

.HOW TO USE ANNUITIES FOR
CORPORATE OR INDIVIDUAL RETIREMENT PLANS

Although qualified retirement plans, such as IRAs, Keogh plans, and corporate pension/profit sharing plans, provide a basic tax shelter for the investments in the plan, equity investments (stocks and the like) fail to provide the guarantees found with annuities. As a result, many investors who desire the guarantees, along with the ability to contribute to the same policy on a regular basis, use a flexible premium annuity to fund a part of their qualified retirement plan when certain guarantees are more important than potential inflation hedging. At retirement, the annuity payout would provide lifetime guarantees, and possible income and federal estate tax savings, while providing a method of distribution that complies with IRS regulations.

HOW TO STRUCTURE
THE DEFERRED ANNUITY FOR MAXIMUM FAMILY BENEFITS

Every annuity contract has an owner, *annuitant*, and beneficiary. Those entities are precisely synonomous with the life insurance contract designations of owner, *insured*, and beneficiary. Ownership is almost self-explanatory. With an annuity, the owner is the person who uses the annuity to position assets. As with the life insurance contract, the owner may or may not be the person who is the insured. Likewise, with an annuity, the owner need not necessarily be the annuitant. Here is how such an arrangement might be used to benefit your client. With life insurance, the death of the insured causes the flow of capital from the insurance company to the beneficiary. With annuities, the death of the annuitant (not the owner) causes the flow of capital (in lump sum or installments), from the insurance company to the beneficiary. With both life insurance and annuities, the death of the owner, if he or she is not the insured or the annuitant, simply causes a change in ownership of the contract, not a collapse of the contract and its attendant flow and possibly taxable proceeds from insurance company to beneficiary.

The understanding of these subtleties will help you recognize that interest earned in a deferred annuity can be sheltered continuously over as many as three generations. For example, suppose Grandfather buys a single-premium deferred annuity contract and, upon purchase, names Grandson as the annuitant and himself beneficiary. His death would then cause the ownership of the contract to pass to his heirs (his wife or children or both), just like any other asset he owns. It would also be included in his gross taxable estate. However, the contract itself would continue, accumulating interest, tax-free, until such time as Grandson/annuitant dies.

Now assume that, after Grandfather dies, Son becomes owner. Son now controls the contract and changes the beneficiary to himself so that the proceeds flow to him in the event of the annuitant's (Grandson's) premature death. Keep in mind that, while the owner and beneficiary designations can always be changed, the annuitant of an annuity (or the insured with a life insurance contract) can never be altered.

Upon Son's subsequent death, the policy can still continue and be inherited by Grandson (the annuitant). The interest can also continue to compound, tax-sheltered in this instance, for three generations. Grandson is now both owner and annuitant, and he will probably change the beneficiary to his wife, trust, or children.

Remember, no one should pay taxes in this generation even if it is only postponed to the next generation, or the generation thereafter, and even if it is only the taxes on the interest earned by your client's most serious cash reserves.

When should US government savings bonds be used to storehouse serious cash reserves

Uncle Sam provides two different kinds of savings bonds: series HH and series EE. Series HH bonds, with maturities of 10 years, provide a current taxable income of 7.5% if held for five years or more and are only available in exchange for Series E and EE bonds and savings notes. HH bonds are therefore not currently competitive with alternative taxable yields. Series EE bonds, however, provide a source of tax deferral. These bonds are sold to us for a discount from the face value when held at least 5 years, they will earn 8.5% of the yield on Treasury Securities with a 5-year maturity. A minimum yield of 7.5% is guaranteed. No local or state income taxes are paid on the interest earned, and we can defer paying income taxes on the interest accumulated in series EE bonds until they are redeemed.

Additionally, we may receive extensions beyond the maturity date, continue to accrue interest, tax-deferred, and thereby defer interest into a later year when our top tax bracket, through real or artificial means, is reduced. (Note that the Department of the Treasury has announced that no further extensions will be granted to old EE bonds issued through April of 1952.) We can exchange our series EE bonds for series HH bonds on a tax-free basis and defer taxes even further by paying income taxes only on the interest paid out by the HH bonds.

When and if Series EE and HH bonds offer competitive interest rates, they may well be tax-advantaged investment alternatives to the annuity or other procedural alternatives for sheltering the interest produced by our most serious cash reserves. But that is nowhere near the case now.

How to maximize income with debt securities

It can be successfully argued that the interest rate gyrations of recent years have injured the reputation of corporate and municipal bonds as havens for stable capital. Inflation has also pulled the carpet out from under the image of bonds as a source of safety of principal from a standpoint of buying power. That is, of course, why some investment advisors think that DANGEROUS TO YOUR WEALTH should also be stamped across excessively large bond portfolios for individual investors. Yet no one can deny that bonds still provide a predictable stream of cash flow during times that are anything but predictable. As such, the task at hand then becomes one of deciding on a type of bond portfolio and how to manage it.

As far as the types of bonds are concerned, we have the basic choice between *taxable* government or corporate bonds and *tax-free* municipal bonds. During recent times, the ratio of long-term tax-free yields to taxable yields have been so high as to make municipals the only sane choice for individuals in a marginal tax bracket of *30%* or higher. Inasmuch as that includes practically every individual interested in the contents of this book, the remaining question relates to the management of municipals.

There wouldn't really be such a problem if it weren't for inflation and if it weren't for the possible need for the emergency liquidation of bonds during periods of higher interest rates. But inflation seems to be a fact of life in modern-day economics, and liquidity is a real need—or we wouldn't be considering bonds. Hence the need to manage bonds to produce greater stability and the potential for increasing income.

HOW TO USE THE MUNICIPAL BOND
CYCLING STRATEGY TO INCREASE STABILITY AND INCOME

A *bond cycling strategy* can be used, particularly in the management of tax-exempt municipal bonds, that can assure greater stability of principal and potentially increasing rather than the fixed tax-free income normally associated with volatile long-term bonds. Specifically, this strategy calls for the acquisition of bonds maturing evenly over a period of one to ten years. For example, in the case of the need for a $250,000 municipal bond portfolio, one might acquire $25,000 of bonds maturing every year for each of the next ten years. As each $25,000 segment of the portfolio matures each year, it would normally be "repositioned" into bonds maturing in ten years. The end result is a $250,000 diversified pool of bonds, of which 10% are maturing each year and no section of which is less stable than the market for ten-year bonds.

Inasmuch as the expiring shortest-term bonds would be replaced annually by higher-yielding ten-year bonds, increasing income should result. Should the interest rate curve reverse, as it did in early 1980, the maturing bonds can be replaced by higher-yielding short-term bonds until such time as the interest rate curve reverts to normalcy.

In actually structuring the bond cycling strategy, you obviously have to consider the type and quality of available bonds. The strategy as explained may therefore not always be precisely achieved. The basic premise of acquiring a portfolio of bonds with segments maturing at intervals over such a ten-year period can always be actuated. The key point is that the type and quality of the bond purchases cannot be allowed to suffer for sake of the preciseness of the strategy itself.

WHAT ARE THE CYCLING STRATEGY'S FAULTS?

The disadvantage of this cycling strategy is that it initially produces less income than purchasing all long-term bonds. There is no doubt that this is a valid argument against it—if the only objective is maximizing after-tax income. But when one must at the same time be concerned about having to liquidate bonds for larger-than-normal emergencies or for estate settlement costs, the price for reaching the highest yield could be more costly than the reward. Conversely, when maximizing today's income is primary and care is taken to otherwise provide for liquidity and estate settlement costs, the best strategy may well be to buy longer-term, higher-yielding municipal bonds, bond funds, or unit trusts.

Why common stocks should be used to build enormous wealth in the '80s

Each chapter in this book has placed a significant emphasis on the erosive impact of inflation on every segment of the financial pyramid. It can therefore be no less important to clarify the impact of inflation upon the stock market—or preferably stated—the market of stocks.

A PREDICTABLE RELATIONSHIP

There is no more predictable long-term stock market relationship than the one between a curve of the inflation rate and price-to-earnings (P-E) ratios. When the inflation rate is high, P-E ratios are low. When the inflation rate is low, P-E ratios are high. Conversely, when inflation is high so are E-P ratios, as can be verified by the chart in Figure 11–1.

ARE STOCKS A HEDGE AGAINST INFLATION?

There may therefore appear to be an inconsistency in the historical recommendation of stocks as a hedge against inflation. The inconsistency arises from its timing. As inflation subsides from its 1980 peak, P-E ratios will ascend—particularly if we and Fort Fumble give supply side economics a fighting chance. That, coupled with the rising earnings and lower interest rates that will surely result as our nation crawls out of its current economic limbo, will cause a doubling or tripling of the prices of quality stocks. Wall Street will then again appear as a route to more predictable gains as existed during the 1960s. You, as a studied contrarian, must accumulate your stocks for your clients now, *before* P-E ratios climb, not after.

A TRIED AND TRUER PATH TO FOLLOW: DOLLAR COST AVERAGING

Today's inflation cannot be expected to go away much quicker than it came. Supply side economics and its attendant increased productivity cannot cure the ill overnight, any more than fiscal and energy irresponsibility created it in a day. Only a person who is capable of parting waters can say *exactly* when the core inflation rate will reach half the recent double-digit rate and then when the average P-E ratio will be twice today's single-digit rate. But it doesn't take the omnipotent to sensibly predict that it will happen in the '80s.

This period of ratio readjustment will also probably precede *ensition*—the period of energy source tran*sition* from the nonrenewable (gas and oil) to renewable (mostly solar-related). That, too, should be on its way to success by the end of the '80s. And when it happens, a slowing of exponentially rising petroleum prices will have halted its intermittent fueling of the fires of inflation. Such a transition period provides us with a rare opportunity to acquire equities for accumulating wealth or for preserving the buying power of what we already have.

The tried and truer path to follow is not the most exciting, but it is, in fact, the safest. Known as *dollar cost averaging*, it involves the systematic monthly or yearly purchase of individual stocks or mutual funds. In so doing, you are mathematically guaranteed to end up with an average "cost" that is lower than the average "price" occurring over the acquisi-

FIGURE 11–1   *The Relationship Between Inflation and P-E Ratios*

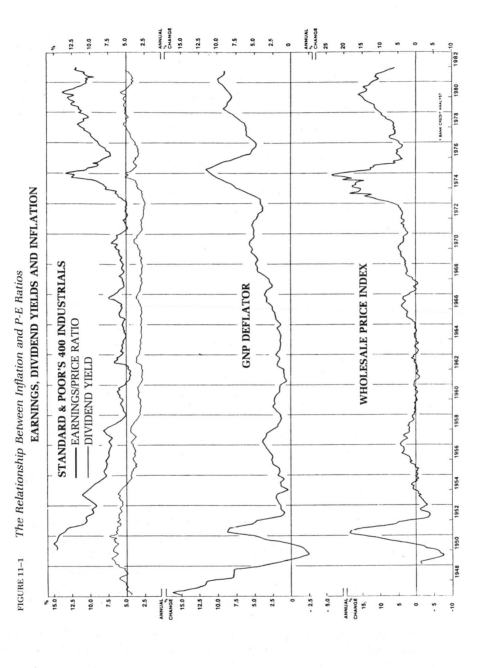

tion period. The key is to invest an equal dollar amount at each interval so that more shares will be bought when prices are lower and fewer shares are bought when prices are higher.

HOW TO BEAT DOLLAR COST AVERAGING

You can even improve on that if you devise a system for increasing the dollar amount of investment when prices are declining and decreasing the amount when prices are ascending. That can, of course, tax even the most contrarian attitudes. On the other hand, *strong profits are not the product of faint hearts.*

HOW THE TAX ADVANTAGES OF STOCKS CAN BENEFIT YOUR CLIENT

What does all this about stocks have to do with any tax advantage? With stocks that are expected to grow in earnings, the chief objective should be capital gains, which in turn provide increased buying power. In 1979, capital gains began to be taxed at a less onerous rate. In effect, only 40% versus the previous 50% of long-term gains are now taxed (unless the alternative minimum tax applies). A safe bet is that the portion of the gain that is subjected to ordinary income taxation will again be reduced in the future. It has already occurred over much of the Western world. Furthermore, any improvement of the double taxation of corporate dividends would send a shock wave (in advance of the actual event) so powerful as to cause more profits to be made in real terms on Wall Street than ever before.

HOW TO GET INCREASING INCOME
AND PROFITS FROM YOUR CLIENT'S INVESTMENT PORTFOLIO

All too often underemphasized is the fact that the stock market, in spite of its often being out of phase with current inflation, is a great source of *increasing* dividend income. Researchers can spotlight segments of the equity market place for especially high and/or reliable increasing income. For instance, while the industrials (typified by the Dow Jones Industrial Average of thirty stocks) have historically increased their dividends at 4% per year, recent years have witnessed an average of 10% annual increase. That yield was 6% in early 1982. Given the more recent rate of increase, based on original investment, that yield could be 15.56% in ten years. Properly sheltered, that could go a long way toward repairing the erosion of, say, an 8–10% annual inflationary Robin Hood. If, in ten years, industrials yield the same 6%, $1 in the market will have grown to $2.59.

If your clients seek higher current income from a given segment of their pyramids than can be provided by industrials, look no farther than utilities. These relatively stable equities provide a yield that is almost double that of the average industrial stock, but they continue to increase their dividends at higher-than-the-historical 4% + rate. An 11% yield today, subjected to only a 4% annual increase, will be 16.28% in ten years, again combating the demoralizing effects of inflation. And if utilities still yield 11% in ten years, every $1 of capital will have grown to $1.48. That's not financial heaven on earth, but it beats just getting back a dollar from a bond. Where inflation has been so bad that one has to liquidate assets to invade principal, it offers a fighting chance to at least stay absolutely whole. Remember, too, that qualified public utilities are allowed to establish dividend reinvestment plans. Shareholders may elect to exclude $750 a year ($1,500 on a joint return) of dividends from taxation when reinvested in that amount.

How the tax-managed trust helps to keep more of what is earned

Another major tax point with regard to equities is that the last few years have witnessed the emergence and survival of the publicly offered tax-managed trust. Simply put, such a trust is an open-end investment company (mutual fund) that has:

1. chosen to be taxed as a corporation,
2. receives 85% of the dividends collected from the shares of other US corporations tax-free, and
3. accumulates the dividends instead of distributing them.

By delaying the taxation of the dividends, the trust effectively transforms them into long-term capital gains whenever *and* if every any appreciated shares are sold. Care must be taken by the trust to so manage its affairs as to avoid accumulating of retained earnings as it is defined by the Internal Revenue Code. As long as the law allows, where the sheltering of dividend income is desirable, while simultaneously seeking professional management and diversification, the tax-managed trust is the epitome of tax sheltering. It makes the variable annuity look like a Model-T.

HOW TO USE THE
TAX-MANAGED TRUST TO REPLACE OR COMPLEMENT BONDS

Utility stocks should continue to provide an attractive dividend yield and an historical source of increasing income rather than fixed dividends. They enjoy less volatility than long-term bonds on the downside, but they are by their very nature a better hedge against inflation than bonds.

Again, a negative factor in holding any high-dividend stock when a high marginal tax bracket is involved is that dividend income is double-taxed. Therefore, rather than investing in individual utility stocks, your client should hold shares in a tax-managed trust that buys the shares for them. After holding such a fund for a year, they can establish a withdrawal plan that distributes the exact amount of cash flow needed, hopefully allowing some of the dividend accumulation to stay in and compound into even higher income in the future.

If they do not currently need the income, no withdrawals need be made. In that instance, triple compounding will occur. That is, they have the opportunity to compound more rapidly for three reasons:

1. The build-up increases from more frequent compounding, as the dividends accumulate daily or weekly instead of once a quarter or once a year. (That can add as much as ½% to the portfolio yield.)

2. They are compounding tax-free.

3. Perhaps most importantly, if history continues to repeat itself, the dividends will increase at a rate of about 5 to 6% or better per year.

HOW TO USE THE
TAX-MANAGED TRUST TO INCREASE FAMILY WEALTH

In larger estates, financial planning must provide for liquid sources to cover estate settlement costs. While the deferred annuity is one tax-advantaged way to build such liquid and guaranteed capital, the tax-managed trust, in certain circumstances, can be one step better. Let's see how that works.

How to Trade in Guaranteed Principal for a Stepped-Up Basis. Assume that Jan Redding is accruing tax-sheltered interest in a $100,000 CD at the bank. Her death requires that the CD be used to pay $125,000 of estate settlement costs upon liquidation. The $100,000 principal was guaranteed, but the $50,000 of accumulated interest (assuming a 50% income tax bracket) really produces net estate enhancement of only $25,000 since income taxes had to be paid along the way. While the CD answer is far better than not preparing at all, a tax-managed trust invested in utility stocks is one step better—assuming a guarantee of principal is not needed.

Under the same assumptions, let's say that this $100,000 estate settlement, "tax-managed" reserve has also grown to $150,000 by the time Jan Redding dies—due only to dividend accumulation. Since ownership of the tax-managed trust for over one year transforms dividend accruals into capital gains from deferred income, a step-up in basis occurs upon death. The entire $150,000 is available to pay the settlement costs of slightly more than $125,000 due to the slight increase in the value of the estate. That then leaves approximately $25,000 more of family wealth than the CD produced.

Do the Cons Outweigh the Pros? The pertinent question obviously relates the the value of guaranteed principal. Going back to the previous example, assuming a 12% CD interest rate and a 12% tax-managed trust dividend rate, the holding period was only 3.58 years. Was the guarantee of $100,000 for 3.58 years worth the "premium" cost of $25,000 or $6,983.24 per year? That's an insurance cost of $69.38 per thousand per year. That's very expensive "casualty" insurance in anyone's book.

If more people knew what it cost to guarantee large amounts of principal in storehouses like the FDIC, they would think twice. On the other hand, if that's what it takes to gain peace of mind during one's older years, it's probably worth the high cost. But then, there is always the single-premium deferred annuity to fall back on—a solution lying, risk-wise, somewhere closer to the CD than to the tax-managed trust.

DIRECT INVESTMENT STRATEGIES

When are direct investment strategies most appropriate?

Direct, as opposed to *indirect* investment strategies, are used when:

1. you wish for the investment valuation to reflect only its underlying economic conditions and not have it elevated or deflated by psychological leverage (the market place),
2. you wish to either avoid double taxation or gain the flow through of business start-up expenses, and
3. liquidity is usually not important.

A perfect example of an investment asset that can easily be acquired through either *direct* or *indirect* format is gold. Gold can be owned indirectly via one of many available stocks of gold mining companies on either US or foreign stock exchanges. The investment will fluctuate upward or downward in value with the market price of gold as well as with the stock market price of the company itself. Alternatively, gold can be owned directly by purchasing gold bullion or coins. The investment will then reflect only the value of gold itself. Your client will not have the upside that could be provided by upward valuations in the stock market nor will he be subject to the risk of such downward valuations.

In this section, we will deal with two major categories of direct investments:

1. precious metals and collectibles and
2. tax-incentive investments.

Using collectibles and precious metals to build wealth

The tax advantages of collectibles and precious metals are similar to those of growth stocks. Any increase in value over more than a one-year holding period results in a long-term capital gain upon sale. If sales are not made prior to death, a stepped-up basis results in no increased taxes being paid upon that accumulation of wealth.

From an economic viewpoint, unless your clients are Hunts or Rockefellers, they will want to restrict their involvements in collectibles and precious metals and stones to the ones that they are most familiar with and can personally enjoy. There are two principal reasons why this is sound and logical.

First, collectibles, precious metals, and stones are costly to own, store, and/or insure. Yet they produce no compensating income to help carry these costs. Conversely, they are attractive storehouses of value. (Being able to enjoy their beauty and utility may sometimes compensate for their cost of ownership.)

Second, the acquisition cost, mark-up, and/or commission costs of acquiring these assets are, in most instances, very high compared to other alternative investments. This has often attracted many less reputable dealers who are in competition with the more reputable people involved in these business areas. The seeming difficulty of finding advisors who can be trusted, who have vast experience, who have demonstrated total results, and whose income is related to expertise, makes these investment areas less attractive on balance.

It is, however, difficult not to be lured to some extent by both their overall performance during inflationary times and by the attractive capital gains tax rates that apply to their ultimate liquidation during life. Additionally, particular precious metals can properly be viewed as insurance against more widespread economic uncertainties. This, however, should be the advice of most financial advisors: Own what can be enjoyed in this area without sacrificing measured income and liquidity needs.

How tax-incentive investments
build wealth for your client and his family

For investors in the higher marginal tax brackets, finding a successful method of converting one's income tax burden into a potential asset or increased income has been a compelling financial planning consideration since the writing of the Internal Revenue Code roughly seventy years ago. Since that time, our federal government has accommodated that goal by attracting capital into certain investment areas via tax incentives. These investments have been mainly in real estate, agriculture, and energy. During the past decade, the purchase of an interest in a limited partnership involved in such tax-favored business endeavors has become a widely accepted practice among both sophisticated and inexperienced investors alike.

There are many ways to explain tax-incentive investments. Actually, the key to any such investment (more commonly called a "tax shelter") is its ability to use "tax" leverage to multiply the appreciation and/or net income produced by that segment of the pyramid. If the benefits of tax leverage are to be clearly understood, a comparison with the more commonly used debt leverage must be made.

HOW TAX LEVERAGE AND
DEBT LEVERAGE WORK DIFFERENTLY ON YOUR CLIENT'S BEHALF

As discussed in Chapter 5, debt leverage exists when, in the process of investing, your client borrows capital from a lending entity, pays interest for its use, and then pays back the capital, occasionally along with part of the profits at some stipulated future point or points in time. For leverage to be successful, the after-tax profitability of using the borrowed funds must be greater than the after-tax cost of the usually deductible interest. Note that complicated legal limitations sometimes apply to the amount of interest that can be deducted in any one year.

Tax leverage, on the other hand, exists when the law allows individuals, trusts, and businesses certain deductions against taxable income and/or tax credits against tax liability as a result of moving capital to stipulated tax-benefitted investment areas. The tax benefits, when they are applied against either related or unrelated income, have the effect of reducing the cost of the investment itself or increasing the return. This reduction in actual out-of-pocket cost or increased return *is tantamount to interest-free borrowing from the government.*

TAX LEVERAGE: A TWO-EDGED SWORD

At some point in time, gradually or all at once, Uncle Sam must be paid back part, all, and sometimes more than the original tax savings. The amount depends on the nature of the investment, the tax situation, and the success of the investment. Not having to pay interest on that "borrowing" is the first plus. The second way tax leverage can beat debt leverage is when your client can effectively pay back less than the original tax savings. Tax planners view that as classic tax sheltering. It occurs when the *rate* at which taxes are saved when investing is greater than the rate at which taxes are paid when exiting the investment. It is commonly referred to as "tax formation," "reduction," or outright "avoidance." Even having to only pay back at an effective rate equal to the original tax savings rate is an obvious advantage. That's called "tax deferral."

Being taxed at the back end more heavily than the rate at which taxes are saved at the front end is a very bad situation indeed. It's a tax hurdle that asks too much of the investment's economics. That is frequently what happens, especially to those who do not watch what is going on with their tax thermometer *each* and *every* year.

No one would ever borrow from a bank knowing that more principal may have to be paid back than was originally borrowed, over and above interest. Why, then, do hoards of tax shelter enthusiasts flock to buy debts (tax benefits) that appreciate? That is exactly what can happen when we look only to today's deductions and credits without considering all of the ongoing and future tax ramifications of tax shelters. I have seen friends and clients alike become heady in the euphoria of multiple tax write-offs and, after April 15, wallow in financial hangover for periods of up to several years. *That's a short-term tax affair that almost always ends up in a divorce with original capital.*

USING DOUBLE LEVERAGE TO GIVE TAX-INCENTIVE INVESTMENTS MORE HORSEPOWER

The most powerful of all tax-incentive investments are those that combine both debt and tax leverage. Some historically more predictable and conservative tax-incentive investment areas—such as income real estate, developmental gas/oil drilling, and existing cable television systems—have found double leverage to be quite profitable without taking undue risk. The less predictable, more volatile areas—such as animal feeding and breeding, movies, government-assisted housing, coal, railway equipment leasing, and start-up cable operations—have in the past often found double leveraging to be financial suicide. Even in times when the average performance of the more aggressive areas may be good, double leveraging will cause the variance between good and bad single investments to be too dramatic for financial planning purposes. Such volatility can be just like a roller coaster ride. The average is not bad but you can lose your lunch.

The big five economic areas for tax shelter opportunity

As pointed out in Chapter 5, all major tax-incentive investments are embodied in the acronym REACT: real estate, energy, agriculture, communication, and transportation. The big five have no magic other than that they represent the largest areas of national economic and social concern. From among these five business areas only, you should select participations in tax-advantaged equity investments. My personal observation is that digressions into other tax-advantaged investment areas, the so-called "exotics" that are made possible by tax loopholes or excessive debt financing, more often than not result in either economic failure, loss of the tax benefits after IRS scrutiny, or both.

NARROWING DOWN THE BIG FIVE

Next, you must act in the most contrarian manner possible to narrow down REACT. Your goal is to pick those two or three areas that seem to offer unusual profit potential. This is best accomplished by searching for specific national economic or social *crises* that are directly related to one of the big five.

Crisis in Perspective. An ancient Arabian proverb held: "four things come not back—the spoken word, the sped arrow, the past life, *and the neglected opportunity.*" All people of worth strive for the *opportunity* to produce or discover something of value. That exercise in search stretches the human spirit toward the potential for greatness. It is not crisis itself but this exercise that creates greatness. Crisis first creates opportunity and then reveals it to us.

We Americans, more than any people in history, quickly learned that the greatest opportunity always appears in companionship with risk. Grasping that opportunity always proves profitable when the crisis is alleviated in so doing. That is why we will limit our strongest areas of investment recommendation to the areas of clear current crisis (real estate, energy, and communications) within the big five.

WHAT TO LOOK FOR WITHIN EACH FAVORED AREA

The final step in the selection process is to pick one or more of the attendant investment opportunities that lie within the favored area. You must take care to align specific segments of available capital with the investment opportunity that best matches your client's desired financial speed, tax circumstances, liquidity needs, and risk tolerance level.

Within each of the REACT areas you select, there will usually be several ways to take advantage of the potential reward. In general, however, you can depend upon there being at least these two:

I. *Purchasing* the asset and/or cash flow stream. Examples: gas/oil income funds in energy, income-producing real estate properties, and existing CATV systems in communications.

II. *Developing* the asset and/or cash flow stream. Examples: gas/oil drilling in the energy area, to-be-built properties in real estate and start-up/expansion of CATV systems in communications.

The main reason for categorizing the opportunities within each favored area into *purchasing* and *developing* the assets is to demonstrate their relative investment objectives. In addition to these two principal ways to seek reward within each area, certain of the REACT areas present opportunities in the ownership of equipment or research and development.

Tax-incentive investments can, in general, also be divided functionally into Types I and II. Type I tax shelters are those that shelter related income, and they are also the same category as "I. Purchasing" in the list. Type II tax shelters create larger amounts of front-end tax benefits that are used mainly to shelter unrelated earned and investment income; these correspond to "II. Developing" in the list.

Now you are beginning to see a relationship between the amount of initial tax benefit and the degree of risk. There is obviously more tax benefit, opportunity, and risk associated with gas/oil drilling than there is with the purchase of existing gas/oil reserves. The same can be said of the differences between to-be-built real estate or start-up CATV systems and existing real estate properties or CATV systems.

As a matter of statistics, you can count on the risk level of any Type II tax shelter being directly proportional to the front-end tax benefit. Tax-incentive investments are usually aggressive enough without leveraging even the good areas so much as to create multiple write-offs. This advice flies in the face of what highly taxed individuals want most and what tax advisors like best to find. But the most rudimentary analysis will support the conclusion that drastically increased leverage—tax or debt—increases risk dramatically. Whenever your clients think they need to travel that fast financially, they usually don't have enough capital with which to travel at all. . . .

The remainder of this chapter highlights those areas that I believe provide the greatest opportunity for total, tax-leveraged economic reward relative to risk.

How to get tax-benefited income and appreciation in real estate

Improved real estate enjoys a jealous position among investment for both income and growth during inflationary as well as more stable times. It is definitely our nation's most popular and widely used source of tax-favored income and appreciation.

Almost a decade ago, long before the stock market had experienced much of the silly seventies, surveys indicated that about twice as many Americans viewed real estate as the preferable source for appreciation and income as did those who favored the stock market. Now, just because it is popular does not make it right. But there is substantial reasoning behind the positive attitude with which investors view improved, income-generating real estate.

TAX BENEFITS CAN MULTIPLY ECONOMICS

Real estate properties such as shopping centers, office buildings, mobile home communities, and apartment buildings have, as primary goals, the production of rental income, appreciation, and the creation of depreciation write-offs to offset income. The amount by which the income exceeds expenses (such as taxes, insurance and upkeep) and loan payments (interest and principal) is the cash flow available for distributing to investors. When depreciation (an artificial "accounting" loss), expenses, and interest costs equal or exceed total income, the cash flow available for distribution is, in effect, tax sheltered, and any excess depreciation shelters other unrelated income.

EXAMPLE: HOW DEPRECIATION SHELTERS INCOME

Let's assume Rex Reynolds is in the 35% tax bracket and invests $10,000 in real estate. Let's also assume that $10,000 cash buys approximately $30,000 of real estate, $5,000 of which is land.

Investment:	
Real Estate Purchase	$ 30,000
Mortgage	(20,000)
Equity Investment	10,000
Cash Flow Analysis:	
Rental Income	$ 5,000
Interest Portion of Mortgage Payment	(2,600)
Principal Portion of Mortgate Payment	(400)
Other Deductible Expenses	(1,500)
	500
Net Cash Available for Distribution yield (Cash Flow as a % of Equity Investment)	5%

Income Tax Analysis:

Rental Income	$ 5,000
Interest Deduction	(2,600)
Other Deductible Expenses	(1,500)
Depreciation ($25,000 ÷ 15 years)	(1,667)
Net Taxable Income (Deduction)	(767)

Tax-Effected Cash Flow:

Net Cash Distributed	$ 500
Net Taxable Income (Deduction)	(767)
Net Savings (35% × $767)	268
Total Tax Effected Cash Flow ($500 + $268)	$ 768

The $767 of net deductions is over and above what was needed to completely shelter the $500 of distributed cash flow. It therefore produced tax savings of $268 plus the taxes that would have otherwise been paid on the $500 of net cash flow had depreciation not been a benefit of real estate investments.

The cost basis of the "$30,000" property is then reduced each year by the amount of depreciation used. The end result is that the use of depreciation eliminates ordinary income taxation on cash flow "today" and transforms it into ordinary income or long-term capital gains taxation upon liquidation "tomorrow," depending on the type of depreciation used. This is, in essence, the definition of true tax sheltering, that is, the deferral and/or transformation of taxation to a later time at hopefully a lower rate.

BENEFITS OF THE LIMITED PARTNERSHIP
IN REAL ESTATE INVESTMENTS

The limited partnership entity is a wondrous tool for investors, particularly in real estate. It allows for the flow-through of business start-up costs or ongoing expenses to the individual investor who really needs it. Since partnerships are themselves not taxed, any taxable income that results from successful operation avoids the double taxation that is associated with the corporate entity. Under the limited partnership concept, the individual investors are limited partners because their liability is limited by law to their capital contribution. The corporation and/or individuals with the investment expertise—the managers—are the general partners. The general partner(s) has unlimited liability and carry out the organization and management of the partnership's activities.

The limited partners, or investors, usually have the opportunity to participate in a highly diversified, professionally managed portfolio of existing and improved real estate through the classic pooling of equity capital. With most types of investments, tax deductions are limited to the amount of capital at risk. Not so with real estate. While real estate limited partners remain limited in capital liability, their *deductions are not limited to their capital contributions.*

Investors in real estate limited partnerships will typically be investing in existing and improved properties or properties under construction. Raw land syndications are generally not recommended by financial planners due to (1) their speculative nature, (2) lack of cash flow relative to ongoing property taxes and carrying costs, and (3) poor track records.

In recent years, certain real estate direct participations have been offered in the form of real estate business trusts, as opposed to limited partnerships. This is a rather innovative move, aimed primarily at institutions like tax-exempt entities which do not need the flow-through of deductions but who do need to avoid the unrelated business income tax.

THE MULTIPLE ADVANTAGES
OF EXISTING REAL ESTATE INVESTMENTS

Five main factors have created a great interest in *existing* real estate:

1. inflation hedge,
2. yield,
3. tax benefits,
4. debt leverage, and
5. safety.

Inflation Hedge. Real estate values in general follow or exceed the upward movement of the cost of living. No wonder that replacement costs consistently move skyward. While building material costs move in an upward bias, they do have corrections from time to time as supply and demand interact. But regardless of demand, labor costs seem to go up every year. In addition to the historical upward revision in real estate values, the borrower incurs debt at today's dollars and repays that debt at tomorrow's cheaper dollars. The net effect is that appreciation is magnified.

Yield. In today's marketplace for large commercial income properties, competitive yields (excluding equity build-up) in the neighborhood of 5 to 10% are available, depending on the growth potential of the property. This tax-benefited income, coupled with appreciation potential, provides a handsome total return picture versus 1982's "core" inflation rate of 8 to 9%. (See the Cash Flow Analysis (Yield), in "How Depreciation Shelters Income.")

Tax Benefits. Let's briefly concentrate on the tax benefits as they relate to the income produced by real estate properties.

1. *Depreciation.* The deduction for depreciation, which permits recovery of the cost of real property in straight line or accelerated fashion over a stipulated period of time, is based on the total cost of the property, exclusive of land.

EXAMPLE:

An investment of $100,000 in real estate, coupled with a modest $100,000 of mortgage debt (a one-to-one debt-to-equity ratio) buys $200,000 of real estate. The $200,000 total represents the purchase of $50,000 of land and $150,000 of building. In accordance with the Economic Recovery Tax Act of 1981, real property may be written off, for tax purposes, under a straight-line method over a 15-year period instead of using accelerated depreciation method. Such an accounting tactic would avoid adverse total depreciation recapture upon the resale of a nonresidential property. As such, the $150,000 would provide $10,000 of depreciation deductions per year for 15 years. That essentially means that our investment could produce as much as $10,000 of otherwise net taxable income from rents before any tax liability would occur.

2. *Regular Interest Payments.* The borrower's regular interest payments are deductible and are used—along with depreciation—to reduce the taxes that would otherwise have to be paid on cash flow. Any excess interest and depreciation deduction over and above that necessary to shelter cash flow would be used to offset the investor's other taxable income. Existing real estate can also become a Type II tax-incentive investment whenever it creates more deductions than are needed to shelter its income.

Debt Leverage. Real estate has historically allowed a greater use of borrowed money that most other types of investments. That in itself says a great deal about the financial world's acceptance of improved real estate as a sound investment. In normal times, 75 to 80% financing is common. The recent scarcity of long-term financing at reasonable and economically acceptable prices makes traditional debt financing more difficult if not impossible. More sophisticated financing arrangements are usually available to the larger real estate buyers.

In any case, here is an illustration of how debt leverage magnifies positive results:

Property Purchase Price	$ 6,000,000
Mortgage (Debt Leverage)	(4,000,000)
Equity Investment	$ 2,000,000

Now assume that a core inflation rate of 8% is in existence for the next seven years and that the property appreciates accordingly. Assume, too, that no debt reduction occurs.

Appreciated Property Value	$ 10,282,946
Mortgate Repayment	(4,000,000)
Net Proceeds After Debt Payment	6,282,946
Original Equity Investment	(2,000,000)
Profit	$ 4,282,946
Profit as a Percentage of Property Purchase Price ($4,282,946 ÷ $6,000,000)	71%
Profit as a Percentage of Equity Investment ($4,282,946 ÷ $2,000,000)	214%

The interest cost of leverage must, of course, be subtracted from this profit. Practically speaking, however, interest costs are typically paid out of annual rental income, which is at least partially sheltered by the deductibility of interest payments.

Leverage can also work to one's disadvantage as well as to one's advantage. It is good only if the after-tax yield and/or increase in value (total return) is greater than the after-tax cost of leverage (interest).

Safety. Real estate is a limited commodity. As long as there are people on earth, there will be a demand for real estate. As people are increasing their appetite for greater convenience, large numbers of people who are not now investing in real estate should and will consider its benefits as a "total return" investment—especially qualified retirement plans.

DISADVANTAGES IN EXISTING REAL ESTATE PROPERTIES

There are naturally some disadvantages to real estate investments:

1. *Risky without proper research and guidance.* As in any complicated investment, the quality of the professional assistance will determine success or failure in the long run. *Location of property, price paid,* and *who manages* it all increase or decrease investment risk. Your clients should steer away from real estate syndicators who lack total expertise in demographics, acquisition, property management, and liquidation.

2. Lower liquidity. This can be only partially offset by diversifying one's investment into many different properties—or by investing via limited partnerships, which could be transferrable if a buyer can be found. Importantly, investments in real estate should be limited to those who have sufficient assets so as not to have liquidity as an important objective insofar as that segment is concerned. Cash reserves and risk management provisions should already be in place before real estate investments are considered.

3. *Difficult to value.* One doesn't actually know what real property is worth until it is sold. Of course, professional appraisers can be employed, but their appraised values cannot be represented as being exact. Unlike stocks and bonds, real estate values are not quoted in the newspaper. If your clients need to know what they are worth each day, real estate is not for them.

4. *Depreciation recapture on sale.* Recapture can be a disadvantage. One must either avoid recapturing accelerated depreciation *at a higher tax bracket* through income timing and planning or via the sheltering of it at the time the property is sold—or pay the consequences.

WHAT TO WATCH FOR IN SELECTING DEPRECIATION METHODS

The write-offs (accelerated recovery percentages per year) are provided in IRS tables. These tables approximate the 175% declining-balance method, switching to straight-line depreciation when it becomes more beneficial. During both the first year and last year of ownership, the depreciation deduction is computed in accordance with the actual number of months held. Distinction is no longer made between new and used real property in determining depreciation allowances.

Instead of using the accelerated recovery percentages introduced by ERTA 1981, real estate may be written off under a straight-line method over 15, 35, or 45 years. This election is made on a property-by-property basis. In many cases, selecting the proper depreciation method is a crucial tax decision.

For instance, gain on the sale of *nonresidential* real estate depreciated under the accelerated recovery percentage will be ordinary income to the extent of the total depreciation used. If the straight-line method is used, all of the gain will be capital gain. On the other hand, gain on the sale of *residential* rental property will be ordinary income only to the extent that the accelerated depreciation exceeds 15-year straight-line depreciation. Also, remember that ERTA 1981 eliminated the use of component depreciation.

The nuts and bolts of all of this will usually result in using *accelerated depreciation with residential properties and straight-line with nonresidential properties.* In both cases, the resulting deductions are

greater than existed prior to ERTA. This bodes well for the future attractiveness of real estate from a tax viewpoint.

How developmental real estate provides more tax shelter

Every great area for tax-incentive investment usually has Type I and Type
II applications. For example, in energy the important issue is the ownership of gas/oil reserves. Type I involves the lower-risk, after-tax investment in existing, producing gas/oil properties that generate tax-
benefited, predictable cash flow. Type II involves the riskier drilling for
those reserves with pretax money which, in turn, dramatically lowers the
risk.

Real estate properties offer the same option. Type I real estate investing, just discussed, involves the purchase of lower-risk existing properties. That offers the advantage of avoiding the risks of the construction
and rent-up phases. Because of its very nature, the investor sees an historical occupancy rate in advance or can contract for one through a
lease-back arrangement. Additionally, the investor usually benefits by immediate tax-sheltered cash flow, as opposed to waiting a year or more
until the building is completed and hopefully occupied.

Conversely, if those risk-cushioning benefits can be given up, there
are distinct advantages to developmental, to-be-built real estate. The
most attractive plus involves the greater tax deductions due to a combination of construction loan interest and other start-up costs. These tax
benefits, properly employed, can have the same effect as buying an existing property at a price well below its replacement cost.

From a pure economic point of view, the widely forecast coming
housing shortage in the '80s should result in big profits for those involved
in the development of apartment complexes. Being very management-
intensive, it is best to have the entity who buys such an investment for
your client also be: (1) a part owner and (2) its manager. It is likely that an
investment, or preferably a series of investments of this type, would provide deductibility of at least your cash investment. More importantly, it
would offer an after-tax anticipated total return of at least 10 percentage
points above the inflation rate expectation, after factoring in leverage.

Recent 1982 *public partnership offerings* comprised mainly of to-be-
built properties offer estimated tax deductions as follows:

First year	40–50%
Second year	30%
Third year	15%
Fourth year	5%

These deductions, expressed as a percentage of capital subscriptions in the partnership, are over and above those estimated to be needed to shelter expected rental income. They are ideally used to offset earned or investment income taxed at the highest tax brackets. Since the vast majority of these deductions are derived from the straight-line portion of the depreciation used and other such nonrecapturable expenses, tax *conversion* or *transformation* occurs.

EXAMPLE:

> Using the percentages from the table, assume that deductions total 100% of capital contribution over the first four years of investment. To illustrate *only* the tax consequences, assume no cash flow, appreciation or equity build-up. All property holdings are presumed sold at the beginning of the fifth year, and the investor is in the 50% maximum bracket.

Capital Contribution	$ 1,000,000
Financing	2,000,000
Total Cost (Basis)	3,000,000
Deductions (100% × $1,000,000)	(1,000,000)
Reduced Cost Basis	2,000,000
Tax Savings (50% × $1,000,000)	500,000
Capital Contribution	$ 1,000,000
Tax Savings	(500,000)
Net Cost of Investment	500,000
Sale of Properties	$ 3,000,000
Reduced Cost Basis	(2,000,000)
Long-Term Capital Gain	1,000,000
Tax Liability ($1,000,000 × 40% × 50%)	$ 200,000
Proceeds of Sale	$ 3,000,000
Debt Repayment	(2,000,000)
Tax Liability	(200,000)
Net Proceeds of Investment	800,000
Net Cost of Investment	(500,000)
Net Profits	$ 300,000

The $300,000 or 30% after-tax profit is simply the result of using the $1,000,000 of deductions against 50% taxed ordinary income and *Uncle Sam* reclaiming them at the effective 20% rate (50 × 40%). That's tax transformation!

Needless to say, few of us could or would often commit the entire $1,000,000 to one partnership or property. Instead, we would probably own one or more $5,000 or $50,000 units of the whole. We would then receive a prorated share of the total tax and economic benefits of the pool.

Private partnerships offered over the past few years, with staged cash investments over two to three years, provide even higher tax deductions. Typical benefits would be a 75–80% deduction of the first-year investment, 125% of the second, and 200% of the third. It usually adds up to about 115% of your total cash investment unless questionable tax ploys and excessive debt leverage are employed to make the tax lures more attractive and the economics more questionable.

EXAMPLE:

A recent typical private offering of a single garden apartment complex under construction totaled $2,755,000 of capital contribution. Each limited partner invested a minimum of $82,000, as follows:

Date	Amount	Percent
Upon execution of Subscription	$34,850	42.5%
February 1, 1983	37,310	45.5%
February 1, 1984	9,840	12.0%

The stated objective of the partnership is to maximize current tax benefits with an emphasis on long-term capital appreciation with interim cash flow, if available. The projected tax deductions per $82,000 investment were as follows:

Year	Cash Invested	Projected Tax Deduction	Deduction as a Percent of Installment
1982	$34,850	$23,016	66.0%
1983	37,310	47,548	127.4%
1984	9,480	23,138	235.1%

The cumulative tax writeoff over three years was projected to be about 114.3%. Financing involved $5,550,000 (callable 83 months after funding) at 13.25% for the first five years and 15.5% thereafter. Conversion to condominiums is anticipated within seven years.

THE PROS AND CONS OF REAL ESTATE DEVELOPMENT

The increased tax benefits of developmental real estate is the chief benefit. Along with the increased risk of construction and rent-up also comes the increased potential for appreciation of such a new project. That must be offset by the usual uncertainty of the amount and timing of cash flow and by illiquidity.

WHO SHOULD INVEST

To-be-built real estate is consequently not for the faint of heart, those with objectives for predictable income, or those who cannot dramatically reduce their "money at risk" via the tax deductions.

After completely understanding the possible drawbacks cited, and still desiring a five- to-seven-year "total return" type of illiquid investment, developmental real estate could be a real winner. That may especially be true if you key in on the coming housing shortage.

How to take maximum advantage of the coming crisis in rents

Recall, if you will, what caused chaos at the gasoline stations in the '70s. It was not the price that had to be paid for gasoline that instigated the fist fights and shootings. It was the threat, real or imagined, of cutting the supply that was so troubling.

If not having enough gasoline to get to work, to shop, or to continue the vacation caused turmoil, what do you expect will happen when Americans cannot, at any price, buy or rent a roof over their heads? If government policy affecting housing does not change immediately, while simultaneously letting rents rise dramatically, this crisis is exactly what the '80s will superimpose upon the energy scenario that has already come to life. Even if our government does act in time to avoid a total catastrophe, it has already set into motion a developing housing shortage that portends a real *crisis in rents*. More succinctly stated, I believe that the second most obviously undervalued "commodity" in our nation today following regulated natural gas is *rents*.

HOW THE SUPPLY OF HOUSING STACKS UP

A combination of (1) price and lack of supply of long-term credit, (2) inability of developers to immediately deduct construction loan interest, and (3) abnormally low rents, has practically halted the construction of new, nongovernment-subsidized residential, rental properties in America. During 1981 and 1982, less than one million new housing units were constructed versus an average of 1.8 million starts per year during the 1970s. In recent years, about two-thirds of the starts represented single-family homes and one-third were multifamily rental units, most of which were government-subsidized.

WHAT WILL DEMAND BE LIKE?

The Bureau of Census (as well as private sources of household formation projections) estimates that the increase in household formations will average approximately 1.5 million per year between now and 1990. Of course, the projection of household formations is only the first step in anticipating the number of household units required. For instance, about 750,000 units per year are lost through demolition, disaster, condemnation, or change to nonresidential use. Some of these re-enter the housing market leaving a conservative estimate of a new loss of 500,000 units or more per year. Without factoring in the decreased expected occupancy per household due to later marriages and increased divorces, or the need to replace substandard housing, an annual shortfall of well over 1,000,000 units per year can easily be forecasted.

WHO CAN AFFORD WHAT?

It is entirely possible that the major thrust of the problem does not center around the 1,000,000±per-year shortage as such. The fact that two-thirds of recent housing production is represented by single-family homes and only one-third by rental units, most of which is government-subsidized, may be a more significant problem. *In other words, what is being made available is no longer affordable and what is affordable is not being made available.*

It is now estimated that less than 20% of all American families are able to afford home ownership costs associated with a median-priced new home. In 1970 the percentage was 46.2%. The reasons for the decline are simple. Using 1967 as a base, by 1980 the CPI rose from 100 to 207 versus 246 for new homes versus only 170.8 for residential rents.

THE SOLUTION SPELLS PROFITS FOR YOUR CLIENTS

Every major crisis has multiple, alternative resolutions. With the crisis in housing looming over the horizon, the answer seems to be (1) the massive re-entry of private industry into new rental housing construction via increased economic and tax incentives, or (2) a major reordering of society in terms of who lives with whom. As all of this comes to pass, I believe that more money will be made in real estate in both absolute terms and in percentage realizations than ever before.

Five years ago or so, we talked in terms of apartment units costing $15,000 or so to build. Then we heard $17,500, then the $20,000 to $25,000 range, and now up to $35,000 per unit. Our federal government began the 80's by allowing developers a total permissible cost per unit of about $34,000. For the last 10 years, those figures have been the harbinger of the average market value of existing apartment units. Yet some units currently under construction and many existing ones can be purchased for nice discounts from that $34,000 figure: Why? Because rents—the measure of return—have not *yet* climbed high enough to warrant higher market values.

So, for those who would contend that the time to invest was yesterday, I disagree. With an estimated $8 to $15 billion of institutional money coming into real estate per year in the '80s—versus $1 to 1½ billion per year in the late '70s, my sights are upward. The institutional demand for all types of properties—coupled with the coming housing crisis—spells out much higher prices for real estate. My opinion is that the great gains are not behind you, but ahead of us all. Here is your best bet for consistent success in real estate.

Join the ranks of the big pros

Your biggest profits are never too far away from a supply/demand ratio that is heavily weighted toward demand. During the previous section, we have gone to great length to tell you why this type of relationship will exist for residential and institutional-type commercial properties during the '80s. But how can the individual investor, small or large, best take advantage of this developing real estate investment scenario?

With very few exceptions, I believe that most investors will do far better by being on the side of the large national syndicators—the "big pros." Most offer limited partnership interests in very diversified public real estate offerings of various property types in units of as little as $2,500 to $5,000. Some also provide occasional single property private syndications similar to the one illustrated on page 231. If coordinated lifetime and estate planning indicates that real estate investing is right for your client, there are a multitude of reasons why investing in publicly registered and private offerings *with the national syndicators* is the best avenue to success.

PROFESSIONAL MANAGEMENT IS A MUST

Professional investment management is, in my opinion, a must in most investment areas. It is even more important in real estate. Because so many Americans own "some" real estate, the temptation to "do it yourself" in such a familiar area is keen. Yet real estate investing always ends up being far more complicated than the uninitiated would ever dream. What to buy, where to buy it, how to finance it, who should manage it, how to diversify, and when to sell are all questions that demand expert answers. While today's opportunities are seemingly giant, so are the problems. Rents are at relative lows while competitive current yields are relatively high. Financings are complicated and changing rapidly. Fundamental economic changes and innovative national planning have to take place before the bright future I see unfolds. That future is in the hands of the "big pros," and you should join them because you won't be able to beat them!

INTEGRITY CAN BE EASILY MEASURED

Nothing is more crucial than integrity in selecting investing management. You must in every instance verify the existence of the highest level of ethical standards in your investment associations. Whether national syndicators on average have more integrity than their local counterparts is not a question to be answered here. Certainly, however, it is easier to check out the nationals. A lot of people you know have access to them—national accounting firms, NYSE member firms, advisory services, and highly regarded law firms. Much more is typically disclosed in their offering documents, particularly with the SEC-registered public offerings.

DIVERSIFIED EXPERTISE IS IN PLACE

In real estate today, national expertise is a real plus. Too often, investors come to believe that real estate in their hometown is the best real estate. Economic patterns, population trends, politics, and demographics are all key considerations. It is not enough to be good with locations, with how to buy and finance, or with how to manage or when to sell. It is necessary to be good at all of that and more to win the big chips. And the big pros have it all. Most of them manage their own properties. An old adage reminds us that no one manages a property as well as its owner!

BEING BIG IN REAL ESTATE IS GOOD

After the rapid inflation of recent years, attractive, well located properties of consequence are valued in millions and tens of millions of dollars. How else can your client participate in properties of such size and prime location than with the large national syndicators? These types of properties are the ones that will be sold to the even larger domestic and foreign buyers of the future.

In addition to single property buying power, the larger public offerings also provide extensive diversification. In the financial planning sense, it is much easier to predict investment performance when you are dealing with a diversified pool of properties. Diversification also provides management with the power to ride out difficulties associated with any one problem property and therefore reduce risk dramatically.

Size provides the freedom to develop investment strategy. Small, local developers are more restricted. They usually "know" apartments, office parks, or shopping centers, and then they know only in their locale. What if what they know best is not the best buy at the time you invest?

Conversely, the national syndicators can stress income properties or to-be-builts, residential or commercial, one region of the country over another. They have the ability to develop and execute a portfolio strategy that will accommodate intermediate or long-term trends.

PAST RESULTS ARE IN A FISHBOWL

Last but not least, you must be able to determine how your real estate money manager has performed in the past. Don't just look at the good times. Find out how he fared during periods like 1974–76. The national syndicators—and there are many who have been around for years—live in a fishbowl. The results you can easily study are impressive. All of their past offering documents are a matter of public record. You can see what past investors were charged and who shared what with whom.

Some would say that the smaller, local syndicators charge less—if in fact you can find out what is, in total, charged. Even if that were not a problem, I would remind you that the cheapest surgeon is not usually the best. It is the same in real estate. You will *get* in direct proportion to what you pay—within reason.

How buying proven gas/oil production can make your client richer by the barrel

Listen to this! Two articles appeared in one of the nation's top newspapers, one of which went so far as to say that there is a great deal of OPEC oil around that cannot find a home and that should undermine OPEC's price structure. The other article noted that oil supplies, currently in abundance, may remain adequate at least through 1990, reducing the likelihood of another extraordinary jump in prices. Don't get too excited, because these articles were written late in 1977—just before oil prices jumped by 170% in early 1979.

The press loves buzz words, and the term "glut" is one such word. As one astute oil analyst recently observed, there is a surplus of oil above the ground right now but he didn't see any surplus below the ground. A "glut" implies some major collapse in oil prices and that simply is not evident. Anyone who thinks that our oil supply is stable and secure is reading only the funny papers and not the international news. Anything that interrupts the oil supply will set off another scramble in higher prices. In early 1979, a shortage of less than 5% created a near panic and led to that 170% increase in price. Other respected sources have spotlighted the probability of Saudi Arabia cutting production whenever it must do so to protect prices.

Even if OPEC prices did drop substantially, don't count on much of a break. The politicians now recognize that we live in a highly unstable world and that the only oil that we can count on is our own. For that reason, Washington is even beginning to discuss the possibility of a tax on imported crude oil to keep prices high so that we can continue to strengthen our domestic oil industry.

I believe that the early '80s will prove to be nothing more than a passing fancy. Better than that, it offers us enormous buying potential in the interim. You should bet on producing oil and gas reserves being an excellent hedge against future inflation.

It is impossible for most of us to go out and select, buy, manage, and market the production of two, three, or more existing oil and gas fields, as attractive as that might sound. We do not have enough capital to dedicate to that one investment area; we do not have enough expertise to pull it off. Fortunately, oil companies can and have been doing that for investors for years. They study producing wells, estimate future production, apply their selling price and producing cost estimates, apply present values to all of that at about 12%, and then bid. If they win, the field goes into a limited partnership and investors then own a part of it. If their pricing estimates were right on the mark, and their engineering estimates were fairly accurate as are most such estimates with fields that have been in production for some years, the investment will have performed as expected.

Due to the use of cost depletion and deductions from other operating expenses, 60% or so of the cash flow over the life of the investment is tax-free. Most of the revenues in the first three to five years should not be taxable and then should become more taxable as the years go on. If, however, prices of oil and gas go up faster than the general partner factored into the winning bids, the total internal rate of return could be well in excess of 12%. Don't overlook the fact, too, that some such investments are internally debt-leveraged, further increasing both potential and risk.

Three additional factors lead me to believe that returns in this investment area have more than a fighting chance of doing better than the 12% discounting factor used in purchasing these properties.

First, because of currently legislated decontrol of natural gas pricing on January 1, 1985 or within 18 months thereafter, the natural gas portion of any reserves owned could actually skyrocket in value, depending upon what oil is selling for in 1985. Note that when oil is at $100 per barrel, decontrolled natural gas should be at $18.48 per 1,000 cubic feet ($100 ÷ 5.72 = $18.48).

Second, and more importantly, there's a great chance that more than expected will be recovered or extracted from your oil fields.

Technological advances in enhanced recovery techniques during the next ten years can legitimately be depended upon to help keep US production from declining as precipitously as it has in recent years. The higher prices go, the more this can be counted on to help both the nation and the investor in energy. Farm-outs of still drillable acreage, too, could and has created larger-than-expected profits.

The third reason why buying reserves via a limited partnership could provide a windfall is the windfall profits tax itself. If a Mr. Big General Partner is bidding on relatively big fields (but with less than 1,000 bbls per day of oil production) against other large buyers, he will factor the maximum windfall profits tax that applies to the majors into his bid. If he wins, and your client is a limited partner in the partnership that contains such a property, the lower case windfall profits tax for independents will apply since he is considered an independent. This, with certain types of properties, could be a major advantage for a limited partnership. Additionally, and perhaps more important, some oil production categories have already become exempt from the windfall profits tax. Others may also—sooner than later.

EXISTING GAS/OIL PRODUCING PROGRAMS
CAN PRODUCE INCOME, APPRECIATION, OR BOTH

It's possible to purchase interests in partnerships engaged in the acquisition of oil and gas properties *and* structure the investment to produce either cash flow, asset build-up or both. You can do this by automatically reinvesting part or all of the cash flow from the sale of oil and gas into subsequently formed partnerships at no sales cost. The amount that is not reinvested can be sent to your client monthly or quarterly just as is usually done through a mutual fund withdrawal plan.

The Prudential Company has historically advocated "owning a

TABLE 11–3a

Hypothetical Analysis When Applying an Investor's One-Time $10,000 Subscription

Gross Investment	$10,000
First Year Administrative and General Overhead Cost	($ 1,400)
Net Proceeds Prior to Adding Borrowed Funds	($ 8,600)
Borrowed Funds (Approximate)	($ 8,600)
Total Amount Available For Property Acquisitions Per $10,000 of Gross Investment	$17,200
Should Purchase:	
Estimated Future Net Revenue (Approximately 2.5–3.0 Times)	$43,000
Loan Repayment P/I — 6-year Note (Average 12% Interest)	($11,000)
Net Distributable Revenue to Partnership	$32,000
Percent of Limited Partner's Interest	×.85
Distributable to Limited Partner Over Life of Partnership	$27,200

TABLE 11–3b
Example: Cash Flow and Taxable Income
Hypothetical $10,000 Investment
($17,200 Purchasing Power)
85% Limited Partner's Share

Hypothetical Cash Flow		Hypothetical Taxable Income			
First Full Year's Gross Revenue*	$4,300	First Full Year's Gross Revenue*	$4,300	Estimate of Equipment Depreciation	($ 430)
					$1,070
Operating Cost (Average 25–35%)	($1,300)	Opeating Cost (Average 25–35%)	($1,300)	Estimated Loan Interest Deduction in Early Years at 14% Average ($8,600 × 85% × 14% = $1,000)	($1,000)
Net Distributable Revenue	$3,000	Net Taxable Revenue	$3,000	Reported as Taxable Income on Average $1,200 of Early Years' Distribution	$ (70)
Loan Repayment (P/I)	$1,800				
Revenue Distributable to Limited Partners	$1,200				

*Net of windfall profits tax payments.

piece *of* the rock." After your client has enough cash reserves and other more liquid assets, you should consider recommending a part of what is *in* the rock—oil and natural gas reserves. With today's seemingly imbedded and "energized" inflation rate (don't let temporary dips to between 5 and 7% placate your fear of this silent embezzler), it would be wise to have your clients own directly a part of the culprit itself. They can do that, *and* get the pass-through of the attendant tax-benefited cash flow *and* limited liability *and* professional management, only by owning their oil and gas wells via the direct participation, limited partnership route. Table 11–3 presents an illustration of how $10,000 units of such an investment are projected to work out during the early years.

THE ADVANTAGES AND DISADVANTAGES OF OWNING EXISTING GAS/OIL WELLS

Owning gas/oil wells is like owning any other business. It simply is not possible to know exactly what the investment is worth on any given day. Gas/oil income programs probably come closer, however, than any other limited partnership investment in providing an impartial estimate of future net revenues. Even so, the formula these programs use to transform the future net revenue figure to a current repurchase price is at best conservative. Besides the proper discounting of future net revenues to present value, the formula generally uses a haircut of 30% to account for possible reserve engineering errors. The fact is, most income program engineering estimates have been too low. These conservative valuations also render the repurchase prices less meaningful from a liquidity view. While this aspect of the investment will provide needed liquidity in an emergency, it certainly is not the kind of liquidity you would want to take advantage of simply to switch investments.

During the first year and a half of the investment—prior to an outside engineering evaluation—your client will show a paper loss of 20% because of the front-end costs of organizing the partnership and its investments. While it is an advantage to have this valuation to use for intrafamily gifting purposes or for estate valuations, it is not typically a valid estimate of economic value. Your client will usually have to wait two to three years before engineering estimates begin to vindicate on paper your decision to invest. I know that from experience over and over again. Even then, the early valuations still do not typically show true potential.

Finally, the greatest negative is the potential for either reserves or prices to turn out lower than estimated when the wells were purchased by the general partner. Diversification goes a long way toward mitigating low reserve estimates. Price-wise, you either believe the wildflower scenario, or you don't!

On the plus side, gas/oil "income" investments are usually a far better way to attach an energy-related cash flow stream to an investor than through oil stocks. Via Texaco or Exxon, the sale of your reserves are taxed twice, once on the corporate level and again on the dividends. That's mainly why the investor can get a much higher tax-advantaged cash flow stream of about 12% initially via the partnership. As a comparison, Exxon common stock provides a 10% "taxable" dividend at the time of this writing. Which would you prefer, 10% taxable or 12% partially tax-sheltered?

Some gas/oil income programs, as they are commonly called, provide an administrative flexibility not available in oil stocks. As previously noted, investors can reinvest all of the cash flow, making the investment a growth vehicle. Or they can receive all of the cash flow to produce maximum spendable income. Being a depleting asset, a gas/oil income program would take on the looks of a ball of investment twine unwinding itself. Finally, investors could take only the cash flow they actually need, say 8 to 10%, and reinvest the remainder in an attempt to keep inflation-hedged reserves level or increasing!

Two less significant advantages are the small size of the required minimum investment—usually $2,500. Whoever dreamed a few years ago that an investor could go directly into the oil business with so little capital. Conversely, large institutions find it very efficient to invest millions of dollars in this area alongside the smallest individual.

All of these pluses make gas/oil income programs ideal partial funding vehicles for charitable remainder trusts, installment sales, private intrafamily annuities and qualified or unqualified deferred compensation plans.

The greatest of all advantages, though, is the ability to own gas/oil reserves directly without having to subject capital to the higher risk of drilling. If your client is in a lower tax bracket or risk-averse, gas/oil income direct participations were designed with this sort of person in mind.

The king of tax shelters: how to use drilling to enhance wealth

The proper conceptual approach to tax-incentive investment planning requires that the probability of profit (aside from the tax benefits) be the prime consideration. Insofar as economic viability is concerned, research indicates that the diversified approach to the exploration and development of gas/oil properties provides unusual opportunity for profit. It has in fact, never appeared more attractive than it does as 1982 ends.

Since the energy crisis slowly developed during the late '60s and early '70s, and especially since October of 1973 when the crisis became so visible, the price of gas and oil has risen far more rapidly than the average cost of finding it. While the price of oil hovers in the low to middle $30s, the average cost of finding oil is currently estimated to be in the area of $7 to $10 per barrel.

Although the drilling for decontrolled oil and "price-controlled" natural gas is quite attractive now, there is a high potential, speculative add-on profit that could occur during the latter half of the '80s after prices are deregulated. Gas above 15,000 feet is currently under federal price control. The current price of that gas averages under $3 per thousand cubic feet (mcf) and is allowed to go up with the gross national product deflater. January 1, 1985 is the date when current law decontrols gas unless the President chooses to extend it for an additional 18 months. Here lies a potential bonanza.

The energy equivalent price of oil is derived by multiplying the natural gas price by a factor of 5.72. That means that if gas is at $2.50 per mcf, oil should be at $14.30 per barrel. We all know that oil is over two times that price, and therefore, if oil goes up only at the inflation rate between now and the mid-'80s and gas quite naturally, under the law, does the same, we will see a *tripling* of the price of shallow natural gas after decontrol. That, less any windfall profits tax that our government may choose to impose on the results of its past natural gas policy mistakes, is inevitable. As evidence of the fact that gas will sell at or in excess of the BTU equivalent of oil, the deeper uncontrolled gas in Oklahoma has recently sold for $6.50 to $9 per mcf.

As a result, the economic viability of drilling for oil and particularly for natural gas has never been more attractive. It enjoys an enviable position among tax-incentive investments due to its ability to produce an attractive return as long as the gap between prices and costs stays wide. It is a potential windfall if at least the discovery of some natural gas is involved and is or becomes decontrolled.

REDUCING RISK THROUGH
DIVERSIFICATION IS REQUISITE TO SUCCESS

In addition to insisting on unusually attractive economic potential before participating, drilling risk can be further controlled through broad and extensive diversification. When exploration is involved, participating in a series of limited partnerships over more than one year is an absolute must. If the involvement is mainly developmental drilling (close to existing production), diversification is also important but not as much as with higher-risk exploration.

WHEN AND WHAT TO EXPECT IN THE WAY OF CASH FLOW

In the case of both developmental and exploratory drilling, investors should expect an average return (future net revenues) of between two to three times the pretax investment, spread over ten to fifteen years subsequent to the year of investment. Cash flow will normally begin nine to eighteen months after the date of investment with developmental partnerships, and three to five years after the year of investment with exploratory ones. Also, balanced programs will fall in between those two parameters.

How the three major income tax benefits
of drilling reduce cost and increase return

Under present law, three important tax benefits are available to investors in gas and oil drilling programs:

1. intangible drilling cost deductions,
2. depletion allowances, and
3. investment tax credits and depreciation of capital equipment.

HOW INTANGIBLE DRILLING EXPENSES
REDUCE THE INVESTOR'S OUT-OF-POCKET COST

The major expenses inherent in a drilling effort are deducted as intangible drilling costs (IDCs). These include well site expenses, actual drilling costs, geological and geophysical expenses, lease expenses on dry holes, plus the cost for items necessary in preparing a well for production that no salvage value. Under current law, these items can be expensed in the year incurred.

For investors in an oil and gas program, this means that from 60% to 90% of their investments may be deducted in the year of their investment, and up to a total of 100% within a two- to four-year period. The extent to which these tax benefits affect individuals will depend on the magnitude of their income and tax bracket.

When the investment is leveraged, illusive multiple deductibility can be achieved. Except for real estate, however, no deductions are valid unless they are produced via the employment of capital, borrowed or otherwise, for which *you are at risk*. That includes the letters of credit often used for collateral for partnership borrowings in leveraged programs.

It must be reemphasized that the IDCs associated with successfully completed wells are preference items that affect the alternative minimum tax computation.

HOW PERCENTAGE DEPLETION
INCREASES THE INVESTOR'S AFTER-TAX RETURN

The best known tax benefit of gas/oil investments is the depletion allowance, which 1975's tax "deform" reduced. This is a perfect example of how our government reduced the attractiveness of gas/oil production just at the moment when it should have been increasing it. If in fact we wanted to strive for domestic energy self-sufficiency, the opposite trend should have been legislated.

In any case, the depletion allowance allows for a portion of the income from the sale of oil and gas production to be tax-free, provided that the investors qualify as "small producers." It, too, can be a preference item if the taxpayer's accumulated depletion deductions exceed the cost basis. A "small producer" is anyone who does not control a sizable retail outlet or who does not refine more than 50,000 barrels of oil on any one day of a taxable year.

Here's a table illustrating the depletion allowance rate by year and by production volume:

Year	Production Exempted	Depletion Rate
1982	1,000 bbls a day or 6.0 mcfs per day	18%
1983	1,000 bbls a day or 6.0 mcfs per day	16%
1984 and thereafter	1,000 bbls a day or 6.0 mcfs per day	15%

To determine the tax-free amount, one applies the depletion rate to the *gross* income before operating expenses, which will result in the tax-free amount (assuming it does not exceed 50% of the net income). Typically, 20% + of the cash flow in a drilling program would currently be tax-free, as the following example illustrates for 1983:

Gross Income	$2,000
Less Operating Costs	500
Net Income	$1,500
Depletion Allowance (16% of gross income)	320 (21% of Net Income)
Taxable Income	$1,180

In this example, an investor would receive a check for $1,500 with $320 (or 21%) being tax-free due to the depletion allowance. A maximum of that amount, $320, may have to be included as a tax preference item but would not be taxed at the 20% minimum tax rate, unless other items of tax preference would trigger the alternative minimum tax.

HOW DEPRECIATION AND TAX CREDITS INCREASE RETURN

The third tax benefit relates to programs whose capital is also used to purchase above-ground equipment used in the production of gas and oil from commercially successful wells. Typical of these "recoverable" or "tangible" expenses would be pipe, storage tanks, separators, valves, and other equipment for which the investment tax credit is available and which can be depreciated.

It becomes readily apparent that these expenses are more apt to be of consequence in developmental programs that have a high drilling success ratio and when the partnership structure provides for the partnership to foot that bill. For example, if a partnership expends as much as 30% of its capital on such equipment, the investor should still end up with the intangible drilling cost deductions that result from the employment of the other funds for drilling. In addition, about 30% of the investment will be depreciated over its first five years and 10% of the 30% (or about 3% of the investment) will result in investment tax credits. These depreciation and tax credit benefits usually serve to make a larger portion of the early years' cash flow tax-free than would be caused by statutory depletion alone.

Conversely, many exploratory and some developmental drilling partnerships are structured in a way that allocates all of the drilling costs to the investor and the equipment purchases to the general partner (functional allocation). In such an arrangement, the investor would get more front-end, IDC deductions (90–100% in the first year or two of the program). But a lesser percentage of the early cash flow would be tax-free. As usual, we always give up one benefit to get another.

WHAT A SUCCESSFUL DRILLING PROGRAM LOOKS LIKE

Tax benefits are usually the initial reason investors are attracted to oil and gas drilling programs, but the drilling program must find profitable quantities of oil and gas for the limited partners to make the investment worth while. To better understand what characterizes a successful program, you need to understand the phases of a drilling program's life. There are as many as four phases in an exploratory program's life.

In the first phase, most of the funds raised are applied to drilling exploratory wells. The objective in this phase is to find new fields that can be profitably developed. While the number of wells completed as producers are few, reserves discovered, which can be developed from the successful wells, can be significant. The first phase can take from six months to three years to complete.

In the second phase, developmental drilling around successful discoveries occurs. There are up to six sources of funds to finance developmental drilling:

1. Some programs retain a portion of the initial capital for development drilling.

2. The next favored source is cash flow from initial discoveries. Rarely is this substantial enough, however, to fund the development of a substantial discovery.

3. New natural gas discoveries are sometimes funded by pipeline companies that advance the necessary funds to develop the field at preferential loan terms, in exchange for the right to the natural gas at a competitive price.

4. If the discovery is oil or in areas where pipeline companies are unwilling to make advances, loans from banks that serve the oil industry are made. Generally, these have been less desirable than advances from pipeline companies because the banks demand a major portion of the production revenue for debt service, thus delaying cash flow to the investor.

5. The least desirable method of funding developmental drilling from the drilling program's perspective is through what is termed a "farm-out." This occurs when there is not enough equity to borrow funds, and another party drills the location. If successful, they receive their money back before the original group participates in a reduced portion of the revenue.

6. Limited partners are often assessed.

The development phase typically takes from six months to five years to complete from the date of the discovery.

The third phase in an exploratory program occurs if loans are involved in the funding of developmental drilling. It consists of the repayment of that debt.

The final phase is cash distributions to the investors, which rarely begin before the second year of a program's life. In an exploratory program, they typically begin in the third or fourth year.

Developmental programs are less involved since they are generally drilling in shallower areas, which require less time to complete. Since less activity is required before completing the program, cash flow generally begins more quickly. However, most developmental programs in the past have not discovered as much reserves as the average exploratory program.

Apparently, larger reserves are usually found by exploratory-oriented programs. However, the cash flow from these programs takes longer to begin. Therefore, an aspect of defining a successful program is to determine which is preferable: an early cash flow program or a program that delays cash flow and finds larger reserves. Obviously, due to the time value of money, funds received five years from now are worth less than funds received in the present year. So if an exploratory program's cash flow is spread over years four through fourteen, it must provide a larger total net revenue before it is economically equivalent to a development program that spreads its income over years one through ten.

Because gas/oil drilling partnerships are compared with alternative investment choices, it is quite natural to want to relate some uncomplicated "rate of return" to the average investment so that we might compare it with the other investment strategies. While that is a natural tendency, doing it does not always come natural to even those investors with mathematical backgrounds. The problem, you see, arises out of the fact that participating in a drilling program is more like going into the petroleum business than it is like buying an investment security. As such, most of us have used "after-tax internal rates of return," which are rather complicated to compute and more complicated to understand. We will therefore attempt to provide a new and easier way to measure and define a simple rate of return for gas/oil programs. But first we will preface our basic calculations with some definitions and assumptions:

EXAMPLE: RATE OF RETURN FOR GAS/OIL PROGRAMS

Definitions:

1. *Payout:* is the total pretax revenues received by the investor within ten years, divided by the pretax cash of his investment. A payout of

two to one means that a $10,000 investor is expected to receive monthly or quarterly cash flow payments totalling $20,000 over the first ten years of the partnership's life.

2. *Tax saving rate* is the total amount of net taxes saved during the first 12 to 36 months of the investment, expressed as a percentage of pretax cash cost of the investment.

3. *Tax paying rate* is the total amount of net taxes paid as a ratio to the taxable portion of the net revenues.

Assumptions:

1. The majority of the front-end tax benefits (intangible drilling costs plus investment tax credits) accrue to the investor during the first 12 months of the life of the partnership.

2. Almost all of the net revenues will be received by the investor within 10 years, with cash flow beginning within 9 to 18 months, peaking around the fifth or sixth year, and depleting by year 10.

3. One-third of the net revenues are tax-free, principally as a result of the depletion allowance plus depreciation of capital equipment.

Fact. Receiving $20,000 of net revenues in the manner described in "the second assumption" is mathematically equivalent to receiving $2,000 per year for 10 years.

Computation. Assume 50% tax saving rate, 50% tax paying rate, and 2:1 payout.

Cash Cost of Gas/Oil Investment	$ 10,000
Total Tax Saving @ 50% Tax Saving Rate	(5,000)
Money-at-Risk	$ 5,000
Total Net Revenues with 2 : 1 Payout	$ 20,000
Total Tax-Free Portion (⅓)	6,666
Total Taxable Revenues (⅔)	13,334
Taxable Revenues After 50% Tax Paying Rate	6,667
Total After-Tax Revenues ($6,666 + 6,667)	13,333
After-Tax Revenues per Year (13,333 ÷ 10)	$ 1,333
That portion of $1,333 annual after-tax revenues considered to be return of principal. $358 invested per year @ 6% will refund the total $5,000 of money-at-risk in 10 years	(358)
Portion of $1,333 annual revenues considered to be profit (after-tax income)	975
After-tax annual simple rate of return ($975 income ÷ 5,000 money at risk)	19.50%

Table. Similar computations of after-tax rates of return can be made for an infinite number of combinations of payouts, tax paying rates, and tax saving rates. We have, however, computed the simple rates of return for the 50% tax rate and six different payouts.

Tax Savings and Tax Paying Rates						
	.5 : 1	1 : 1	1.5 : 1	2 : 1	2.5 : 1	3 : 1
50%	− .5%	4.18%	12.84%	19.50%	26.16%	32.84%

These results are quite significant. In the 50% tax savings and paying rates, investors would need to average a payout of less than 1 : 1 before they would have been better off in a ten-year investment that paid 4.18% tax-free or 8.36% taxable.

AN INVESTMENT STRATEGY FOR THE SUITABLE INVESTOR

Throughout this chapter, we have stressed the necessity of considering economic potential the primary factor for selecting a tax-incentive investment. You must then weigh the clarity of the initial, ongoing, and future tax ramifications as well as the extent to which your client can benefit by them.

In general, the investors should be able to use all of the deductions created by a drilling investment to offset income that would otherwise be taxed at a 48% rate or higher on the federal income tax level. They should also have a substantial net worth prior to considering the purchase of a series of gas and oil investments. They should not impair the required level of estate liquidity. Finally, they should have a temperament that will allow them to be comfortable with the fact that their investment value may be totally unknown for as long as a year and not accurately known for as long as three to four years. They should also understand the meaning of "after-tax capital at risk" and learn enough about potential investment merits and risks to understand the major factors that are important beyond the initial tax benefits. They should recognize that risk is reduced to a sensible level only when their investment capital is spread over a series of separate limited partnerships. Investors who possess these traits are ideally suited to seek the multiple benefits offered by gas and oil drilling programs.

HOW GAS/OIL DRILLING
CAN REDUCE GIFT AND ESTATE TAXES

Besides using gas/oil drilling partnership investments to simply transform tax liability into wealth, there are a number of other important financial planning applications.

Basically, what investors own, when they own a successful gas/oil drilling program, is a stream of future net revenues. The cash liquidating value of a drilling program, acceptable to the IRS for intrafamily gifting or estate valuation purposes, is usually a severely discounted "present value" of all the future net revenues, haircutted for possible engineering error. Investors should therefore never sell a drilling partnership at its posted cash liquidating value. Also, a potentially large percentage of the drilling deductions taken, depending on the years of participation, get recaptured as ordinary income. The combination of discounting, haircutting, and adverse tax ramifications make it foolish in most instances to liquidate such an investment for cash or exchange it on a "taxable" basis for an existing security. Most often, even exchanging it on a tax-free basis should be closely scrutinized.

It is not at all uncommon to find mature and very successful drilling partnerships with estimated future net revenues of two and one-half to three times the computed cash liquidating value. That is because the future stream of income is discounted to present value at perhaps as much as two to three percentage points above the prime rate and then haircutted by as high as 33½%. The future revenues often include only the production from existing producing zones, not from other formations and reserves that can be tapped later on. All this typically produces too low a price at which to sell or gift to charity *but a very good one for estate valuation or intrafamily gifting purposes.*

HOW TO USE GAS/OIL DRILLING
TO REDUCE COLLEGE EDUCATION COSTS BY 75%

EXAMPLE

Geneva Walters estimates the future cost of her child, Katherine's, education to be $50,000 after considering inflation. If she were to achieve an average two-to-one result in a series of drilling programs, she would have to invest $25,000 five to ten years in advance of Katherine's college freshman year. Because of her 50% marginal tax bracket, Geneva waits until the investment provides her with the equivalent of $12,500 in combined tax savings and tax-sheltered cash flow, before she gifts it to Katherine or to Katherine's trust.

The future net revenues of $50,000 produce a haircutted, discounted present value of only $20,000. That amount she can gift to Katherine over 2 years without gift taxes or the use of any of her unified transfer credit. Her cost is actually 50% of the $25,000 investment, or $12,500 versus $50,000 had she gifted cash instead. She will, in actual fact, provide Katherine with four times her outlay of $12,500, assuming Katherine receives the $50,000 in the zero to very lowest tax brackets. That's the magic—taking the deductions against her high bracket and taking in the predominately taxable cash flow at the child's lower to nonexistent bracket.

These figures admittedly do not factor in the time value of money. However, it is also true that your client would not have to invest as much in this example had the program's cash flow been invested in a money market fund while waiting for the child to pay tuition. This same concept can easily be used to pay for part or all of an elderly relative's nursing home expenses.

HOW TO SIZABLY REDUCE
CHARITABLE GIFTING COSTS WITH DRILLING PROGRAMS

At the very outset, we must spotlight the lack of desire for making charitable gifts of mature gas/oil drilling partnerships due to the severely discounted and haircutted cash values that are typically computed. There is, however, a clever alternative if investors can afford to use the fruits of their drilling efforts to fund charitable obligations. Consider this. Investors in gas/oil drilling can keep the one-quarter to one-third of the overall cash flow that is tax-free due to depletion and other business expenses. Then they can gift the rest to charity each December, by which time they should have a very good idea what it is and how much is taxable. That is like having their cake and eating it, too.

EXAMPLE

Dr. Ducos could gift $5,000 of cash to charity, deduct it, save $2,500 in the 50% bracket, and end up with a net cost of $2,500. Alternatively, he could invest $5,000 in an assumed two-to-one ($10,000) drilling program, deduct the $5,000, save $2,500 in a 50% bracket, and again end up with a $2,500 initial cost. He then gifts the otherwise taxable two-thirds of the cash flow, or $6,667 to the charity as it arrives each year, and keeps the tax-free one-half, or $3,333. The charity gets $6,667 tax-free, and he reduces his cost from $2,500 to a negative $833. In other words, he makes money by giving money. All he has to do is average two-to-one. This should not be a major problem with today's drilling economics and extensive diversification helping him along.

One step better would be for him to gift appreciated securities in amounts exactly equal to the taxable portion of the gas/oil income he wishes to donate. The gas/oil cash flow is sheltered by the charitable gift. He can then replace the gifted securities with the gas/oil flow and have a higher cost basis.

How to capture the strong economics of drilling with lower-risk royalty interests

If we can call gas/oil drilling the king of tax-incentive investments, royalty interests would be the prince. While it is attractive for investors in all tax brackets, it becomes increasingly so as one's bracket becomes lower. It is therefore an ideal investment strategy for your client's tax-exempt accounts, such as IRAs, Keogh plans, and corporate retirement programs, as well as other tax-exempt institutions.

HOW ROYALTY INTERESTS WORK

A royalty interest is the percentage of future production retained by landowners when their land is leased to an oil company for gas and oil exploration or developmental drilling. In the exploration and development of gas and oil, there are effectively two sides of the business. One side, the working interest, pays for all the expenses and receives roughly three-quarters to seven-eighths of the net fruits of the effort. This is often a drilling program. The other side, the royalty interest, owns the mineral rights, puts up none of the capital to prove up and produce the gas/oil reserves, but receives anywhere from roughly one-eighth to one-quarter of the gross gas/oil production. More and more, you will see individual investors and institutions taking a more active role in this side of the business as well as in drilling, depending upon tax situations, experience, and risk tolerance.

Basic conservatism drives an energy-oriented investor toward royalty interest investment partnerships. Today, large amounts of conservative capital are being steered toward gas/oil income programs. For the risk-averse energy-oriented investor, income programs are perfect in many ways. These programs involve relatively low risk, strong tax-benefited cash flow, and a hedge against inflation. The upside potential is, however, limited just as is the downside risk.

As we have pointed out, there are also very attractive upside opportunities for the highly taxed investor in drilling. Very high returns are quite possible with commensurate risks being partially reduced by diversification, tax benefits, and careful management selection. Royalty interests are, however, able to minimize the risk on the downside yet maximize upside potential, making it an attractive direction in energy, as you will learn, for individuals and fiduciaries alike.

WHERE SHOULD ROYALTY INTERESTS BE PURCHASED?

After the Arab embargo in 1973, the major oil companies dramatically increased their domestic drilling budgets. Higher prices made deeper drilling very much more feasible. Energy "elephant hunting" took on a sane complexion.

Deeper drilling—where the larger deposits of natural gas are found—automatically assumes bigger profits and higher risks than shallower activities. The significance of deep gas drilling is also spotlighted by the Natural Gas Policy Act of 1978, which deregulated gas produced from depths below 15,000 feet. Over this whole span of time, the price of such gas rightfully went from 20¢ per thousand cubic feet to anywhere from $6.50 to $9 because of its basic energy value. The marketplace *is* honest!

These facts suggest that the time has been—and continues to be—right to purchase royalty interests in the deep gas plays of the Gulf Coast, Oklahoma, and the Rocky Mountain basins. The royalty interest buyer—statistically knowledgeable and loaded with cash—can indirectly use the geological, geophysical, and research staffs of the major oil and gas companies and the larger independents. You see, you don't buy a royalty interest until the oil company has "staked a well" on someone's property. Staking effectively represents a decision on the part of the oil company to spend anywhere from $10 to $50 million on a well. *The royalty interest investor rides piggyback on that decision.*

Current royalty owners may be willing to sell an investor or limited partnership a part of their royalty interest as a "stop loss" tactic. If the oil company hits, they will take in more than they ever dreamed possible. If it's a dry hole, as it is likely to be at least three times out of four in the more active deep gas basins, they are out of the big money. So they often opt to sell a part of their interest for a price that will average the royalty buyer perhaps 20 or more times their money if the well is successful.

If royalty investors buy enough such royalty interests and hit only one-quarter of them, their *average* return should be about five times their money spread over the next fifteen or so years. It is significant to note how much better this is than having your money grow to five times its current worth in fifteen years (11.3%). Although this is worth smiling about, having it come back to you *over* the fifteen-year period, instead of *at the end* of it, doubles the return!

HOW TO TURN THE RISK-TO-REWARD RATIO UPSIDE DOWN

Besides the normal experience and expertise that the general partners of a royalty interest program must possess, two more ingredients should be in place. First, vast diversification is necessary! If investors are to face the odds of striking oil one out of every four to five trys, they must be spread over 50 or more prospects during any planned investment period. Second, it's wise to split the royalty interest investment perhaps 50% into proven or tested areas and 50% under lands on which those deep, very expensive, exploratory wells will be drilled.

The downside risk on the proven areas will be minimal and should at least return one's investment. The exploratory areas will provide the upside of exploratory drilling *or more* without assuming the relatively higher risks of such activity.

In drilling, there are two main risks: first, finding the reserves and second, completing and producing the well. When clients buy a royalty interest, they take on the finding risk, but they aren't concerned about how much it costs to complete and produce the well. Avoiding the completion cost overruns goes a long way toward making royalty interests attractive to lower-risk investors.

On the exploratory side, another factor levers your client's gains as no other type of investment. Suppose the interest that a partnership buys has room for two or more wells and the first one strikes. The partnership not only gets royalty checks from that first well, but then, without investing another dime beyond the original purchase price, gets a share of the gas/oil sales of the developmental wells too. That's called "royal" leverage and it, more than anything else, makes this investment most intriguing on the upside.

WHAT TYPE OF RETURN CAN YOU EXPECT?

Vastly diversified and professionally managed, experienced experts in this area advise that average returns of four to six times one's-pretax investment over a fifteen-year payout period are probable. If we assume that, overall, 50% of the wells in a balanced program hit, the other 50% will be deducted over the first three or so years of the partnership's life. Assuming that the investor is in a 50% top bracket, that would reduce each $1 invested to $.25 to an out-of-pocket cost of $.75. The estimated $5 (5 : 1) returned over the next fifteen years would be about 80% taxable. The 50% bracket would therefore tax the $4 (80% × $5) to the tune of $2, providing a net after-tax payout of $3 ($5 − $2).

When the simplified rate of return computation investments is applied, that would mean average annual after-tax cash flow of $.20 per year for fifteen years. About 3.2¢ would have to be storehoused at 6% to return the out-of-pocket cost of $.75 in fifteen years, leaving 16.8¢ of after-tax annual return. That, divided by the $.75 at risk, creates a 22.4% average annual after-tax rate of return. That's *twice* what you earn if an investment grows five fold in fifteen years!

WHY ROYALTY INTERESTS ARE
EVEN BETTER FOR LOWER TAX BRACKETED INVESTORS

Let's take the opposite extreme and assume that investors pay no taxes! The bad news is that they cannot benefit from the front-end deductions and consequently must risk the whole $1 without support from Uncle Sam. The good news is that the $5 of assumed return is not taxed, and they average 33.3¢ per year of cash flow for fifteen years. Subtracting the 4.3¢ that must be put aside at 6% to get the original $1 back in fifteen years, 29¢ is left as income. That 29¢, divided by their money at risk of $1, elevates the return to 29%.

We can conclude that a shift from the 50%-bracketed investor to a 0%-bracketed investor, increases the returns by 29.5% from 22.4% to 29%. This makes royalty interests very attractive to a wide array of investors who, due to risk-tolerance limitations or lower tax brackets, would not otherwise benefit from the extraordinary profitability of gas/oil drilling.

However, there's still the liquidity problem. But after understanding the higher potential and lower risk of royalty interests, you too will come to understand the meaning of the question, "What price liquidity?"

THREE FINANCIAL PLANNING APPLICATIONS THAT UP THE FAMILY UNIT'S TOTAL RETURN

Just as with drilling, royalty interest programs have discounted present values that work to the whole family unit's advantage:

1. The unrealistic repurchase values, acceptable to any IRS agent, are ideal for valuing an estate and reducing estate taxes.

2. The low valuations allow much more to be gifted to a family member without using up any of the unified transfer tax credit or paying gift taxes.

3. Holding a royalty interest investment *until* (a) the investor gets most of the front-end tax benefits and until (b) taxable cash flow starts, and *then* gifting the investment and its 80% taxable cash flow stream to a lower-tax-bracketed family member, spells even more tax leverage. The family keeps more of what is made!

Alternatively investors can keep the investment and use the taxable part of their cash flow to fund charitable inclinations or obligations. But they must plan ahead!

How to garner the economic reward and tax shelter of gas/oil equipment

Three of the four direct participation investment opportunities that appear opposite the risk side of the *energy* coin have now been explained: drilling, existing properties, and royalty interests. In recent years, a fourth major thrust has been made available to the investing public: the direct ownership and operation of large equipment used in the pursuit of gas/

oil production. The direct ownership and operation of offshore jack-up rigs, barge and land drilling rigs, work-over rigs, and larger offshore support vessels has and will again one day soon offer unusually attractive opportunity for both economic reward and tax shelter. The dire need to finance the building of a capital-intensive energy search has again highlighted the great validity of the limited partnership's role in capital formation. Not very long ago, we were caught up in the throes of a natural gas shortage, and an ever increasing level of oil imports as a percentage of domestic consumption seemed inevitable. But then a funny thing happened on the way to potential disaster. A shy but developing free market set in. Price ceilings were raised on natural gas. Gradual decontrol of oil prices began, and the prospect for total decontrol of both gas and oil appeared real.

It all caused nothing less than a mountain of petroleum activity. All of a sudden, oil and gas from smaller reserves, or from less readily producible ones, was not ignored. Drillers reemphasized their search for natural gas instead of viewing it as a sometimes bothersome byproduct of oil. More numerous and expensive projects for the development of existing fields and the exploration for new ones appeared in the budgets of both independents and majors alike. Despite the slowness of the move toward full price decontrol, all of this activity caused domestic production of gas and oil to increase for the first time since 1973.

Amazing what a return to free market capitalism can do! The stark reality is that what is being found is still a nonrenewable energy resource. To fend off a potential doomsday, *ensition* has to happen. An *energy source transition* must evenutally occur, switching us gradually to reproducible, renewable, solar-related energy sources, but it will literally take years if not decades.

TWO POTENTIAL ECONOMIC BENEFITS OF EQUIPMENT PARTNERSHIPS

The principal economic reward appears in the form of attractive cash flow distributions, which typically begin during the first or second year after the investment is made. Partnerships are usually structured so as to project taxable distributions of about four times the pretax investment over ten years. Second, energy-related equipment has historically appreciated at about twice the inflation rate. It would appear more reasonable today to expect a residual value in ten years of about equal to original value.

TWO TAX BENEFITS THAT HELP TO INCREASE NET WORTH

The timing of the two major tax benefits of an equipment financing investment, tax credits and depreciation, depends on the year in which the equipment is placed into service. For sake of simplicity, we will categorize these investments as:

1. *Current year transactions.* Generally speaking, *a current year transaction* should experience a first-year tax deduction of between 25% and 50% of the investment plus an investment tax credit (ITC) of about 25%. More deductions generally fall into year two before taxable income begins in year three or four.

2. *Next-year transactions.* This usually anticipates deductions of about 5% in the year of investment and deductions of 45% or so, plus ITCs of approximately 25% in the next year.

Many partnerships will invest in both this-year and next-year transactions. The effect is to split the tax benefits into two separate calendar years.

HOW TAX CREDITS REDUCE TAXES

The major tax benefit is the investment tax credit (ITC), which falls into the year in which the equipment is placed into service. It is, of course, *a direct offset against income tax liability*, not against taxable income. Tax credits therefore shelter more income for taxpayers in the 50% marginal bracket than they did when the top bracket was as high as 70%.

The credit is now established by law at 10% of investment in Section 38 property. This includes tangible personal property and other tangible property (not including a building and its structural components) used as an integral part of manufacturing, extraction, or production processes. Thus a drilling rig and related equipment is Section 38 property. If such equipment has a recovery period of five years, it qualifies for the full credit.

WHAT TO GUARD AGAINST WITH TAX CREDITS

Property does not qualify for the tax credit if it is under a net lease. Therefore, equipment financed by partnerships should not be subject to such leases, contracts, or agreements. Day rates received by the partnerships should be *gross* rates, and operating costs such as labor, energy, and food must be borne by the partnerships. Additionally, such operating costs must exceed the 15% of revenues requirement during the first year and, in fact, typically averages 35%–40% of such income. Any contract or agreement under which equipment is operated should be for less than one-half of the equipment's useful life.

Finally, if Section 38 property is disposed of prior to the end of the original estimated life, usually five years, the investment tax credit taken in excess of what was due for the actual holding period is recaptured.

The greatest potential tax planning pitfall with investment tax credits involves the investor with large long-term capital gains. Without tax counsel's consent, extreme care must be exercised not to have ITCs transform the investor's tax computation method into the alternative minimum tax. ITCs cannot be applied against tax liability when the alternative minimum tax is used. It is not currently clear that tax credits can be carried back three years and forward seven.

HOW DEPRECIATION ALLOWANCES WORK

Tangible personal property, such as drilling rigs and offshore vessels, may be depreciated over a five-year period at a rate of up to 150% of the straight-line amount. While accelerated depreciation on *"leased"* personal property *is* a tax preference item, the equipment that is owned by worthy partnerships should *not be subject to a net lease. It will therefore not result in causing the depreciation to be a tax preference item*, a clear benefit to many investors who border on paying the alternative minimum tax.

It should be emphasized that these nonpreference item deductions are ideally suited to sheltering levels of income subject to the highest brackets, while the ITCs can then be used to reduce taxes at either the very highest rate *or* the rates beneath 48%–50%. It is the only way I would ever recommend to shelter your clients down to "zero" taxes.

Finally, if tangible personal property used in a trade or business is disposed of at a gain, the gain is taxable as ordinary income to the extent that deductions for depreciation have previously been allowed, or to the extent of the gain, whichever is less.

HOW THE ECONOMICS AND TAX BENEFITS OF EQUIPMENT INTERACT TO CREATE WEALTH

The best way to demonstrate the combined benefits of an equipment partnership is via a pro forma illustration of a typical this-year transaction. The illustration in Table 11–4 is taken from an early 1982 private offering of a partnership investment in seven offshore support vessels. This 11t after-tax projection represents an overly optimistic 29.27% internal rate of return and is typical of anticipated results of well-structured partnerships offered over the past two to three years.

WHAT ARE THE RISKS?

Aside from possibly getting involved with general partners who lack integrity and/or management experience, the major risks involve:

TABLE 11–4
Pro Forma Illustration of an Equipment Partnership
($25,000 Investment)

Year	Cash Investment	Taxable Income (Loss)	Tax Savings (Requirement) (1)	Investment Tax Credit	Cash Distribution	Cumulative Cash Distributions	Annual Tax Effected Cash Flow	Cumulative Tax Effected Cash Flow
1982	$25,000	$(12,128)	$ 6,064	$5,975	$ 0	$ 0	$12,039	$ 12,039
1983	0	(5,151)	2,575	0	0	0	2,575	14,614
1984	0	0	(345)	0	9,447	9,447	9,102	23,716
1985	0	0	(1,451)	0	7,253	16,700	5,802	29,518
1986	0	0	(1,489)	0	7,443	24,143	5,954	35,472
1987	0	7,922	(4,113)	0	8,683	328,263	4,570	40,042
1988	0	5,996	(3,833)	0	10,172	42,998	6,339	46,381
1989	0	12,092	(6,106)	0	12,405	55,403	6,299	52,680
1990	0	13,470	(7,048)	0	14,885	70,288	7,837	60,517
1991	0	17,366	(8,683)	0	17,366	87,654	8,683	69,200
1992(2)	0	69,847	(34,924)	0	67,384	155,038	32,460	101,660

(1) Includes tax requirements in 1984–1990 created by cash distributions in excess of "at risk" basis.

(2) Assumes sale of the Vessels in 1992 at 100% of original cost, resulting in taxable income of $43,005, tax requirement of $21,502 and cash distribution of $36,847.

1. changing economics,
2. lack of liquidity, and
3. changing tax laws.

Changing Economics. The energy equipment business is a cyclical one. Supply and demand for equipment are both variable. Government interventions, through taxes, price controls, and federal land leasing policies, can influence economics. An oversupply of equipment or lack of demand for drilling can, as they did in late 1982, cause disruptions in usage or depress income and/or liquidation values. A key consideration in any energy equipment investment is how well it and the investors can weather the market fluctuations. Today, vessels seem to be even less vulnerable than rigs. Contrarian philosophy says that now should be an excellent time to be purchasing existing "excess" supplies of drilling equipment.

Lack of Liquidity. Any type of equipment is generally viewed as relatively illiquid. Moreover, the larger pieces of equipment, such as rigs and boats, are even more so. Fewer investors can afford them. Additionally, when owned by limited partnerships, no market can be expected to exist for partnership units.

Changing Tax Laws. During the course of any illiquid investment, tax law changes could change the benefits you anticipated. Remember, the example of the tax benefits and cash flows shown in the illustration was based on 1982 tax laws and the accompanying market for energy equipment.

All of these risks, while existent, seem minimal over the long pull. Because of the stark reality of this nation's need to keep itself very busy trying to keep our oil and gas production at least level over the next 10 to 25 years, the equipment, not withstanding the over-supply situation of 1982, should both maintain value and keep busy over the long pull. Concentration in areas of equipment investment—including both offshore and onshore drilling and work over rigs, especially boats involved directly in those activities—should eventually prove quite profitable.

All of these energy investments properly diversified and structured for investors by sponsors with impeccable integrity and successful past experience, offer after-tax economic potential very much in excess of any currently anticipated inflation rate.

How to Exploit the Evolving Communications Opportunity

In 1980, President Carter's Congress completed its work on our nation's first formalized synthetic fuels legislation. Several leaders in the field of investments and energy economics indicated during the week of passage that oil would have to be at about $75 per barrel in 1980 dollars to make the production of the average barrel of synthetic fuel commercially successful. We can then safely project that this $75 price will at least rise at the rate of inflation.

Even so, as each year's projection of existing, nonsynthetic oil becomes an increasingly larger part of the reserves that remain, we can also predict with some degree of comfort that the current price will continue to rise more rapidly than the cost of producing synfuels. Otherwise, the production of synfuels will never be economically viable. There will then obviously be a crossover point sometime in the next 10 to 20 years, creating a very strong economic incentive to produce and use alternative, replaceable, solar-related energy sources. We will have then undergone one of our nation's most crucial periods, a period of energy source transition or, for short, "ensition." That period would be very much shorter than I envision if Arab supplies are interrupted again as they were in 1973.

During ensition, our nation has no choice but to succeed in two rather formdiable tasks. The first, already begun with vigor, involves an all-out attempt to reverse the sharp downward slide in domestic production of oil and gas. The second involves the tapping of our second greatest existing energy source, *conservation*. The extraordinary need for conservation dictates that the transformation of transportation to communication become a national priority.

CATV: A MAJOR IDENTIFIABLE ANSWER TO CONSERVATION

The move toward dramatically increased national conservation will cause a burst in technological advancement that will rival both the industrial revolution and space age technology for pages in our future history books. Yet, far in advance, there is a practical tax-advantaged way for investors to participate quite handsomely via the cable television industry. Let's see how that is developing.

While the industrial revolution was characterized by the more efficient production of mass, this decade's gigantic moves toward conservation will best be characterized by the cheaper and quicker flow of bits of information. Major advances will therefore be made in the use of two-way electronic pipeline that is today called the "coaxial cable." The principal beneficiaries of that advancement will be owners and users of America's cable television systems.

COAXIAL CABLE TO THE RESCUE

While a telephone wire can carry only several voice channels, the coaxial cable used by cable television systems can carry 100+ television channels, 1,000 voice channels, and up to 100,000 "bits of information" or data channels all at the same time and in both directions. Today's technology will allow only for the use of about half of that capacity.

When you realize that only a very small percentage of today's limited technological capacity is currently being used, you come to understand how much more in the way of information will be flowing in and out of America's homes *and* offices via the coaxial cable in the future. That is why I believe that what we know as cable television today is just the beginning of a massive wiring of our nation with this remarkable electronic pipeline, the coaxial cable.

CATV: A MEANS TO PROVIDE
INEXPENSIVE ENTERTAINMENT TO HELP OVERCOME ENERGY-
INDUCED INFLATION

While conservation will help to alleviate our country's significant dependence on oil and natural gas, it cannot eliminate it. We will continue to be subjected to the effects of rising gas and oil prices both directly and indirectly through our energy requirements, as well as through the myriad byproducts of petroleum and petrochemicals.

This continuing inflationary impact calls for consumers to search for less expensive alternatives to meet their basic needs, including entertainment. We no longer can routinely treat ourselves to movies or sporting events when these activities cost a family twenty dollars or more to enjoy. Home entertainment through cable television therefore becomes an economically viable alternative. How else can a family enjoy unlimited movies, sporting events, and entertainment specials at a monthly expense equal to attending just one such activity? This rapidly increasing demand for cable television services as an inexpensive entertainment vehicle simply compounds the growth opportunity of the ownership of cable television systems.

HOW TO LOCK IN CATV'S DRAMATIC GROWTH POTENTIAL

In 1948 in Astoria, Oregon, the first cable television system in the US began operation. Today there are over 4,500 such wired communities in America. According to cable television industry experts, the average system has had revenue gains of about 24% during each of the past five years, and it has only just begun. It only takes a 15% annual compounding rate to double a system's value in five years.

Here lies the ability to make cable television capital grow fast. Those 4,500 systems, many of which change hands from year to year for a multitude of reasons, are generally valued at some relationship to gross revenues less operating expenses. Today's revenues come mainly from the basic monthly fees charged the homeowner–subscribers. Additional revenues are often derived by offering additional levels of entertainment services, such as Home Box Office or Show Time.

Sources of future revenues are limited only by our imaginations. In addition to a wealth of possible entertainment channels, there is *now* the capability to wire all of your home alarm (fire, smoke, burglar) systems for greater efficiency through cable television or to read your utility meters. But I can envision so much more. Shopping for both goods and services, electronic games, education, banking, information access, book and magazine reading, telephonic vision, financial planning, office-at-home-arrangements may all soon be available to you without ever having to get into your five-figure petroleum guzzling automobile. Actually, some of these services are already being successfully used in certain areas of the country.

In addition to revenue increases from these and other exotic services, there are the more mundane but significant sources of increased income from improving subscriber penetration, expanding the system into newly developed neighborhoods, rate increases, and advertising. As in any successful business operation, the dire necessity is to have a greater growth in revenues than in operating expenses. That, of course, is management's premier task. It is interesting to note that only about 3% of a CATV system's operating costs are energy-related.

HOW CABLE TELEVISION'S TAX BENEFITS WORK

The ability to shelter current unrelated income with cable television is, like real estate, principally a result of *depreciation* of the equipment used in its operation. That, plus the ability to write off the cost of the franchise or license to operate (which is granted by the local government), operating expenses, and the interest paid on debt service, as well as some investment tax credits, produces attractive tax shelter. During the first three years of operation, assuming about a two-to-one debt-to-equity ratio, these deductions should amount to about 90 to 100% of your equity in an existing cable television investment. Very significantly, because CATV equipment is not real property, the accelerated depreciation thereof is not a preference item.

HOW LIMITED PARTNERSHIPS
PROVIDE ACCESS TO DIRECT CABLE TELEVISION OWNERSHIP

Few of us have the financial wherewithal to go out and buy one or more small to middle-sized cable television systems. That would require millions of dollars. We must therefore search out a management company that will pool the smaller amounts of capital from many investors. Then, with the fewest possible conflicts of interest and the greatest possible expertise and efficiency, buy, manage, and then sell the assets for capital gains.

Again, the best route to the maximum economic potential and tax benefits through direct participation is the limited partnership. This format should allow for the flow-through of the 90% to 100% deductibility of your investment spread fairly evenly over three to four years. In accordance with a recent opinion of a major accounting firm, it may be possible to then plan on the recapture of those deductions as long-term capital gains upon sale. Even if only the deferral of taxes results, it is plenty worthwhile.

It is, as with all tax-incentive investments, not the shelter but mainly the economic potential that should attract your client. In the final analysis, the USA's forced move toward conservation should result in people staying at home more (not a bad idea!) and being entertained at home more. CATV will be a major beneficiary. That, plus the continued rapid technological advances, augur well for unusually attractive economic rewards through *both* growth of capital *and* tax shelter.

HOW THE ECONOMICS AND TAX BENEFITS
OF CABLE TELEVISION JOIN FORCES TO MAKE CAPITAL GROW

The illustration in Table 11–6 serves to demonstrate how CATV economics and tax shelter act in concert to provide handsome capital growth. For simplicity's sake, we will use a $10,000 segment of your client's "growth"-oriented capital, assuming a two-to-one debt-to-equity ratio and a 15% compounded growth rate in the revenues and therefore in the value of the system. We will also assume that your arrangement with a "CATV money manager" requires the sharing of profits on a 75%-to-25% basis, after all of your client's original capital is returned, and the payment of commissions as shown.

THE PLUSES AND MINUSES OF CABLE TELEVISION OWNERSHIP

We have demonstrated the potential performance of an *existing* CATV system. As with drilling versus existing gas/oil wells, and as with to-be-built versus existing real estate properties, greater deductibility can

TABLE 11–5
Assumed Example of Pretax Results

Equity investment in a Cable TV Partnership	$10,000
Start-up Costs	(1,400)
Net Equity in a CATV System	8,600
Borrowing (assumes 2:1 debt-to-equity ratio)	17,200
Market Value of CATV System Acquisition	$25,800
Less 5% Commission	(1,290)
Subject to Appreciation	$24,510
Compounded for 5 Years (vs. 24.7% average for last 5 years)	× 15%
Sale Proceeds 5 Years Later	$49,298
Remaining Debt ($17,200 less $5,160 of debt reduction)	12,040
Net Proceeds to the Partnership	$37,258
Return of Principal to the Limited Partner as per Partnership Sharing Arrangements	10,000
	$27,258
Less: 25% of Profits to General Partner	6,816
	$20,443
Plus: Return of $10,000 of Original Principal	10,000
Total Value of Investment After 5 Years (3.04 × Pretax Investment)	$30,443

be achieved via start-up CATV operations than with existing systems. The opportunity for both economic gain and aggressive tax shelter is exceeded, however, by the attendant risks. The game of developing a brand-new CATV system, versus buying or expanding an existing one, is fraught with political payoffs. Most of the negatives associated with CATV are therefore eliminated by sticking with the Type I tax shelter in this area—existing systems that can be better marketed, better expanded, or both. Even so, operating CATV systems cannot be expected to provide current income. Upgrading, expanding, marketing, and debt service all place heavy demands on available cash flow. CATV systems should therefore be viewed as a "growth of capital" investment vehicle, not as a generator of income.

While preservation of the future purchasing power of capital is a strong objective of CATV ownership, the ratio of system value to gross revenues cannot be guaranteed to stay in the 10% to 12% area at any one point in time. Investors in CATV need patience. It requires time and talent to bring an existing system up to top potential—and patience to wait for it to sell for a proper ratio-to-gross revenues in the CATV market.

The cable television industry also faces competition from a number of sources including the three major networks of broadcast television

TABLE 11–6

50% Continuing Marginal Bracket	
Assumed Example of After-Tax Results	

Investment	$10,000
Deduction (over 3 years)	9,000
Federal Tax Savings	4,500
Money-at-Risk After 3 years	$ 5,500
Assumed Pretax Proceeds to Limited Partner (from previous page)	$30,443*
Less: Gains Taxes at 50% on 40% of front-end deductions*	(1,800)*
Less: Gains Taxes on 50% on 40% of Remaining Proceeds of $21,443	(4,289)
After-Tax Proceeds (4.43 × Money-at-risk)	$24,354

Ideal Financial Planning Application

Client Investment in 50% Bracket	$10,000
Deduction over First 3–4 Years	9,000
Tax Savings	4,500
Out-of-Pocket Cost	$ 5,500

Client gifts partnership to child after receiving 3 to 4 years of deductions.

Assumed Pretax Proceed to Child Spread Over 2–3 Years	$30,443
Assume Little or No Income Taxes	0
Net Proceeds to Child	$30,443

RESULT: Parent paid $5,500 for $30,443 of college education costs or start-up business costs for child, or down payment on child's first home.

*Note: These examples are of course based upon growth expectations of 15% or better on revenues and therefore cable system value. The capital gains nature of the recapture of front-end deductions of $9,000 is a result of the deductibility of the 25% profits fee to the general partnership plus the fact that the depreciation of the franchise is not recaptured as ordinary income. Note that the tax treatment of the 25% management fee is cloudy at this time. Competent authorities currently disagree on this issue.

and more recent advances via rooftop antenna satellite reception. Many view the latter as a real threat. Quite the opposite, I see nothing on the horizon that comes close to equaling the almost magical capacity of the coaxial cable.

For example, the most advanced home satellite receiving system now being developed (known as a Direct Broadcast Satellite system) involves purchasing a small rooftop satellite receiving antenna for as little as $100 to $200. These antennas will be able to receive signals from special satellites, which send signals powerful enough to be received by the smaller antennas. A maximum of three to six channels of programming will be offered at a cost of $20 to $25 per month. Obviously such a system can be successful only in areas that are not or will not be served by a cable television system. Why would a consumer choose such a service when for roughly the same monthly cost he can have cable television with 36, 54, or more channels of programming, *plus* the two-way communication capabilities of the coaxial cable?

There are also legislative and regulatory risks. Because of the very nature of CATV, government entities may one day view it as a public utility and attempt to regulate in that way. Should the current trend toward decreased government regulation reverse itself under a different federal administration, CATV could be a victim to some extent or another. Even then, this would only provide a slowdown in what we view as the continuing growth in CATV usage.

CABLE TELEVISION: GROWTH OPPORTUNITY FOR THE 1980s

For three decades cable television has existed in relative anonymity as a stepchild of the communications industry. Its intended purpose was to bring improved television reception to predominantly rural areas of the country. Now, however, as we enter the 1980s, cable television is strongly and rapidly asserting itself in its progress toward reaching its eventual potential of what could become the principal means of comprehensive communication to and from our nation's homes. Due to rapidly developing technological advances, coupled with sharply curtailed government regulations, we have already seen cable television become an inexpensive source of total home entertainment. In addition, the two-way interactive communications capability of the coaxial cable opens up the reality of home security systems, data transmission and retrieval, shopping and banking at home, and so on. The revolutionary aspects of cable television as an electronic pipeline to our homes is dramatically changing our country's television viewing habits, and to some degree our very lifestyles. Considering that the bulk of this explosive change in the cable industry has occurred only within the last five or six years, the ultimate uses of cable television as a comprehensive communications system can now only be imagined. In sum, I feel that the ownership of cable television systems through professionally managed limited partnerships offers investors an extraordinary opportunity to achieve meaningful capital appreciation in an exciting and rapidly developing growth industry.

This chapter has clearly shown that there is a tax-advantaged investment strategy for appropriately positioning your client's every dollar of assets and/or cash flow. After having identified the various alternatives for a particular segment of capital, it is simply a matter of determining how much capital must move in what direction, at what time, and for what specific reason.

The zenith in overall financial problem solving is reached when you are capable of objectively selecting, from the major categories of problem solvers, the *procedural tools* in chapter 10 and the *investment strategies* of this chapter. Next, chapter 12 closes with a discussion of several key concepts for assuring continued financial planning success.

12

Key Concepts for Assuring a Continued Successful Financial Plan

All great ideas go through the three stages of rejection, acceptance, and finally enthusiastic espousal. Financial planning is no less than a grand concept. It is great because it is right. And it is right because it creates order out of chaos for individuals who are living and dying in the greatest nation on earth.

This nation is, however, also one that has unfortunately allowed its laws and taxes to become more complex and burdensome than even their authors envisioned or can fathom. And every effort toward tax reform ends up as more tax deform. Even so, most taxpayers are trying desperately to get from point "A" to point "B," financially speaking, with anything but clear roadsigns ahead. Comprehensive financial planning clearly becomes a most profound, yet practical, total delivery system.

Coordinating plan creation, implementation, and updating

Simply *designing* a financial plan or road map is not enough.

It has been imaginatively said that when a tree falls in the forest with no one there to hear it, a profound question arises as to whether there was a noise. Similarly in financial planning, does a plan cost if it is not *implemented?*

A comprehensive plan, however brilliantly conceived and properly implemented, cannot be carved in marble. Changing laws, interpretations of the law, the economic scenario, market conditions, and personal objectives force a good plan to be ever growing, ever evolving, and often *updated.*

I do not know which of the three steps of design, implementation, and updating in the financial planning process is the most important any more than I know whether the brain, heart, or lungs serve the most important physical purpose. I am certain that each is equally essential to physical life, just as I have no doubt but that plan creation, plan implementation, and plan updating must all be inextricably interwoven in the life of financial planning.

Why other professionals are needed in the financial planning process

Several final considerations assure a continued successful financial plan. One such consideration involves the selection and use of complete professional assistance every step of the way. Most clients are too busy to even consider implementing their own plans. In general, they have neither the time, talent, nor temperament to do so. Clients can never be expected to write their own wills and trusts, manage their own stock and bond portfolios, or select their own general partners or insurance policies. Even if your clients were able to develop a meaningful plan of action, they would likely, sooner or later (and hopefully sooner), realize the importance of professional implementation assistance. Business executives, for example, cannot hope to spend less than an hour a day on something that is, in total, more complex and important than what they spend eight to eighteen hours doing at work. It is easy to forget that, with the exception of workaholics, most of us work to live and die comfortably more than we live and die to work.

Admitting that professionals are needed to help achieve one's financial goals for life and death is therefore not just a big step forward. It is absolutely crucial to financial success. You cannot just turn over all of these plan implementation functions to just anyone who is impressive or known. How then do you help your client to select professionals—be they lawyers, accountants, trust officers, insurance specialists, or investment advisors—to implement certain parts of the plan? What can you believe from among all the conflicting advice about whom to use for what?

What your client should consider in selecting "implementation" professionals

First, some professionals participate in the overall plan *creation* process. Others are selected to *implement* specific procedural and investment solutions. All must be selected on the basis of their *expertise* and *integrity*— and little else. Clients cannot just get bids as they might do in business or in the construction industry.

Nothing is more important in the business of your clients' financial lives than the integrity of their advisors. Absolutely nothing! It is necessary to find out all about a professional's reputation from a number of different sources. It will prove helpful to talk to someone either who has used the professional or who knows of others who have successfully and economically used the professional's services. It is frequently necessary to even check out the person or entity that is doing the checking out for you or your client. This entire milieu is one which, of its very nature, proliferates in conflicts of interest. But it is a cornerstone of a lasting financial pyramid.

Secondly, the professional should have the *specific* expertise that *your client needs* now. All accountants, for example, are not savvy in accomplishing or even reviewing income tax planning, nor do they pretend to be. All investment advisors/brokers are not competent in both areas of corporate tradable securities and direct participations. In fact, most tend to lean too far in one direction or the other. All attorneys are not experienced in taxation or wills and trusts. Your client's current attorney may not be the one who should implement all of the procedural solutions to a financial plan. Any highly professional attorney or accountant will be quick to agree with this philosophy. On the other hand, your client's current attorney or accountant may be associated with others who have the specialized expertise needed. In this case, ride piggyback on their integrity. It is doubtful that they will risk losing clients by referring you or your client to someone in their firms whom they do not respect and trust.

In the beginning of this discussion, I mentioned that little other than integrity and expertise should be considered when selecting implementation professionals. The little else that is a consideration is cost, particularly among the professionals who implement procedural solutions. There is no greater example of getting what you pay for than in the area of final tax advice. Advisors in this area should never be chosen on the basis of cost alone. *If* that were the sole determinant, it would be better to hire the most expensive than the cheapest. After all, free tax advice can be acquired from the next door neighbor or Aunt Minnie. In general, what you get is worth exactly what you pay for it. Also remember that the portion of the financial planning, accounting, and legal fees that is related to tax advice is deductible.

Here is some final advice relative to seeking tax implementation assistance. Accountants and attorneys overlap in the gray area of tax matters. Both professions will readily admit that there is no less than controversy as to who does what in the area of giving final tax advice. Neither do they agree on who is best employed to review the tax advice of competent overall financial planners who are perhaps not themselves accountants or tax attorneys. I have become convinced, over all these years, that the professional designation is not the key ingredient. Cost—as you compare what an accountant versus a lawyer would charge per hour for similar advice is also not the principal determinant. The deciding factor is simply who has the better reputation for accomplishing the work at hand. Once you have determined the individual who is most accomplished in performing the services in question, I again advise that your client not be stingy about paying for the best. The key, however, is to have a very clear understanding in advance of how and what will be charged.

What criteria should be used in selecting an investment management team

In spite of all of the pitfalls, my experience has been that the process of selecting a professional to implement the procedural problem solvers is easier and less costly than finding the best possible professional manager of investments. Particularly in the broad area of direct participations, you must be prepared to exercise extreme due diligence in selecting management teams for your clients' investments.

It is one thing to decide that a procedure, such as an outright gift, a reversionary trust, or an interest-free loan, is an applicable solution to your client's overriding problem. As was discussed in the immediately prior section, selecting the individual or firm to implement the decision is an equally serious undertaking. Properly implementing investment solutions is an even more demanding task. What goes on in the world of investment management is less visible and meaningfully regulated. Therefore, while it is again one thing to evolve the proper investment directions and strategies, it is quite another to determine who should implement and/or manage them.

Twenty years of experience in the world of investment securities and financial planning have taught me that four major characteristics or aspects of any investment manager must be painstakingly evaluated before your client ever commits to "money under management":

1. integrity,
2. experience,
3. past results, and
4. vehicular structure.

The use of these four criteria is quite valid, as you shall see, no matter what professionally managed investment involvement you are considering.

With investments ranging from stocks to bonds, gold to Persian rugs, gas/oil wells to leased drilling rigs, cable television systems to garden apartment complexes, your clients are doing so much more than simply buying an investment product. They are in reality making a profound investment management decision. More succinctly, they are searching for a person or institution who can *and* will best conduct the affairs of an economically viable business involvement. Consideration of the details of the particular vehicular structure as it compares with the various alternatives is but a part of that total process.

Here then is your four-part guide to selecting professionally managed investments:

WHY INTEGRITY COMES FIRST

Your clients can be involved in the most economically attractive investment area, have the best legal structure, the fairest sharing of costs and proceeds, and then lose money if their investment manager is without integrity. There is no doubt but that the unethical advisor will find a legal way to get to the investor. Therefore, *after* it has been decided that the economic activity being considered is unusually attractive, go about the business of identifying possible management teams of the highest integrity.

There is no better way to identify integrity than by communicating with many people who know the investment managers well and/or who know of them through others who have used their services. Outside advisory services can never be totally relied upon. They cover—seldom adequately—the three other criteria of experience, past results, and structure, which definitely need evaluation. But never do they tell you who is thoroughly principled and who is not. Yet, as I purposefully emphasize, that is the most important part of the evaluation process.

Clients should be able to rely upon existing relationships among trusted advisors or advising institutions to study the integrity of various management teams. It is therefore crucial that, if your client is depending upon you for such advice, you establish a systematic, professional approach to verifying integrity above all else.

If you do not have a long enough history with advisors or services that you are using in the "due diligence" process, you must check out their ability to select investment managers before you have them check someone out for you and your clients. Don't be misled by big names either. Just because the individual or investment firm you now use to help select investments and managers is a big one, because it is generally well known, or because it is well advertised locally or nationally, does not mean that a top job will be done in thoroughly checking out management integrity. In other words, "big" is not automatically good in this respect anymore than "small" is automatically bad.

If you are depending on a law firm, bank, independent financial planning firm, a securities brokerage house, an insurance company, or an accounting firm to help you select investment managers of high integrity, first determine who owns the recommended management team. If your source of due diligence owns the investment manager, chances are you should be suspect. While there will be many exceptions, asking your investigative sources to select objectively between the advisor they own and all else that is available is frequently asking too much. The world of NASD and NYSE investment firms and financial planning firms are beginning to proliferate in the creation of subsidiaries to buy, manage, and eventually sell this or that. You must determine whether this has come to pass because of a conviction that a better job can be done for their clients or whether it is because the continuing fees involved in investment, creation, and management are usually larger than those involved in investment marketing. In any case, I would at least do some further investigation if my "medical" doctor manufactured his own medicine.

Always review the relative stability of a given "list" of recommended management teams and check to see why deletions were made. But don't ever say why you are asking. You see, if the proper homework is being accomplished in the first place, big changes in the recommendations made from year to year do not usually occur. This is likewise a good test of the validity of the work you may be doing for your clients with respect to rating integrity. If you are changing your mind from year to year about whom you can trust, that may be an indication that you should be relying upon someone else to help you evaluate the integrity of the investment managers you recommend to your clients or choose for yourself.

I stress integrity, seemingly inordinately, only because it is so often under-emphasized by investment advisors. That is because it is such a costly and time-consuming endeavor. I have observed for many years that practically every segment of the financial services industry pays far too much attention to vehicular structure and past results. Even so, investment history is seldom properly measured. Studies of vehicular structures are little understood and often characterized by sweeping generalities. I know for a fact that selections for recommendations are often made without ever *really* getting to know management. Even worse, selections are sometimes made because there is enough product to meet demand or because a wholesaler appears impressive. You would be amazed to know how much product is selected by some advisors due to the attractiveness of the book "cover." I am intentionally hammering away at the crucial need to get to know and trust the management team of each and every investment area you recommend. The fact that the sales brochure or marketing approach is impressive is nowhere near enough if you are to meet the minimum obligations to your client.

HOW EXPERIENCE FITS INTO THE MANAGEMENT EQUATION

The length, breadth, and depth of a management team's business experience is your second most crucial consideration. Many a brochure advertises the many years of real estate experience of the principals without saying anything about whether it was in purchasing, managing, or selling properties. Little is sometimes revealed about the nature of the properties involved in the past relative to the activity that is now being proposed. Many years of experience of one sort or another with apartments in California doesn't make one a sudden expert with office buildings in Louisiana or New York.

I recall studying an oil company several years ago for the purpose of exploring and developing gas and oil properties for my firm's clients. Practically all of this company's successful drilling experience had been in another area while current proposed activities mainly involved the Gulf coast states. Their using past performance as an indication of future results therefore seemed meaningless to me, possibly a measure of some lack of integrity. I was in doubt and stayed out. It proved to be a very correct decision indeed.

The same is true of the management of indirect investments such as equity and debt securities. If you see a well known manager of equities suddenly form one type of a pool or another of managed debt securities, watch out. The motivation may be a desire to benefit at your expense by capturing part of the "income market" without paying for the acquisition of experienced debt managers. Similarly, just because a firm on "Blue Blood" Street in Boston has vast experience in the management of federal government and corporate debt securities does not automatically indicate an inherent ability to manage a new municipal bond fund. Check to see who has been attracted to the money management firm prior to the offering and whether they have extensive experience in managing tax-exempt issues.

Never let a management team practice on your client or on the money you control. You must find experience *coupled* with integrity. You will have to search for it. That search costs time and money, but its benefit to cost ratio is great.

In selecting *experienced* management teams for the various segments of your client's financial pyramid, you must also consider the matter of "prime activity." Do the managers you are considering have as their prime business activity the experience you need most? If not maybe you ought to stay away. For example, is the drilling program business the main purpose of the oil company's business life? Or it is just a way to add diversification funds to those that will be spent drilling for the manager's own account—or for keeping a drilling subsidiary's rigs busy? Those, you see, are the types of questions that have to be explored. The person asking must be able to judge and document the substance *and* sincerity of the response.

You must be particularly tuned in to measuring experience when a given economic activity becomes "hot." I watched real estate partnerships come into being in the early '70s. They were often managed by sharp and aggressive legal minds whose real estate experience was limited to watching how much more real estate brokers earned than lawyers. Gas/oil, real estate, and research/development programs have been put together by some brokerage firms who also suffer from the expertise transfer syndrome. They sometimes get involved due mainly to an involvement of interest in their geographical area or because it can be very profitable and it's "selling" well. Seldom is the motivation, "We see an extraordinary opportunity for high total return for our clients, *and* we truly do not know anyone who can manage it better than us." Instead, there is a strong business nature to go where the action is, even when it is only distantly related to a business entity's prime area of expertise.

Guard against new entries into the market place of wealth management. It is fraught with automatic conflicts of interest. And that is why you need to study very closely things other than the prospectuses. Offering circulars and prospectuses seldom tell you all that you should know about experience and integrity or even past results. Sometimes I get the impression that prospectuses are designed to keep you from learning all that you need to know.

HOW PAST RESULTS CAN
GUIDE YOU TO FUTURE SUCCESS

While "the record," particularly the recent record, can be of great assistance, it has to be viewed through the glasses of relativity. That is true in every area of investment, indirect securities, and direct participations alike.

To begin with, apples cannot be compared with oranges. Because a speculative growth portfolio has done dramatically better than a quality, big research-oriented growth stock list during the past ten years does not mean that one management team is better than the other. Study the milieu in which the two teams have operated. Perhaps the marketplace accommodated one activity and not the other. Instead, study how the speculative portfolio manager performed relative to a similar index and likewise for the quality growth stock manager. Remember, too, that history seldom immediately repeats itself. Circles repeat themselves, but they go nowhere!

All of the same principles hold true in direct participations. In gas/oil drilling, for example, the performance of an exploration manager cannot be compared with that of a development group. Each will hopefully be in that particular activity due to a combination of personal talent and temperament. There will be periods when one activity is more attractive than the other relative to risk. So compare exploration with exploration, and development drilling with development drilling. Don't compare stocks with bonds, so to speak, for a given segment of capital or discretionary cash flow. Even in development drilling, the risk-to-reward ratios have varied dramatically from time to time between west of the Mississippi activities and eastern drilling. The comparative results of two different general partners may therefore be due more to geological province than to management expertise. Don't forget, too, that you cannot expect an oil company's existing staff to jump from one province to another every few years. Geological and engineering expertise is simply not quite that transferable. It is, however, acquirable.

Make sure that you study volatility as well as average performance. If you put your hands on a block of ice and a hot stove, the average is not bad but it hurts! So, too, with investments. Be certain that your mathematical formula for measuring rates of return considers both *what* you get back and *when* you get it. For this purpose, consider using the internal rate of return method. Under most circumstances it will not measure exactly what you should earn on your money because of the unlikely event of reinvesting cash flow in investments precisely equal to the original investment. The internal rate of return calculation will, however, enable you to adequately compare the past results of different investments. Finally, with the internal rate of return, as well as with any other such calculation, always factor in prognostications of current, ongoing, and future tax ramifications. As previously noted, pretax rate of return is meaningless. Only the after-tax rate of return measurements tell you the true story.

In the final analysis, your first decision is whether or not your clients should participate in a given economic activity with a measured segment of their capital or cash flow. You then key in on the subordinate areas of who with integrity has what experience in successfully managing what. After circling in on potential money managers based upon these first most significant considerations, you compare "comparable" results. Only then should you go on to consider the more popular matters such as the sharing of costs/revenues, and fees.

THE DIFFERENCE VEHICULAR STRUCTURE MAKES

It is somewhat difficult to come up with an adequate single phrase to describe all that must be considered in this last category. You should begin however by recognizing that every professionally managed investment involvement has a choice of legal structure. Management exercises its talent within some vehicle, such as a trust, corporation, general or limited partnership, or outright ownership. In any case, there are associated agreements as to who puts up how much capital and/or expertise, what sales costs are paid to whom, what final amount actually gets directly involved with the economic activity at hand, what and how debt financing is or might be employed, what initial and ongoing professional management fees are involved, who pays for what costs, how profits are shared, and what fees are paid to whom upon liquidation.

Sweeping generalizations about this or that structure for any kind of any investment should be looked upon with a jaundiced eye. If integrity exists, the structure of the vehicular arrangement is probably sound. I actually know of no case where thoroughly principled sponsors of a given professionally managed investment do not, upon close scrutiny, also use a fairly structured vehicle.

The question of high fees will sometimes come up. But then, the most capable money managers of any sort are not usually the cheapest. The cheapest are usually so because they have to be "on sale" to sell. Again it is just like the medical world! You will not get the lowest price for advice on the treatment of juvenile diabetes at the Joslin Clinic in Boston! Ochsner Clinic in New Orleans may not be your cheapest medical bet, but they will search every nook and corner of your very physical and mental existence to uncover your ills. In professional money management, too, your clients should expect to pay for what they get. They can never expect to buy good money managers or general partners in a bargain basement. A pro who is top-notch and in demand is not likely to be on sale.

What's on the horizon for financial planning?

Total financial planning must be comprised of all its parts. It must consist of the creation of the financial path, the religious traveling of that map, and the occasional revising of the financial itinerary.

The planning process espoused in this book was conceived in the realization that it cannot be made to appear meek in its scope. It must be comprehensive in terms of both breadth and depth. Financial planning can therefore be very powerful in its ability to either help or hurt over long periods of time. Much like nuclear power in energy or genetic research in medicine, it is fraught with the best and worst intentions of mankind. But the power of financial planning can be harnessed to serve all its most noble purposes.

Conversely, financial planning can and often is used to cloak the most devious financial schemes in respectibility. Especially during these formative years, clients are having difficulty distinguishing between the money doctor and the financial quack, between the legitimate financial medications and worthless placebos.

As the realization of the need for financial planning assistance becomes even more widespread, and the availability of professional financial planning consultants more widespread, potential clients have to be more discerning than ever. You must come to know that it is not the expensive brochure that tells your story; it is your expertise and integrity, and that of the implementing professionals with whom you associate that will really count. Watch for the forthcoming availability of the International Association For Financial Planning's *Registry of Financial Planning Practitioners.*

On a flight from New Orleans to Atlanta one day in 1975, I read a remarkable article on management in *Sky Magazine* by Dr. M. H. Mescon of Georgia State University. The article stayed with me as few articles ever have. In it, Mike Mescon, whom I fortunately came to know shortly thereafter, made one statement that stood out like no other. "As a matter of fact," Dr. Mescon wrote, "one point I try to communicate to my students is that in a free society there should be a linear or straight-line relationship between what you do and what you get, between pay and productivity, investment and reward, compensation and contribution . . . people are quick to sense gulfs between mouth and movement, between stated philosophy and overt behavior."

I hope you too can get an exponential lift from a philosophy like that, especially when you apply it to the planning of your client's financial future. When financial planning is conducted in a way that always considers uppermost the benefits to the one whose future is planned, planners need never worry about their own financial future. It will have already been assured. Output will have always equaled input. Action will have replaced articulation.

As the evolution of the practice of financial planning ensues, it will continue to be defined in a multitude of proper and acceptable ways. But every definition, however short or long, must incorporate all three major facets of (1) examining the client *in relationship to* financial goals, (2) identifying the principal hurdles to getting there, and (3) selecting, implementing, *and* updating the alternative procedural and investment strategies for success.

Financial planning will also continue to be practiced somewhat differently by professionals who legitimately have varying confidence levels in certain procedural tools and investment strategies. This is not to even speak of the still existing differences in how to best examine facts and diagnose problems. All of this will cause competent specialists in the legal, risk management, accounting, and investment professions to thrive as they fill in and implement the parts of the plan that central planners cannot and/or should not themselves accomplish. The specialists will, however, have to learn to perform their functions with greater financial peripheral vision.

More than anything I sense that we will see less and less of the home practice of do-it-yourself financial planning and more reliance upon experienced professional help. That is the main reason why this book has been written—primarily for you who would choose to enter into or broaden a career in financial planning, those of you who are already professional planners, and those clinets who would want to better understand the total financial planning process.

As all of this promising future unfolds, for client and practitioner alike, it will have unbelievable staying power if one all-encompassing golden rule of personal financial planning is routinely applied. This principle must permeate the application of all of the others that this book espouses. Simply stated, *the perfection of purpose in financial planning is reached when you succeed in objectively managing wealth instead of letting wealth manage you.*

I wish you the former, always.

IV

MODEL
FINANCIAL
PLANS

The case studies in this section are designed to give you the nuts and bolts that represent many of the concepts discussed throughout this book. You will find hypothetical cases that consider age, salary level, number of dependents, and marital status.

Case Study I. A typical financial plan for a 31-year-old, single, middle-management executive.

Case Study II. A typical financial plan for a 54-year-old, married, business owner of a closely-held corporation.

Case Study III. A typical financial plan for a 40-year-old, married, upper-income executive.

Case Study IV. A typical financial plan for a 47-year-old, self-employed professional.

At the end of each plan, you will be shown what a completed, typical financial planning questionnaire looks like. These questionnaires help to avoid errors in the financial planning process and enhance both the client's and planner's understanding of how calculations, strategies, and options for specific situations were arrived at.

Special note: While the plans have been developed with the 1983 tax law in mind, conceptually, the same basic financial planning principles may be applied in any given year.

I

A Total
Financial Plan
Prepared for:
Susan M. Lane

by
Mary O. Pitts, CFP
Financial Planning Consultant

Preface

Ms. Lane, our intent is to provide you with an analysis of your personal financial situation which will assist you in planning a program to meet your financial goals. No investment program is ideal for everyone to follow; a financial plan must be tailored to each person's unique situation and also provide a degree of flexibility to accommodate changing circumstances and objectives. In designing an appropriate financial program three fundamental elements must be balanced. These elements include:

1. *Accumulation* of assets by converting income to capital.
2. *Conservation* of assets by prudent investment management, tax planning and risk management.
3. *Distribution* of assets to your heirs according to your testamentary objectives.

After taking into consideration your personal investment, legal, and tax circumstances as well as your financial goals and risk temperament, we have prepared an analysis of your situation and offer a prudent financial program that, when followed consistently, will help you to achieve your economic goals without placing you in financial jeopardy. This plan, of course, will be of no value to you unless implemented.

In our analysis we have used certain approximations and reasonable estimates based on information you provided. In our assumptions we have tried to be conservative. Our exhibits are for illustrative purposes, and we urge you to discuss these exhibits with your tax counsel for exact computations concerning your situation. Whenever reference is made to laws affecting the disposition of your property the references are for your general information only. The specific application of these laws to your situation is within the exclusive province of your attorney.

Although we have discussed alternatives to your present status which will improve your financial condition, this plan, once implemented, should be considered as the beginning of a constantly evolving process. Changes in your personal situation, in laws, regulations, and the economy make it necessary to periodically review, and, if necessary, revise your financial program.

Table of contents

Personal balance sheet

Assets:

Checking Accounts	$ 500
Savings Accounts	1,000
Certificates of Deposit	20,000
Home	60,000
Personal Property	19,000
Total Assets	$100,500
Liabilities:	
Credit Cards	1,000
Mortgage on Home	50,000
Total Liabilities	$ 51,000
Net Worth	$ 49,500

Cash flow analysis

Income:	
Salary	$ 35,000
Interest	2,453
Insurance Costs	35
Adjusted Gross Income:	$ 37,488
Less: Personal Exemptions	(1,000)
Excess Itemized Deductions	(8,872)
Estimated Taxable Income	$ 27,616
Estimated Federal Income Tax Liability	(5,553)*
	$ 22,063
Add: Personal Exemption	1,000
Less: Remaining Itemized Deductions	(2,300)
FICA Tax	(2,170)
Insurance Costs	(35)
Net Cash Flow After Taxes	$18,558
Less: Living Expenses	(7,800)
Insurance Premiums	(708)
Discretionary Cash Flow	$ 10,050

*Tax calculation assumes use of Income Averaging; using the appropriate tax rate schedule would result in a tax liability of $5,666.

Introduction

Formulating a sound lifetime and estate financial plan begins with a careful analysis of your present resources and their positioning as well as your income, its taxation and subsequent direction—all relative to your personal financial goals. We have therefore included at the beginning of this report a Personal Balance Sheet and a Cash Flow Analysis.

Your Balance Sheet indicates a net worth of $49,500. Although you have investable assets of $21,000, the major concentration of your asset base is in your home and personal property. Such concentration is fairly normal considering your age and the relative length of time you have spent in developing a career. However, now that you have established a financial base of personal assets, it is essential to achieving financial success that you begin a properly structured investment program.

At this stage in your financial program the major consideration should be asset accumulation by the systematic conversion of income to capital. However, a successful accumulation program cannot be achieved without a strategy to conserve your capital base by choosing appropriate investment vehicles. Proper diversification of your present assets as well as the investment of your annual discretionary cash flow into suitable areas will balance and thereby enhance your total financial picture.

A review of your Cash Flow Analysis indicates an estimated federal income tax liability of $5,553, assuming that the Income Averaging method of tax computation is used. Your attendent marginal tax bracket is 32%, that is, each additional dollar of taxable income will be taxed beginning at the rate of 32%. Based on your current income, tax level, and living expenses, we have estimated that during 1983 you should have a cash flow investment capability of $10,000. Positioning these funds in an appropriate manner will initiate a plan designed to ensure financial success.

You have indicated that you want to create a financial system of checks and balances which will allow you to enjoy your present income without jeopardizing your future financial security. A major obstacle in achieving your goal will be the erosion of your income and capital by inflation and progressive taxation. Therefore, the funds you allocate for investment must be positioned in vehicles that are compatible with your personal level of risk tolerance but which will increase your asset base, thereby counteracting the effects of inflation. Also, the ramifications of income taxation must be considered so that investment income is generated in a manner that does not unnecessarily reduce that income by taxation.

Lifetime planning

ASSET ACCUMULATION

One of the basic principles of sound financial planning is the systematic conversion of income to capital. Many savings and investment programs have failed because of the following reasons:

1. Lack of definite plan or goal.
2. Reversal of priorities. A plan to save whatever is left over generally results in nothing left for savings.
3. Imbalance in spending. Current luxuries are put ahead of future necessities.

If you are to reach financial security, you must begin to convert a portion of your present income, through regular savings and investments, to capital. To ensure the success of your financial program you should begin a constructive strategy to accumulate capital now. Although it might sound very elementary, the first step in beginning a program of asset accumulation is defining a realistic budget. By reviewing how you have spent money in the past you can develop a flexible budget that is neither austere nor restrictive, but one that reduces the total outlay of cash by limiting wasteful spending.

Prior to beginning our study we asked you to complete an Expense Worksheet which would indicate your annual living expenses. Based on the information you provided us, we have projected that in 1983 you should have investable income of $10,000 or approximately 27% of your gross income. However, you have indicated that you are finding it difficult to save any money. You obviously have taken a great deal of care in determining your annual expenses and have indicated that the Expense Worksheet is fairly accurate according to your records. Since this is your first attempt at budgeting, we suggest that you "try out" the budget (Expense Worksheet) you have designed for the first six months of 1983. In June you should review each category to compare actual results with your budgeted allocation then adjust each category as needed. However, we recommend that you include a category for investment in your present budget. We will discuss an appropriate allocation and distribution of investment funds later in this report.

INVESTMENT STRATEGY

As we have indicated, our present economic environment makes it imperative to consider the effects of inflation and taxation on the components of your investment portfolio. An appropriate combination of suitable investment vehicles needs to be designed to minimize the erosion caused by both of these elements. An investment strategy for you will be choosing investment media that will provide capital appreciation and increasing income to combat inflation, as well as tax-benefited income resulting from deferral, exemptions, and legal deductions to minimize the effect of taxation.

You have acknowledged the need for beginning an investment strategy, but you are concerned about your lack of knowledge and experience in appraising investment alternatives. Therefore, we recommend, as a part of your overall strategy, that you adopt a policy at this time of investing in vehicles offering professional management. A lower-risk complexion results from your investment dollars being directed by professionals with both experience and expertise in specific areas. You would also have the additional advantage of greater diversification than could be provided by investing in individually owned vehicles since most investments under management pool investors' money.

Although diversification of one's assets is a good prevention measure against financial catastrophe, you need to be careful not to position your investment funds into too many vehicles. By establishing a solid financial base through directing your existing capital into a limited number of areas, then gradually building on this base with other investments from future cash flow, you can best achieve a proper balance and integration of your investment portfolio. This strategy will also allow you to become more comfortable with investment decisions thereby raising your risk-reward tolerance level.

In this section of our study we will discuss areas that we feel are appropriate for your existing capital. While we will limit our comments to those investments that can be accommodated by the funds you have available, these areas are by no means the only investment media appropriate for you. As you accumulate investment funds, we'll want to discuss additional areas that will align your Balance Sheet with your financial objectives.

ASSET ANALYSIS

1. Cash Reserves. You currently have cash equivalents of $1,000 in savings and $20,000 in Certificates of Deposit. Although the first criteria of a sound investment program is to provide a cash emergency fund, fixed-dollar assets are eroded by inflation, which results in declining purchasing power. However, considering your total financial scenario, including your risk-management program, we recommend that you maintain an emergency fund of $10,500 or approximately one year's living expenses.

Since you have expressed some anxiety about beginning an investment program because you have recently accepted the financial responsibility of home ownership, we suggest that you maintain $8,000 in a highly liquid medium. Rather than using a time deposit vehicle that might carry a substantial penalty for early withdrawals, we recommend that you place this reserve of $8,000 in a very accessible medium such as a money market fund. Money market funds buy short-term, high-interest instruments, such as US Treasury bills and notes, commercial paper, and repurchase agreements. While you could purchase these instruments individually, professional managers are generally able to receive a higher rate of return due to their experience in following the money market and also due to the large amounts purchased with "pooled" funds from investors. These funds are also considered a relatively safe investment—especially those funds with portfolios having a very short average maturity. Generally, funds are available to the investor upon request and some funds offer check writing privileges.

Normally, we would suggest that a minimum of short-term reserves be maintained and that more emphasis be placed on serious, long-term reserves. For your situation, until you become accustomed to budgeting and feel more comfortable with an investment program as well as your present financial obligations, we have reversed the allocation for short-term and long-term reserves. However, we recommend that you begin to build an appropriate level of long-term reserves.

As a storehouse for long-term, serious reserves, a deferred annuity has several characteristics that are appropriate for your situation:

1. Your principal is fully guaranteed.
2. Your interest accumulates tax-sheltered at a competitive rate.
3. Irregular withdrawals of uneven amounts can be made.
4. Probate costs, delays, and publicity are avoided.

A deferred annuity serves as a sure and convenient source of tax-sheltered accrual of interest while simultaneously guaranteeing your most serious cash reserves. We recommend that the remainaing $2,500 of your cash reserves be positioned into a deferred annuity. The balance of your present cash equivalents should be invested in more appropriate areas.

2. Equity Securities. One investment area in particular that you should consider as an appropriate medium for accumulating capital is the equity market place. Our opinion is that, historically speaking, quality common stocks are intrinsically undervalued. This undervaluation can be measured in terms of:

1. the relationship of the averages to the book values of the companies they reflect;
2. the relationship between current price levels and corporate earnings (P-E ratios); and
3. the possibility of increased dividend payouts as corporate earnings experience the cyclical upswing that normally accompanies a recovery from a recession.

The increasingly favorable tax treatment of capital gains gives additional incentive toward equity participation. Also, an inflationary period, such as we are now experiencing, is an excellent opportunity for accumulation as demonstrated by the curve of inflation rates and the ratio of earnings to price being almost coincident. In addition, after this period of inflation subsides, the normal upward trend of equities due to rising P-E ratios could be accentuated by a restructuring of corporate taxation to alleviate the double taxation of dividends.

To provide growth of your capital, an appropriate low-risk segment of the equity marketplace in which you should invest is the area of quality, high-dividend paying issues. A very negative factor for you, however, in owning any dividend-paying stock is that the dividend income is taxable. Therefore, to alleviate the loss of income by taxation we recommend that you participate in the ownership of quality issues through a tax-managed trust.

As well as the acquisition of excellent professional management, such a trust would cause you to eliminate for now, and transform for the future, the tax ramifications of any dividend income. The trust invests in quality, dividend-paying issues, and by internally reinvesting rather than distributing dividends and using the 85% corporate dividend exclusion, tax-free accumulation occurs. This also provides for a tax-free reinvestment of an important portion of the total expected return. The only income tax consequence to you would be favorable capital gains treatment of the dividend and growth portion of any future cash withdrawals.

We recommend that this year you invest $3,000 in a tax-managed trust for quality issues to provide a source of growth of capital as well as a future source of tax-benefited income. Investment in a tax-managed trust is an ideal way to achieve capital growth as both dividends and appreciation increase the value of your shares. When income is needed, a systematic withdrawal program can be established where shares are liquidated on a monthly, quarterly, or annual basis to provide income.

3. Energy-Related Investments. Our research indicates that energy-related investments provide unusual opportunity for economic reward. This opportunity is directly related to our present energy scenario. A principal cause of the long-term inflation we face is the gradually rising cost of energy, particularly oil and natural gas. Rising oil prices not only affect us directly at the gas pumps, but also indirectly through fuel costs to industry, as well as petroleum byproducts of plastics, fabrics, chemicals, and drugs. Therefore, we feel it is essential that a carefully structured investment program include a significant allocation to the direct ownership of oil and gas reserves.

An appropriate method for you to use for participating in energy-related investments is oil/gas income programs. Such programs, in limited partnership format, do no drilling, but rather acquire producing reserves. Typically, historic rates of return, as well as current projections in such programs, are in excess of 12%. At least 60% of the cash flow should be tax-free over the 10-to-15-year life of each partnership, with a larger percentage being sheltered in the early years and a lesser amount in the later years. It should be noted that, if a partnership experiences above-average results due to substantial reserve or price increases in excess of what was estimated when the properties were acquired, the percentage of cash flow sheltered will decline as economic return increases.

When investing in such programs, you will have the options of:

1. automatically reinvesting all cash distributions, or
2. depleting your investment over a 10-to-15-year period by receiving both the income and return of principal portions of the cash distributions.

Some programs may allow a third option of receiving a specified portion of the distribution in cash and reinvesting the remainder.

In addition to offering the opportunity of increasing income and capital appreciation through a vehicle with moderate risk, oil/gas income programs offer substantial liquidity. Such programs have a provision where the general partner will purchase the interest of a limited partner. During the first few years of your investment this would be at a discounted value, but the value would increase with time as deregulated oil and gas prices increase and as recoverable reserves increase.

To provide the opportunity for capital appreciation that direct ownership of oil and gas reserves offers, we recommend that you invest $3,000 in oil/gas income programs. This investment can also provide you with substantial liquidity and current income. However, we suggest that you opt to have all cash distributions reinvested to allow for a greater opportunity for capital growth.

4. Communications. The area of communications seems to provide an unusual opportunity for capital growth. To share directly in the growth provided by this business area, you should consider participating in the acquisition of a diversified portfolio of cable television systems. The unique two-way communicative properties of the coaxial cable used in cable television systems are making this medium an essential component of our society. In addition to entertainment, cable television systems will be used for burglar and fire alarms, banking, shopping, education and instruction, information retrieval, and a variety of other applications. Our strong attraction to this area is also indirectly related to our domestic energy scenario. The rising costs of energy will encourage families to plan more of their entertainment around the home. CATV systems will be a major beneficiary of this cost-enforced energy conservation movement.

The objective of a typical CATV partnership is to purchase existing systems, to upgrade the cash flow of the systems (increasing viewer base, raising monthly fees, and adding other features), and then to sell the systems in five to seven years for capital gains. An attractive byproduct of owning CATV systems via a limited partnership format is that various expenses of the partnership, such as depreciation, flow-through to the individual investor. As a result, it is estimated that 90%–100% of an investment in such a program will be deductible over a three- to four-year-period.

In the final analysis the continued rapid growth and technological advances forecast for cable television should result in attractive economic growth. Since this area provides an unusual opportunity for capital appreciation and a hedge against inflation, we recommend that you invest $2,500 this year into CATV systems programs.

CASH FLOW ANALYSIS

1. Income Taxation. You have indicated that one of your primary objectives is to reduce your current tax liability. At the beginning of this report we presented a cash flow analysis which is summarized below:

Adjusted Gross Income	$37,488
Estimated Taxable Income	$27,616
Estimated Federal Income Tax Liability	$ 5,553
Net Cash Flow after Taxes	$18,558
Marginal Tax Bracket	32%

Our approach to designing a tax-reduction strategy involves a process of using low-risk procedures to reduce taxable income. Then, where appropriate, we further reduce taxable income by creating legal deductions or exemptions in certain economically viable, tax-favored investment areas.

As a method of reducing taxes we recommend that you establish an individual retirement account. Current law allows individuals with earned income to contribute and to deduct a maximum of $2,000 or 100% of earned income to such a plan. Contributing to an individual retirement account will not only allow you to reduce your taxable income but will also allow for the tax-free accumulation of assets for your retirement program. Since you have available cash reserves for emergencies and other contingencies, an individual retirement account is an excellent method for you to accumulate capital.

Earlier in this report we recommended that you reposition $19,000 of your capital. Assuming an average annual rate of 12%, maintaining $8,000 in a money market fund will generate approximately $960 in taxable income. Placing capital in a deferred annuity and tax-managed trust for quality issues will not generate taxable income, but allow for tax-deferred accumulation of capital. Approximately 60% of the income generated over the lifetime of an oil/gas income program is tax-free. During the first year of such an investment, all the income should be sheltered from taxation. An investment in a CATV systems program should create deductions against unrelated income of 90%–100% of the investment over the first three to four years. In the first year of investment, the level of deductions depends on how early in the year the investment is made, as well as other factors such as how quickly the partnership can acquire existing systems after the partnership is formed. Assuming that you invest in a CATV program in the first quarter of the year, however, you could expect to deduct approximately 15% of the capital contributed.

The following cash flow illustration indicates that implementing our recommendations will result in a tax liability of $4,428 or a tax savings of $1,125. You will note that your discretionary cash flow has decreased slightly. However, this discretionary cash flow does not take into consideration the accumulation of income, which will be working for you in the tax-advantaged vehicles we have recommended.

Income:	
Salary	$ 35,000
Interest	960
Insurance Costs	35
CATV Program Deductions	(375)
IRA Contribution	(2,000)
Adjusted Gross Income:	$ 33,620
Less: Personal Exemption	(1,000)
Excess Itemized Deductions	(8,872)
Estimated Taxable Income	$ 23,748
Estimated Federal Income Tax Liability*	(4,428)
	$ 19,320

Add: CATV Program Deductions	375
Personal Exemption	1,000
IRA Contribution**	2,000
Less: Remaining Itemized Deductions	(2,300)
FICA Tax	(2,170)
Insurance Costs	(35)
Net Cash Flow After Taxes	$18,190
Less: Living Expenses	(7,800)
Insurance Premiums	(708)
Discretionary Cash Flow	$ 9,682

*Assumes use of appropriate tax rate schedule.
**Assumes initial contribution to IRA is made from existing capital and does not affect cash flow except that a portion of taxable income is sheltered from taxation.

To reduce materially your current income tax liability it would be necessary for you to participate in a deep shelter investment area. Generally, the risk level of a tax-incentive investment has a direct correlation to the level of deductions generated in the first year. When first-year deductibility approaches the level of 50% of the investment, it is crucial to generate the same level of tax savings not only to reduce the risk level of the investment but also to increase the return on the investment. When determining the suitability of a deep sheltering, tax-incentive investment, our approach requires the weighing of four major considerations:

1. the probability of profit aside from the tax benefits;
2. the clarity of the tax benefits in current law as well as your ability to use the tax deductions to the fullest extent;
3. the effect of such investments on your estate liquidity; and
4. your temperament and risk-taking ability.

Economically profitable sheltering vehicles are available, and we are in a position to assist you in identifying appropriate investment areas. You have sufficient liquidity in cash reserves, and your estate has sufficient liquidity provided by insurance coverage. Your willingness to expose 20% of your investment assets to moderate and high-risk levels indicates that your risk tolerance level is high enough to accept the risk inherent in such an investment.

However, the second consideration (2)—your ability to use the tax deductions to the fullest extent—would make such an investment inappropriate for you at this time. When taxable income does not include a large long-term capital gain, the maximum amount of deductions that should be created from tax-incentive investments is an amount equal to taxable income in excess of $55,300, the level at which the 50% bracket begins. Since your taxable income this year is approximately $24,000, an investment in a deep shelter area would create deductions that would be applied against income taxed at less than 49%. You would, therefore, not be using such deductions to the maximum extent.

2. *Cash Flow Distribution.* While we have discussed allocation of your existing capital into suitable investment vehicles, we have not discussed the investment of your discretionary cash flow. However, we have recommended that you set aside a specific amount in your budget *for investing*. According to our Cash Flow Analysis on page 284, you should have a cash flow investment capability of $9,682 or $807 a month. We recommend that you allocate this monthly cash flow as follows:

1. Allocate $150 per month as "mad money." Maintain these funds in your checking account for unexpected expenses. If these funds have not been spent by the end of the month, transfer this money to your money market fund. Having this "mad money" available will help make budgeting easier for you, and the funds not spent can be saved for large purchases (furniture, appliances, and the like) or allocated for pleasure trips.

2. Invest $285 per month into equities. These funds should be invested in the tax-managed trust for quality stocks we have already recommended. By investing a given amount monthly into this vehicle, you will be employing a plan of dollar cost averaging. This calls for the same dollar amount to be invested at regular monthly intervals, each time purchasing as many shares as the dollar amount permits. Over the long run, this plan has historically allowed the acquisition of shares at or below average price. Dollar cost averaging calls for continuous periodic investments regardless of price levels. The plan does not assure a profit and discontinuing a program when the value of accumulated shares is less than their cost would result in a loss. However, we believe this to be a very viable method of accumulating capital.

3. Because our research indicates energy-related investments appear to provide unusual opportunity for economic reward, we feel that an investment program should include a significant allocation to this area. Therefore, we recommend that you direct $220 per month to increase your initial investment in an oil/gas income program. Also, we reiterate that you should choose to have all cash distributions from this program reinvested.

4. Accumulate additional investment funds of $150 each month in your money market fund. Since most investment vehicles would require an initial investment greater than your monthly discretionary cash flow, you should "collect" funds on a monthly basis so that when investment opportunities become available you will have the funds necessary to take advantage of these opportunities. For exam-

ple, we have already mentioned that eventually you should consider investing in individually owned equity issues. Another area that we feel would be appropriate for you is a professionally managed real estate program. Therefore, while building your asset base in a limited number of investments, you should also accumulate funds that will allow you to diversify into additional investment areas.

3. Retirement Planning

A. RETIREMENT INCOME.

You have indicated that you plan to retire at age 65. At that time you would like to have annual purchasing power of $25,000. The following chart indicates your present status in relation to your retirement goal:

	Age 65
Annual income need adjusted for a 9% annual rate of inflation*	$ 429,550
Capital required to provide income needed assuming an after-tax rate of return of 10%	$ 4,295,500
Less: Capital available from retirement plans**	(2,084,052)
Capital available from individual retirement account***	(444,503)
Present investable assets of $21,000 compounding at 10% after-tax annually	(487,728)
Additional capital needed	$ 1,279,217
Annual investment required to provide additional capital assuming:	
An 8% after-tax annual rate of growth	$ 8,765
A 10% after-tax annual rate of growth	$ 5,756
A 12% after-tax annual rate of growth	$ 3,736

*Annual income need is not adjusted for any Social Security benefits that might be available to you. Our present economy and political scenario suggest that your future financial independence should not be dependent upon social programs. We suggest that you consider Social Security as a hedge against inflation in your post-retirement years.

**Capital from retirement plans assumes current value of $6,000 compounding at 10% annually, as well as contributions of 25% of salary each year compounding at 10%.

***Capital from IRA assumes annual contributions of $2,000 compounding at 10% a year.

This chart indicates that, given your present resources and cash flow, it should be financially comfortable for you to achieve your goal. The importance of this chart is that it illustrates the necessity of long-range planning and of investing a portion of your annual cash flow. The key to a secure retirement is to create a balanced and diversified mixture of assets designed to meet your objectives. Such an asset base, in your case, must be accumulated by developing a serious, systematic, and continuous program of periodic investment.

B. INDIVIDUAL RETIREMENT ACCOUNT.

We have recommended that you establish an individual retirement account as a tax-benefited method of accumulating capital for your retirement needs. The preceding chart indicates that by positioning $2,000 a year in an IRA, assuming that these funds grow at 10% per year, at age 65 you would have funds of $444,503. If you did not utilize an IRA, $2,000 of taxable income, assuming a 32% marginal bracket, would provide you with investable funds of $1,360. Investing $1,360 a year to grow at 10% annually would provide you with funds of $302,262 at age 65.

Obviously, an individual retirement account is an advantageous method of helping you achieve your retirement goals. Although an IRA is an excellent method of accumulating wealth, you should be aware that its purpose is to provide a source for retirement income. The favorable income taxation provisions for an IRA are given by the government as an incentive to stimulate personal savings for retirement needs. Consequently, you should understand certain restrictions regarding distributions.

Distributions from an IRA may begin at age 59½ (except in the case of death or permanent disability) and must begin by age 70½. Any distribution taken prior to age 59½ is subject to a penalty of 10% on the distribution, which is treated as ordinary income. Therefore, an IRA should be viewed as a long-term commitment. Distributions may be received in a lump sum or in periodic payments and are treated as ordinary income in the year received. In the event the investor dies before the account is completely distributed, the beneficiary receives ownership of the account, chooses a method of payment, and assumes the identical tax liability of the deceased. If the beneficiary chooses to take a lump sum distribution, the value of the IRA will be included in the deceased's estate.

As the preceding chart indicates, continuous inflation will result in your needing a substantial amount of capital to meet your retirement objectives. Therefore, your IRA should be positioned to allow for maximum growth. You could use a high-yielding investment, such as Certificates of Deposit or money market funds to take maximum advantage of the tax-free accumulation of income within an IRA. However, fixed-income investments have historically never kept up with inflation over the long pull.

Although interest rates on fixed-income vehicles seem attractive, consider the scenario that assumes a rate of return of 12% on a money market instrument and an annual inflation rate of 9%. The maximum real growth of such an investment is 3%. While our present high inflation rate should subside, the loss of real growth during high inflationary periods will result in minimal growth in real value.

Earlier in this report we discussed our attraction to the equity marketplace and indicated that a period of inflation is an excellent time to accumulate equity securities. Quality stocks can be purchased at prices that are low relative to the earning power of the companies they represent as well as the underlying values of the assets of the companies.

Historically, as inflation rates decrease, P-E ratios increase. The adage of "buy low, sell high" is extremely applicable in a period of high inflation in that the underlying assets of a company can be purchased at bargain prices. As this period of inflation winds down, the stock market will correct itself to more accurately reflect the values of the companies that common stocks represent, as well as the income streams generated by these companies.

Since the major objective of your individual retirement account should be capital appreciation, we recommend that you direct your current contribution to the equity marketplace. Specifically, we recommend that you position this year's contribution in a mutual fund with an aggressive growth objective. Such a vehicle will provide professional management and diversification for these funds, as well as the opportunity for the growth of capital.

4. Risk Management. Proper overall risk management of your cash flow stream, as well as your assets, is crucial. The most valuable asset you have is your earning power. If it were disrupted as the result of a disabling accident or sickness, you could be in financial jeopardy. You have indicated that you presently have group disability coverage that would provide monthly benefits of $1,750 until you reach age 65. The Expense Worksheet that you completed indicates that, in the event of disability, you would have monthly living requirements of $1,360. You should realize, however, that the disability income you receive will be taxable to you. If certain requirements are met, an individual can exclude a maximum of $5,200. However, this exclusion is reduced dollar-for-dollar for adjusted gross income, including disability payments, above $15,000. Consequently, there is no exclusion allowed if adjusted gross income is above $20,200 ($15,000 + $5,200). Your disability income would be above this level and therefore fully taxed.

However, assuming that in the event of disability your itemized deductions would not be reduced significantly, you would incur a minimal tax liability. It therefore appears that you have sufficient disability income protection at this time. However, we recommend that you purchase personal disability coverage to provide lifetime benefits. A disabling illness or accident would prevent you from completing your financial plan, but your income needs would continue past your scheduled retirement. Lifetime disability coverage would protect you from financial dependence.

At this time we would also recommend that you review your risk management program in the area of personal liability. Since you are becoming financially visible, we recommend that you protect your assets by purchasing an excess liability policy. Such coverage acts as a suprapolicy, which extends the limitations of your homeowner's policy—usually to $1,000,000. This is very inexpensive coverage, and it is vital for the protection of the assets you have already accumulated as well as those you hope to accumulate.

Lifetime planning summary

The principal thrust of our recommendations is to design an investment strategy for you that will provide diversification and balance by directing capital to areas that will align the overall structure of your Balance Sheet with your stated objectives. After reviewing your financial scenario, including your risk parameters and the level of taxes you pay, we have suggested a matrix of investment vehicles that, given your financial resources, will provide a solid asset base for achieving financial security. Specifically, we have made several investment recommendations for repositioning your cash reserves and for directing your discretionary cash flow. These recommendations regarding the structure of your financial program are as follows:

1. Utilize a money market fund for short-term reserves but limit such reserves to $8,000; direct long-term, serious cash reserves of $2,500 to a deferred annuity.

2. Invest $3,000 into a tax-managed trust for quality stocks and also direct $285 of your monthly cash flow to this investment area.

3. Direct $3,000 into an oil and gas income program and augment this investment by $220 each month.

4. Position $2,500 in CATV systems programs.

5. Accumulate investment funds by allocating $150 each month for future investments. Such funds should be accumulated in your money market fund.

Finally, we stress that our analysis of your financial situation and the resulting recommendations should be considered only as the beginning of your lifetime planning process. To ensure that you maintain the proper financial posture toward attaining your financial objectives we should review and monitor your situation on a timely basis to determine when and if appropriate adjustments should be made.

Estate planning

The following is an illustration of your present estate and associated expenses:

Estate at Death

Estate Assets:	
Checking Accounts	$ 500
Savings Accounts	1,000
Certificates of Deposit	20,000
Proceeds Life Insurance	205,000

Retirement Plan		*
Home		60,000
Personal Property		19,000
Gross Taxable Estate		305,500
Administration and Probate (4%)	$(12,220)	
Estimated Final Expenses	(5,000)	
Liabilities	(51,000)	
Adjusted Gross Estate		$237,280
Net Taxable Estate		$237,280
Taxes:		
Gross Federal Estate Tax	$ 66,730	
Unified Transfer Credit	(66,730)	
State Death Tax Credit	0	
Net Federal Estate Tax	$0	
State Death Tax (Georgia)	0	
Total Taxes		$ 0
Total Estate Settlement Costs		$ 17,220

*Value not included in taxable estate if proceeds are left to a named beneficiary (other than "estate"), and proceeds are *not* left in a lump sum. Proceeds left in a lump sum can be excluded from taxable estate if beneficiary does not elect special income tax provisions such as 10-year averaging or capital gains.

WILL

A properly drafted will is the cornerstone of any sound estate planning program. Where no will exists, the eventual distribution of your property will be in accordance with state law, which may be totally inconsistent with your desires. We recommend you contact an attorney to have a will drafted.

ESTATE LIQUIDITY

You need to be fully aware of the liquidity needs of your estate. Based on your present gross estate of $305,500, the cash needed for estate settlement costs would be $17,220. Estate settlement costs includes administration and probage costs, final expenses, and taxes. Generally, the best method of coping with the liability of estate settlement costs is to provide an adequate reserve through either estate assets or life insurance. You presently have life insurance coverage of $205,000 on your life, which is more than adequate for your present estate liquidity needs. However, as you accumulate assets and your personal situation changes, you should monitor your estate settlement needs and maintain sufficient liquidity for these costs.

LIFETIME TRANSFERS

You have indicated that your parents will retire in ten years. If necessary, you would like to be in a position to supplement their income. While it is not appropriate for you to consider substantial gifts at this time as you are just beginning an asset accumulation program, you should be aware of how gifts are taxed.

Current gift tax regulations allow an annual exclusion of $10,000 per donee. Gifts above this exclusion are subject to tax, but the unified transfer credit is applied against any taxes due. The unified transfer credit is a credit against estate or gift taxes. This credit is $79,300 this year but will increase each year until 1987 when it reaches $192,800 which is equivalent to an exemption for taxable transfers of $600,000. The gifted value of all taxable gifts, that is, gifts above the annual exclusion, is added back to the donor's estate but not the present value of the asset.

Should you need to supplement your parent's income, rather than gifting assets or income that you might need for your financial program, you may wish to consider making an interest-free demand loan to them. Such a loan could be invested in high-yielding securities and the resulting investment income would be shifted to your parents where it would be taxed in a lower tax bracket. You should be aware, however, that the IRS has unsuccessfully challenged that interest-free demand loans are in fact taxable gifts. Although various courts have recently held that interest-free demand loans among family members do not constitute taxable gifts, the Service will probably continue to strengthen its case against this planning tool. However, assuming that the precedence established by the courts continues to be followed, income earned on such loans can be effectively transferred to family members at little or no tax cost.

Depending on your parents' needs and the level of wealth you have accumulated, another alternative to providing them with income would be a short-term or Clifford trust. This involves putting income-producing property into a trust with a life of more than ten years for the benefit of your parents. If properly handled, the income from this trust would be payable to your parents and could be used for their future needs. Upon expiration of the trust, the trust corpus would be returned to you. This arrangement is often preferable to outright gifts to parents where the children need to retain their capital for retirement programs. A short-term trust must be carefully designed to avoid having the income taxed to the grantor. Proper funding is very important. You should discuss this planning technique with your tax advisor.

Estate planning summary

Our major recommendation regarding your estate planning arrangements is that you consult an attorney to have an appropriate will drafted. Since you are in the process of beginning to build an estate, we suggest that your estate plan be as flexible as possible. As the mixture of your assets change or unusual circumstances develop, we recommend that we review your total estate plan along with your other financial advisors.

Total Investment
Planning
Confidential
Questionnaire

The very first step in the financial planning process is the examination of your total financial wherewithal. In addition to this questionnaire, the following documents are considered:

DOCUMENTS

☒   Copies of your last four years income tax returns and any gift tax returns.

☐   Copy of your will

☐   Copy of your spouse's will

☐   Copies of trust agreements or contracts (if applicable)

☐   Copies of business buy-sell agreements (if applicable)

☐   Others _____

☐   _____

Your life, health, and other insurance policies should also be included for analyzing your present coverage.

PERSONAL INFORMATION

Client's Name ___ Susan M. Lane ___ Social Security No. __294-68-5543__

Home Address __6436 Park Drive__ Phone __813-7734__

Business Address __901 East Main__ Phone __343-6845__

Date of Birth __6-22-51__ Birth Place __Ocala, Florida__

Occupation __Systems Engineer__ How Long? __1 Year__

Who is your attorney? __None__

Who is your accountant? __None__

Do you have any other professional advisors of whom we should be aware? __No__

Registered Representative_____ Date Information Obtained __January, 1982__

Branch Office _____

(1)

FAMILY INFORMATION

Spouse _____ Date of Birth _____ Social Security No. _____

Occupation _____ How Long? _____

CHILDREN	DATE OF BIRTH	DEPENDENT	SELF-SUPPORTING
N/A		☐	☐
		☐	☐
		☐	☐
		☐	☐
		☐	☐

Are all family members in good health? Yes __X__ No _____

If not, explain: _____

Are any relatives other than spouse and children depending on you for support now or will need support in the future?

Yes __X__ No _____ If so, explain: My parents will retire in about 10 years. I'm afraid that inflation will prevent them from enjoying their retirement years. If they need financial assistance, I'd like to be in a position to supplement their income.

Do you have any alimony or child support obligations? Yes _____ No __X__

If so, how much? _____ For how long? _____

Is your estate obligated to continue these obligations? _____

EDUCATION

Do you want to send your children to college? Yes _____ No _____

How much do you estimate it will cost per child, per year? (In today's dollars) $_____

Have you set aside any assets for your children?   Yes _____ No _____

Are they to be used for their college education?   Yes _____ No _____

DESCRIBE:

CHILD	TYPE OF ASSET	AMOUNT	HOW HELD*

*Custodianship, trust or other. Give custodian, trustee, and donor: _____

_____

(2)

CASH RESERVES — FIXED DOLLAR ASSETS

	HUSBAND	WIFE	JOINT	YIELD/MATURITY
Cash				
Checking Accounts		500		
Savings Accounts		1,000		5 1/4%
Credit Union				
Certificates of Deposit		20,000		12%
Money Market Funds				
Deferred Annuities				
Government Bonds				
Notes Receivable				
Mortgages Receivable				
Other:				

HOME AND PERSONAL PROPERTY

Market value of your home $ 60,000* _____ Cost basis $ 60,000 _____

Remaining mortgage $ 50,000 _____ Number of years 30 _____ Interest rate 17 %

Who is the owner? Self
*Purchased August, 1982.
Do you have mortgage insurance in case of disability or death? Yes X No _____ If so, how much? $50,000

PERSONAL PROPERTY	HUSBAND	WIFE	JOINT
Home furnishings		10,000	
Automobiles		6,000	
Silver, jewelry, coins		--	
Clothing, furs		3,000	
Antiques		--	
Boat, airplane, trailer		--	
Other_____			

REAL ESTATE

List all real estate holdings other than your home and those included under tax incentive investments. Use separate sheet if necessary.

Description	Market Value	Remaining Mortgage	Cost Basis	Gross Annual Income	Expenses, Depreciation (annual)	Owner	What are your plans for this property?

(3)

STOCKS, BONDS, AND MUTUAL FUNDS

Owner	No. Shares or Face Amount	Security Description	Listed or NASDAQ Symbol	Present Market Value	Total Cost	Annual Dividend	Coupon	Maturity Date

TAX-INCENTIVE INVESTMENTS

Do you have any tax-incentive investments?
(Oil and gas exploration, real estate, cattle, coal, railway cars, etc.) Yes _____ No _____

Description	Year Purchased	Amount Invested	Expected Annual Deductions	Present Value (if known)	Current Annual Income	Owner

(4)

307

BUSINESS INTEREST OR PROFESSIONAL PRACTICE

Sole Proprietorship ☐   Sub-chapter S ☐
Partnership ☐   Corporation ☐

Business

I. Name _____ I.D. Number _____

II. Valuation

a). What is your estimation of the present market value of *your* share of the business?

_____

b). What do you estimate your estate would collect for the business (liquidation value)?

_____

or

Professional Practice

List the present value of *your* share of the following:

Checking Account _____

Accounts Receivable _____

Equipment or Furniture _____

Building _____

Other _____

_____

Any liabilities? _____

Would your estate be able to collect the above values? Yes _____ No _____
If no, which ones would decrease and by how much?

_____

_____

_____

Business or Professional Practice

Ownership:

Name	% of Ownership	Relationship (if any)
_____	_____	_____
_____	_____	_____
_____	_____	_____

For Corporations Only:

Do you have any of the following corporate fringe benefit programs?

Pension Plan   Yes _____ No _____

Profit Sharing Plan   Yes _____ No _____

105(b) Medical Expense Reimbursement Plan   Yes _____ No _____

Corporate Disability Plan   Yes _____ No _____

Group Life Insurance   Yes _____ No _____

Deferred Compensation Plan   Yes _____ No _____

Thrift or Salary Savings Plan   Yes _____ No _____

If not a corporation, have you ever considered incorporation?

If so, explain: _____

_____

(5)

Business or Professional Practice (Continued)

Employee Information (Complete for Employee Benefit Plan Proposals)

Name	Sex	Date of Birth	Employment Date	Full Time Part Time	Current Annual Compensation

Disposition of Interest

What would happen to your business in the event of a long disability or your death? Would you want it retained by your

heirs or sold or dissolved? _____

_____

Do you have a Buy-Sell or Stock Redemption Agreement? Yes ____ No ____

What is the purchase price? $_____

Is there an escalation clause (to provide for increasing values)? Yes ____ No ____

Is your agreement funded? Yes ____ No ____

With what? _____ How much? _____

RETIREMENT INFORMATION

Type of Plan	Present Vested Interest	Value at Death	Beneficiary	Value of Voluntary Contributions	How Funded?	Monthly Retirement Income at Age ____
Keogh						
I.R.A.						
Pension	*		Parents			
Profit Sharing	*		Parents			
Thrift						
Salary Savings						

Are you satisfied with your retirement plan? Yes ____ No ____

Explain *My interest in my company's retirement plans is $6,000; however, this interest
is not fully vested.

(6)

LIFE INSURANCE

If you do not send us your life insurance policies for an analysis, please complete the following for yourself and your spouse:

Insured	Face Amount	Company	Type	Issue Date	Cash Value	Annual Premium	Beneficiary	Owner
Self	$155,000	Group (Term)				Co. Pays	Parents	
Self	$ 50,000	Mortgage Insurance (Decreasing Term)		8/82		$158	Parents	Self

Insured	Company	Disability Income	Benefit Period	Daily Benefit (Hosp.)	Major Med.	Acc. Death Benefit
Self	Group	60% of Mo. Income up to $3,000	Age 65			
"	"			Basic	$1,000,000	

OTHER INSURANCE

When was your property and casualty insurance last reviewed? __Purchased August, 1982__

Do you have personal excess liability coverage? Yes _____ No __X__ How Much? _____

LIABILITIES

What other indebtedness do you have aside from mortgages previously mentioned?

	Total Amount	Due Date	Monthly Outlay	Obligor (Husb., Wife, Jt.)
Notes Credit Cards	$1,000			
Installment Obligations				
Cash Value Loans				
Taxes Payable				
Margin Accounts				
Other				

(7)

310

ESTATE INFORMATION

Do you have a will? Yes ＿＿ No _X_ Date Drawn ＿＿＿＿＿＿＿＿＿＿＿＿＿ Date Reviewed ＿＿＿＿＿＿

What are the provisions of your will? ＿＿＿＿＿＿＿＿＿＿＿＿＿＿＿＿＿＿＿＿＿＿＿＿＿＿＿＿＿＿

＿＿

＿＿

Does your spouse have a will? Yes ＿＿ No ＿＿ Date Drawn ＿＿＿＿＿＿＿＿ Date Reviewed＿＿＿＿＿＿

What are the provisions of the will? ＿＿＿＿＿＿＿＿＿＿＿＿＿＿＿＿＿＿＿＿＿＿＿＿＿＿＿＿＿＿＿

＿＿

Do you expect any inheritances? <u>Last year received $25,000 from great aunt's estate; used $10,000 for down payment on house.</u> Amount? ＿＿＿＿＿＿＿＿＿＿

Does your spouse expect any inheritances? ＿＿＿＿＿＿＿＿ Amount? ＿＿＿＿＿＿＿＿＿＿

Have you made any gifts to relatives? Yes ＿＿ No _X_

When? ＿＿＿＿＿＿＿＿ How Much? ＿＿＿＿＿＿＿＿＿＿＿＿＿＿＿＿＿＿＿＿＿＿＿＿＿＿＿＿＿

Have you made any substantial gifts to any charities? Yes ＿＿ No _X_

Are you interested in making such gifts? Yes ＿＿ No _X_   (not at this time)

Now or in your will? ＿＿＿＿＿＿＿＿＿＿＿＿＿＿＿＿＿＿＿＿＿＿＿＿＿＿＿＿＿＿＿＿＿＿＿＿＿

TRUSTS

Have you created any trusts? Yes ＿＿ No _X_

If yes, please give (a) type, (b) date created, (c) how it is funded, and (d) who is the beneficiary.

＿＿

＿＿

＿＿

Are you the beneficiary of any trusts? Yes ＿＿ No _X_

If yes, please give (a) type, (b) donor, (c) annual income

＿＿

＿＿

＿＿

(8)

CURRENT INCOME AND EXPENSES

Estimate of Current Year's Income   **Expenses**

Salary	$35,000	
		DEDUCTIBLE
Bonus	_____	Interest	8,250
Self Employment Income (Net)	_____	Taxes (Property, State Income)	2,592
Director or Trustee Fees	_____	Contributions	_____
Pension, Annuity	_____	Other Deductible Expenses	_____
Interest (Taxable)	2,453	**NON DEDUCTIBLE**
Dividends	_____	Principal Reduction	_____
Real Estate (Net)	_____	Living	7,800
Net Short Term Gains/Losses*	_____	Education	_____
Net Long Term Gains/Losses*	_____	Insurance Premiums	708
Social Security	_____	Savings	--
Spouse's Income	_____	Investments	--
Other Insurance excess premium costs	35	Other_____	--
	37,488	TOTAL	19,680

*Please give details of any installment sale income, capital gains or losses you expect this year._____

_____

Do you expect any significant changes in your income or expenses in the next 5 years? Yes __X__ No ____ Please
explain _My income should increase about 15% per year; expect to receive bonus of 10% of my salary each year after 1983._

INCOME OBJECTIVES

RETIREMENT

At what age do you plan to retire? _____   (Turn to the end of this questionnaire for Susan M. Lane's Expense Worksheet.)

What annual aftertax (spendable) income would you want at retirement? (In today's dollars) $ _____

DISABILITY

If you became disabled, how much annual income would you and your family need to maintain your present

standard of living? $_____

SURVIVOR'S INCOME

If you died today, what principal amount would you want to provide for:

Home Mortgage? $_____   Education Fund? $_____

Debts? $_____   Other $_____

How much annual income would your family need to maintain their standard of living? $_____

(9)

312

OVERALL FINANCIAL AND INVESTMENT CONCERNS

How would you best position your investment assets to coincide with your current investment temperament?

_____20___% Very Conservatively. Conserving present capital is more important than making it grow.

_____60___% Conservatively. High quality investments that provide an opportunity for appreciation and relative safety are important.

_____15___% Subject to moderate risk. Aggressive growth is important.

_____5___% Subject to high risk. Speculative growth is acceptable.

Do you have any preferences or objections to any particular investment areas?

Please explain ___I have never made any investments._____

_____

Which of the following best describes your attitude towards your income needs?

☒ My present income is adequate for my needs.

☐ I need more current income.

☐ I can forgo current income to be better able to provide for future retirement income.

Indicate areas of major concern to you by rating numerically in order of importance:

_____Current Income   _____Education of Children

___3___Retirement Income   ___2___Reduction of Current Income Taxes

___4___Further Building of Estate   _____Reduction of Estate Taxes

_____Conservation of Assets for Heirs   ___1___Other ___See Below_____

What would you consider to be your primary financial objective or concern?___I want to enjoy my financial status now, but I'm concerned about the future._____

Is there any thing else we should know? _____

_____

_____

_____

(10)

Expense Worksheet
(State whether annual or monthly)

	CURRENT MONTHLY	IN EVENT OF DISABILITY	IN EVENT OF DEATH
LIVING EXPENSES:			
Food, Household Supplies	150	150	
Allowances, Subscriptions	15	15	
Household or Yard Help, Pool Maintenance			
Clothes, Cleaning	75	35	
Miscellaneous Cash Expenses			
Auto Expenses (Gas, OVIL, Tires Repairs)	75	40	
Utilities (Phone, Electricity, Gas, Water)	120	120	
Commuting (Other Than Use of Auto)			
Vacations			
Recreation, Club Dues	15	15	
Entertainment	100	75	
Hobbies	20	20	
Family Gifts	30	30	
Boat, Airplane, etc., Maintenance			
Other			
SUBTOTAL (LIVING EXPENSES)	600	500	
DURABLES (PURCHASES)			
Autos			
Boats, Airplanes			
Furniture, Appliances			
Other			
SUBTOTAL (DURABLES)			
INSURANCE			
Life	14	14	
Health			
Home	20	20	
Auto	25	25	
Liability			
SUBTOTAL (INSURANCE)	59	59	
	CURRENT MONTHLY	IN EVENT OF DISABILITY	IN EVENT OF DEATH
OTHER			
Medical and Dental	10	10	
Education			
Mortgage (Excludes Taxes and Insurance)	700	700	
Rent			
Debts (Other Than Mortgage	40	40	
Charitable Contributions			
Professional Advice (Lawyer, Accountant)			
Alimony			
Child Support			
Political Contributions			
Unreimbursed Business Expense			
Property Taxes	41	41	
Intangibles Tax			
Ad Valorem Tax	10	10	
State Income Tax	165		
Miscellaneous			
SUBTOTAL (OTHER)	966	801	
GRAND TOTAL OF EXPENSES	1,625	1,360	

II

A Total
Financial Plan
Prepared for:
Robert F. Murphy

by
Jeannie B. Wright, CFP, CLU
Financial Planning Consultant

Preface

Mr. Murphy, we have prepared an analysis of your present financial resources taking into consideration your personal, investment, legal and tax circumstances. We have discussed certain procedural and investment changes that should prove advantageous and desirable in helping you to achieve your financial goals.

These recommendations are, of course, useless unless implemented. We urge you to first review this report with your attorney and/or tax advisor in implementing the recommendations at your earliest convenience.

And finally, no financial plan, however well conceived and individually tailored, is an end in itself. Changing laws, regulations, economics, and forecasts require this in-depth financial program, once implemented, to be periodically reexamined and possibly revised. We strongly encourage you to consider this plan as the beginning of an annual or bi-annual process of reviewing your total financial condition.

Table of contents

Personal balance sheet

	Owned by Mr. Murphy	Owned Jointly	Owned By Mrs. Murphy
Assets:			
Checking Accounts	$ 4,000	$	$ 1,500
Savings Accounts			5,000
Certificates of Deposit	35,000	15,000	
Treasury Bills	30,000		
Municipal Bonds	75,000		
Life Insurance Cash Values	30,000		
Pension Plan	75,000		
Profit Sharing Plan	115,000		
Stocks	230,000		55,000
Real Estate (see schedule)	105,500		7,000
Oil and Gas Drilling Programs	35,000*		
Business Interest	2,000,000		
Home	225,000		
Personal Property	35,000	80,000	40,000
Total Assets	$2,994,500	$95,000	$108,500
Liabilities:			
Notes Payable	7,000		
Cash Value Loans	25,000		
Mortgage on Home	45,000		
Margin Account	50,000		
Total Liabilities	$ 127,000	$ –0–	$ –0–
Net Worth	$2,867,500	$95,000	$108,500
Combined Net Worth		$3,071,000	

*Represents amounts invested.

Real estate schedule

Robert Murphy		
Condominium—Myrtle Beach	$ 75,000	
Less Mortgage	57,000	$ 18,000
Commercial Building	$225,000	
Less Mortgage	80,000	
Total Equity	$145,000	
Your Interest (50%)		72,500
Mercer Properties, Ltd.		
(10% Interest)		15,000*
Total Real Estate Equity		$105,500
Jane Murphy		
Mountain Lot		$ 7,000

*Represents amount invested.

1983 Estimated cash flow analysis

Income:		
Salary		$ 145,000
Bonus		35,000
Director Fees		1,000
Interest		11,300
Dividends		17,000
Real Estate Income	$(12,000)	
Less Expenses, Depreciation	(15,000)	(3,000)
Trust		6,000
Oil and Gas		
Income		2,500
Deductions		(1,900)
Insurance Cost		3,500)
Adjusted Gross Income		$216,400
Less: Excess Itemized Deductions		(28,100)
Personal Exemptions		(2,000)
Estimated Taxable Income		$186,300
Estimated Federal Income Tax Liability		(77,150)
		$ 109,150
Add: Oil and Gas Deductions		1,900
Real Estate Depreciation		3,000
Tax Free Interest		5,200
Personal Exemptions		2,000
Less: Remaining Itemized Deductions		(3,400)
Insurance Cost		(3,500)
Net Cash Flow After Taxes and Deductible Items		$ 114,350
Less: Living Expenses		(60,000)
Principal Reduction		(3,000)
Insurance Premiums		(4,000)
Gifts to Angela		(10,000)
Net Discretionary Cash Flow		$ 37,350

Estate at Death

Estate Assets:		
Checking Accounts		$ 4,000
Certificates of Deposit		42,500*
Treasury Bills		30,000
Municipal Bonds		75,000
Proceeds Life Insurance	$300,000	
Less Loans	(25,000)	275,000
Pension Plan		350,000**
Profit Sharing Plan		15,000**
Stocks		230,000
Real Estate		105,500
Oil and Gas Programs		35,000
Business Interest		2,000,000
Home		225,000
Personal Property		75,000*
Gross Taxable Estate:		$3,462,000
Administration and Probate (4%)	$(138,500)	
Estimated Final Expenses	(5,000)	
Liabilities	(127,000)	
Adjusted Gross Estate:		3,191,500
Marital Deduction	(1,595,750)	
Net Taxable Estate		$1,595,750
Taxes:		
Gross Federal Estate Tax	598,887	
Unified Transfer Credit	(79,300)	
State Death Tax Credit	(70,530)	
Net Federal Estate Tax	449,057	
State Death Tax (Georgia)	70,530	
Total Taxes		$ 519,587
Total Estate Settlement Costs		$ 663,087

*One-half of jointly held property included in estate.

**An aggregate exclusion of $100,000 is available for proceeds of qualified retirement plans if proceeds are left to a named beneficiary (other than "estate"), and proceeds are *not* left in a lump sum. Proceeds left in a lump sum can be excluded from taxable estate if beneficiary does not elect special income tax provisions such as 10-year averaging or capital gains.

Introduction

Formulating a sound lifetime and estate plan begins with a careful analysis of your present resources and their positioning, your income and its taxation and subsequent direction, and both your assets and cash flow—all relative to your personal financial goals. We have included at the beginning of this report a Personal Balance Sheet, a Cash Flow Analysis, and an Estate at Death illustration.

A review of your Balance Sheet shows that you and Mrs. Murphy have a combined net worth of $3,071,000. About 65% of this is concentrated in your business interest, and the remainder of your assets (exclusive of home and personal property) appear to be equally divided between liquid and nonliquid investment areas.

The Cash Flow Analysis indicates your taxable income this year will be about $186,300 resulting in a federal tax liability of $77,150. You should have about $37,000 available after all taxes and expenses for saving and investing.

The Estate at Death illustration shows that you now have a potential gross estate of $3,462,000, and cash of approximately $663,000 would be needed by your executor for estate settlement costs.

Your major concern at this time is whether or not you should sell your business. You recently received an offer for $2,000,000, which you feel is very attractive. However, your daughter Angela has been working in the business for ten years now. She feels, as you do, that she could successfully continue the business when you retire or in the event of your premature death. You would consider retaining the business only if you can provide for a comfortable retirement for you and Mrs. Murphy without the capital value of the business. You have asked us to examine this possibility, and you would also like to know, if you sold the business, what the tax consequences would be and what you should do with the after-tax proceeds. Your other financial objectives include reducing your current income tax liability and future estate taxes. In addition, you should be concerned about providing adequately for the liquidity needs of your estate.

You have indicated that you would like to retire at age 65 with an annual income of $60,000 in today's dollars. The following illustration shows the capital that will be required to provide this income:

Retirement

Annual income needed at age 65	$ 60,000
Adjusting for a 10% annual rate of inflation, at age 65 you would need	188,305

Less: Estimated Social Security Benefit[1]	(34,380)
Estimated After-Tax Pension Benefit[2]	(52,500)
Net annual income needed	$ 101,425
Capital required to provide $101,425 annually, assuming an 8% after-tax rate of return	$ 1,267,812

Present-capital-at-work[3]	$580,500	
Assuming an 8% after-tax rate of growth, at age 65 these assets would be worth		1,461,797
Estimated value of profit-sharing plan at age 65[4]		681,683
Additional Capital needed		–0–
Annual income provided from available capital of $2,143,480, assuming an 8% after-tax rate of return		$ 171,478

[1]*Based on present benefit levels and adjusted for inflation.*
[2]*Assumes an 8% annual increase in present vested benefit of $42,000 and assumes a 50% marginal tax bracket.*
[3]*Assets that are or could be invested other than home, personal property, lake lot, and business.*
[4]*Assumes present value of $115,000 and annual contributions of $15,000 compounding 10% annually.*

Based on this projection, your retirement benefits and the capital outside of the business would be adequate to provide for your retirement. In fact, your income at retirement would be more than you need, thus allowing you to continue to accumulate additional capital as a hedge against inflation after retirement. In the illustration, we have assumed that your present capital, outside of your retirement plans, would increse 8% after taxes annually.

In the following sections of this report, we will present our recommendations for the proper positioning of your assets and for the investment of the assets in your retirement plans. We will then analyze the tax consequences of the sale of the business and the investment of the after-tax proceeds. Finally, in the Estate Planning section, we will discuss in detail the liquidity needs of both your estate and Mrs. Murphy's, particularly if you retain the business for your family.

Lifetime planning

ASSET ANALYSIS

Cash Reserves. A closer review of your Balance Sheet indicates you and Mrs. Murphy are maintaining fixed-dollar assets of $90,000 including the savings account, certificates of deposit, Treasury bills, and net insurance cash values. While we recognize the need to maintain adequate fixed-dollar cash reserve assets for emergencies, future investment opportunities, or other unforeseen contingencies, we recommend that you limit your reserves to about six month's to one year's living expenses.

Fixed-dollar assets do not allow for any capital appreciation and are consequently very vulnerable to inflation. Furthermore, the yields on traditional fixed-dollar assets such as certificates of deposit or Treasury Bills, while appearing attractive, are reduced significantly by income taxation. For example, your top tax bracket is 50%. This means your last dollar of interest income is reduced by $.50, or, the 15% rate of return on your certificates of deposit is reduced to an effective after-tax yield of only 7.5%. After applying the effects of today's inflation, such assets are losing future purchasing power for you.

We recommend you limit your cash reserve holdings to $50,000. To help maximize your return on this capital, we suggest you position $40,000 of this into a deferred annuity. This will allow the interest earned from the majority of your reserves to accumulate without being subject to current income taxation. Your $40,000 principal in the annuity will be fully guaranteed, and withdrawals can be made if cash is needed. As long as your cumulative withdrawals do not exceed your original principal, there will be no income tax consequences. We recommend you reposition the $35,000 of certificates of deposit registered in your name and the $5,000 in Mrs. Murphy's savings account into two deferred annuities. Current first-year guaranteed rates for deferred annuities are in excess of 12%.

The remainder of your reserve holdings should be comprised of your net insurance cash values and a very liquid fund for emergencies, major purchases, tax payments, and the like. For these short-term reserve holdings, we recommend a money market fund. Money market funds buy short-term high interest bearing instruments, such as US Treasury Bills and notes, government agency securities, commercial paper, bank certificates of deposit, and other corporate notes and repurchase agreements. By pooling large amounts of investors' money, professional managers are usually able to receive a better return from these instruments than individual investors.

Money market funds offer immediate liquidity, relative safety of principal, and current rates of about 9%. They are also very attractive vehicles for accumulating funds for investments to be made during the year. We caution you, however, not to let excess funds accumulate and be eroded by taxation and inflation. We suggest you position $5,000 of the jointly held certificates of deposit into a money market fund. The remaining $10,000 of certificates and your $30,000 of Treasury bills needs to be positioned in areas that will provide a greater overall return. We will refer to this $40,000 as your "excess" cash reserves.

Securities. You have indicated that one of your "preferred" investment areas is common stocks, and this is apparent from the $285,000 you and Mrs. Murphy currently have positioned in this area. We favor your continuing participation in equities, and we feel that now is an attractive time to be increasing your portfolios.

Historically speaking, quality common stocks appear to be undervalued in terms of the relationship between current price levels and corporate earnings (P-E ratios) and the relationship of the market averages to the book values of the companies they reflect. The increasingly favorable tax treatment of capital gains gives additional incentive toward equity participation, as does an apparent trend towards annually increasing dividend payouts. Furthermore, the possible restructuring of our tax system to reduce or eliminate the double taxation of dividends could have a dramatic effect on future equity values.

The disadvantage of owning equity securities for your situation is your overall return is reduced by taxation of dividend income. This can be avoided by acquiring shares of a professionally managed, tax-sheltered trust. Such a trust is a mutual fund that elects to be taxed as a corporation. Consequently, 85% of the dividends received from domestic corporations in which the trust invests are received tax-free. These dividends are internally accumulated rather than distributed to shareholders. Thus, fully taxable dividends are effectively transformed into more favorably taxed capital gains, realized when and if any shares are sold.

We suggest you reposition $100,000 of the capital currently committed to individual equities into shares of a tax-managed trust. More specifically, you can reduce your holdings of ABC, DEF, and GHI. These stocks comprise the majority of your equity portfolio and should be diversified. You can realize $100,000 as follows:

800 Shares ABC at $35 per Share	$ 28,000
900 Shares DEF at $50 per Share	$ 45,000
900 Shares GHI at $30 per Share	$ 27,000
	$100,000
Basis for All Shares Sold	75,000
Total Gain	$ 25,000

To offset this $25,000 capital gain, we recommend you sell your current municipal bonds and replace them with shorter-term issues. All of your bonds have maturities in excess of twenty years. Recent rises in interest rates have caused the value of most bonds to decline, and longer-term issues have suffered the greatest decreases. By using issues with maturities of five to ten years, your capital value should not decline as drastically as longer-term issues when interest rates rise. We feel it is appropriate for you to maintain $75,000 to $100,000 in municipal bonds to provide liquidity in your net worth and tax-free income. We can assist you in identifying bonds that are appropriate for your situation.

At the present time, you should be emphasizing capital appreciation in your equity portfolio. The tax-managed trust is an ideal vehicle to use for this because both appreciation and accumulated dividends increase the value of your shares. In the future, if you need additional income, a systematic withdrawal program could be utilized. Enough shares could be sold on a monthly, quarterly, or annual basis to provide the desired income.

Consider the following simplified example, which shows how this would occur and the tax consequences:

Assume 10,000 shares are acquired for $10 per share or $100,000. At the end of one year, assume the 10,000 shares are worth $112,000 or $11.20 per share due to a 6% net dividend yield that was reinvested and 6% net dividend yield that was reinvested and 6% appreciation. To receive $6,000 (the 6% dividend yield):

Sell 535 shares at $11.20 or	$ 6,000
Basis is 535 shares at $10.00 or	(5,350)
Gain (Assume Long-Term)	$ 650
Taxable Gain (40% of $650)	$ 260
Tax Liability (50% Bracket)	$ 130
Proceeds Received	$ 6,000
Tax Liability	(130)
After-Tax Income	$ 5,870

This $5,870 of after-tax income is certainly greater than the $3,000 you would have if $6,000 of dividends were subject to tax in a 50% top tax bracket.

Real Estate. Your real estate holdings are currently comprised of a vacation condominium at the beach, a mountain lot, a limited partnership interest in some undeveloped land, and a 50% interest in a commercial building. In addition to the opportunity for attractive capital appreciation, real estate investments can offer several tax advantages. As you are aware, interest and taxes provide deductions against ordinary income, and improved properties offer additional tax savings through depreciation.

You question the value of the undeveloped land in the limited partnership. There has been little interest in the property by any outside developers, and the partnership itself has no plans for development. Your attitude towards this property is "wait and see."

Your commercial building, however, appears to be a profitable investment; the building has appreciated an average of 18% annually, and your rental income has also increased. Your depreciation deductions and other expenses are currently in excess of your income so you are receiving a tax-sheltered cash flow.

The condominium at Myrtle Beach also appears to be a wise acquisition. It has appreciated about 15% over the past year and a half. Although you do not have any plans now to rent the property, in the future you may want to consider this alternative.

You want to continue to invest in real estate, and we can help you select those particular investments that are appropriate for you. We do not recommend any additional acquisitions of undeveloped land. As you have discovered, this is a very speculative area of real estate that can take many years to show a profit. At the present time we are particularly attracted to the areas of existing income properties and new construction of conventional income properties with emphasis on multi-family housing.

Several factors have contributed to what we envision as a coming crisis in this nation's housing situation. Due to a combination of (1) the high cost and scarcity of long-term credit, (2) the inability of developers to immediately deduct construction loan interest, and (3) abnormally low rents, the construction of new, nongovernment subsidized residential rental housing has almost halted, thus reducing the available supply of housing.

Demand for residential rental properties has been increasing and will continue to do so for many years. The Bureau of the Census projects 1.5 million household formations each year for the next decade. Home ownership for many of these new households will be prohibitively expensive. This increasing demand, together with the loss of about 500,000 housing units each year due to fire, conversion, disaster, and other reasons, and the lack of new housing construction will result in a housing shortage.

The tax benefits associated with real estate properties have been significantly enhanced as a result of the Economic Recovery Tax Act of 1981. Under the legislation, real estate acquired in 1981 or later has been assigned a 15-year recovery period for depreciation purposes with a 175% declining balance method available for all properties other than low-income housing. The nature of any gains on the disposition of properties will depend on whether the property is residential or nonresidential.

For nonresidential properties when the accelerated method is used, the gain, up to the amount of deductions taken, will be ordinary income and any excess will be capital gain.

If the property was residential, the gain will be recaptured as ordinary income only to the extent that the deductions under the accelerated method exceeded those that would have been allowed under a straight-line method over the 15-year period.

These provisions will make residential properties in particular very advantageous, and help ease the coming crisis we see in this area.

You should invest in both new construction and existing income properties through professionally managed limited partnerships. Publicly offered partnerships offer diversification into several properties in different geographic locations and add greater safety through expert decision making in the acquisition, management, and ultimate sale of the properties. We are in a position to recommend to you those partnerships that are managed by real estate firms of high integrity, extensive experience, and excellent past results for our clients. Initially we recommend you invest $25,000 of your "excess" cash reserves into limited partnerships that are involved in new construction of income properties. As attractive opportunities become available in the acquisition of existing properties, we will point them out to you.

Tax-Incentive Investments. One of your overall objectives is to reduce your current income tax liability. We have already discussed some ways of accomplishing this. For example, interest can accumulate tax-sheltered in a deferred annuity and fully taxable dividends can be transformed into future capital gains by acquiring shares of a tax-managed trust. In addition, deductions against taxable income can be created through investment in certain economically viable tax-incentive areas. You have invested in two oil and gas drilling programs in the past that have provided deductions against your highly taxed income, and you are now beginning to receive income from both programs.

When considering any investment and, in particular, an investment in tax-incentive areas, you need to consider four major factors:

1. the probability of profit aside from any tax benefits;
2. the clarity of any tax benefits under current law, as well as your ability to use any tax deductions to the fullest extent;
3. the effect such investments have upon your estate liquidity; and
4. your temperament and risk-taking ability.

We have identified several investment areas in particular that appear to provide unusual opportunity for both economic reward and high tax deductions against unrelated income. The first is new construction of conventional real estate income properties, which we have already discussed.

The next area of tax-incentive investments we favor is direct participation in the acquisition of a diversified portfolio of cable television systems. The rising costs of energy will encourage families to plan more of
their entertainment around the home and therefore their television sets.
The unique two-way communicative properties of the coaxial cable that
is used in cable television systems are making this medium an essential
component of our society. In addition to entertainment, we will be able
to use our televisions, through cable systems, for burglar and fire alarms,
banking, shopping, educational instruction, information retrieval, and
the like. By investing in this increasingly important vehicle in our lives,
one can achieve significant economic gains as well as tax benefits, both of
which are desirable in meeting your financial objectives.

It is estimated that the investor will be able to deduct 90% to 100%
of the investment over three to four years. A typical CATV partnership attempts to purchase existing systems with an eye toward upgrading the
cash flow of the systems (increasing viewer base, raising monthly fees,
adding other features, and so on) and selling the systems in five to seven
years for capital gains. In the final analysis, the continued rapid growth
and technological advances that we forecast for cable television should
result in attractive economic gains. As with any tax-incentive investment,
this, not the tax savings, should be the primary motivation for investment.

The third great opportunity we see is more directly related to our
energy outlook. This is in very diversified oil and natural gas exploration
and developmental drilling. Given proper diversification, we see an attractive opportunity for investment with risk being significantly reduced
by substantial tax savings. Our experience indicates that average performance over a very diversified series of gas and oil drilling program investments should provide future net revenues of between 1.5 to 3 times
one's "pretax" investment over a period of 10 to 15 years. Under current
law approximately 20–30% of net revenues from drilling programs should
be tax-free over the life of the investment due to statutory depletion allowances and other business deductions.

As you are aware, investments in oil and gas drilling programs generate deductions of 60% to 90% in the year of investment, depending on
the structure of the partnership and the timing in which the investment
is made. Most will provide additional deductions, bringing the total up to
100% over the next one to four years. With few exceptions, the higher-risk
exploratory programs, because of their partnership structures, provide
greater first-year deductions than the more conservative developmental
programs.

Cash flow distributions from developmental programs usually begin within nine to 18 months after the investment, while distributions of
cash flow from exploratory programs begin in about the third or fourth

year after the investment. When more emphasis is placed on the investments in exploratory programs, we recommend even greater than normal diversification to spread out one's risk. In the Cash Flow Analysis section of this report we will discuss our recommendations for the specific allocation of funds toward real estate, drilling programs, and cable television.

Another energy-related investment in which we see attractive economics provided by continually rising domestic energy prices is the acquisition of existing income-producing oil and gas properties. Investments in this area can be classified as "tax incentive" due to the tax-favored cash flow they provide rather than heavy front-end deductions. Investments in limited partnerships that have acquired existing, producing properties have demonstrated historic rates of return in excess of the 12% area. At least 60% of the cash flow should be tax-free over the ten-to-fifteen-year life of such a program, with a larger percentage being sheltered in the early years and a lesser amount in later years. Should a partnership experience above-average results due to substantial increases in the oil and gas reserves sold, the percentage of cash flow sheltered will decline as economic return increases.

When investing in such programs, you will have the options of (1) automatically reinvesting all cash distributions or (2) depleting your investment over a ten to fifteen-year period by receiving both the income and return of principal portions of the cash distributions. Some programs may allow a third option of receiving a portion of the distribution in cash and reinvesting the remainder. We recommend you invest the remaining $15,000 of your excess cash reserves into an oil and gas income program and that you elect to reinvest all cash distributions. Upon your retirement, you can then elect to begin receiving some portion or all of the cash distributions to meet your income needs at that time.

Retirement Plans. You have two qualified retirement plans in Murphy and Murphy, a defined benefit pension plan funded with life insurance, and a profit sharing plan that is invested in a bank common trust account. You feel the performance of the profit sharing plan has been poor, and you are exploring other alternatives. We feel that, for reasons discussed earlier, quality equities should certainly account for a portion of a retirement plan's assets, but diversification of these assets is also important.

One particularly appropriate investment vehicle for qualified retirement plans is participation in a real estate financing technique known as "wrap-around mortgages." A wrap-around mortgage is a new loan, secured by property, that is "wrapped" around a first or existing mortgage with no change in the existing lien. The resulting amount of the wrap-around includes both the unpaid principal balance of the first mortgage and whatever additional sum is advanced by the lender.

Investors can participate in large, well diversified pools of these mortgages with minimum investments as low as $5,000. These ten-to-twelve-year self-liquidating portfolios of wrap-around mortgages are exclusively limited to tax-exempt accounts. The investor can expect an average annual return of 15% +. The differential between the debt service on the existing loan and that on the wrap-around mortgage will account for about 9 to 10% of the total return. The remaining 5 to 6% is due to the equity build-up feature, that is, the principal balance on the initial loan is being reduced at a faster rate than the balance on the wrap-around mortgage. In addition to this, most of the loans will have "equity kickers." These are provisions that allow the investor to participate in the higher returns traditionally associated with real estate ownership without having to assume the risk of property developers.

Your retirement plans should also make a commitment to energy-related areas. Oil and gas income programs would be one way to participate in this area, but any taxable income from the partnership would be unrelated business income for the retirement trusts. However, an investment in royalty interests could avoid this negative tax consequence because royalty income is specifically excluded from the trust's unrelated business income.

A royalty interest represents a landowner's share in the future cash flow from mineral rights on property that he or she has sold to oil and gas drillers and developers. Generally, the landowner retains the right to one-eighth of the future cash flow from any oil and gas discovered and developed. The remaining seven-eighths is the "working" interest; the owner of this interest bears all the costs and assumes the risk of drilling and developing the oil and gas reserves.

Royalty interests can be acquired through limited partnerships that purchase a landowner's royalty rights. Such partnerships will acquire royalties on a mixture of tested properties (producing and/or proven reserves) and exploratory properties located in known trends. Cash flow normally begins twelve to fifteen months after the partnership is formed, and future net revenues from a diversified royalties program are expected to be at least three to five times one's investment over an average fifteen-year life of the investment.

We would suggest the $115,000 in your profit-sharing plan be allocated as follows:

Equity Securities	$50,000
Real Estate—Wrap-around Mortgages	$35,000
Oil/Gas—Royalty Programs	$30,000

As you continue to make contributions to your plan, we can assist you in properly investing the funds.

A provision of the Economic Recovery Tax Act of 1981 allows you to participate in an Individual Retirement Account, even though you are covered by your own corporate plans. Up to $2,000 or 100% of earned income, if less, can be contributed and deducted each year. Since Mrs. Murphy is not working, you can have a spousal IRA and contribute up to $2,250 each year. Assuming a 12% annual rate of growth, by your retirement at age 65, you could accumulate an additional $60,815. We recommend these annual contributions currently be positioned under a prototype plan offered by many mutual fund companies. This will allow you to select a growth-oriented vehicle with a very nominal administrative fee and to benefit from professional management. We can assist you in selecting a fund that would be suitable for you.

CASH FLOW ANALYSIS

Current Cash Flow. Here is a summary of the Cash Flow Analysis at the beginning of this report:

Adjusted Gross Income	$216,400
Estimated Taxable Income	$186,300
Estimated Federal Income Tax Liability	$ 77,150
Net Discretionary Cash Flow	$ 37,350

Your top tax bracket this year will be 50%. We recommend your discretionary cash flow be used to reduce your tax liability through investments in some of the previously recommended tax-incentive areas. More specifically, we recommend $25,000 be directed to oil and gas drilling programs. Considering your net worth and your willingness to aggressively position a portion of your investment capital, we suggest diversification into two programs whose emphasis is exploratory drilling.

First-year deductions created from these investments would be $20,000 to $22,000. We further recommend the remaining $12,000 or so of cash flow be directed to limited partnerships that are acquiring cable television systems; this would generate 1983 deductions of about $1,500. We have already recommended $25,000 of your excess cash reserves be directed to real estate investments involved in new construction of income properties. This investment should provide about $7,500 of deductions for this year.

If all of these investments are made within the next few months, and our other recommendations for repositioning your capital are implemented, your cash flow for 1983 would approach the following:

Income:		
Salary and Bonus		$ 180,000
Director Fees		1,000
Interest		3,000*
Dividends		12,000*
Real Estate (Current Holdings—Net)		(3,000)
Trust		6,000
Oil and Gas (Current Holdings—Net)		600
Insurance Cost		3,500
Long-Term Capital Gain	$ 25,000	
Long-Term Capital Loss	(25,000)	–0–
New Investments		
Real Estate		(7,500)
Oil and Gas Drilling		(21,000)
Oil and Gas Income		(600)**
Cable Television		(1,500)
Individual Retirement Account		(2,250)
Adjusted Gross Income:		$ 170,250
Less: Excess Itemized Deductions		(25,600)***
Personal Exemptions		(2,000)
Estimated Taxable Income		$ 142,650
Estimated Federal Income Tax Liability		(55,330)
		$ 87,320
Add: Oil and Gas Deductions—Current		1,900
Real Estate Depreciation		3,000
Tax-Free Interest		5,200
Partnership Deductions—New Investments		30,600
Personal Exemptions		2,000
Less: Remaining Itemized Deductions		(3,400)
Insurance Cost		(3,500)
All Living Expenses		(67,000)
Gifts to Angela		(10,000)
New Investments		
Oil and Gas Drilling		(25,000)
Cable Television		(12,000)
Reinvestment of Oil and Gas Income Program		(1,350)
Distributions		
Net Discretionary Cash Flow		$ 7,770****

Reduced to reflect repositioning of assets.

**Assumes income of $1,350 (mostly interest while acquisitions are being made), and deductible expenses of $1,950.*

***Reduced to reflect about $2,500 reduction in state income taxes.*

****Does not reflect tax sheltered accrual of interest in deferred annuity or reinvestment of dividends in tax-managed trust.*

The overall effect of our recommendations is to reduce your 1983 tax liability by about $21,800 and to diversify your net worth into areas that will provide an opportunity for capital appreciation and tax-favored returns. The remaining $7,770 of cash flow should be used for an investment in a real estate partnership involved in the acquisition of existing properties.

Sale of Business. You have received an offer of $2,000,000 for Murphy and Murphy, Inc. It is our understanding that you would receive all cash and a five-year employment contract beginning in 1984 with a salary of $145,000 annually. The following table shows the effect of such a sale on your current year's cash flow, assuming none of our previous recommendations are implemented:

Income:	
Salary	$ 180,000
Director Fees	1,000
Interest, Dividends	28,300
Real Estate	(3,000)
Trust	6,000
Oil and Gas	600
Insurance Cost	3,500
40% of Long-Term Capital Gain	680,000*
Adjusted Gross Income	$ 896,400
Less: Excess Itemized Deductions	(68,900)**
Personal Exemptions	(2,000)
Estimated Taxable Income	$ 825,500
Estimated Federal Income Tax Liability	(396,750)
	$ 428,750
Add: Oil and Gas Deductions	1,900
Real Estate Depreciation	3,000
Tax-Free Interest	5,200
Nontaxable Portion of LTCG	1,020,000
Return of Principal	300,000
Personal Exemptions	2,000
Less: Remaining Itemized Deductions	(3,400)
Insurance Cost	(3,500)
All Living Expenses	(67,000)
Gifts	(10,000)
Net Discretionary Cash Flow	$1,676,950

*Assumes: Sale Price: $2,000,000
                Basis   (300,000)

     Long-Term Gain $1,700,000
**Increased to reflect additional state income taxes of about $40,800.

If we compare this cash flow to our original projection on page 320, about $360,000 more would be paid in federal and state income taxes if Murphy and Murphy, Inc., were sold this year. Ideally, you would want to shelter the taxable portion of the gain by creating deductions through tax-incentive investments or certain itemized deductions.

For example, you could prepay the $40,800 of estimated Georgia state income tax before the end of 1983 so it could be used as a deduction on your federal return. However, when taxable income includes a sizable gain, the alternative minimum tax may limit the amount of deductions that you want to create.

This tax is computed by first adding one's items of preference income to adjusted gross income. The most common preference items include: the long-term capital gain deduction; intangible drilling costs of successful oil and gas wells; accelerated depreciation on real or leased personal property in excess of straight-line depreciation; excluded interest on All-Savers certificates and future net interest exclusions and the dividend exclusion. From the sum of one's preference income and adjusted gross income, the following itemized deductions are subtracted: medical expenses, casualty losses, charitable contributions, home mortgage interest and other interest to the extent of net investment income. A specific exemption is then applied against the resulting alternative minimum taxable income. This exemption is $40,000 for joint returns, $30,000 for single returns and $20,000 for married individuals filing single returns. A 20% tax rate is then applied after subtracting the applicable exemptions.

The alternative minimum tax is payable when it exceeds one's regular tax liability including any regular minimum tax on preference items. Taxable income should not be reduced by creating deductions through tax-incentive investments or itemized deductions below the level where the alternative minimum tax becomes applicable.

At this point, the maximum possible tax savings for each additional dollar of deduction is only $.20. This tax savings is not sufficient to warrant exposure to the risks associated with tax-incentive investments, nor would you want to incur itemized deductions that could be postponed to save only $.20 per $1 of deduction.

We have calculated that you could create about $83,000 of deductions, in addition to prepaying your state income tax, before the alternative minimum tax would become payable. This assumes no additional items of tax preference are created. Your taxable income would be $742,500, and your taxes would be calculated as follows:

Tax Schedules		$ 355,252
Income Averaging		$ 355,252
Alternative Minimum Tax:		
Adjusted Gross Income	$ 813,460	
Preference Income:		
Excluded Portion of Gain	1,020,000	
Allowable Deductions:		
Charitable Contributions	(5,000)	
Interest	(12,000)	
Exemption	(40,000)	
AMT Base		$ 1,776,400
Tax at 20%		$ 355,280

The alternative minimum tax would be just slightly higher than your tax from the schedules, and it would therefore be the applicable tax.

We would recommend you create $83,000 of deductions through investments in the previously discussed tax-incentive areas. Such investments, however, would have to be coordinated with other recommendations. For example, the reduction of your interest and dividend income from the repositioning of some of your assets would decrease your taxable income. This would, in turn, decrease the amount of deductions to be created from tax-incentive investments.

In addition, our recommendation for the positioning of your cash flow from the sale may create additional investment income. We have considered carefully the overall effects on your cash flow and offer the following summary of recommendations should your business be sold this year:

1. Current "excess" cash reserves ($40,000)—follow previous recommendations for $25,000 directed to new construction of real estate income properties and $15,000 to oil and gas income programs.

2. Changes in securities portfolio—follow previous recommendations to reduce concentration in certain issues with reinvestment in tax-managed trust and to obtain shorter-term municipal bonds.

3. Discretionary cash flow—your cash flow should be directed as follows:

   a. $55,000 to oil and gas drilling programs with emphasis on exploratory drilling;

   b. $50,000 to new construction real estate;

   c. $100,000 to cable television limited partnerships;

   d. $650,000 to individual equities with emphasis on aggressive, growth-oriented companies;

e. $300,000 to shares of a tax-managed trust;

f. $200,000 to oil/gas income programs;

g. $200,000 to real estate partnerships acquiring existing properties; and

h. $200,000 to municipal bonds.

4. Position $290,000 in tax anticipation notes for the payment of your tax liability. These notes represent short-term municipal financing and will provide tax-free interest. This assumes $75,000 will be withheld from your compensation for taxes.

5. Prepay your estimated state income tax liability of about $36,500 before the end of the year.

Assuming all of these recommendations are implemented, your cash flow for the year would approach the following:

Income:	
Salary and Bonus	$ 180,000
Director Fees	1,000
Interest	3,000
Dividends	44,500[1]
Real Estate (Current Holdings—Net)	(3,000)
Trust	6,000
Oil and Gas (Current Holdings—Net)	600
Insurance Cost	3,500
40% of Net Long-Term Capital Gain	680,000
New Investments	
Real Estate	(22,500)
Oil and Gas Drilling	(50,000)
Oil and Gas Income (Net)	(8,610)
Cable Television	(15,000)
Real Estate	8,000[2]
Individual Retirement Account	(2,250)
Adjusted Gross Income	$ 825,240
Less: Excess Itemized Deductions	(64,600)
Personal Exemptions	(2,000)
Estimated Taxable Income	$ 758,640
Estimated Federal Income Tax Liability	(364,148)[4]
	$ 394,492
Add: Oil and Gas Deductions—Current	1,900
Real Estate Depreciation	3,000
Tax Free Interest	43,000[5]
Nontaxable Portion of L.T.C.G.	1,020,000
Return of Principal	300,000
New Partnership Deductions	96,110
Personal Exemptions	2,000

Less: Remaining Itemized Deductions	(3,400)
Insurance Cost	(3,500)
All Living Expenses	(67,000)
Gifts to Angela	(10,000)
New Investments	
Real Estate—New Construction	(50,000)
Real Estate—Existing	(200,000)
Oil and Gas Drilling	(55,000)
Oil and Gas Income	(200,000)
Cable Television	(100,000)
Equities	(650,000)
Tax Managed Trust	(300,000)
Municipal Bonds	(200,000)
Reinvestment of Oil and Gas Income	
Programs Distributions	(19,350)
Net Discretionary Cash Flow	$ 2,252

[1]Assumes $32,500 of dividend income from new equities.
[2]Assumes interest earned while acquisitions are being made.
[3]Reduced to reflect reduced state income tax of approximately $36,500.
[4]Alternative minimum tax calculation; regular tax would be $363,322.
[5]Includes interest from project notes.

Our recommendations for the positioning of the stock sale proceeds would provide an opportunity for capital appreciation with a minimum of tax consequences. Your capital would certainly be adequate to provide your future retirement income.

LIFETIME PLANNING SUMMARY

As shown on page 323, you have potential to provide for your retirement needs outside of Murphy and Murphy, Inc. Based on our discussions with you, we feel that you would prefer to keep the business, and we have elaborated on the investment alternatives available to help you achieve your retirement objectives. We feel it is most important that you direct your capital not only to areas that will provide capital growth as a hedge against inflation but also to investments that have favorable tax consequences.

We have therefore made the following specific recommendations based on this overall investment objective:

1. *Cash Reserves:* Reduce fixed-dollar assets to about $50,000. This $50,000 should be comprised of $40,000 in a deferred annuity, $5,000 in a money market fund, and $5,000 of net insurance cash values.

2. *Securities:* Reposition $100,000 of your individually held equities into a tax-managed trust and reposition your municipal bonds into shorter-term issues. The tax-managed trust will transform fully tax-

able dividends into more favorably taxed capital gains; shorter-term bonds will help protect this principal value as interest rates fluctuate.

3. *Tax-Incentive Investments:*

   a. Invest $25,000 in limited partnerships that are involved in new construction of conventional real estate properties.

   b. Direct $25,000 to oil and gas drilling programs.

   c. Position $12,000 in partnerships that are involved in the acquisition of cable television systems.

   d. Invest $15,000 in oil/gas income programs and elect to automatically reinvest all cash distributions.

   Total 1983 deductions from these investments would be about $30,600. These deductions, together with the $2,250 IRA deduction and the $13,300 reduction in taxable interest and dividend income, will result in tax savings of approximately $22,000.

4. *Retirement Planning:* The capital in your profit sharing plan should be diversified into areas outside of equities. We recommend $50,000 be retained in stocks, $35,000 be invested in a pool of wrap-around mortgages, and $30,000 be directed to oil/gas royalty programs. You should establish an individual retirement account for you and Mrs. Murphy and make the maximum $2,250 contribution. A mutual fund prototype plan would be appropriate for your IRA.

We have discussed the tax ramifications of the sale of your business and made recommendations for the reinvestment of the stock sale proceeds on page 336 and 337. We feel you will not sell; if you do sell, we will want to discuss our recommendations in more detail with you.

Finally, if all our recommendations are implemented, you will have a solid, diversified capital base that will be available for your retirement income. You need to add to this base each year from your discretionary cash flow. We will be available to assist you in properly positioning not only your cash flow but also your retirement plan contributions.

Estate planning

WILLS

A properly drafted will is the cornerstone of any sound estate planning program. Without one, much of your capital may be dissipated unnecessarily. Your will, which was written in 1975, is designed to pass half of your property outright to Mrs. Murphy. This property will qualify for the marital deduction and not be subject to taxes in your estate.

The remainder of your estate, after deducting all taxes and expenses, will pass to a residuary trust for eventual distribution to Angela. Mrs. Murphy has an income interest only in this trust during her lifetime, and none of the trust assets will be included in her estate at her subsequent death.

Mrs. Murphy's will is designed to pass all of her property to you. It may be more advantageous for her assets to pass directly to Angela. Based on the size of Mrs. Murphy's current estate, no taxes would be due because of the unified transfer credit. This credit is $79,300 in 1983 and will increase to $192,800 by 1987. A $79,300 credit is equivalent to a tax-free transfer of $275,000; a $192,800 credit will allow $600,000 of property to be transferred without any taxes.

We understand your wills have not been reviewed since they were originally drafted. You should make a practice of reviewing your wills with your attorney every three to five years. Changes in laws, in the attitudes of the courts and the Internal Revenue Service, and in the components of your estate, your age, health and desires—all make this necessary. A current review is particularly appropriate for you due to your desire to pass some stock in Murphy and Murphy directly to Angela, should you decide not to sell the business. In addition, the Economic Recovery Tax Act of 1981 contained several provisions relating to estate taxes with which you need to become familiar.

For example, under the new law there is an unlimited marital deduction for estate tax purposes for property that passes to one's spouse. While the use of this provision would eliminate all taxes in the event of your death, all property would then be taxed in Mrs. Murphy's estate. The following compares the overall tax consequences under (1) your present estate arrangement and (2) the use of the unlimited marital deduction.

Present Estate Arrangement

	Mr. Murphy Dies	then	Mrs. Murphy Dies
Gross Taxable Estate:	$ 3,462,000		$ 1,851,750
Administration and Probate (4%)	(138,500)		(74,070)
Final Expenses	(5,000)		(5,000)
Liabilities	(127,000)		—
Adjusted Gross Estate:	$ 3,191,500		$ 1,772,680
Marital Deduction	(1,595,750)		——
Net Taxable Estate	$ 1,595,750		$ 1,772,680

Tax Calculations

Gross Federal Estate Tax	$ 598,887	$ 678,506
Unified Credit	(79,300)	(192,800)
State Death Tax Credit	(70,530)	(83,230)
Net Federal Estate Tax	449,057	402,476
State Death Taxes	70,530	83,230
Total Death Taxes	$ 519,587	$ 485,706
Total Shrinkage	$ 790,087	$ 564,776
Total Shrinkage—Both Estates	$ 1,354,863	

[1]Assumes Mrs. Murphy's death occurs after 1986. Her estate would be comprised of the marital deduction share of Mr. Murphy's estate ($1,595,750), the proceeds of the retirement plans not taxed in Mr. Murphy's estate ($100,000), one-half the jointly held property ($47,500) and her assets ($108,500).

[2]Total shrinkage includes administration, probate, final expenses, liabilities, and taxes.

Use of Unlimited Marital Deduction

	Mr. Murphy Dies	then	Mrs. Murphy Dies
Gross Taxable Estate:	$ 3,462,000		$ 3,447,500
Administration and Probate (4%)	(138,500)		(137,900)
Final Expenses	(5,000)		(5,000)
Liabilities	(127,000)		—
Adjusted Gross Estate:	$ 3,191,500		$ 3,304,600
Marital Deduction	(3,191,500)		—
Net Taxable Estate	$ 0		$ 3,304,600

Tax Calculations

Gross Federal Estate Tax	$ 0	$ 1,428,100
Unified Credit	0	(192,800)
State Death Tax Credit	0	(210,440)
Net Federal Estate Tax	0	1,024,860
State Death Taxes	0	210,440
Total Death Taxes	$ 0	$ 1,235,300
Total Shrinkage	$ 270,500	$ 1,378,200
Total Shrinkage—Both Estates	$ 1,648,700	

[1]Assumes Mrs. Murphy's death occurs after 1986. Her estate would be comprised of the marital deduction share of Mr. Murphy's estate ($3,191,500), the proceeds of the retirement plans not taxed in Mr. Murphy's estate ($100,000), one-half the jointly held property ($47,500) and her assets ($108,550).

[2]Total shrinkage includes administration, probate, final expenses, liabilities, and taxes.

As you can see from these illustrations, the use of the unlimited marital deduction would actually increase the total estate settlement costs. You could have your will designed to take advantage of the unified transfer credit by passing the credit's equivalent exemption to a residuary trust.

For example, in the previous illustration, you would have a taxable estate of $275,000; the tax due of $79,300 would be eliminated by the unified credit. Mrs. Murphy's estate would be $275,000 less, and the total shrinkage would decrease by $137,500 to $1,511,200. This would still be greater than under your present arrangement. However, our illustration has not considered the time value of money.

By eliminating all taxes at your death, Mrs. Murphy would have $519,600 of additional capital. Since there is no way of knowing when her death would occur, it is impossible to account for the use of this capital, but it should be considered. You will want to discuss using the unlimited marital deduction and other estate tax provisions of ERTA in more detail with your attorney when you have your wills reviewed.

ESTATE LIQUIDITY

You need to be fully aware of the liquidity needs of your estate. Based on your present gross estate of $3,462,000, cash of about $663,000 would be needed by your executor for estate settlement costs. This includes administration and probate costs, final expenses, and taxes. One of the most advantageous means of meeting such expenses is with life insurance.

Life insurance (1) provides immediate cash, (2) avoids the liquidation of assets to meet expenses, thus preserving the value of an estate for one's heirs, and (3) if properly arranged, the proceeds can be excluded from the insured's taxable estate.

You now have $275,000 of net insurance coverage, all of which is payable to Mrs. Murphy. She can make the proceeds available to your executor by lending them to the estate or "buying" assets from the estate. In addition to your insurance, the other liquid assets in your estate (stocks, bonds, cash reserves) could be used for estate settlement costs. To the extent that you did not want these assets used for estate liquidity needs, you could consider other means of providing liquidity in your net worth.

For example, a Section 303 stock redemption with Murphy and Murphy could be utilized. This would allow an amount of stock equal in value to your estate taxes and other death expenses to be redeemed from your estate without the redemption being considered a dividend.

To take advantage of Section 303, the value of your stock must be more than 35% of your adjusted gross estate. Life insurance carried by the company on your life could be used to finance the redemption or part of it. The insurance proceeds would be received by Murphy and Murphy income-tax-free, but the value of the proceeds would increase the value of your stock for estate tax purposes. To avoid this problem, Angela could purchase insurance on your life and lend the proceeds to the corporation. We suggest you discuss using a Section 303 redemption with your attorney.

The insurance in your pension plan could also be used for liquidity needs, but you need to be fully aware of the income and estate tax implications. As noted on the Estate at Death illustration (page 323), up to $100,000 of the proceeds from your retirement plans would be excluded from your taxable estate if they are paid to a named beneficiary such as a person or a trust, and they are not paid in a lump sum. If the proceeds are paid in a lump sum, they can be excluded from the estate if the beneficiary does not elect special income tax treatment such as ten-year averaging or capital gains; that is, the proceeds would all be fully taxable to the beneficiary in the year received. Furthermore, the proceeds cannot be "receivable by or for the benefit of" the decedent's estate; thus if they were used directly for estate settlement costs, the proceeds would be included in the estate.

When the death benefit of a qualified plan is paid from life insurance, the income tax consequences are not as severe. The difference between the cash surrender value and the face amount is treated as death proceeds of life insurance and is therefore income-tax-exempt. The taxable value for income tax purposes is the cash surrender value, which may be reduced by a $5,000 death benefit exclusion and the previously reported P.S. 58 insurance costs. For example, if your death were to occur today, the portion of the pension plan proceeds reportable for income tax purposes would be calculated as follows:

Cost Surrender Value	$ 75,000
Death Benefit Exclusion	(5,000)
P.S. 58 Accumulated Costs	(7,500)
Taxable Portion of Distribution	$ 62,500

As the cash values increase in a greater proportion to the insurance costs, the taxable portion of the distribution will increase. Therefore, as time passes, using the insurance in the pension plan will be less attractive.

You need to consider ways of reducing your taxable estate and thus your liquidity needs. Because you are the owner of all of your present insurance policies, the proceeds will be included in your taxable estate. By transferring all ownership rights to an irrevocable trust, the proceeds can be excluded from your taxable estate. The trustee would receive the proceeds at your death and could have the right, but not the obligation, to purchase assets from your estate or to lend money to the estate. Mrs. Murphy can have an income interest only in the trust, and none of the trust assets would be included in her estate at her subsequent death. The trust could also be named beneficiary of your pension and profit-sharing plans. This would keep these proceeds from being taxed in Mrs. Murphy's estate at her subsequent death.

Your attorney can advise you further on the use of an irrevocable insurance trust; the following illustration shows that about $179,200 more could eventually pass to Angela by using such a trust:

Use of Irrevocable Insurance Trust

	Mr. Murphy Dies	then	Mrs. Murphy Dies
Gross Taxable Estate:	$ 3,187,000		$ 1,619,760
Administration and Probate (4%)	(127,480)		(64,790)
Final Expenses	(5,000)		(5,000)
Liabilities	(127,000)		—
Adjusted Gross Estate:	$ 2,927,520		$ 1,549,970
Marital Deduction	(1,463,760)		—
Net Taxable Estate	$ 1,463,760		$ 1,549,970

Tax Calculations

Gross Federal Estate Tax	$ 540,217		$ 578,286
Unified Credit	(79,300)		(192,800)
State Death Tax Credit	(62,080)		(67,598)
Net Federal Estate Tax	398,837		317,888
State Death Taxes	62,080		67,598
Total Death Taxes	$ 460,917		$ 385,486
Total Shrinkage	$ 720,397		$ 455,276
Total Shrinkage—Both Estates		$ 1,175,673	
Total Shrinkage—Present Estate Arrangements:		$ 1,354,863	
Savings:		$ 179,190	

[1] Assumes $275,000 of life insurance is transferred to an irrevocable trust and the proceeds of the retirement plans are made payable to this trust.

[2] Assumes Mrs. Murphy's death occurs after 1986. Her estate would be comprised of the marital deduction share of Mr. Murphy's estate ($1,463,760), one-half the jointly held property ($47,500) and her assets ($108,500).

[3] Total shrinkage includes administration, probate, final expenses, liabilities, and taxes.

RECAPITALIZATION

If you retain Murphy and Murphy, you will want to consider ways of "freezing" the value of the business in your estate. A tax-free corporate recapitalization could be considered. Two classes of stock could be issued, voting preferred and nonvoting common. Almost all of the current value of the corporation would be allocated to the preferred stock. You could then gift the common shares to Angela.

The preferred stock's value will remain the same at its call value while all the appreciation in the business will accrue to the common stock. The preferred stock could have a dividend feature that would be a source of future retirement income to you. This is a highly technical procedure, and it is essential you have the assistance of professionals who specialize in this area. But we feel a corporate recapitalization would be very appropriate for your circumstances if you do not sell Murphy and Murphy.

GIFTS

You have been making annual gifts to Angela, and you need to be completely familiar with gift tax laws and how they relate to estate tax laws. Present gift tax regulations allow a donor to give up to $10,000 to any individual in any given year without any gift tax consequences. The value of a gift within this exclusion allowance would be removed permanently from the donor's estate. Through a gift-splitting privilege, if a spouse consents to a gift, the exclusion would be $20,000.

Gifts above these exlcusion allowances are subject to tax, and the unified transfer credit can be applied against any taxes due. The taxable value of all gifts is added to the donor's taxable estate at death for purposes of computing estate taxes. Therefore, it is possible to remove the appreciation and income from a gifted asset from the donor's estate but not the present value of the asset.

For gifts to one's spouse, there is an unlimited marital deduction. This unlimited marital deduction should be used to increase Mrs. Murphy's estate so she can fully utilize the unified transfer credit. Over the next few years, you should consider gifting enough assets to increase Mrs. Murphy's estate to $600,000 by 1987. As previously mentioned, this will be the maximum amount of property that can pass tax-free through the use of the unified transfer credit. You will want to discuss any gifting plans with your attorney.

Estate planning—summary

It is important that you make plans now to assure that your and Mrs. Murphy's estates will be distributed according to your desires. We urge you to meet with your attorney and discuss the following:

1. The estate and gift tax provisions of the Economic Recovery Tax Act of 1981 and their effect on your situation. In particular you should review using the unlimited marital deduction for both gift and estate taxes.

2. A change in Mrs. Murphy's will that would provide for all of her property to pass to Angela.

3. The use of an irrevocable insurance trust.

4. The possible recapitalization of your business.

We suggest you continue gifting assets to Angela and that you transfer property to Mrs. Murphy to maximize the unified transfer credit. We will want to discuss in more detail with you the liquidity needs of your estate and how to best provide for them.

347

The very first step in the financial planning process is the examination of your total financial wherewithal. In addition to this questionnaire, the following documents are considered:

DOCUMENTS

☒ Copies of your last four years income tax returns and any gift tax returns.

☒ Copy of your will

☒ Copy of your spouse's will

☐ Copies of trust agreements or contracts (if applicable)

☐ Copies of business buy-sell agreements (if applicable)

☐ Others _____

☐ _____

Your life, health, and other insurance policies should also be included for analyzing your present coverage.

PERSONAL INFORMATION

Client's Name __Robert F. Murphy__ Social Security No. __487-66-7320__

Home Address __207 Homewood Ave, Atlanta, Ga 30329__ Phone __386-7770__

Business Address __100 S. Market St., Atlanta, Ga 30323__ Phone __266-6000__

Date of Birth __11/1/30__ Birth Place __Rochester, NY__

Occupation __President, Murphy & Murphy, Inc.__ How Long? __14 years__

Who is your attorney? __Paul R. Shivers - Smith, Shivers, & Vain__

Who is your accountant? __Thomas McNeil__

Do you have any other professional advisors of whom we should be aware? __Vince Shaeffer - Insurance__

__Agent__

Registered Representative __Jim Smith__ Date Information Obtained __1/5/83__

Branch Office __Atlanta, Ga__

(1)

348

FAMILY INFORMATION

Spouse __Jane E. Murphy__ Date of Birth __9/15/27__ Social Security No. __466-07-1121__

Occupation __Housewife__ How Long? __36 years__

CHILDREN	DATE OF BIRTH	DEPENDENT	SELF-SUPPORTING
Angela J. (Single)	8/11/49	☐	☒
		☐	☐
		☐	☐
		☐	☐
		☐	☐

Are all family members in good health? Yes __x__ No _____

If not, explain: _____

Are any relatives other than spouse and children depending on you for support now or will need support in the future?

Yes _____ No __x__ If so, explain: _____

Do you have any alimony or child support obligations? Yes _____ No __x__

If so, how much? _____ For how long? _____ _____

Is your estate obligated to continue these obligations? _____

EDUCATION   N/A

Do you want to send your children to college? Yes _____ No _____

How much do you estimate it will cost per child, per year? (In today's dollars) $_____

Have you set aside any assets for your children?   Yes _____ No _____

Are they to be used for their college education?   Yes _____ No _____

DESCRIBE:

CHILD	TYPE OF ASSET	AMOUNT	HOW HELD*

*Custodianship, trust or other. Give custodian, trustee, and donor: _____

(2)

CASH RESERVES — FIXED DOLLAR ASSETS

	HUSBAND	WIFE	JOINT	YIELD/MATURITY
Cash				
Checking Accounts	4,000	1,500		
Savings Accounts		5,000		5.5%
Credit Union				
Certificates of Deposit	35,000		15,000	15% 3/83
Money Market Funds				
Deferred Annuities				
Government Bonds				
Notes Receivable				
Mortgages Receivable				
Other: ___T Bills___	30,000			14%

HOME AND PERSONAL PROPERTY

Market value of your home $ __225,000_____ Cost basis $ __90,000 + $30,000 for addition__

Remaining mortgage $ __45,000_____ Number of years _____ Interest rate _____ %

Who is the owner? _____Robert F._____

Do you have mortgage insurance in case of disability or death? Yes ____ No __X__ If so, how much? _____

PERSONAL PROPERTY	HUSBAND	WIFE	JOINT
Home furnishings			75,000
Automobiles	15,000	10,000	
Silver, jewelry, coins		30,000	
Clothing, furs			
Antiques			5,000
Boat, airplane, trailer	20,000		
Other_____			

REAL ESTATE

List all real estate holdings other than your home and those included under tax incentive investments. Use separate sheet if necessary.

Description	Market Value	Remaining Mortgage	Cost Basis	Gross Annual Income	Expenses, Depreciation (annual)	Owner	What are your plans for this property?
Condominium – Myrtle Beach, SC	75,000	57,000	65,000	–	–	RFM	Family Use
Commercial Bldg	225,000	80,000	120,000	24,000	30,000		Keep
(I own one-half of this with my neighbor – acquired in 1977)							
Lot--N.C. Mountains	7,000	–	5,000	–	–	JEM	Possible Retirement or Vacation Home

(3)

STOCKS, BONDS, AND MUTUAL FUNDS

Owner	No. Shares or Face Amount	Security Description	Listed or NASDAQ Symbol	Present Market Value	Total Cost	Annual Dividend	Coupon	Maturity Date
RFM	Various Blue			230,000	150,000	12,000		
JEM	Chips			55,000	30,000	5,000		
RFM	Municipals			75,000	100,000		5.2%	2002-2010
			Schedule Included					

TAX-INCENTIVE INVESTMENTS

Do you have any tax-incentive investments?
(Oil and gas exploration, real estate, cattle, coal, railway cars, etc.) Yes __X__ No ____

Description	Year Purchased	Amount Invested	Expected Annual Deductions	Present Value (if known)	Current Annual Income	Owner
Mercer Properties	1977	15,000	$400 (1983)	?	None	RFM
(10 partners - undeveloped land)						
Absco Oil	1980	20,000	400		2,000	RFM
Vesco Gas & Oil	1981	15,000	1,500		500	RFM

(4)

BUSINESS INTEREST OR PROFESSIONAL PRACTICE

Sole Proprietorship ☐   Sub-chapter S ☐
Partnership ☐   Corporation ☒

Business
I. Name Murphy & Murphy, Inc. _____ I.D. Number _____
II. Valuation
a). What is your estimation of the present market value of *your* share of the business?
   $2,000,000--based on recent offer
b). What do you estimate your estate would collect for the business (liquidation value)?
   $2,000,000

or
Professional Practice
List the present value of *your* share of the following:

Checking Account _____

Accounts Receivable _____

Equipment or Furniture _____

Building _____

Other _____
_____

Specialty Chemical Co. started by
my father in 1960. I inherited
all of the stock at his death in
1967. Value at that time was
$300,000.

Any liabilities? _____

Would your estate be able to collect the above values? Yes ____ No ____
If no, which ones would decrease and by how much?

_____
_____
_____

Business or Professional Practice

Ownership:

Name	% of Ownership	Relationship (if any)
Robert F. Murphy	100%	

For Corporations Only:
  Do you have any of the following corporate fringe benefit programs?

Pension Plan   Yes _X_ No ____

Profit Sharing Plan   Yes _X_ No ____

105(b) Medical Expense Reimbursement Plan   Yes _X_ No ____

Corporate Disability Plan   Yes ____ No _X_

Group Life Insurance   Yes _X_ No ____

Deferred Compensation Plan   Yes ____ No _X_

Thrift or Salary Savings Plan   Yes ____ No _X_

If not a corporation, have you ever considered incorporation?

If so, explain: _____

(5)

Business or Professional Practice (Continued)

Employee Information (Complete for Employee Benefit Plan Proposals)

Name	Sex	Date of Birth	Employment Date	Full Time Part Time	Current Annual Compensation

Disposition of Interest

What would happen to your business in the event of a long disability or your death? Would you want it retained by your heirs or sold or dissolved? __See note at end of questionnaire.__

Do you have a Buy-Sell or Stock Redemption Agreement? Yes _____ No _____

What is the purchase price? $_____

Is there an escalation clause (to provide for increasing values)? Yes _____ No _____

Is your agreement funded? Yes _____ No _____

With what? _____ How much? _____

RETIREMENT INFORMATION

Type of Plan	Present Vested Interest	Value at Death	Beneficiary	Value of Voluntary Contributions	How Funded?	Monthly Retirement Income at Age _____
Keogh						
I.R.A.						
Pension	75,000	350,000	JEM	0	Life Insurance	3,500
Profit Sharing	115,000	115,000	JEM	0	Bank Common Trust Fund	?
Thrift						
Salary Savings						

Are you satisfied with your retirement plan? Yes _____ No __X__

Explain __Performance of profit sharing plan has been poor.__

(6)

LIFE INSURANCE

If you do not send us your life insurance policies for an analysis, please complete the following for yourself and your spouse:

Insured	Face Amount	Company	Type	Issue Date	Cash Value	Annual Premium	Beneficiary	Owner
RFM	150,000	New Eng. Mut.	WL	Various	30,000	2,000	JEM	RFM
RFM	150,000	Group	Term					

Insured	Company	Disability Income	Benefit Period	Daily Benefit (Hosp.)	Major Med.	Acc. Death Benefit
RFM & JEM	BC–BS		$500 deductible / $ 1,000,000 Max.			
RFM	Union Mutual	3,000	to Age 65			
RFM	Provident	1,500	for Life			

OTHER INSURANCE

When was your property and casualty insurance last reviewed? __1981__

Do you have personal excess liability coverage? Yes _x_ No ___ How Much? _$ 1,000,000_

LIABILITIES

What other indebtedness do you have aside from mortgages previously mentioned?

	Total Amount	Due Date	Monthly Outlay	Obligor (Husb., Wife, Jt.)
Notes	7,000	6/83		RFM
Installment Obligations				
Cash Value Loans	25,000			RFM
Taxes Payable				
Margin Accounts	50,000			RFM
Other				

(7)

354

ESTATE INFORMATION

Do you have a will? Yes __x__ No ____ Date Drawn _____ 1975 _____ Date Reviewed __ Never __

What are the provisions of your will? __1/2 of estate to Jane, remainder to trust for her benefit__

_____

_____

Does your spouse have a will? Yes __x__ No ____ Date Drawn _____ 1975 _____ Date Reviewed _____

What are the provisions of the will? __All property passes to spouse__

_____

_____

Do you expect any inheritances? _____ No _____ Amount? _____

Does your spouse expect any inheritances? _____ No _____ Amount? _____

Have you made any gifts to relatives? Yes ____ No ____

When? ____ Annually ____ How Much? __For past 5 years, I've given $6,000 annually to__
__Angela. Will increase to $10,000 this year.__

Have you made any substantial gifts to any charities? Yes ____ No ____

Are you interested in making such gifts? Yes ____ No ____

Now or in your will? _____

TRUSTS

Have you created any trusts? Yes ____ No __x__

If yes, please give (a) type, (b) date created, (c) how it is funded, and (d) who is the beneficiary.

_____

_____

_____

Are you the beneficiary of any trusts? Yes __x__ No ____

If yes, please give (a) type, (b) donor, (c) annual income

Jane is an income beneficiary of a trust created by her mother's will. Annual income is
$6,000. Her share of trust corpus is $100,000, and it will pass to Angela at Jane's death.
Assets are currently positioned in stocks and corporate bonds. Jane has tried unsuccessfully
to have trust assets diversified.

(8)

CURRENT INCOME AND EXPENSES

Estimate of Current Year's Income   (1983)   **Expenses**

Income		Expenses	
Salary	145,000	DEDUCTIBLE	
Bonus	30,000 - 40,000	Interest	12,000
Self Employment Income (Net)	_____	Taxes (Property, State Income)	12,000
Director or Trustee Fees	1,000	Contributions	5,000
Pension, Annuity	_____	Other Deductible Expenses	2,500
Interest (Taxable)	11,300	NON DEDUCTIBLE	
Dividends	17,000	Principal Reduction	3,000
Real Estate (Net)	5,000	Living	60,000
Net Short Term Gains/Losses*	_____	Education	_____
Net Long Term Gains/Losses*	_____	Insurance Premiums	4,000
Social Security	_____	Savings	_____
Spouse's Income	_____	Investments	_____
Other_Trust_	6,000	Other___Gifts___	10,000
Tax Free Interest	5,200		

*Please give details of any installment sale income, capital gains or losses you expect this year._____

_____

Do you expect any significant changes in your income or expenses in the next 5 years? Yes ____ No ____ Please

explain _Possible sale of business; salary will increase 5% - 10% annually_

INCOME OBJECTIVES

RETIREMENT

    At what age do you plan to retire? ____65____

    What annual aftertax (spendable) income would you want at retirement? (In today's dollars) $ _60,000_

DISABILITY

    If you became disabled, how much annual income would you and your family need to maintain your present

standard of living? $_60,000_

SURVIVOR'S INCOME

    If you died today, what principal amount would you want to provide for:

    Home Mortgage? $____0____ Education Fund? $__N/A__

    Debts? $_57,000_ Other $_____

    How much annual income would your family need to maintain their standard of living? $_50,000_

(9)

OVERALL FINANCIAL AND INVESTMENT CONCERNS

How would you best position your investment assets to coincide with your current investment temperament?

___5___ % Very Conservatively. Conserving present capital is more important than making it grow.

___30___ % Conservatively. High quality investments that provide an opportunity for appreciation and relative safety are important.

___55___ % Subject to moderate risk. Aggressive growth is important.

___10___ % Subject to high risk. Speculative growth is acceptable.

Do you have any preferences or objections to any particular investment areas?

Please explain ___I like Oil and Gas, Real Estate & Common Stocks___

Which of the following best describes your attitude towards your income needs?

☐ My present income is adequate for my needs.

☐ I need more current income.

☒ I can forgo current income to be better able to provide for future retirement income.

Indicate areas of major concern to you by rating numerically in order of importance:

_____Current Income _____Education of Children

__1__Retirement Income __2__Reduction of Current Income Taxes

_____Further Building of Estate __3__Reduction of Estate Taxes

_____Conservation of Assets for Heirs _____Other _____

What would you consider to be your primary financial objective or concern? __Provide for my retirement with an income that will keep pace with inflation.__

Is there any thing else we should know? __My dad started Murphy & Murphy after he retired from the Navy and I inherited the business from him. I've recently been offered $2,000,000 cash for the business, which I feel is a fair price and I would consider selling. However, my daughter has been working closely with me in the business. I feel she is capable of continuing the business if something happened to me or I retired. She has urged me not to sell if I can otherwise provide for my retirement. I want you to tell me: 1) If I sell, what the tax consequences would be and what I should do with the cash and 2) If I do not sell, can I provide for my retirement?__

(10)

III

A Total
Financial Plan
Prepared for:
Stanley E. Jones

by
Mel Brian Locklear, CPA, CFP
Financial Planning Consultant

Preface

Mr. Jones, this plan represents a comprehensive analysis of your existing financial resources. It offers both investment and procedural advice on how you might better direct these resources towards attainment of your personal goals.

We encourage you to study our recommendations carefully and to then consult with your other financial and legal advisors, in implementing them, at your earliest convenience. We also encourage you to view this plan in its totality and to recognize the interrelationships that exist among our recommendations.

Finally, changes in the laws and the economic environment, as well as changes in your personal circumstances, require this initial plan to be updated periodically. Therefore, you should consider this plan as the beginning of a regular process for reviewing your financial situation.

Table of contents

Personal balance sheet

	Owned By Mr. Jones	Owned Jointly	Owned By Mrs. Jones
Assets:			
Checking Accounts	$ 1,000	$ 2,000	$ 2,000
Money Market Fund	38,000		
Cash Values of Life Insurance			10,200
Stocks	100,000		
Thrift Incentive Plan	30,000		
Stock Options*	156,250		
Real Estate	115,000	90,000	
Tax-Incentive Investment**	43,000		
Employee Stock Ownership Plan	85,000		
Pension Plan	33,000		
Home		240,000	
Personal Property	14,000	40,000	12,000
Total Assets	$615,250	$372,000	$24,200
Liabilities:			
Note Payable	$ 10,000		
Cash Value Loans			$ 8,500
Credit Cards		$ 1,200	
Mortgages on Real Estate	75,000	30,000	
Mortgages on Home		90,000	
Total Liabilities	$ 85,000	$121,200	$ 8,500
Net Worth	$530,250	$250,800	$15,700
Combined Net Worth		$796,750	

*Represents difference between fair market values and exercise prices on 12,500 shares.
**Represents amount invested.

1983 Estimated cash flow analysis

Income:		
Salary		$ 85,000
Bonus		20,000
Interest		5,800
Dividends		1,375
Dividend Exclusion		(200)
Real Estate		
Rentals	$14,300	
Depreciation	(4,500)	
Other Expenses	(9,000)	800
Taxable Portion of Net Long-Term Capital at 40%		3,668
Tax-Incentive Deductions		(7,200)
Employer Paid Insurance Premiums		2,300
Adjusted Gross Income		$111,543
Less: Excess Itemized Deductions		(14,300)
Personal Exemptions		(4,000)
Estimated Taxable Income		$ 93,243
Estimated Federal Income Tax Liability		(30,947)
		$ 62,296
Add: Dividend Exclusion		200
Depreciation		4,500
Excluded Portion—LTCG		9,632
Return of Basis—LTCG		6,700
Sales Proceeds—STCL		18,000
Tax-Incentive Deductions		7,200
Personal Exemptions		4,000
Less: Remaining Itemized Deductions		(3,400)
Employer Paid Insurance Premiums		(2,300)
Net Cash Flow After Taxes and Deductible Items		$ 106,828
Less: Living Expenses		(40,000)
Principal Reduction on Home Mortgage		(3,000)
Insurance Premiums		(1,765)
Social Security Contributions		(2,392)
Thrift Plan Contributions		(5,100)
Net Discretionary Cash Flow		$ 54,571

Estate at death

Estate Assets:	
Checking Accounts	$ 2,000*
Money Market Fund	38,000
Stocks	100,000
Thrift-Incentive Plan	30,000
Stock Options	156,250
Real Estate	160,000*
Tax-Incentive Investment	43,000
Employee Stock Ownership Plan	85,000
Pension Plan	**
Home	120,000*
Personal Property	34,000*
Gross Taxable Estate:	$ 768,250
Administration and Probate (4%)	(30,730)
Estimated Final Expenses	(5,000)
Liabilities	(145,600)
Adjusted Gross Estate	$ 586,920
Martial Deduction	(586,920)
Net Taxable Estate	$ 0
Taxes:	
Gross Federal Estate Tax	$ 0
State Death Tax Credit	0
Unified Transfer Credit	0
Net Federal Estate Tax	$ 0
State Death Taxes (Georgia)	0
Total Taxes	$ 0
Total Estate Settlement Costs	$ 35,730***

*Includes one-half of jointly owned property.

**Values not included in taxable estate if proceeds are left to a named beneficiary (other than "estate") and proceeds are *not* left in a lump sum. Proceeds left in a lump sum can be excluded from taxable estate if beneficiary does not elect special income tax provisions such as ten-year averaging or capital gain treatment.

***Includes administration, probate, and final expenses.

Introduction

Developing a personalized, comprehensive financial plan that properly integrates both lifetime and estate goals must begin with careful analyses of your existing resources and their positioning, your income and its taxation and subsequent direction. Only then we can identify specific changes to bring these resources in line with your objectives. We have included, at the beginning of this report, a Personal Balance Sheet, a 1983 Estimated Cash Flow Analysis, and an Estate at Death illustration.

A review of your Balance Sheet shows that you and Mrs. Jones have a combined net worth of about $796,750. Of this, about $330,500, or 41%, is connected with your employer (stocks, options, ESOP, pension plan), while another $293,000, or 37%, is positioned in real estate (condo, duplex, public housing project, home). Your Balance Sheet also reveals a high level of liquidity, as provided by the cash items, stocks and options.

The Cash Flow Analysis indicates that your taxable income this year will be about $93,200 which will result in a federal tax liability of $30,947. After all expenditures for living and paying taxes, you should have about $54,500 to direct towards your financial objectives.

The Estate at Death illustration shows that you would have a gross estate of $768,250, were you to die today, and that approximately $35,730 would be needed by your executor for estate settlement costs.

You have indicated that your primary financial objective is to accumulate as much wealth as you can between now and retirement without taking undue risks and without altering your present family lifestyle. Other financial objectives you have identified include reducing your income tax exposure and maximizing employee benefit opportunities available from Varden Corporation, your employer.

Lifetime planning

To develop a strategy for achieving your primary financial objective, we'll begin by analyzing each of your assets, attaching an investment objective to each based upon its most desirable characteristics, consider the resulting effects on your cash flow, and, if necessary, offer recommendations for the repositioning of certain assets.

Since the largest segment of your assets is connected with your employer, and since this will be the primary source of funding for the wealth you plan to accumulate, we believe it is appropriate to begin our discussion with an analysis of certain of these assets and how you might better direct them towards attainment of your goals. Fundamental to this discussion will be the desire for investment diversification.

ASSET ANALYSIS

Company Benefits 1. STOCK OPTIONS.

Presently the "bargain element" of all stock options held by you is $156,250. It is our understanding that these options were granted to you at various intervals pursuant to a qualified plan established by your employer in 1970 and that the exercise prices of all options equaled the market values at date of grant. Obviously, the market values of the options at the date of granting vary significantly since Varden is an aggressive and volatile equity issue.

As you know, the Tax Reform Act of 1976 enabled you to exercise options, hold the resulting shares for at least three years, and then receive long-term capital gain treatment on the difference between your basis (market value at date of grant) and the market values at the date the shares are sold. This was true as long as they were exercised prior to May 21, 1981. The difference between share purchase price and share market value at date of exercise was a tax preference item subject to the minimum tax. During April of 1981, you took advantage of this by exercising a number of options.

Your employer has now informed you that they plan to elect certain favorable tax treatment accorded stock option plans under the Economic Recovery Tax Act of 1981. This election will have the same effect on options you now hold as it will on future options granted to you. You are interested in gaining a better understanding of this new treatment and how you might incorporate it into your overall financial plans.

The ERTA creates a new type of stock option known as an "incentive stock option." These new options provide for no tax consequences at either the date of grant or date of exercise of the option. Instead, you would receive long-term capital gain treatment upon sale of the shares, provided:

1. that you hold the stock two years after the option is granted and one year after the date of exercise and
2. that you are employed by Varden continuously from date of grant until three months before exercise.

Otherwise, you would recognize ordinary income at the time of sale equal to the lesser of (1) the gain upon sale or (2) the difference between the option price and the market value of the stock on the date of exercise.

There are several disadvantages, such as the requirements that options be exercised chronologically and that the stock be held for a certain period. This new treatment, however, presents outstanding planning opportunities for you. These opportunities arise from the fact that: (1) you anticipate receiving a significant number of options in the future, (2) wise investment requires diversification, (3) the options receive favorable tax treatment, and (4) a framework for implementing an orderly wealth accumulation process presents itself.

To illustrate how these can be coordinated with your financial objectives, we offer the following strategy: Begin a process of exercising a predetermined number of options each year consistent with your "insider" knowledge of the company and the market conditions prevalent at the time. You might consider exercising about 20% each year. As these options are exercised and the shares received, you would hold the shares at least one year before liquidation. The purpose of this process is two-fold.

First, and most important, is to create a more diversified asset base. As stated in the "Introduction," about 41% of your net worth is connected with your employer. We believe it is important at this stage of your career to gather many different assets as a hedge against the highly uncertain and volatile environment in which we live. Note that you will still be able to participate in the growth of Varden via your ESOP, bonus, and existing Varden stock.

Second, and the factor that will probably dictate the timing of sales more than anything else, is to serve as a major source of liquidity (along with your Net Discretionary Cash Flow) for funding tax-incentive investments and other capital growth investments. We will discuss these areas in more detail later on in this report. The major consideration at this point is to recognize the segmented and therefore more manageable approach to accumulating diversified wealth on a tax-favored basis. Since this is a cornerstone of our recommended wealth accumulation strategy, proper implementation will require regular communication with your stockbroker and tax advisor.

2. THRIFT INCENTIVE PLAN.

Based upon the thrift incentive plan statement of account dated December 31, 1982, your total contributions since 1971 of $18,800 (net of withdrawals) have resulted in a vested equity of about $40,000. Of this $21,200 growth, approximately $10,390 resulted directly from employer contributions, and the remainder, or $10,810, reflects the plan's tax-deferred earnings. Presently, your equity is invested in a fund, which is guaranteed by an insurance company to return 11% for the 1983 plan year.

You have indicated an interest in permanently withdrawing from this plan in order to consider alternative investments. Even though 11% tax-deferred yields should be easily obtainable elsewhere, we encourage you to continue maximizing your contributions (6% of salary) while your salary is high. Although your contributions of $18,800 have generated only $21,200 of growth, much of these contributions were made in low income years and therefore the tax-free compounding effect was not as dramatic as it could be in the future. Consider the following illustration:

Assume:
  18 years until retirement
  Annual salary of $85,000
  Average return of 11%
  Maximum employeecontributions and half matching employer
  contributions (6% and 3% of salary, respectively)

  Value of $40,000 in eighteen years $261,720
  Add: Value of $7,650 (9% of $85,000) contributed annually   427,933

  Total Estimated Value $689,653

This analysis reveals that your total equity could increase by about $650,000 in eighteen years. It also reveals that your annual contributions of $5,100 (6% of $85,000) would generate a principal amount of almost $428,000. This equates to an annual growth rate on your contributions of about 15% and is attributable in large part to your employer's matching contributions. Although it would be conceivable to achieve such returns on alternative investments, we doubt it could be achieved with such a low level of risk.

3. Employee Stock Ownership Plan (ESOP).

Your participation in the Varden ESOP represents one of four retirement plans available to you, the others being the Varden pension plan, individual retirement accounts, and the Social Security system. Presently, your vested equity in the ESOP approximates $115,000 but will not be accessible to you until employment termination or retirement.

From a lifetime planning standpoint, we believe there are two areas of consideration regarding your ESOP. The first relates to our prior discussion about investment diversification and your heavy equity interest in Varden. We view the ESOP as another timing determinant for stock option exercisings and eventual share liquidations. As the value of Varden shares in the ESOP appreciate and reach levels of apparent support, we would recommend increased option exercisings, share liquidations, and further asset diversification. Continuing this process on an annual basis should help to reduce the volatility in your net worth and facilitate your planning activities over the next several years.

The second area of consideration relates more directly to the "financial speed" necessary for you to achieve a comfortable retirement. If Varden share values do not appreciate over the years as expected, obviously you will need other assets to rely upon. This in turn may require that you position other assets in a more risky attitude to enable a greater potential for return. For instance, you would need to reconsider our recommendation for maintaining your thrift incentive plan as is. Although there is little you can do about this second consideration now, it does emphasize the point that periodic review of your financial resources and objectives is critical.

4. PENSION PLAN.

Your vested benefits in this plan currently equal $33,000 and offer the most conservative segment of your company benefits since there is little risk of default by the well established plan underwriter (an insurance company). Presently, there is not much you can do to control your financial destiny with regard to this plan. There will be important future lifetime considerations, however, such as the method and time for receiving benefits upon disability, job change or retirement. Therefore, your major emphasis with regards to this plan should be to keep alert for any plan amendments, changes in insurance carriers or methods of funding and to seek advice on how these changes may affect your financial plans.

Cash Reserves. A primary consideration in developing any financial plan is providing an adequate level of cash reserves. Cash reserves are needed to provide for emergencies and investment opportunities and to act as a parking place between investments.

Your cash reserves consist of $5,000 in checking, $38,000 in a money market mutual fund, and $2,700 (net) in life insurance cash values. To instill greater manageability, we encourage you to view your reserves as being either short-term or long-term. Your short-term reserves should consist of checking accounts and money market funds. As you probably know, money market funds offer outstanding liquidity and very competitive yields with minimal risk. You should develop an efficient and habitual system of moving cash from the fund to checking accounts for living expenses.

Yields and other factors considered, you should also consider the All Savers Certificate for shorter-term reserves. These certificates were created as a result of the Economic Recovery Tax Act of 1981. They would allow you to earn 70% of the yield on current 52-week Treasury bills and would enable you to exclude up to $2,000 of interest income for a period in excess of two years. Today you could expect yields of about 8%.

For your long-term reserves, we recommend that you purchase a single-premium deferred annuity. Deferred annuities are guaranteed by insurance companies to return an attractive yield (currently 12%) over the longer term with no immediate income taxation. You would be taxed on the income from the annuity only when withdrawals are made. A deferred annuity should be viewed as your most serious cash reserves.

For your short-term reserves, we recommend that you maintain not more than $10,000 in your checking accounts and money market fund. You should also reposition: (1) not more than $10,000 of your money market fund into an All Saver's Certificate and (2) between $10,000 and $20,000 of your money market fund into a deferred annuity. The total of these amounts should approximate six to nine month's living expenses. This amount should be reasonable given the conflict between your family financial responsibilities and the desire for rapid wealth accumulation, which requires a greater exposure to capital growth-type assets.

After providing for these cash needs, you should have about $15,700 of investable cash, determined as follows:

Total Cash Available	$ 45,700
Less: Short-Term Reserves*	(10,000)
Long-Term Reserves**	(20,000)
Investable Capital	$ 15,700

*Via checking accounts and money market fund.
**Via All Savers Certificate, deferred annuity and net life insurance cash values.

In subsequent discussions, we will refer to this $15,700 as your "excess cash."

Equity Securities. Equity securities currently appear to offer one of the greatest opportunities for growth of capital over the next decade. When measured in "real" terms, the stock market is undervalued. This undervaluation can be measured by both the relationships of share market values to book values and of market values to corporate earnings. In addition to these apparent undervaluations, the domestic political environment seems more attuned to improving fiscal and monetary policies. This should eventually allow for improved corporate earnings and, therefore, increased equity values. We recommend that you plan upon significantly increasing your equity securities position over the next several years.

Currently your equity securities (not including stock options) represent about 13% of your total net worth but consist of only three individual issues. We believe a much more diversified approach to equity investing is necessary. Alternatively, we offer the following strategy for accumulating greater wealth via equities during the "bull" market that we foresee for the 1980s.

Initially establish a significant position in a couple of quality, growth-oriented mutual funds. These mutual funds are managed by professionals and provide·instant share diversification, thereby reducing risk. You should review the prospectuses of several mutual funds and identify the ones suiting your investment philosophy and temperament. We then recommend that you make regular purchases of the mutual funds at a predetermined amount. This should allow you to obtain the highest value per share at the lowest cost per share as equities appreciate.

As a complement to your quality, growth-oriented mutual funds, we encourage you to establish a portfolio of more aggressive individual equity issues. The best source for opportunities in this respect is regional brokerage firms. These firms tend to follow local companies with above-average growth potential.

The majority of issues should be selected on the basis of their long-term potential, but it is obviously appropriate at times to trade for the shorter term. When attractive issues are periodically identified, we encourage you to purchase them but also continue to make regular contributions to the mutual funds you have selected. We believe this is a most appropriate strategy for accumulating wealth via equities when the investor has neither the time nor the required knowledge to constantly select and monitor a significant portfolio of individual issues. Therefore, we recommend that you commit $32,000 of your 1983 discretionary cash flow to the ownership of additional equities with the majority going to quality, growth-oriented mutual funds.

Real Estate. Your current real estate holdings consist of a condominium that is used both for personal leisure and rental income, a duplex that provides rental income, and a public housing limited partnership that you purchased primarily for the tax benefits. It appears that both your condominium and duplex have been good investments since the market values are significantly greater than the cost basis. Furthermore, they are providing substantial tax-sheltered cash flow. You have indicated you are satisfied with the way these two real estate investments fit into your financial plan and have no desire to sell them. You would also be particularly interested in any future real estate opportunities.

Your public housing investment appears to have generated the tax deductions you expected and has allowed you to direct these tax dollars into other investments. However, from an investment point of view, we discourage your further participation in these partnerships. Rents from public housing may be subject to government regulation and therefore may restrict your ability to raise rents in tandem with inflation. Quite often these partnerships encounter operational problems, and the properties typically are not of the quality to offer strong appreciation potential.

Furthermore, the high degree of debt used in these partnerships may create taxable income in later years with no attendant cash flows. We doubt if you want to pay taxes on something you will not directly receive.

Our research has uncovered one area of real estate investment that we feel has outstanding potential for growth during the 1980s. This is in residential rentals. Due to a combination of: (1) the high cost of long-term credit, (2) the inability of developers to immediately deduct construction period interest expenses, and (3) abnormally low rents, the construction of new, nongovernment subsidized residential rental housing has almost halted. Combine this with the continued destruction, obsolescence, and condominium conversion of existing apartments, the lack of adequate housing is evident. On the demand side, the Bureau of Census projects 1.5 million household formations each year for the next decade and home ownership will be prohibitively expensive for many. Therefore, we see an opportunity for real capital growth in this area.

There are basically two ways you should participate in this forecasted crisis. The first is the new construction of income-producing properties via professionally managed limited partnerships offering diversification into several geographic locations. This method would also generate substantial tax losses during the first few years to offset unrelated income.

The second method is participating in existing income-producing properties. This method also allows for professional management and geographic diversification but does not offer the same level of tax deductibility. However, you could expect cash flows to begin sooner.

Given your high tax bracket and lack of time for personal management, we recommend that you plan upon initially committing $10,000 to the new construction of professionally managed income-producing properties. We also recommend that you fund this purchase from discretionary cash flow as opposed to excess cash.

Energy. During the last ten-to-fifteen-year period, our nation has become aware of its dependency on energy resources, particularly oil and natural gas. Over the next several decades, many factors will serve to reduce this dependency. In the meantime, however, we believe any prudently structured investment plan should include a significant commitment to these energy resources.

As with real estate, equity securities and other investment areas, there are a number of ways to directly participate in energy investing. One is by owning income-producing oil and natural gas reserves. This can be accomplished by investing in oil and gas "income" limited partnerships. With these investments you could expect revenues equal to about 2½ times your initial outlay over a ten-to-fifteen-year period. Current cash-on-cash yields would start in the 10% to 12% range and follow the inflation rates thereafter. At least 60% of these cash flows would be tax-free over the life of the investment.

Owning oil income programs would be the more conservative way to incorporate energy into your investments. In addition, they offer the flexibility for converting from an income vehicle to a growth-oriented one, since you could elect either to receive cash distributions or have them reinvested.

Another way to directly own energy reserves is by investing in "drilling" programs. The programs offer significant early tax deductions, which can be used to offset your other income, much like your public housing investment. However, cash flows from the investment might not begin until one to four years when they would benefit from 20% to 30% depletion allowances and other deductible business expenses. Overall, you could expect future net revenues of 1.5 to 3 times your pretax investment over a ten-and-fifteen-year period.

We believe you should concentrate upon the use of drilling programs as the prime vehicle for converting income tax liabilities into personal wealth over the next several years. This should be supplemented by direct ownership of real estate and other economically viable areas. In these areas more than any, you should concentrate upon diversification and competent management. In the Cash Flow Analysis, we will make specific oil and gas drilling recommendations to be funded from both your excess cash and your net discretionary cash flow.

Communications. Another capital growth opportunity with attractive tax attributes is the ownership of cable television systems. We believe the entertainment features of cable television will create widespread use of the coaxial cable and eventually more sophisticated uses of the cable. Examples of these uses would include security and fire alarms, banking, shopping, educational instruction, information retrieval, and the like. A typical CATV partnership purchases existing systems, upgrades the cash flows of the system by increasing rates and penetrating the market and then selling the system in five to seven years for capital gain treatment. You could deduct the amount of your investment over a period of four or five years, but there is little cash flow during these years of operation.

We recommend that you direct $10,000 of your 1983 cash flow into the ownership of cable television systems. This will represent an additional illiquid investment, which you should expect to hold for several years. Therefore, it is important that you continually maintain sufficient liquidity via cash reserves, equities and company benefits.

Individual Retirement Account. As a supplement to your corporate retirement benefits, you may establish an individual retirement account.

Contributions of up to $2,000 may be made to your IRA and will be deductible against your other taxable income. These contributions will also be allowed to grow tax-free until you retire. Since Mrs. Jones is not employed, she can have a spousal IRA thus allowing for a total of $2,250 to be contributed to both IRAs. Assuming a 12% annual rate of growth, by your retirement at age 60, you could accumulate an additional $181,570 of wealth.

We recommend that you commit $2,250 of your discretionary cash flow to two IRAs and fund them as early as practical in the year to gain the advantage of tax-free growth for the full year.

For your situation we recommend that you invest your IRA contributions in a family of mutual funds. This will allow the flexibility to invest in either equities, bonds, or a money market fund. You would be allowed to switch between funds as economic conditions change. Furthermore, the charges for administering the IRAs would be reasonable in relation to other alternatives.

CASH FLOW ANALYSIS

We have made recommendations for the repositioning of certain assets that should enhance the potential for greater wealth accumulation. We have also recommended that you direct portions of your 1982 discretionary cash flow into several investment areas. The following table illustrates funds available for investing based upon these prior recommendations:

	Excess Cash	Discretionary Cash Flow
Beginning Balance	$15,700	$ 54,571
Individual Retirement Account		(2,250)
Equities		(32,000)
Real Estate		(10,000)
Cable Television		(10,000)
Totals	$15,700	$ 321

This table indicates that you currently have about $16,000 of cash available.

Since you are at the early stages of your high earned income years, it is most important that you direct annual cash flows into investments in a diversified and recurring manner. However, it is also important that you take advantage of incentives provided by law for converting income tax liabilities into personal wealth. Accordingly, this section of the plan will identify a strategy for accomplishing this without taking undue risk. It will also present a revised cash flow analysis, which will quantify the potential tax savings, and finally it will recommend where to reinvest these resulting tax savings.

Income Taxation. Here is a summary of the Cash Flow Analysis on page 362 of this report:

Adjusted Gross Income	$111,543
Estimated Taxable Income	$ 93,243
Estimated Federal Income Tax Liability	$ 30,947
Net Discretionary Cash Flow	$ 54,571

Based upon taxable income of $93,243, you will have over $7,600 taxed at a highest marginal bracket of 48%. It is this highly taxed income that should be removed from taxation via tax-incentive investments. At this level of taxation you may use about a dollar of your own plus a dollar of Uncle Sam's to control $2 in assets. Surely the risks inherent in most tax-incentive investments can be mitigated by such an equitable sharing. Furthermore, these inherent risks can be lessened over a period of time by increased diversification. This increased diversification must occur as you commit to an annual process of converting tax liabilities into personal wealth.

Tax-Incentive Investing. We have recommended your investment in two areas that will provide substantial deductions over the next four or five years. Those include the new construction of income-producing real estate properties and the ownership of cable television systems. To complement these investments and to participate in an area with a higher level of first-year deductibility, we recommend that you develop a portfolio of oil and gas drilling programs. (See page 362 for a discussion of these energy investments.)

More specifically, we recommend that you invest your excess cash into one or two different drilling programs. We also recommend that these programs have a significant exploratory emphasis. Exploratory activity, although more risky, may provide greater returns over the long run and thus will satisfy the aggressive portion of your investment temperament.

By investing in these drilling programs, you could expect first-year tax deductions ranging from 60% to 100% with the remaining deductions available in the next couple of years. You could expect to save $3,000 to $5,000 in taxes per $10,000 invested. However, you should be aware of the effect of preference income generated by certain drilling programs. Intangible drilling costs associated with successful oil and gas wells are considered preference income. To the extent your total preference income for one year exceeded one-half your federal tax liability, you would be liable for the add-on minimun tax. A tax rate of 15% would then be applied to the excess preference income and added to your normal income tax. Our recommendations have properly considered these facts for your 1983 investments.

To illustrate how this $16,000 commitment to oil and gas drilling, the $20,000 committed to real estate and CATV, and our other recommendations would effect your 1983 cash flow, consider the following revised analysis:

1983 Revised Cash Flow Analysis

Previous Adjusted Gross Income	$ 111,543
Add: Dividends	1600[1]
Less: Oil/Gas Drilling Deductions	(12,000)[2]
Real Estate Deductions	(5,000)[3]
CATV Deductions	(2,000)[4]
Interest Income	(3,000)[5]
Individual Retirement Accounts	(2,250)
Revised Adjusted Gross Income	$ 88,893
Less: Excess Itemized Deductions	(12,500)[6]
Personal Exemptions	(4,000)
Revised Taxable Income	$ 72,393
Revised Federal Income Tax Liability	(21,467)
	$ 50,926
Add: Dividend Exclusion	200
Depreciation	4,500
Capital Gains/Losses	34,332
Old Tax-Incentive Deductions	7,200
New Tax-Incentive Deductions	19,000
Personal Exemptions	4,000
Less: Remaining Itemized Deductions	(3,400)
Employer Paid Insurance Premiums	(2,300)
Living Expenses	(40,000)
Principal Reduction on Home Mortgage	(3,000)
Insurance Premiums	(1,765)
Social Security Contributions	(2,392)
1983 Investments Funded From Cash Flow	(59,500)
Revised Discretionary Cash Flow	$ 7,801

[1]Assumes a 5% yield from 1983 equity investments.

[2]Assumes 80% first-year deductibility on drilling investments.

[3]Assumes 50% first-year deductibility on real estate investments.

[4]Assumes 20% first-year deductibility on CATV investments.

[5]Represents interest income that would have been taxed in money market fund if not repositioned.

[6]Adjusted for reduction in deductible state income taxes.

This revised analysis indicates that implementing our recommendations would reduce your federal liability by about $9,480 or 31%. In addition, you would have created another $7,800 of investable funds, which represent primarily the tax savings from 1983 investments. With this newly created discretionary cash flow, we recommend that you invest $5,000 in existing income-producing real estate and $2,500 in another CATV partnership. This should create additional opportunities for the capital growth you desire while still observing the liquidity constraints that are so important when investing in limited partnerships.

Lifetime planning summary

Our recommendations have been designed primarily to provide an operational framework for achieving your wealth accumulation goals. We have shown you how to utilize your employee benefits, how to position your existing assets, and how to direct your 1983 discretionary cash flow towards this objective. These recommendations can be used as a basic reference for activity in subsequent years and modified when necessary. A summary of these recommendations follows:

1. Plan upon periodically liquidating stock options for the purpose of investment diversification and as a source of liquidity for tax-incentive investing.
2. Maximize contributions to your thrift plan.
3. Continually monitor the value of Varden shares held in the ESOP in order to determine its effect upon your other investment activities.
4. Be alert for any employer or regulatory changes that may affect your pension plan.
5. Maintain not more than $10,000 of short-term cash and between $10,000 and $20,000 of long-term cash.
6. Direct $32,000 of your 1983 discretionary cash flow into quality growth mutual funds.
7. Plan upon developing a portfolio of individual equity issues.
8. Concentrate your real estate investments in professionally managed limited partnerships owning quality properties. For 1983, direct $10,000 of your discretionary cash flow into the newly constructed rental properties and another $5,000 into existing rental properties.
9. Direct $15,000 of discretionary cash flow into one or two oil and gas drilling programs.

10. Invest $12,500 of your discretionary cash flow into the ownership of cable television systems.

11. Establish your individual retirement accounts early in 1983.

Estate planning

Based upon the order of your financial priorities as represented in the planning questionnaire that follows, you are not too concerned with saving estate taxes or conserving assets for your heirs. You feel this will become more important as your wealth grows. Therefore, this section is designed to inform you of how the Economic Recovery Tax Act of 1981 (ERTA) will affect your present estate arrangement over the coming years. It will also offer ideas that you might consider implementing immediately to gain the advantages of ERTA with little inconvenience or cost on your part.

WILLS

Your will was drawn in 1979 and provides that all your estate pass to your wife. If she predeceases you, then your estate would pass to your children equally. Likewise, your wife's will provides for her estate to pass to you or to your children equally if you predecease her.

As can be seen from the Estate at Death illustration, this arrangement would result in no taxes payable by your estate. This results from the fact that all property qualifies for the marital deduction and ERTA now allows for unlimited use of this deduction. Upon the death of your wife, however, all estate assets would be subject to taxation. Therefore, it is most meaningful to view your estates together and to identify the combined shrinkage that would result after both deaths. The following analysis shows this combined effect if you were to die in 1983 and your wife after 1986:

	Mr. Jones Dies	*then*	*Mrs. Jones Dies*
Gross Taxable Estate:	$ 768,250		$ 1,196,920[1]
Administration and Probate (4%)	(30,730)		(47,877)
Estimated Final Expenses	(5,000)		(5,000)
Liabilities	(145,600)		(69,100)
Adjusted Gross Estate:	$ 586,920		$ 1,074,943
Marital Deduction	(586,920)		(0)
Net Taxable Estate	$ 0		$ 1,074,943

	Taxes	
Gross Federal Estate Tax	$ 0	$ 376,527
State Death Tax Credit	(0)	(37,397)
Unified Transfer Credit	(0)	(192,800)
Net Federal Estate Tax	$ 0	$ 146,330
State Death Taxes (Georgia)	0	37,397
Total Taxes	$ 0	$183,727
Total Shrinkage[2]	$ 181,330	$305,704
Combined Shrinkage	$487,034	

[1]Assumes Mrs. Jones' estate consists of the marital deduction share of Mr. Jones' estate ($311,920), one-half of jointly owned property ($186,000) and her assets ($14,000).
[2]Total shrinkage includes administration, probate, final expenses, liabilities, and taxes.

This analysis shows that both your estates would be subject to shrinkage of $487,000. Of this, only $183,727 results from estate taxes. (Note that this analysis does not consider any appreciation of assets between the dates of death, nor does it consider any invasion of principal between these dates.) A good portion of these taxes could be reduced by amending your will to provide that enough taxable estate remain after the marital deduction to fund the unified transfer credit.

This unified transfer credit, as amended by ERTA, equals $79,300. This means that, in 1983, you can transfer $275,000 to heirs without tax consequence. This tax-free transfer increases to $600,000 by 1986. Your will could be amended to provide that the credit's equivalent exemption pass to a residuary trust. The income from this trust could then be available to your wife during her life, but the principal would escape taxation upon her subsequent death.

Another means for reducing estate shrinkage would be to transfer ownership of your life insurance policies to an irrevocable insurance trust. This would allow the insurance proceeds to escape taxation in your estate. The trustee would receive the proceeds at your death and could have the right, but not the obligation, to purchase assets from your estate or to lend money to the estate. Mrs. Jones could have an income interest only in the trust, and none of the proceeds would be included in her estate at her subsequent death. The trust could also be named beneficiary of your pension plan. This would keep these proceeds from being taxed in your wife's estate at her subsequent death.

A significant problem with this approach is that Mrs. Jones already owns the life insurance contracts on your life. The law does not allow an individual to establish a trust for personal benefit and then have the trust assets excluded from that individual's estate. To circumvent this, it would be necessary to have your wife transfer ownership of the insurance policies back to you and then you could establish the insurance trust.

To illustrate how funding the unified credit and establishing an irrevocable insurance trust might reduce estate shrinkage, we have prepared the following revised analysis:

	Mr. Jones Dies	then	Mrs. Jones Dies
Gross Taxable Estate	$ 768,250		$ 511,920[1]
Administration and Probate (4%)	(30,730)		(20,477)
Estimated Final Expenses	(5,000)		(5,000)
Liabilities	(145,600)		(69,100)
Adjusted Gross Estate:	$ 586,920		$ 417,343
Marital Deduction	(311,920)		(0)
Net Taxable Estate	$ 275,000		$ 417,343
	Taxes		
Gross Federal Estate Tax	$ 79,300		$ 127,697
State Death Tax Credit	(0)		(0)
Unified Transfer Credit	(79,300)		(127,697)
Net Federal Estate Tax	$ 0		$ 0
State Death Taxes (Georgia)	3,000		9,275
Total Taxes	$ 3,000		$ 9,275
Total Shrinkage[2]	$ 181,330		$ 103,852
Combined Shrinkage		$285,182	

[1]Assumes Mrs. Jones' estate consists of the marital deduction share of Mr. Jones' estate ($311,920), one-half of jointly owned property ($186,000) and her assets ($14,000).

[2]Total shrinkage includes administration, probate, final expenses, liabilities, and taxes.

This revised analysis indicates that the combined shrinkage could be reduced by $201,850. This results primarily from the death tax savings and the reduction in administrative and probate costs. These attractive savings, however, need to be weighed against the personal desires you may have. For instance, your wife would not have control over those assets in the residuary and insurance trusts. You may feel that the tax savings are not worth her inability to significantly invade principal. We encourage you to discuss these possibilities with your attorney.

You also need to consider revising Mrs. Jones' will to take advantage of the unified credit if she were to die first. Currently she does not own enough assets to fund this credit, so it would be necessary to transfer assets to her. This is another area that needs to be discussed with your attorney.

Finally, we encourage you to have your wills reviewed regularly. There will surely be regulatory and personal changes that necessitate this review. You should consider having this review performed every three to five years.

ESTATE LIQUIDITY

Because your present will provides for using the unlimited marital deduction, the liquidity needs of your estate are not significant. In fact, if your executor decided not to settle your share of real estate and other liabilities, less than $50,000 would be needed. Your insurance proceeds are certainly adequate to cover this. There is also sufficient liquidity via equities and cash items. In the future, however, you will want to review your estate liquidity needs as your wealth grows, and if you revise your will as discussed previously.

FAMILY INCOME

In the event of your premature death during 1983, your surviving family would have the following assets available to provide income:

Total Assets	$ 1,011,450
Add: Insurance Proceeds	310,000
Pension Proceeds attributable to Life Insurance	67,000
Less: Life Insurance Cash Values	(10,200)
Home	(240,000)
Personal Property	(66,000)
Mr. Jones' Share of Liabilities	(145,600)
Estate Settlement Costs	(35,730)
Total Capital Available	$ 890,920

Assuming all capital could be positioned to generate an 8% aftertax return, an annual income of $71,274 would be available. Based upon your family's present standard of living and your goal of $30,000, it appears that this would be more than adequate.

Estate planning summary

Although planning for your estate disposition is not of critical importance for you at this time, it is important that you understand the basic estate law provisions and how they might be utilized to your advantage in the future. Accordingly, we have discussed certain ideas that you should consider, as follows:

1. Have your wills reviewed regularly.
2. Consider using a residuary trust to take advantage of the unified transfer credit.
3. Consider using an irrevocable insurance trust.
4. Consider transferring assets to your wife so that the unified credit could be utilized if she were to die first.

Q

The very first step in the financial planning process is the examination of your total financial wherewithal. In addition to this questionnaire, the following documents are considered.

DOCUMENTS

- ☒ Copies of your last four years income tax returns and any gift tax returns.
- ☒ Copy of your will
- ☒ Copy of your spouse's will
- ☐ Copies of trust agreements or contracts (if applicable)
- ☐ Copies of business buy-sell agreements (if applicable)
- ☒ Others Varden Employee Benefit Handbook
  Life Insurance Policies (3)
- ☒ Real Estate Investment Projections/Correspondence

Your life, health, and other insurance policies should also be included for analyzing your present coverage.

PERSONAL INFORMATION

Client's Name __Stanley E. Jones__ Social Security No. __123-45-6789__

Home Address __1702 Victoria Way__ Phone __586-7240__

Business Address __14 Corporate Square__ Phone __731-1826__

Date of Birth __7/13/42__ Birth Place __Atlanta, Georgia__

Occupation __Vice President - Marketing - Varden__ How Long? __12 Years__
Corp.

Who is your attorney? _____

Who is your accountant? _____

Do you have any other professional advisors of whom we should be aware? _____

_____

Registered Representative_____ Date Information Obtained _____

Branch Office _____

(1)

FAMILY INFORMATION

Spouse _____Pamela A. Jones_____ Date of Birth __8/27/45__ Social Security No. __987-65-4321__

Occupation _____Housewife_____ How Long? __14 years__

CHILDREN	DATE OF BIRTH	DEPENDENT	SELF-SUPPORTING
Robert S. Jones	2/15/69	☒	☐
Shelia M. Jones	8/21/72	☒	☐
		☐	☐
		☐	☐
		☐	☐

Are all family members in good health? Yes __x__ No _____

If not, explain: _____

Are any relatives other than spouse and children depending on you for support now or will need support in the future?

Yes _____ No __x__ If so, explain: _____

_____

Do you have any alimony or child support obligations? Yes _____ No __x__

If so, how much? _____ For how long? _____

Is your estate obligated to continue these obligations? _____

EDUCATION

Do you want to send your children to college? Yes __x__ No _____

How much do you estimate it will cost per child, per year? (In today's dollars) $ __5,000__

Have you set aside any assets for your children?   Yes _____ No __x__ **Grandparents have provided for their educations.**

Are they to be used for their college education?   Yes _____ No _____

DESCRIBE:

CHILD	TYPE OF ASSET	AMOUNT	HOW HELD*

*Custodianship, trust or other. Give custodian, trustee, and donor: _____

_____

(2)

CASH RESERVES — FIXED DOLLAR ASSETS

	HUSBAND	WIFE	JOINT	YIELD/MATURITY
Cash				
Checking Accounts	1,000	2,000	2,000	
Savings Accounts				
Credit Union				
Certificates of Deposit				
Money Market Funds	38,000			12%
Deferred Annuities				
Government Bonds				
Notes Receivable				
Mortgages Receivable				
Other:				

HOME AND PERSONAL PROPERTY

Market value of your home $ 240,000 _____ Cost basis $ 185,000 _____

Remaining mortgage $ 90,000 _____ Number of years 25 Interest rate 8 3/4 %

Who is the owner? Joint _____

Do you have mortgage insurance in case of disability or death? Yes _____ No X If so, how much? _____

PERSONAL PROPERTY	HUSBAND	WIFE	JOINT
Home furnishings			40,000
Automobiles	10,000	8,000	
Silver, jewelry, coins		3,000	
Clothing, furs		1,000	
Antiques			
Boat, ~~airplane, trailer~~	4,000		
Other_____			

REAL ESTATE

List all real estate holdings other than your home and those included under tax incentive investments. Use separate sheet if necessary.

Description	Market Value	Remaining Mortgage	Cost Basis	Gross Annual Income	Expenses, Depreci-ation (annual)	Owner	What are your plans for this property?
Beach Condo	90,000	30,000	50,000	4,500	5,000	Joint	personal/rental
~~Duplex~~	115,000	75,000	80,000	9,800	8,500	SEJ	rental

(3)

STOCKS, BONDS, AND MUTUAL FUNDS

Owner	No. Shares or Face Amount	Security Description	Listed or NASDAQ Symbol	Present Market Value	Total Cost	Annual Dividend	Coupon	Maturity Date
SEJ	6,250	Stock Option	VRN	156,250*	–0–	–	–	Various
SEJ	750	Common	VRN	26,250	27,500	375		
SEJ	1,000	Common	ABC	28,750	21,250	1,000		
SEJ	100,000	Common	MNO	45,000	15,000	–		

* Represents "bargain element."

TAX-INCENTIVE INVESTMENTS

Do you have any tax-incentive investments?
(Oil and gas exploration, real estate, cattle, coal, railway cars, etc.) Yes _X_ No ____

Description	Year Purchased	Amount Invested	Expected Annual Deductions	Present Value (if known)	Current Annual Income	Owner
Section 8						
Ltd Partnership	1981	25,000	42,000	–	–	SEJ
	1982	18,000	23,000	–	–	
	1983	–	7,200	–	–	

(4)

BUSINESS INTEREST OR PROFESSIONAL PRACTICE

Sole Proprietorship ☐   Sub-chapter S ☐
Partnership ☐   Corporation ☐

Business

I. Name _____ I.D. Number _____

II. Valuation

a). What is your estimation of the present market value of *your* share of the business?

_____

b). What do you estimate your estate would collect for the business (liquidation value)?

_____

or

Professional Practice

List the present value of *your* share of the following:

Checking Account _____

Accounts Receivable _____

Equipment or Furniture _____

Building _____

Other _____

_____

Any liabilities? _____

Would your estate be able to collect the above values? Yes _____ No _____
If no, which ones would decrease and by how much?

_____
_____
_____

Business or Professional Practice

Ownership:

Name	% of Ownership	Relationship (if any)

For Corporations Only:

Do you have any of the following corporate fringe benefit programs?

Pension Plan	Yes _X_ No _____
Profit Sharing Plan	Yes _X_ No _____
105(b) Medical Expense Reimbursement Plan	Yes _____ No _____
Corporate Disability Plan	Yes _X_ No _____
Group Life Insurance	Yes _X_ No _____
Deferred Compensation Plan	Yes _____ No _____
Thrift or Salary Savings Plan	Yes _____ No _____

If not a corporation, have you ever considered incorporation?

If so, explain: _____

_____

(5)

Business or Professional Practice (Continued)

Employee Information (Complete for Employee Benefit Plan Proposals)

Name	Sex	Date of Birth	Employment Date	Full Time Part Time	Current Annual Compensation

Disposition of Interest

What would happen to your business in the event of a long disability or your death? Would you want it retained by your

heirs or sold or dissolved? _____

_____

Do you have a Buy-Sell or Stock Redemption Agreement? Yes ____ No ____

What is the purchase price? $_____

Is there an escalation clause (to provide for increasing values)? Yes ____ No ____

Is your agreement funded? Yes ____ No ____

With what? _____ How much? _____

RETIREMENT INFORMATION

Type of Plan	Present Vested Interest	Value at Death	Beneficiary	Value of Voluntary Contributions	How Funded?	Monthly Retirement Income at Age ____
Keogh						
I.R.A.						
Pension	33,000	100,000	PAJ	N/A	Insurance	
Profit Sharing	40,000	40,000				
Thrift						
Salary Savings						
ESOP	115,000	115,000	Estate of SEJ	30,000		

Are you satisfied with your retirement plan? Yes _X_ No ____

Explain _____

_____

LIFE INSURANCE

If you do not send us your life insurance policies for an analysis, please complete the following for yourself and your spouse:

Insured	Face Amount	Company	Type	Issue Date	Cash Value	Annual Premium	Beneficiary	Owner
SEJ	250,000	Life of Va	Group Term				PAJ	PAJ
SEJ	10,000	Mass Mutual	Ordinary	2/65	2,100	450	PAJ	PAJ
SEJ	25,000	Lincoln Life	x	7/69	4,700	615	PAJ	PAJ
SEJ	25,000	Lincoln Life	x	1/74	3,400	700	PAJ	PAJ
	Plus Pension Plan (see pg 6)							

Insured	Company	Disability Income	Benefit Period	Daily Benefit (Hosp.)	Major Med.	Acc. Death Benefit
SEJ	Life of Va	2/3 Base Pay	26 wks			

OTHER INSURANCE

When was your property and casualty insurance last reviewed? 2 years ago

Do you have personal excess liability coverage? Yes ____ No _x_ How Much? _____

LIABILITIES

What other indebtedness do you have aside from mortgages previously mentioned?

	Total Amount	Due Date	Monthly Outlay	Obligor (Husb., Wife, Jt.)
Notes	10,000	Every 90 days	interest only	SEJ
Installment Obligations				
Cash Value Loans	8,500			PAJ
Taxes Payable				
Margin Accounts				
Other Credit Cards	1,200			Joint

(7)

389

ESTATE INFORMATION

Do you have a will? Yes __x__ No ____ Date Drawn ___1979___ Date Reviewed ___Never___

What are the provisions of your will? __All to PAJ; if she dies, then to children equally.__

_____

_____

Does your spouse have a will? Yes __x__ No ____ Date Drawn ___1979___ Date Reviewed ___Never___

What are the provisions of the will? ___All to SEJ; if he dies, then to children equally.___

_____

Do you expect any inheritances? ___Negligible___ Amount? ___?___

Does your spouse expect any inheritances? ___No___ Amount? _____

Have you made any gifts to relatives? Yes ____ No __x__

When? _____ How Much? _____

Have you made any substantial gifts to any charities? Yes ____ No __x__

Are you interested in making such gifts? Yes ____ No __x__

Now or in your will? _____

TRUSTS

Have you created any trusts? Yes ____ No __x__

If yes, please give (a) type, (b) date created, (c) how it is funded, and (d) who is the beneficiary.

_____

_____

_____

Are you the beneficiary of any trusts? Yes ____ No __x__

If yes, please give (a) type, (b) donor, (c) annual income

_____

_____

_____

(8)

CURRENT INCOME AND EXPENSES

Estimate of Current Year's Income   **Expenses**

Salary	85,000	DEDUCTIBLE	
Bonus	20,000	Interest	8,000
Self Employment Income (Net)	_____	Taxes (Property, State Income)	8,500
Director or Trustee Fees	_____	Contributions	1,000
Pension, Annuity	_____	Other Deductible Expenses	200
Interest (Taxable)	5,800	NON DEDUCTIBLE	
Dividends	1,375	Principal Reduction	3,000
Real Estate (Net)	800	Living	45,000
Net Short Term ~~Gains~~/Losses*	(4,130)	Education	_____
Net Long Term Gains/~~Losses~~*	13,300	Insurance Premiums	1,765
Social Security	_____	Savings	_____
Spouse's Income	_____	Investments	_____
Other_____	_____	Other___ _____	_____

*Please give details of any installment sale income, capital gains or losses you expect this year._____

_____ from stock trades; _____

Do you expect any significant changes in your income or expenses in the next 5 years? Yes _____ No _X_ Please

explain _____ Normal salary increases _____

INCOME OBJECTIVES

RETIREMENT
   At what age do you plan to retire? ___60_____

   What annual aftertax (spendable) income would you want at retirement? (In today's dollars) $ __50,000____

DISABILITY
   If you became disabled, how much annual income would you and your family need to maintain your present

   standard of living? $___40,000____

SURVIVOR'S INCOME
   If you died today, what principal amount would you want to provide for:

   Home Mortgage? $_60,000_____   Education Fund? $_____

   Debts? $__15,000_____   Other $_____

   How much annual income would your family need to maintain their standard of living? $_____

(9)

OVERALL FINANCIAL AND INVESTMENT CONCERNS

How would you best position your investment assets to coincide with your current investment temperament?

_____% Very Conservatively. Conserving present capital is more important than making it grow.

___55___% Conservatively. High quality investments that provide an opportunity for appreciation and relative safety are important.

___35___% Subject to moderate risk. Aggressive growth is important.

___10___% Subject to high risk. Speculative growth is acceptable.

Do you have any preferences or objections to any particular investment areas?

Please explain ____No_____

_____

Which of the following best describes your attitude towards your income needs?

☒ My present income is adequate for my needs.

☐ I need more current income.

☐ I can forgo current income to be better able to provide for future retirement income.

Indicate areas of major concern to you by rating numerically in order of importance:

___5___Current Income   ___4___Education of Children

___2___Retirement Income   ___3___Reduction of Current Income Taxes

___1___Further Building of Estate   ___6___Reduction of Estate Taxes

___7___Conservation of Assets for Heirs   _____Other _____

What would you consider to be your primary financial objective or concern? __To accumulate greater wealth so we can enjoy life before and during retirement.__

Is there any thing else we should know? __Would like advice on:__

_____1)   maximizing corporate benefits_____

_____2)   reduction of income taxes_____

_____3)   overall investment direction_____

(10)

IV

A Total
Financial Plan
Prepared for:
Thomas J. Wright, M.D.

by
Harold W. Gourgues, Jr., CFP
Financial Planning Consultant

Preface

Dr. Wright, all of the enclosed recommendations for rearranging your financial affairs fall into two main categories: (1) legal and accounting procedures and (2) investment strategies and are carefully coordinated to achieve, as a whole, your stated objectives. This plan is therefore not to serve as a set of independent suggestions for your possible consideration; proper use of this plan calls for the gradual implementation of all of the major recommendations. Since most of these recommendations have current, ongoing, and future income tax and/or unified transfer tax ramifications, we suggest that you seek the assistance of your tax advisor in reviewing this plan in advance of its implementation.

Finally, this comprehensive plan, no matter how well designed and carefully implemented, cannot be carved in stone. Changing laws, legal interpretations of the law, economic conditions, market forces, and your personal considerations act in concert to force a need for updating. You must therefore periodically have your plan examined and revised.

Table of contents

Personal Balance Sheet

	Owned By Dr. Wright	Owned Jointly	Owned By Mrs. Wright
Assets:			
Checking Account	$ 3,000	$	$ 1,000
Savings Account	8,000		
Municipal and Corporate Bonds	65,000		
Life Insurance Cash Values (Net)	0		13,885
Common Stocks	31,185		
Real Estate			$ 60,000
Keogh Plan	12,750		
Pension Plan	60,000		
Profit Sharing Plan	80,750		
Personal Holding Co.	66,000		
Wright Radiology Professional Corporation	30,000		
Tax-Incentive Investments	30,000		
Home			165,000
Personal Property		50,000	
Total Assets	$386,685	$50,000	$239,885
Liabilities:			
Mortgage on Lake House			30,500
Mortgage on Home			99,500
Demand Note	31,500	–0–	–0–
Total Liabialities	$ 31,500	$ –0–	$130,000
Net Worth	$355,185	$50,000	$109,885
Combined Net Worth			$515,070

Cash Flow Analysis

Income:	
Salary	$ 110,000
Interest	1,250
Dividends From Professional Corp*	4,560
Personal Holding Company (Sub S Corp.)	6,000
40% of Net Long-Term Gains	4,000
Business Deductions	(3,500)
Tax Incentive Investment Deductions	(10,000)
Adjusted Gross Income	$ 112,310
Less: Excess Itemized Deductions	(21,600)
($25,000–$3,400)	
Personal Exemptions	(4,000)
Taxable Income	$ 86,710
Federal Income Tax Liability	(27,811)
	$ 58,899
Add: Tax-Incentive Investment Deductions	10,000
Dividend Exclusion	200
Personal Exemptions	4,000
Tax-Free Income	4,200
Excess Itemized Deductions	21,600
	$ 98,899
Less: Taxable Gain	(4,000)
Living Expenses	(48,424)
Discretionary Cash Flow	$ 46,475
Less: Tax-Incentive Investment Commitments	(10,000)
Remaining Discretionary Cash Flow	$ 36,475

*After the $200 dividend exclusion.

Estate at death analysis

Estate Assets:		
Checking Accounts		$ 3,000
Savings Account		8,000
Municipal Bonds and Corporate Bonds		65,000
Proceeds Life Insurance		0
Common Stocks		31,185
Keogh Plan		0*
Pension Plan		0*
Profit Sharing Plan		53,500*
Personal Holding Company		66,000
Wright Radiology Professional Corporation		30,000
Tax-Incentive Investments		30,000
Personal Property		25,000
Prior Taxable Gifts (Split Gift made to children within 3 years of death)		26,000
Gross Taxable Estate:		337,685
Administration and Probate (4½%)	$(15,195)	
Estimated Final Expenses	(5,000)	
Liabilities	(31,500)	
Adjusted Gross Estate:		$285,989
Marital Deduction	$(78,500)	
Net Taxable Estate:		$207,489
Prior Taxable gifts	–0–	
		$207,489
Tentative Tax Base:		
Tentative Federal Estate Tax	$ 57,196	
Unified Transfer Credit	(79,300)	
State Death Tax Credit	–0–	
Net Federal Estate Tax	–0–	
State Death Tax	–0–	
Total Taxes		$ –0–
Add: Administration and Probate	$15,196	
Estimated Final Expenses	5,000	
Liabilities	31,500	
Total Estate Settlement Costs		$ 51,696

*First $100,000 of proceeds excluded from taxable estate if left to a named beneficiary (other than "estate") and not paid in a lump sum. $100,000 of proceeds paid in a lump sum can be excluded if beneficiary elects not to use special income tax provisions such as capital gains or ten year averaging.

Introduction

Personal Financial Planning consists of both lifetime and estate planning. The entire process begins with a careful portrayal of your current financial posture. This will allow our analysis to align your assets and cash flow with your objectives for accumulating, preserving, and distributing wealth. We have therefore placed your Balance Sheet, your 1983 Cash Flow Analysis, and your current Estate at Death illustration at the very beginning of this analysis.

Keep in mind that you can build your financial future with two tools: (1) the investment assets you now have and (2) the assets that can be acquired with your future discretionary income. How you position these assets and direct your annual cash flow are central to building a successful financial pyramid.

A review of your current Balance Sheet indicates that you and Mrs. Wright have total assets of $676,570, $161,500 of long-term debt liabilities and a resulting combined net worth of $515,070. Of that, $447,570 is represented by personal investment assets and qualified retirement plans. The net worth is currently weighted more toward yourself since the major leveraged assets are owned by your spouse. An acceptable 31.9% of your assets is reflected in the current valuation of your home and personal property.

The Cash Flow Analysis indicates that, with no further tax planning for 1983, your federal income tax liability will approximate $27,811. After this expense plus your normal living expenses of $48,424 and the $10,000 tax-incentive investment commitment, $36,475 of discretionary cash flow can be directed during 1983 toward your multiple objectives.

The Estate at Death illustration indicates a current gross estate of $337,685. You have a cash need of about $51,696 for administration and probate of your estate, final expenses, and debt liabilities that should be paid off in the event of your immediate death. Alternatively, your spouse's Estate at Death analysis would result in an even lesser and inconsequential estate settlement problem and shrinkage at this time.

In our conversations, as well as throughout your questionnaire, you indicated a prime concern to transform some of your income tax liability into the further building of your estate for future income and to adequately prepare for the financial strains of properly educating your two children. Conserving assets for heirs and reducing estate taxes do not figure prominently in your overall plan for now or the future. More specifically, you would like your children to own only such assets as to fully fund the preparation for their future financial independence. Simultaneously you are planning for an assured $55,000 of annual after-tax income in today's dollars by age 65 or earlier and $50,000 of such income should you become disabled or upon your death.

In planning for these goals, your risk tolerance indicates a heavy weighting of investments toward the middle of the risk spectrum, a secondary attachment to the conservative and very conservative positions, and only a minor interest in the higher-risk opportunities.

Lifetime planning

ASSET ANALYSIS

While your Balance Sheet provides us with an accurate measure of what you now have, the financial pyramid that follows helps demonstrate, visually, your current financial condition. As you proceed upwards within your pyramid, increased risk and return, and/or decreased short to immediate-term liquidity and/or availability is implied.

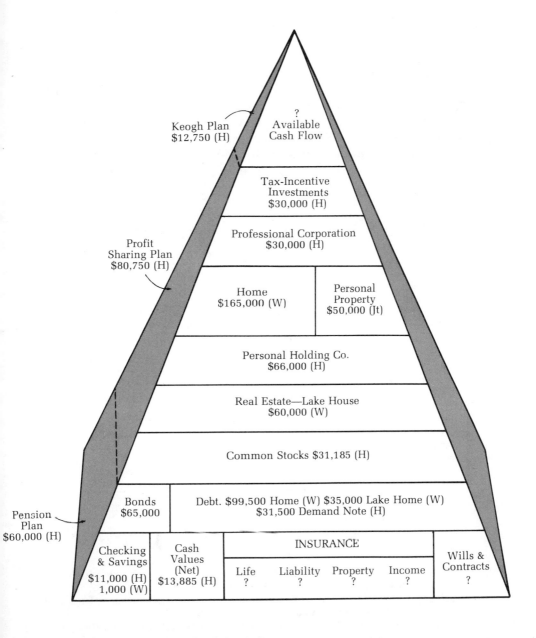

Keogh Plan
$12,750 (H)

?
Available
Cash Flow

Tax-Incentive
Investments
$30,000 (H)

Professional Corporation
$30,000 (H)

Profit
Sharing Plan
$80,750 (H)

Home
$165,000 (W)

Personal
Property
$50,000 (Jt)

Personal Holding Co.
$66,000 (H)

Real Estate—Lake House
$60,000 (W)

Common Stocks $31,185 (H)

Pension
Plan
$60,000 (H)

Bonds
$65,000

Debt. $99,500 Home (W) $35,000 Lake Home (W)
$31,500 Demand Note (H)

Checking
& Savings

$11,000 (H)
1,000 (W)

Cash
Values
(Net)
$13,885 (H)

INSURANCE

Life
?

Liability
?

Property
?

Income
?

Wills &
Contracts
?

RATE OF RETURN MATRIX STUDY

In diagnosing the hurdles that lie between your current condition and your desired future, we must first study how your segments of investment assets relate to your major overall lifetime goals. If you are not properly segmented and aligned with these objectives, the following rate of return matrix study will guide us toward appropriate adjustments.

We have already determined that you and Mrs. Wright have $294,070 of personal investment assets plus the $153,500 in the various qualified retirement plans. Let us therefore segment all of these various investment assets into the various pyramid and subpyramid components, make assumptions as to their expected after-tax return on investment (ROI), and then compute the overall weighted average return on investment (ROI).

Assets	January 1, 1983 Amount	Assumed Average ROI	% Of Total	Weighted Average ROI
Savings	$ 8,000	5.25%[1]	2%	.10%
Cash Values	13,885	4.00%	3%	.12%
Tax-Exempt Bonds	65,000	6.46%[2]	15%	.97%
Common Stock Fund	31,185	9.00%[3]	7%	.63%
Real Estate (Lake House)	60,000	10.00%	13%	1.30%
Personal Holding Co.				
Note	31,500	6.00%[4]	7%	.42%
Utility Stocks	34,500	12.00%[5]	8%	.96%
Professional Corp.	30,000	0%[6]	7%	.00%
Tax-Incentive Investments				
Gas/Oil	10,000[7]	20.00%[8]	2%	.40%
Real Estate	10,000	15.00%[9]	2%	.30%
Keogh Plan	12,750	10.00%[10]	3%	.30%
Pension	60,000	9.50%[11]	13%	1.24%
Profit Sharing Plan	80,750	9.00%[12]	18%	1.62%
Totals	$447,570		100%	8.36%

[1]Passbook Savings rate of 5¼%.

[2]6% of $70,000 face amount = 6.46% of current market value.

[3]Average Stock Market performance of 9% is also assumed to be Dr. Wright's average performance of a conservatively run tax-managed trust.

[4]$31,500 note times 6% interest.

[5]$34,500 Utility Stocks produce $4,110 dividend.

[6]Assumes that assets of the Professional Corporation will not appreciate.

[7]$20,000 present value of gas/oil drilling investments is reduced by contemplated gift to children of his $10,000 present value of the 1981 investment.

[8]An internal rate of return of 20% is assumed as a compounding rate. It is therefore assumed that all tax savings and cash flow that result from this investment will be reinvested into an investment whose performance will be identical to the investment which creates it.

[9]15% return is assumed for these two existing and occupied, income-oriented commercial real estate portfolios.

The sum total of this analysis for planning purposes is that we are to project an average rate of return of 8.36% on your $447,570 of available investment assets. This will be important when developing the rate of return matrix that guides your discretionary cash flow during the year or two between updating your financial plan.

But before we analyze your cash flow, let's proceed with our review of your investment assets with the objective of improving their after-tax return without taking undue risk.

Cash Reserves. You are currently maintaining cash reserves of $25,885 including the two checking accounts, a savings account, and net life insurance cash values.

The foundation for every solidly structured financial pyramid is an adequate cash reserve for emergencies, pending investment opportunities and estate liquidity needs. While we will pinpoint your estate liquidity needs in later sections of this report, we will now address your need for short-term to intermediate emergency reserves. Your particular circumstances warrant the maintenance of cash or equivalents of about $25,000. This amount represents approximately six months of living expenses, which also closely parallels your short-term cash needs during the first months of any long-term disability. A reserve pool of this size for you is also a "well" from which totally unexpected expenses can be drawn and subsequently replenished, without strain, from future annual discretionary cash flow.

As you realize, inflation is an important factor in financial planning. Fixed-dollar holdings such as cash reserves are particularly vulnerable to this silent embezzler. Yet due to the very nature of this type of reserve, sanctity of principal must be the prime characteristic. Accumulating high, tax-sheltered income is part of the answer to repairing the damages inflicted upon that principal by inflation.

After continuing to maintain about $1,000 in each of your checking accounts, you should move about $5,000 into a money market fund for short-term reserves. Such a fund buys short-term, higher-yielding instruments such as US Treasury bills and notes, US government agency securities, bank Certificates of Deposit, banker's acceptances, commercial paper, and other corporate paper. Daily accrual of interest, substantially above your current passbook savings rates, is available along with immediate liquidity and safety of principal.

---

[10]Keogh plan consists of a quality corporate bond fund currently paying a 10.00% compounded annual rate of return tax-sheltered by the plan's qualified status.

[11]The mixture of CD's at 10% and Bank Common Funds @ 9% is assumed to produce an average tax-sheltered return of 9.5%.

[12]The tax-sheltered rate of return on the combination of common stocks selected by you and your broker and the equity mutual funds is assumed to average 9%.

The life insurance cash values owned by Mrs. Wright are increasing at the very conservative rate of 3.5% and could be used more productively. For example, the interest rate for borrowing the cash value is 5%. While it might seem appropriate to borrow these funds at this low rate, a reinvestment into low-risk, tax-advantaged alternatives such as a single-premium deferred annuity or short-term municipal bonds would create a problem. Section 264 of the Internal Revenue Code disallows the interest deduction on indebtedness incurred to purchase or carry annuities or tax exempt bonds. For this reason and others to be demonstrated under "Estate Planning," the $100,000 HiLife should be cancelled after first acquiring a $125,000 annual renewable term policy (see "Estate Planning—Capital Needs"). The resulting $13,885, plus the $5,000 of excess savings, should be used to purchase an $18,885 single-premium deferred annuity.

Such an annuity is an excellent vehicle for maintaining one's intermediate emergency cash reserves. Principal is fully guaranteed. Interest at very competitive rates accumulate tax-free until such time as it is withdrawn. Probate costs, delays, and publicity are avoided on cash reserves so held. While not a technical description, a single-premium deferred annuity does serve as a sort of tax-sheltered "Certificate of Deposit" with a legal reserve life insurance company and can serve purposes similar to those traditionally served by CD's. Annuities also have early surrender fees, just as government regulations impose penalties for early withdrawals from CD's.

In summary, we recommend you reduce your checking accounts to $1,000 each. Move $5,000 to a money market fund with check writing privileges, and position $18,885 of remaining savings and cash values into a single premium deferred annuity.

Bonds. Your marginal tax bracket of 48% would traditionally warrant some participation in tax-exempt bonds. Because of the duality of the imbedded 8% to 12% inflation we envision for the forseeable future and due to your overall objective of accumulation, we think otherwise. On the other hand, you desire to maintain about 40% of your investment assets in relatively conservative positions. The answer, as we see it, is to reposition the bonds into quality utility common stocks that provide high, increasing, and potentially tax-benefited income coupled with moderate appreciation potential whenever interest rates moderate. We believe that your downside risk from this point in utilities would be only about 70% as much as your long-term bonds while, as indicated, offering the same or more upside potential.

The disadvantage of having any taxable dividend income in your marginal bracket is obvious. Fully taxable dividends can, however, be transformed into deferred and ultimately reduced taxation via a tax-managed trust. Such a professionally managed entity first chooses to be taxed as a corporation, invests in high-dividend stocks such as utilities, and accumulates and internally reinvests the dividend income. As a result, the 85% corporate dividend exclusion applies. With the 15% taxable portion of the dividend build-up offset by administrative and management changes, tax-free dividend accumulation occurs without taking more risk, and perhaps less, than now exists in your bond portfolio.

Also, up to $1,500 (on a joint return) of public utility dividends reinvested in the utility's stock can be excluded from income.

In your case, the $10,000 capital loss due to the switch can be of further benefit as will be discussed under "Cash Flow Analysis." More importantly, abotu 10% to 12% after-tax annual accumulation would result ($6,500 to $7,150) versus the current $4,500.

Equity Securities. You have made an important commitment to certain assets and cash flow streams via liquid corporate equity securities. Besides the more sizable $120,000 commitments in your pension and profit sharing plans, you also have committed $31,000 to a tax-managed trust, which emphasizes industrial equities. We commend you for this decision and would like to reiterate our feelings about the serious undervaluations of the quality, dividend-paying segment of the stock market. This undervaluation can be viewed in several ways.

Quantitatively, we now have an historically low relationship between the Dow Jones Industrial Average and the book values of the shares it represents. Price-to-earnings ratios are also relatively low. That is mainly a reflection or mirror image of the inflation rate. We believe that, as inflation eventually moderates due to more conservative fiscal and monetary policies during the 80s, P-E ratios will ascend. In less measured fashion, we would speculate that the probability of lower future capital gains rates, coupled with the return to some semblance of supply side economics and the future elimination or reduction of the double taxation of corporate dividends, would augur well for future equity prices. As will be quantified in "Cash Flow Analysis," we will want you to increase your personal participation in the equity marketplace.

Real Estate. In addition to your $165,000 home, you now have $60,000 invested in a lake house for both investment and personal reasons and $10,000 in two real estate partnerships. This total of $235,000 represents 35% of your total asset picture. The lake house and partnerships, however, represent only 15% of your investment assets. Because of our strong feelings about the developing housing shortage/crisis, and because rents have in general not yet caught up with the inflationary spiral, a greater participation is probably warranted.

Real estate, as you know, enjoys a jealous position among inflation and "1040" fighters. Leveraged appreciation potential due to many factors, including rising rents and replacement costs, is a strong incentive toward investments in improved real estate properties. Tax incentives, mainly in the form of depreciation and interest deductions, act as a further lure to highly bracketed individuals such as yourself.

Two warning signs must however be pointed out. First, real estate is less liquid than your other holdings. This means that coordinating lifetime and estate planning is essential. Second, real estate needs professional management, particularly when it is owned by investors like yourself who can give it only scant attention. We will therefore direct you toward professionally managed real estate involvements under the "Retirement Planning" section.

Tax-Incentive Investments We will discuss only the areas of investment in direct participation format that provide up-front deductions and credits. These investments may be used to reduce the tax liability on unrelated income such as your dividends, interest, and then salary income.

All major tax-incentive investments appear within the acronym RE-ACT: *r*eal estate, *e*nergy, *a*griculture, *c*ommunications, and *t*ransportation. To gain tax incentives, the investor must risk capital directly in the ownership of "activity for profit" in these areas or in the ownership of equipment involved in the activity. To reap consistent economic benefits via tax-incentive investments, participation should be restricted to only those areas of business that represent unusually attractive opportunities appearing opposite the risk side of a coin of economic crisis. Consistent with this philosophy, three areas we currently see as being unusually attractive are real estate, energy and communications.

1. REAL ESTATE.

We have already discussed the general benefits of improved real estate. Involvements in the construction of such residential and commercial properties now offer very attractive potential. Start-up expenses followed by today's more rapid depreciation schedules provide handsome, early tax deductions. Rapidly increasing material, labor, and land costs make yesterday's building appear inexpensive today. Long-term conventional financing, when available at reasonable costs, multiplies the appreciation potential. The major risk here involves the uncertainty related to attracting and maintaining quality tenants at hopefully increasing rents. But when all is said and done, it will probably be the coming housing shortage that will become this nation's second greatest crisis, outdone only by energy.

2. ENERGY.

The dynamic opportunities that appear opposite the risk side of the energy crisis can best be directly acquired via first the exploration, development and ownership of gas/oil properties and second through the ownership of major equipment used in that pursuit.

Since the energy crisis, the price of what is found has risen far more rapidly than the average cost of finding it. With 60% to 90% of the finding costs immediately deductible, your out-of-pocket cost of such an involvement is quickly reduced. The resulting cash flow, on average two to three times your pretax investment, is partially tax-free due to depletion allowances and other business expenses. You are already taking advantage of this area for both accumulation and distribution planning purposes, and we want you to continue that to the extent your future marginal tax bracket allows for it.

The second opportunity periodically exists due to (1) the strong longer-term demand versus supply of major drilling and related equipment, (2) the high rentals that result from a high rate of usage of it, and (3) the depreciation and tax credits that result from owning it. The added tax benefit results from such equipment being considered "personal" versus "real," and therefore depreciation produces no items of preference income. Because participations here are usually in such large denominations, because we are temporarily facing a soft market in such equipment, and because drilling already provides you with enough activity on this risk level, you must, at least for the time being, postpone an involvement in equipment.

3. COMMUNICATIONS.

The increasing expense of mobility, due to the effect of the energy crisis on the cost of transportation, places a spotlight on the demand for improved communications. Stated differently, while a return to the free market in gas/oil will continue to result in accelerated energy price increases and an important halt in the rapid decline of domestic production, it is conservation that should become our nation's greatest new source of energy. Conservation requirements will result in advanced communications frequently replacing transportation.

Cable television at long last becomes a major answer. Wiring our nation with CATV's coaxial cable, we believe, will allow people to stay at home more for entertainment at first, then for services such as shopping, alarm systems, banking, surveys and then, finally, work. Owning, operating, and expanding existing CATV systems appear to offer a great ratio of potential benefit to risk.

There are also important tax benefits. With leverage of about a two-to-one debt-to-equity ratio, deductibility of 90% to 95% of the investor's equity can be secured over a three-to-four-year span. A lesser write-off could, however, result whenever leverage is lower or abnormally high cash flow is automatically sheltered within the partnership itself. Additionally, as in the case of equipment in energy production, CATV equipment is "personal" equipment not subject to a lease. Investment tax credits are available, and the accelerated depreciation thereon is not a preference item.

Tax-Incentive Investments Summary. In your specific case, real estate has not provided you with important tax benefits other than the interest deductions due to personal usage. You have, however, successfully participated in gas/oil drilling, and we believe that you should not only maintain your holdings but continue this participation in the mannner described under "Cash Flow Analysis." You should also become involved in the purchase of existing gas/oil properties, real estate, and cable systems as indicated in the "Personal Holding Company" section of this analysis.

Retirement Plans. A qualified retirement plan is axiomatically the most perfect tax shelter. It allows for the 100% deductibility of the cash that is so positioned, defers the taxation on its income and appreciation, and under certain circumstances provides for tax-advantaged receipt of the proceeds. You have taken handsome advantage of qualified retirement planning, and we congratulate you for it. Currently 22.7% of your total assets and 34.3% of your investment assets are so positioned. We would encourage you to do exactly what you suggested in your questionnaire and increase your contributions to the plans to a level of at least $10,000 per year. Make every attempt to also increase it by whatever the inflation rate is each year. This can be facilitated by having salary increases keep pace with inflation.

We also have strong recommendations with regard to the investment of the assets already in your various plans. The corporate bond fund in the frozen Keogh Plan is providing a yield equal to or slightly in excess of the inflation rate. It has provided a pattern of increasing income as well. Maintain that position for the time being.

As for the pension plan, your bank has performed relatively well with common stocks in their common fund. While you should continue to monitor their performance relative to other professional managers, we can find no fault with that stance at this time. Keeping one-half of your pension plan in CD's is, however, a bad recommendation on their part. Since you wish to remain relatively conservative with these funds, we suggest that you take advantage of another opportunity offered by the real estate market through "all-inclusive mortgage trust deeds," more familiarly called "wrap-around mortgages."

Due to the unique structure of this type of mortgage financing, it is particularly attractive to tax-exempt investors such as charities, endowment funds, and qualified retirement plans. "Wraps" enable the tax-exempt investor to currently achieve an average annual total return in excess of 16% including current income, equity build-up, and equity kickers, after all management fees and front-end costs. Such a commitment lasts about ten to fifteen years and should be entered into only with the funds that can be positioned in such less liquid format. A most attractive feature is the ability of these mortgages, when professionally selected and managed, to offer an attractive current yield and total return with a minimum risk to your principal. We, therefore, suggest that your $30,000 CD commitment be repositioned into a pool of wrap-around mortgages.

The commitment to equities in your profit sharing plan should be maintained. The individual quality growth equities remain undervalued in their own right as well as relative to the market as a whole. The growth funds have performed admirably relative to the market, and we suggest a definite hold and/or buy attitude about them, too.

We have also mentioned in previous meetings the attractive opportunities in royalty interest programs. We agree, however, with your desire to balance your personal energy-related holdings with nonenergy investments in your retirement plans.

Personal Holding Company. Your Personal Holding Company is being maintained as a vehicle for future business involvements or as a tool for minor estate planning objectives in the future. Its assets are, in our opinion, ill positioned. First you should arrange your debt so as to have it paid off in cheaper future dollars to a bank instead of indirectly to yourself. That would also free up $31,500 for investment in the PHC at a rate higher than the interest rate.

Furthermore, the utility stocks are producing highly taxed dividend income. Because we have already transformed your municipal bonds to such utilities principally via a tax-managed trust (see "Asset Analysis—Bonds"), we believe that this $34,500 could be invested more aggressively to produce more appreciation and a type of tax-benefited cash flow that is dictated by the sub-chapter S status of the PHC. Therefore, the total of $66,000 should be divided equally into:

1. a pool of residential real estate,
2. existing cable television properties partnerships, and

3. partnerships involved in the acquisition of proven, income-producing gas/oil properties.

While we have already discussed real estate and existing cable operations, we have not yet mentioned the lowest-risk method for participating in the ownership of existing gas and oil reserves. Such an investment is very suitable for investors in practically all tax brackets who find the risk level or high tax deductions of drilling not appropriate or applicable. These investments are likewise formed via the limited partnership format, typically every month or quarter. The funds purchase, on a present value basis, the future net revenues of literally hundreds of existing wells on a basis of about three-to-one ratios of future revenues to capital at risk. Usually some modest level of leverage is involved and about 50% to 60% or more of the cash flow is tax-free over the ten- to 20-year life of the investment due to cost depletion allowances and other business expenses.

Children's Assets. We find no problem with either of the investments your children own. We also admire the trust arrangements created for them by your attorney. The stipulations contained therein better assure that the capital will be used for the educational purpose that was intended.

We recommend, however, that you discontinue the $6,000 ($3,000 per child) cash gifting you began in 1981 and resume the gifting of gas/oil drilling partnerships after you have personally received the major tax benefits.

For instance, the $10,000 drilling investment (two units) made in 1981 have been fully deducted. It conservatively projects $21,000 of future net revenues plus further prospective development activity. This investment has a current repurchase agreement of only $6,000 due to the effect of interest rates and other "haircutting" upon the computation of present values. As soon as possible, gift one unit each to Jean and David. That would actually fulfill your intended commitment to Jean's college fund and probably take care of most of David's as well. David also has the added cushion of four more compounding years that Jean now does. Should Jean's trust not provide sufficient early cash flow to fund all of the costs by 1986–87, you will want to consider an interest-free loan to her, which can be repaid to you out of eventual gas/oil sales or mutual fund liquidations.

Revised Rate of Return Matrix. As a result of the minor alterations made in the investment complexion of your assets, the following revision of your weighted average return on investment (ROI) can be made:

Assets	Current Amount	Assumed After-tax Average ROI	% Of Total	Weighted Average ROI
Money Market Fund	$ 5,000	10.0%[1]	1%	.10%
Deferred Annuity	18,885	11.3%[2]	4%	.45%
Tax-Managed Utility Trust and Utility Shares	65,000	10.0%[3]	15%	1.50%
Common Stock Fund	31,185	9.0%[3]	7%	.6%
Real Estate (Lake House)	60,000	10.0%	13%	1.30%
Personal Holding Co.				
Real Estate	22,000	15.0%	5%	.75%
CATV	22,000	15.0%	5%	.75%
Gas/Oil Income	22,000	12.0%[4]	5%	.60%
Professional Corp.	30,000	0%[5]	7%	.0
Tax-Incentive Investments				
Gas/Oil	10,000[7]	20.0%	2%	.40%
Real Estate	10,000	15.0%	2%	.30%
Keogh Plan	12,750	10.0%	3%	.30%
Pension Plan	60,000	12.5%[6]	13%	1.6%
Profit Sharing Plan	80,750	9.0%	18%	1.62%
Totals	$449,570		100%	10.33%

[1]Money market rate of 10%.

[2]11.3% current tax deferred rate.

[3]These assumed rates are very conservative due to expectations for both appreciation plus the reinvestment of increasing dividend rates. A higher rate is assumed for the utility trust because of the dramatically higher dividend yield currently available in that sector of the market.

[4]Assumes 12% current income and no appreciation.

[5]Assumes no appreciation.

[6]The mixture of common funds at a minimum 9% and wrap-around mortgages of at least 16% produces a conservative tax-sheltered average simple return at 12.5%.

[7]$2000 more than before due to decreased committment to checking accounts.

Note that slightly altering the posture of your existing assets, particularly from a tax viewpoint, dramatically increases the conservative estimated weighted average ROI from 8.36% to 10.33% without any added risk. This, as you will see, will dramatically *decrease* the need for you to earn an abnormally high rate of return on your discretionary cash flow to reach your asset/income goals for the future.

Risk Management. We are pleased to see that you have acquired all of the types of insurance protection needed by you to avoid the formidable potential burden of replacing existing assets. Your homeowner's policy, liability insurance coverage, and auto policies all appear adequate to us. We urge you to review all of this coverage with Mel Nunn, your certified property and casualty underwriter, at least every two years.

CASH FLOW ANALYSIS

Income Taxation/Discretionary Cash Flow. It will be helpful for you to now review particularly the federal income tax aspects of the Cash Flow Analysis, which appeared at the beginning of this report:

Adjusted Gross Income	$112,310
Taxable Income	86,710
Federal Income Tax Liability	27,811
Remaining Discretionary Cash Flow After Tax Incentive Investment Commitments	$ 36,475

The Taxation Thermometer on the next page is used to illustrate the taxation of your income as it was estimated prior to the recommendations made in this plan.

After income taxes and other appropriate adjustments, $46,475 remains for investments. During the past year, you allocated your discretionary cash flow proportionately as follows and have anticipated accomplishing about the same in 1983.

Tax-Incentive Investments	$10,000
Cash Gifts to Children	6,000
Personal Property Purchases	16,975
Additional Common Stock Purchases	8,000
Additions to Cash Reserves	2,500
Reduction of Demand Note	3,000
	$46,475

In accordance with the changes in cash reserves and in the Personal Holding Company assets, your Cash Flow Analysis would change as follows:

Revised 1982 Cash Flow Analysis

Income:	
Salary	$ 110,000
Interest	765
Dividends (Professional Corp.)	4,560
Gains $ 10,000 Long-Term Gain	
($10,000) Long-Term Loss (Bonds)	
0	0
Personal Holding Co. (sub S)	
$22,000 Real Estate (20% first-year deduction)	(4,400)
22,000 CATV (10% first-year deduction)	(2,200)
22,000 G/O (little or no tax effect)	0

Taxation Thermometer for Joint Returns–1983

Taxable Income	TAX BRACKET	TAXABLE INCOME	INCOME TAX
	50% ×		
$109,400			
	48% ×	$ 1,110	$ 533
$86,710			
$ 85,600			
	44% ×	25,600	11,264
$ 60,000			
	40% ×	14,200	5,680
$ 45,800			
	35% ×	10,600	3,710
$ 35,200			
	30% ×	5,300	1,590
$ 29,900			
	26% ×	5,300	1,378
$ 24,600			
	23% × to 0%	$24,600	3,656
	TOTALS	86,710	27,811

EID $ 21,600
PE $ 4,000
AL $ 13,500
TOTAL $ 39,100

TAX CREDITS (0)

TOTAL TAX 27,811

Gas/Oil Drilling Deductions	
1982 Investments	(8,000)
Previous Investments	(2,000)
Business Deductions	(3,500)
Adjusted Gross Income	$ 95,225
Less: Excess Itemized Deductions	
($25,000 − $3,400)	(21,600
Personal Exemptions	(4,000)
Taxable Income	69,625
Federal Income Tax Liability	(20,249)*
	$ 49,376
Add: Tax-Incentive Investment Deductions	16,600
Dividend Exclusion	200
Personal Exemptions	4,000
Excess Itemized Deductions	21,600
Less: Living Expenses	(45,924)
	$ (45,852
Less: Gas/Oil Drilling Investment	(10,000)
Remaining Discretionary Cash Flow	$ 35,852

*Via the tax schedules or Tax Thermometer.

On the surface, it would seem that our recommendations have reduced your cash flow when, in fact, they were intended to do the opposite. In actuality, your financial posture is much improved, but it is disguised by the investments themselves.

Some $2,134 of tax-sheltered income is built up within the deferred annuity and therefore did not appear as taxable interest income in the cash flow.

Also, approximately $6,500 of tax-free dividend income will be built up per year in the utility stocks and tax-managed utility trust, versus the $4,500 of tax-free income that was originally included in cash flow. All of the net income and growth of capital created in the real estate and CATV investments in the Personal Holding Company will be withheld as working capital or otherwise used to reduce debt and produce equity build-up.

Additionally, the oil income program will reinvest approximately $2,640+ per year into the acquisition of further income-producing properties.

These three measurable sources of income accumulation (deferred annuity, tax-managed trust, and gas/oil income) would produce approximately $11,274 of additional cash flow were you to factor it into the Cash Flow Analysis instead of allowing it to be automatically reinvested or accumulated in the programs that are themselves creating it. Additionally, we have shown its effect in your revised Rate of Return Matrix Study.

Direction of Discretionary Cash Flow. You have indicated income needs of $55,000 in today's dollars in nineteen years when you expect to retire at age 65 or earlier. Given this precise objective, as well as the updated average weighted return of 10.33% on your existing investment assets, we can now determine the rate of return or "financial speed" at which you must proceed with your remaining $36,475 of discretionary cash flow.

Current Income Needs in Today's Dollars at Age 65 or Earlier	$ 55,000
Less: Estimated $1,000/Month Social Security Tax-Free Income	(12,000)
Income Needed after Social Security	43,000
Current Income Needs Inflated at 10% for 19 Years	262,984
Capital Needed Assuming 8% Yield	3,287,301
Less (1) Current Investment Assets ($449,570) Compounded at Current Projected ROI Matrix of 10.33% for 19 years	(2,897,609)
(2) Current Annual Qualified Retirement Plan Contribution of $10,000/year Increased 12% per year Compounded at 9.21% per year	(1,283,731)
Capital Surplus (Shortage)	$ 894,039

While you would now have $46,475 ($36,475 + $10,000) of discretionary cash flow, after considering your typical $16,975 of personal property purchases, $29,500 is actually available for investments and debt reductions.

Of this $29,500, $10,000 is already allocated to gas/oil drilling investments, which is your only more aggressive involvement. The additional $19,500 of discretionary cash flow should be available for building the more conservative segments of your pyramid.

In essence, we can conclude that you should actually have very little problem at all in meeting your lifetime financial objectives. In fact, you have the flexibility of probably being able to retire very shortly if you were to invest the entire $29,468 annually.

Quite importantly, you do not have to assume even close to the risks you had probably expected prior to this analysis. We suggest continuing the modest drilling investments only because of your emphasis upon saving taxes. Investing your assets or discretionary cash flow at risk levels very much higher than necessary subjects your principal to perils not required for you to reach financial independence at a reasonable age.

On the other hand, our projections are at best speculations when we reach out as far as 19 years. The actual inflation rate, the investment performance achieved, the tax brackets that will exist then, and the availability of sources for tax-advantaged income will all profoundly affect the level of capital you will need to produce the spendable income you desire. This all further highlights the need for frequent updating of your plan.

Here are, however, some general guidelines that we can provide to help you decide upon the direction of your annual discretionary cash flow:

1. You could adopt a plan for the prudent investment of the entire $29,500 of cash flow, which may cause you to reach financial independence well before age 65. Beefing up any combination of our recommended investment directions with part or all of these funds in accordance with your particular preferences and risk tolerance level is our best advice.

2. You can sizably increase your standard of living without sacrificing tomorrow's income needs.

3. You can further reduce the average risk associated with your current investment assets if you become so inclined and then also take a very low-risk profile with some or all of the discretionary cash flow.

4. You can dramatically increase your *lifetime* charitable gifting to, for example, the Juvenile Diabetics Foundation mentioned as a possible recipient of some of the wealth distributed from your estate. You could also set up a separate fund for Jean's possible future medical expenses as has been suggested by her pediatric endocrinologist, Ed Dennis.

5. To increase future benefits to your loyal employees, you can further increase your qualified retirement plan contributions. You could also add up to $2,250 to an IRA for you and your wife.

Having come to know you and your family, your current lifestyle, and your future aspirations well during the creation of this plan, we would offer the following more specific suggestions for starters.

Just to be safe, you should protect against even higher inflation and tax rates than we have assumed. Position your current assets as we have suggested, invest the annual $10,000 in gas/oil, donate about $5,000 more to charity each year, further reduce the demand note with about one-third of what remains ($4,000), add another $4,000 to your position in the equity markets, and use the final third or $6,468 to buy some insurance against the small chance of unforeseen economic problems—gold. We should review this mix very carefully again when we update your lifetime plan in the next year or so.

Risk Management/Disability Income. The most valuable asset you now have is your earning power. And yet it is the riskiest. It can not only be disrupted through death, but it can also end as a result of a disabling accident or illness.

With current investment assets of about $447,000, it may be possible for you to transform them entirely into an investment matrix that would produce $35,000+ of after-tax income. That, plus Social Security and your current disability income benefits, may provide you with sufficient monthly income if the disability period is brief.

Due to inflationary expectations, in tandem with probable economic, tax, or temperament reasons for not wanting to immediately alter the nature of your entire investment asset pyramid, we counsel increasing your disability benefits to $3,000 per month. Your corporation currently pays and deducts the premium for your first $1,500 of coverage. As a result, those benefits would be taxable to you. Because of your exemptions and the zero bracket amount, very little taxes would be paid on this income and the other minor amounts of taxable income that you would be receiving.

The additional policy that we suggest you personally buy would produce tax-free income, as does Social Security, in the event of your disability. We suggest only $1,500 of additional coverage with a six-month deductible, which your cash flow can easily absorb. The six-month deductible makes the cost reasonable. The absence of disability income during the first six months is just one more reason for at least a six-month budget of the cash reserves we discussed at the outset.

The following worksheet can be used as a guide for determining your desired level of disability coverage. It summarizes your long-term disability insurance needs:

Long-Term Disability Income Needs Worksheet *Dr. Tom Wright*	
After-Tax Income Needs	$ 55,000
Reduction (Reduced Business, Entertainment and other expenditures during disability period)	(5,000)
Social Security (Monthly Benefit × 12)	(11,040)
Spouse's After-Tax Income	(3,600)
After-Tax Investment Income	(11,220)
Preinflation-Adjusted Disability Income Needs	$ 24,140

Adjustment for Inflation:

Long-Term Inflation Rate Assumption	5%
Preinflation-Adjusted Disability Income Needs Compounded at 5% for Life Expectancy (29 years)	$ 99,364
Add: Preinflation-Adjusted Disability Income Needs	24,140
Total	$ 123,504
Average Annual Need (Total ÷ 2)	$ 61,752
Inflation Adjusted Average Monthly Disability Income Need (Annual Need ÷ 12)	$ 5,146

Note that the $5,146 per month computation is an average for you over your entire life expectancy of 29 years. Even if $3,000 were not a limit for you, it is unlikely that we would recommend more. Note too, that we have only used the *current* after-tax investment income shown in your questionnaire. Actually, as per our increased disability income recommendation, plus the possible future total revamping of your portfolio toward the production of higher tax-benefited current cash flow, your disability income needs should be easily met. This analysis, too, must be reviewed every year or two.

Estate planning

CAPITAL NEEDS

While most estate plans immediately key in on the need to provide liquid assets for estate settlement costs, a much greater concern exists for families like yours who are still in the capital accumulation phase of their financial development. We have therefore used the information contained in your questionnaire, Balance Sheet and Estate-at-Death Analysis to complete the following Capital Needs Worksheet:

Capital Needs Worksheet

Capital Needs For Family Income:	
After-tax Income Needs	$ 50,000
Less: Estimated Social Security Benefits	(14,000)
Pension Income	–0–
Income Needs from Investment Capital	36,000
Capital Needed Assuming 8%	450,000

Capital Needs for Debt Repayment:

Home Mortgage	$ –0–
Charge Cards	1,000
Bank Notes	31,500
Other	–0–
Total Debts	32,500

Other Side Funds:

Emergency Reserves	25,000
College Education Funds	15,000
Other	
Total	40,000

Estate Settlement Costs:

Funeral Expenses	$ 5,000
Administration and Probate	15,196
Federal Estate Taxes	–0–
State Death Taxes	–0–
Uninsured Medical Costs	1,000
Other	
Total	21,196
Total Capital Needs	$543,696

Current Assets Available or Convertible to Income Producing Investments	224,070

Lump Sum Distributions from Qualified Retirement Plans:

IRA	–0–
Keogh	12,750
Pension	60,000
Profit Sharing	80,750
Other	–0–
Current Life Insurance	150,000
Total Capital Available	$527,570

Net Capital Needs (Surplus)—Capital Needs Less Capital Available	$16,126

First note that your current level of life insurance protection is just about adequate for your needs. Inasmuch as we have recommended extracting the $13,885 of cash values from your $100,000 whole life policy (for tax reasons) versus borrowing it, you will need to purchase another policy of an equal or slightly higher amount such as $125,000. As your need for this insurance is measured and determined only by the previous worksheet, it is likely that your capital gap will diminish with time. As such, your need is temporary and therefore term insurance is warranted. $125,000 of annual renewable term insurance should be purchased prior to cancelling your current whole life coverage. In so doing, you will also increase your annual cash flow by another $400 to $500, which will offset the purchase of your additional disability coverage.

Observe also that your estate settlement costs total $21,196 assuming that your state has no estate tax at the time of your death. Your current cash reserves would again serve to easily cover this need. This is further evidence that your estate and lifetime plans are properly synchronized.

WILLS

A properly drafted will is the cornerstone of any sound estate planning program. Without one, much of your capital may be needlessly dissipated and the distribution thereof made inefficient. Your wills, which were prepared in 1975, properly employed the basic two trust marital deduction provisions. You should have your attorney immediately draft new wills designed to take proper advantage of all aspects of the marital deduction and other pertinent aspects of the 1981 Economic Recovery Tax Act. Your Estate-at-Death Analysis assumes this to have already been accomplished. Additionally, we would advise very strongly to use the following insurance trust concept in your total estate plan.

INSURANCE TRUST

Under your present insurance program, Mrs. Wright is the owner of both the $50,000 group term policy, as well as the policy with HiLife. The advance replacement of this policy should be purchased and owned by an irrevocable trust named the "Thomas J. Wright 1983 Trust" with Mrs. Wright as co-trustee with your bank's trust department. Your attorney should create this trust at the same time he draws your new wills—*as soon as possible*. Arranging a meeting with your attorney, Kenneth Reeves, should be your first priority.

You should donate to the trust an amount of cash equal to the annual premium. The premium can be paid by the trustee and still have the proceeds escape estate taxes at your death and at Mrs. Wright's. Actually this trust should have your wife as the income beneficiary and your children as remaindermen, and, via your will, it will also act as the trust into which assets not passing directly to your wife or proceeds of your retirement plans would be positioned.

The trust should also own the $50,000 group term policy and would therefore receive the total insurance proceeds of $175,000 upon your death, as well as other assets in accordance with your will. This trust would pay the income from the trust to Mrs. Wright for life. At her death, the trust assets would pass to your two children.

The trustee can be given the right, but not the obligation, to purchase assets from your estate or to lend money to the estate. This would provide your executor (presumably Mrs. Wright with the help of myself) with the cash needed for estate settlement costs. Ken Reeves and Bud Greene can advise you further on the details of the use of these estate planning techniques.

We urge that you consult with your tax and legal professionals for implementing this and all other legal and accounting procedures recommended in this comprehensive plan for your future. My staff and I remain completely available to work in concert with them to reach your intended financial destiny.

The very first step in the financial planning process is the examination of your total financial wherewithal. In addition to this questionnaire, the following documents are considered:

DOCUMENTS

☒   Copies of your last four years income tax returns and any gift tax returns.

☒   Copy of your will

☒   Copy of your spouse's will

☒   Copies of trust agreements or contracts (if applicable)

☐   Copies of business buy-sell agreements (if applicable)

☒   Others __(such as Personal Holding Co. documents)__

☐   _____

Your life, health, and other insurance policies should also be included for analyzing your present coverage.

PERSONAL INFORMATION

Client's Name __Thomas J. Wright__ Social Security No. __123-45-6789__

Home Address __1385 Medical Hall Rd. NE, Atlanta, Ga 30319__ Phone __404-123-4567__

Business Address __2 Peachtree Bark St. NW, Atlanta, Ga 30303__ Phone __404-765-4321__

Date of Birth __9-23-36__ Birth Place __Macon, Ga.__

Occupation __Medical Doctor, Radiologist__ How Long? __14 years__

Who is your attorney? __Ken Reeves__

Who is your accountant? __Buddy Greene__

Do you have any other professional advisors of whom we should be aware? __Investment Broker, Bootsie__

__Carmichael; Banker, Reed Jones; CPCU, Mel Nunn.__

Date Information Obtained __January 1983__

(1)

FAMILY INFORMATION

Spouse _____ Mary _____ Date of Birth _Oct. 22, 1941_ Social Security No. _101-11-2131_

Occupation _____ Housewife _____ How Long? _16 years_

CHILDREN	DATE OF BIRTH	DEPENDENT	SELF-SUPPORTING
Jean	6-07-68	☒	☐
David	6-25-72	☒	☐
		☐	☐
		☐	☐
		☐	☐

Are all family members in good health? Yes _____ No _x_

If not, explain: Jean is a juvenile diabetic, good health now but complications could set in later, which I will want to help take care of financially.

Are any relatives other than spouse and children depending on you for support now or will need support in the future?

Yes _____ No _x_ If so, explain: _____

Do you have any alimony or child support obligations? Yes _____ No _x_

If so, how much? _____ For how long? _____

Is your estate obligated to continue these obligations? _____

EDUCATION

Do you want to send your children to college? Yes _x_ No _____

How much do you estimate it will cost per child, per year? (In today's dollars) $_5,000_

Have you set aside any assets for your children? Yes _x_ No _____

Are they to be used for their college education? Yes _x_ No _____

DESCRIBE:

CHILD	TYPE OF ASSET	AMOUNT	HOW HELD*
Jean **	Gas/Oil Drilling Prog.	$6,000 (Present Value)	Trust, Mary, trustee
	Growth Mutual Fund	10,000	
David	Gas/Oil Drilling Prog.	4,000 (Present Value)	Trust, Mary, trustee
	Growth Mutual Fund	6,000	

*Custodianship, trust or other. Give custodian, trustee, and donor: Trustee, Mary; donor, Tom.

(2)

**I would like to concentrate now on bringing this up to $20,000 or more ASAP, since Jean is only 4 years away from college. My cost estimates may also be too low.

424

CASH RESERVES — FIXED DOLLAR ASSETS

	HUSBAND	WIFE	JOINT	YIELD
	-	-	-	-
Cash				
Checking Accounts	$ 3,000	$ 1,000	-	
Savings Accounts	8,000	-		
Credit Union				
Certificates of Deposit				
Deferred Annuities				
Government Bonds				
Notes Receivable				
Mortgages Receivable				
Other:				

HOME AND PERSONAL PROPERTY

Market value of your home $ _____ 165,000 _____ Cost basis $ _____ 135,000 _____

Remaining mortgage $ _____ 99,500 _____ Number of years _____ 25 _____ Interest rate _____ 9 _____ %

Who is the owner? _____ Wife _____

Do you have mortgage insurance in case of disability or death? Yes _____ No __X__ If so, how much? _____

PERSONAL PROPERTY	HUSBAND	WIFE	JOINT
Home furnishings			15,000
Automobiles			9,000
Silver, jewelry, coins			20,000
Clothing, furs			3,000
Antiques			1,000
Boat, airplane, trailer			2,000
Other_____			

REAL ESTATE

List all real estate holdings other than your home and those included under tax incentive investments. Use separate sheet if necessary.

Description	Market Value	Remaining Mortgage	Cost Basis	Gross Annual Income	Expenses, Depreci- ation (annual)	Owner	What are your plans for this property?
Lake House	60,000	30,500	50,000	-	-	Wife	hold for pleasure, appreciation

(3)

STOCKS, BONDS, AND MUTUAL FUNDS

Owner	No. Shares or Face Amount	Security Description	Listed or NASDAQ Symbol	Present Market Value	Total Cost	Annual Dividend	Coupon	Maturity Date
Myself	2599 shs	Tax-Managed Trust		12.00 or $31,185	$ 25,000	–	–	
Myself	$ 75,000	Municipal Bonds	OTC	65,000	75,000	–	5.6%	1987

TAX-INCENTIVE INVESTMENTS

Do you have any tax-incentive investments?
(Oil and gas exploration, real estate, cattle, coal, railway cars, etc.) Yes __X__ No ____

Description	Year Purchased	Amount Invested	Expected Annual Deductions	Present Value (if known)	Current Annual Income	Owner
Real Estate LTD.						
Partnership	1978	5,000	–	?)	0	Myself
Partnership	1979	5,000	–	?) (Over 10,000)	0	Myself
Gas/Oil Drilling*	1981	10,000	0	?	0	Myself
	1982	10,000	$2,000 in 83?		0	Myself

*$10,000 invested in 1980 was gifted to the children.

(4)

426

BUSINESS INTEREST OR PROFESSIONAL PRACTICE

Sole Proprietorship ☐   Sub-chapter S ☐
Partnership ☐   Corporation ☒

Business
I. Name __Wright Radiology Professional Corp.__ I.D. Number _____

II. Valuation

a). What is your estimation of the present market value of *your* share of the business?
__$30,000__

b). What do you estimate your estate would collect for the business (liquidation value)?
__$30,000__

or
Professional Practice
List the present value of *your* share of the following:

Checking Account ____$10,000____

Accounts Receivable ____20,000 (1/2 probably collectable)____

Equipment or Furniture ____10,000____

Building _____–_____

Other _____–_____

Any liabilities? _____–_____

Would your estate be able to collect the above values? Yes __X__ No ____
If no, which ones would decrease and by how much?
__Could collect all but about 1/2 of the accounts receivable.__

Business or Professional Practice

Ownership:

Name	% of Ownership	Relationship (if any)
Dr. Thomas J. Wright	100%	

For Corporations Only:
Do you have any of the following corporate fringe benefit programs?

Pension Plan	Yes __X__ No ____
Profit Sharing Plan	Yes __X__ No ____
105(b) Medical Expense Reimbursement Plan	Yes __X__ No ____
Corporate Disability Plan	Yes __X__ No ____
Group Life Insurance	Yes __X__ No ____
Deferred Compensation Plan	Yes ____ No ____
Thrift or Salary Savings Plan	Yes ____ No ____

If not a corporation, have you ever considered incorporation?

If so, explain: _____

(5)

*I also own a Personal Holding Co. with a net worth of $66,000. $31,500 is a note from me and $34,500 is in blue chip stocks. This was originally a corporation that owned the pharmacy I bought from my father after graduating from pharmacy school.

Business or Professional Practice (Continued)

Employee Information (Complete for Employee Benefit Plan Proposals)

Name	Sex	Date of Birth	Employment Date	Full Time Part Time	Current Annual Compensation
Clara Florence Slater	F	1-1-30	1-1-70	Full-Time Sec'y	$12,000
Cheryle Miller	F	2-2-50	2-2-75	Med. Tech	$18,000

Disposition of Interest

What would happen to your business in the event of a long disability or your death? Would you want it retained by your

heirs or sold or dissolved? __Dissolved__

Do you have a Buy-Sell or Stock Redemption Agreement? Yes ____ No __x__

What is the purchase price? $____-____

Is there an escalation clause (to provide for increasing values)? Yes ____ No ____

Is your agreement funded? Yes ____ No ____

With what? _____ How much? _____

RETIREMENT INFORMATION

Type of Plan	Present Vested Interest	Value at Death	Beneficiary	Value of Voluntary Contributions	How Funded?	Monthly Retirement Income at Age ____
Keogh	$12,750 100%	Same	Wife	-	Corp. Bond Mutual Funds	?
I.R.A.						
Pension	$60,000 100%	Same	Wife	-	1/2 Common Funds 1/2 CD's	?
Profit Sharing	$80,750 100%		Wife	-	Stocks & Stock Mutual Funds	?
Thrift						
Salary Savings						

Are you satisfied with your retirement plan? Yes ____ No ____

Explain __Pension plan is administered by bank; profit sharing plan is administered by my brokerage firm. An average of about $5,000 went into my plans during previous years. I'd like that to be about $10,000 from now on.__

(6)

428

LIFE INSURANCE

If you do not send us your life insurance policies for an analysis, please complete the following for yourself and your spouse:

Insured	Face Amount	Company	Type	Issue Date	Cash Value	Annual Premium	Beneficiary	Owner
Myself	$ 50,000	1st Life	Group Term	1970	–	Pd by P.C.	Wife	Wife
Myself	$100,000	Hi Life	Whole Life	1968	$13,885	$ 1,500	Wife	Wife

HEALTH INSURANCE

Insured	Company	Disability Income	Benefit Period	Daily Benefit (Hosp.)	Major Med.	Acc. Death Benefit
Myself	1st Mutual	$ 1,500	5 years – after six months			
Family	BC-BS			Basic	$ 250,000	

OTHER INSURANCE

When was your property and casualty insurance last reviewed? __1977__

Do you have personal excess liability coverage? Yes _X_ No ___ How Much? _$1,000,000_

LIABILITIES

What other indebtedness do you have aside from mortgages previously mentioned?

	Total Amount	Due Date	Monthly Outlay	Obligor (Husb., Wife, Jt.)
Notes (Demand) 1st Atlanta Bank	$ 31,500	6 mos	–	Myself
Installment Obligations				
Cash Value Loans				
Taxes Payable	for cars, boat, down payment on lake house.			
Margin Accounts				
Other				

(7)

ESTATE INFORMATION

Do you have a will? Yes __X__ No ____ Date Drawn _____1975_____ Date Reviewed ___–___

What are the provisions of your will? __See attached—Basic two-trust marital deduction will.__

_____

_____

Does your spouse have a will? Yes __X__ No ____ Date Drawn ____Same____ Date Reviewed _____

What are the provisions of the will? __Same__

_____

_____

Do you expect any inheritances? ____Yes____ Amount? __Small, less than $50,000__

Does your spouse expect any inheritances? _____Yes_____ Amount? __$250,000 or so, but everyone in her family lives forever. We're not counting on any of this in time to enjoy it.__

Have you made any gifts to relatives? Yes __X__ No ____

When? __Past 3 years__ How Much? __See children's assets, no gift taxes paid. Gave less than $6,000 per child per year.__

Have you made any substantial gifts to any charities? Yes ____ No __X__

Are you interested in making such gifts? Yes ____ No ____

Now or in your will? __Now, and more later in will (if financial plan is successful) to Juvenile Diabetes Foundation.__

TRUSTS

Have you created any trusts? Yes __X__ No ____

If yes, please give (a) type, (b) date created, (c) how it is funded, and (d) who is the beneficiary.

__Three years ago, I created irrevocable trusts (attached) for each of the children to contain assets given to them for college and other expenses that I am not legally required to provide.__

_____

Are you the beneficiary of any trusts? Yes ____ No __X__

If yes, please give (a) type, (b) donor, (c) annual income

_____

_____

_____

(8)

430

CURRENT INCOME AND EXPENSES

Estimate of Current Year's Income

Expenses

Salary	$110,000	DEDUCTIBLE	
Bonus	_____	Interest	$ 15,000
Self Employment Income (Net)	_____	Taxes (Property, State Income)	8,000
Director or Trustee Fees	_____	Contributions	2,000
Pension, Annuity	_____	Other Deductible Expenses	3,500
		(Bus. Entertainment)	
Interest (Taxable)	1,250	NON DEDUCTIBLE	
Dividends **(from P.C.)**	4,760	Principal Reduction	1,500
Real Estate (Net)	-	Living	16,024 **
		(**Other than deductible**)	
Income from Sale of Asset	10,000*	Education	3,900
In PHC for '83 only			
(Basis $____0____)		Insurance Premiums	2,000
		F.I.T.	27,811
Social Security	-	Savings	0
Spouse s Income	-	Investments	10,000
Other___PHC___	6,000	Other__Disc. Cash Flow__	36,475
Tax Free Income	4,200		
			126,210
TOTAL	126,210*	TOTAL	126,210

*LTCG proceeds excluded from total since it stayed
in PHC.
Please give details of any installment sale income, capital gains or losses you expect this year. _____ _____

_____ _____ _____

Do you expect any significant changes in your income or expenses in the next 5 years? Yes ____ No ____ Please

explain **We are pleased with our current income status and have no big desire to improve on the lifestyle we now enjoy. We're more interested in assurring ourselves of tomorrow's standard of living.**

INCOME OBJECTIVES

RETIREMENT
At what age do you plan to retire? **Whenever I feel like it.**

What annual aftertax (spendable) income would you want at retirement? (In today's dollars) $ **55,000 or more by no later than age 65. I'd like to be able to reach that earlier if possible. In fact, I'd like to reach that level of independence as soon as possible without taking undue risk.**
DISABILITY
If you became disabled, how much annual income would you and your family need to maintain your present

standard of living? $__50,000__

SURVIVOR'S INCOME
If you died today, what principal amount would you want to provide for:

Home Mortgage? $____-_____ Education Fund? $__15,000_____

Debts? $__31,500_____ Other $____-____ _

How much annual income would your family need to maintain their standard of living? $__50,000__ ____

(9)

** Includes $2,170 of Social Security taxes plus $13,854 of other living expenses.

OVERALL FINANCIAL AND INVESTMENT CONCERNS

How would you best position your investment assets to coincide with your current investment temperament?

___10___% Very Conservatively. Conserving present capital is more important than making it grow.

___30___% Conservatively. High quality investments that provide an opportunity for appreciation and relative safety are important.

___50___% Subject to moderate risk. Aggressive growth is important.

___10___% Subject to high risk. Speculative growth is acceptable.

Do you have any preferences or objections to any particular investment areas?

Please explain ___I hate paying this much in taxes.___

_____

Which of the following best describes your attitude towards your income needs?

☒ My present income is adequate for my needs.

☐ I need more current income.

☒ I can forgo current income to be better able to provide for future retirement income.

Indicate areas of major concern to you by rating numerically in order of importance:

___5___ Current Income   ___2___ Education of Children

___4___ Retirement Income   ___1___ Reduction of Current Income Taxes

___3___ Further Building of Estate   ___7___ Reduction of Estate Taxes

___6___ Conservation of Assets for Heirs   _____ Other I want to save all the income
                                            taxes I can but I don't want to loose
                                            my money just to save taxes.

What would you consider to be your primary financial objective or concern? __Accumulate more assets for__ __future income needs.__

Is there any thing else we should know? __I am not anxious to gift more to my kids than they will__ __need for college. I want them to have to work successfully.__

__I like to keep track of my investments but I would like someone else to be responsible__ __for picking and managing them.__

(10)

Index

Index